WILEY

Financial Reporting
under IFRS

Financial Reporting under IFRS

A Topic Based Approach

Wolfgang Dick   Franck Missonier-Piera

A John Wiley and Sons, Ltd., Publication

This edition first published 2010
© 2010 John Wiley & Sons, Ltd

Registered office
John Wiley & Sons Ltd, The Atrium, Southern Gate, Chichester, West Sussex, PO19 8SQ, United Kingdom

For details of our global editorial offices, for customer services and for information about how to apply for permission to reuse the copyright material in this book please see our website at www.wiley.com.

Library of Congress Cataloging-in-Publication Data

Dick, Wolfgang, 1965–
    Franck, Missonier-Piera, 1968-Financial reporting under IFRS : a topic based approach / Wolfgang Dick, Franck Missonier-Piera.
        p. cm. – (Wiley regulatory reporting ; 1)
    Includes bibliographical references and index.
    ISBN 978-0-470-68831-1 (pbk.)
        1. Financial statements.   2. Accounting–Standards.   3. International finance.
I. Missonier-Piera, Franck.   II. Title.
    HF5681.B2D515 2010
    657'.3–dc22

                                                                        2010021933

A catalogue record for this book is available from the British Library.

ISBN 978-0-470-68831-1 (paperback), ISBN 978-0-470-97385-1 (ebk),
ISBN 978-0-470-97162-8 (ebk), ISBN 978-0-470-97161-1 (ebk)

Typeset in 10/11pt Times-Roman by Aptara Inc., New Delhi, India

CONTENTS

FOREWORD

This textbook is the outcome of collective thinking and the experience of professors from several institutions. Accountability and responsibility for this book lie with Wolfgang Dick and Franck Missonier-Piera. Wolfgang Dick is a Professor at the ESSEC Business School (France) and co-holder of the ESSEC-KPMG Chair in Financial Reporting. The interests of Wolfgang Dick relate to accounting harmonization, IFRS, intangible assets and corporate governance. Franck Missonier-Piera is a Professor at the University of Geneva (Switzerland). His interests relate to IFRS, corporate governance, financial analysis and accounting for financial instruments.

A French version of the book has been developed with the cooperation of the following colleagues. Corinne Bessieux–Ollier, Professor of Accounting at Montpellier Business School (France). Roger Dinasquet, Professor of Accounting at the ESSEC Business School. Bernard Esnault, Professor of Accounting at the ESSEC Business School. Jean-Luc Rossignol, Senior Lecturer at the University of Franche-Comté (France) and Peter Walton, Professor at the ESSEC Business School and the Open University (UK).

INTRODUCTION

The European Commission now requires companies in the European Union (EU) which use public savings to present their accounts according to the standards of the IASB (*International Accounting Standards Board*). This has implications for a majority of them. Until 2004, companies listed in the EU could use national accounting standards. For example, in France, consolidated financial statements had been prepared in accordance with rule CRC 99-02. This rule now applies only to the consolidated accounts of non-listed groups. The introduction of the standards of the IASB, i.e. IFRS (*International Financial Reporting Standards*), has imposed a major change in the presentation of accounts. The accounting and finance departments of listed companies, as well as all users of financial statements, should be able to understand the principles of the IFRS. This book therefore refers to international rather than national accounting standards. For the various actors of the economy, harmonization of rules of measurement and presentation of financial statements will facilitate comparison of the financial situation and performance of firms across different countries. However, before presenting the principles of preparation and presentation of accounting information, one should understand the role of that information and the objectives of the IASB.

1. USERS OF FINANCIAL AND ACCOUNTING INFORMATION

The financial statements meet the information needs of many users, who are:

- **Current and potential *investors* (shareholders).** Early users of financial information, they are concerned by the risk inherent in their investment and its profitability. They seek information to determine if they should buy, hold or sell shares in a particular company. Shareholders also want to estimate the company's ability to pay dividends.
- ***Creditors.*** The information they seek is to enable them to determine whether their loans and interest related thereto will be paid at maturity dates.
- ***Suppliers.*** The information they seek is to enable them to determine if the amounts that are due will be paid at maturity.
- ***Customers.*** They seek information on business continuity, especially when they have long-term relationships with the firm (i.e. the supplier).
- ***Employees and their representatives.*** They seek information on the stability and continuity of the operations of the company that employs them. They are also concerned by the profitability of the company, reflecting its ability to pay employees, provide benefits on retirement and employment opportunities.
- ***States and their agencies.*** They care about including the allocation of resources generated by businesses. They thus determine the appropriate tax policies based on national income statistics (for example). It is therefore necessary to impose disclosure requirements.
- ***The public.*** They are interested in the firm's activities, because it contributes substantially to the local economy, including employing a large staff or using local suppliers. The financial statements can inform them of trends and recent changes to the company's prosperity and the extent of its activities.

2. THE ROLE OF ACCOUNTING INFORMATION

The many users of financial statements have specific information needs. The financial statements serve two main functions – not mutually exclusive – and thus meet the needs of most users:

- **An informational role.** Numerous users need to estimate the value of a company. Thus, when evaluating, potential investors (insurance companies, investment companies, pension funds, etc.), financial analysts and other market participants are concerned both with the results of the company and its future performance. Accounting earnings are one of the variables used by investors. Similarly, the estimated cost of credit depends in part on the financial health of the company. Thus, incurring excessive debt and poor earnings may affect the granting of new loans. From the simple evaluation of the financial position of a firm wishing to borrow from a bank to the complex system of assessment of rating agencies (e.g. Standard & Poor's, Moody's), performance, leverage and solvency ratios are at the heart of the assessment process of capital suppliers. They are based on accounting data published by the company.
- **A contractual role.** Accounting data can also help to control the proper execution of contracts between the firm and its business partners. Special contracts govern the relationship between the firm and its stakeholders (e.g. creditors, suppliers, staff, company management, etc.). The contracts of the firm based on accounting data are contingent on the peculiarities of each company. For example, the employment contracts of executives link some of their compensation to performance indicators (return on equity, return on assets, etc.) to encourage them to maximize the value of the firm. Loan agreements may include specific covenants to protect the interest of creditors. For example, the contract may limit the level of debt (measured with accounting data) and may restrict the payment of dividends.

The financial statements do not meet all information needs of users. However, these latter have common needs. Investors are providers of risk capital to the entity, and the IASB considers that when the financial statements satisfy the needs of investors, they also satisfy most users.

3. OBJECTIVES OF THE IASB

To meet the needs of shareholders and investors regarding financial and accounting information, the IASB has three objectives of standardization, in its preface to the IFRS:

- To develop, in the public interest, a single set of global standards, understandable and applicable, that must provide information of high quality, transparent and comparable with regards to financial statements and other accounting data. This helps users of information, including those involved in capital markets, to make economic decisions.
- To promote the use and rigorous application of these standards.
- To work actively with the standard setters in different countries to bring about convergence of accounting standards in different countries with IFRS, in order to obtain high-quality solutions.

The *Framework for the Preparation and the Presentation of Financial Statements* of the IASB presents in greater detail the objectives of financial statements, their qualitative characteristics and their components. In theory, when decisions on standards are taken, the IASB should ensure compliance with the framework, which states that the objective of financial statements is to provide information on the financial position, performance and change in the financial position of an entity that is useful to a wide range of users in making economic decisions.

The economic decisions taken by users of financial statements require evaluation of a company's capabilities to generate cash and cash equivalent, and their maturity or the assurance of their realization. The financial position of a company is affected by the economic resources it controls, its financial structure, liquidity and solvency and its ability to adapt to environmental changes.

Structure Plan

The financial statements are crucial in decision making and should reflect the resources that the company controls. Components of financial statements are explained in terms of assets and liabilities. The balance sheet shows the assets and liabilities of the company, and the difference represents the residual interest of the shareholders.

Chapter 1 ("Financial Statements and Accounting Mechanisms") presents the structure and mechanisms of preparation of financial statements. Chapter 2 ("Income from Ordinary Activities") addresses the company's performance, measured by the difference between the revenues and expenses of the company for a given period. Revenues and expenses are in a financial statement: the income statement (*Profit or Loss account*). Revenues come from an increase in assets or a decrease in liabilities. As for expenses, they come from a decrease in assets or an increase in liabilities. Any designer of accounting rules has to decide whether to start from the income statement when making measurements (i.e. by looking at the commercial transactions) and then consider the balance sheet as a remainder, or to start from the balance sheet (i.e. what wealth the company has generated and what are its obligations) with changes in the balance sheet items expressed within the income statement.

Chapters 3 ("Current Assets") and 5 ("Non-current Assets") handle the assets used for business operations. They generate a number of obligations towards suppliers when goods or raw materials are purchased on credit and towards the employees in terms of compensation, but also pension contributions (Chapter 4, "Non-financial Liabilities").

Chapter 6 ("Financing") presents the main financial obligations, for example *vis-à-vis* credit institutions. Chapter 7 ("Taxation") deals purely with fiscal obligations. The presentation of financial statements of a group of companies requires specific accounting treatments, presented in Chapter 8 ("Group Accounts").

Chapter 9 ("Financial Analysis and Communication") analyzes all of the information provided both from the perspective of credit risk and profitability for shareholders.

Finally, Chapter 10 ("The IASB and Development of the IFRS") reviews the history of the IASB and the continuous process of developing future international standards.

ACKNOWLEDGEMENTS

We wish to thank the companies that have allowed this book to be richly illustrated and thus promote the understanding of the complex topic that is the IFRS. These are Accor, Arcelor Mittal, AstraZeneca, Bic, BP France, British Airways, Cap Gémini, Club Med, Danone, Deutsche Telekom, Fiat, Lafarge, L'Oréal, LVMH, PSA Peugeot-Citroën, Publicis, Renault, Rolls Royce, Schneider Electric, Suez Environnement, Total, TUI, Unibail Rodamco, Unilever, Vinci, Vodafone and Volkswagen.

We also wish to thank Thomas Dumoulin, Vincent Ferry, Thomas Gaimard, Rachel Gorney, Stefan Jensen and Kanchan Rabadia for their help in copy editing the chapters, Jérémy Borot for his valuable contribution in drafting the exercises, and Guillaume Pech and Fanny Sergent for managing relationships with the quoted companies.

This book has received the financial support of the ESSEC Research Center, the ESSEC-KPMG Chair in Financial Reporting, and the EMLyon CERA Chair in Growth firm.

1 FINANCIAL STATEMENTS AND ACCOUNTING MECHANISMS

Financial disclosure has become a critical function for businesses. Today, firms are under pressure from various stakeholders (financial markets, the State, clients, employees, etc.) and are therefore engaged in information policies, in order to meet changing requirements. Thus, we can see that annual reports are providing a growing supply of information. It covers not only the needs of corporate governance, through the establishment of a management report and description of the principal organs of corporate control (for example, the structure of the Board and capital, the firm's Audit committee, the salaries, etc.), but also those related to the firm's environmental responsibility. Other documents and summary tables – the financial statements – also provide various business partners with a wide range of information about the nature and performance of the firm's activity. They perform various functions. On the one hand, they can serve as evidence or control tools for monitoring the performance of contracts between the firm and its partners. On the other hand, they provide investors and other users with relevant information for economic decision making. Financial statements are therefore supposed to better reflect the economic situation of the company so that investors can properly evaluate the performance (section 1.1). In order to produce useful and relevant information, the preparation of financial statements is based on a number of principles, uses its own mechanisms of information processing (section 1.2) and allows a rigorous synthesis.

1.1 FINANCIAL STATEMENTS

The objective of financial statements is to inform all stakeholders about the business situation at a given date. We can identify several groups of regular users of financial statements. The current or potential owners of the company (shareholders for limited liability companies) are the first to be concerned by the financial statements. They are interested in the performance of the company in order to measure the profitability of their investment. On a long-term basis, it is also useful to know the evolution of business investments in order to evaluate if the company will be able to generate profits in the future, and therefore to distribute dividends. For similar reasons, the management team is also concerned by the information contained in the financial statements. Indeed, shareholders have delegated the management of their capital invested to them. Financial statements therefore provide a means for controlling the financial performance of the management team, by informing the owners of the quality of their decisions. In that matter, financial analysts are an important group of users. Their objective is to assess the company as a whole and to make recommendations on whether to invest in it or not. Many banks and other current and potential investors use the recommendations of these experts for decision-making purposes. Thus, the company must necessarily "supply" them with the most complete information possible. Although analysts do not exclusively base their decision on the financial statements, the latter represent a fundamental element of their analysis.

Other users of financial statements are the bankers, suppliers and other creditors who wish to know whether the company is – and will be – able to meet its financial commitments. This is related to both the reimbursement of debts and the payment of interest on loans. Moreover, the State, local authorities and social organizations refer to the accounting records to calculate the contributions and corporate taxes payable by the company. Finally, employees and their representatives also need information on the situation of the firm. It allows them to determine the outlooks on job security and define their social demands.

All these groups of users need information, in near real time, on the **financial situation**, **performance** and the status of the company's **cash account**.

> The **financial situation** consists in identifying the assets used by the company (lands, buildings, machinery, vehicles, inventory, receivables, and cash) and the financial resources, evaluating them and analyzing the evolution of their value over time.

The **financial situation** consists, at first, in identifying the assets used by the company (for example, lands, buildings, machinery, vehicles, inventory, receivables and cash), evaluating them and analyzing the evolution of their value over time. Meanwhile, the evolution of the financial resources, which enabled the acquisition of those assets, must also be carefully monitored. For instance, the more the company gets into debt, the more difficult it will be to reimburse its debts. Even a slight increase in debt can have significant consequences on the business, when a bank decides that it has crossed a particular risk threshold and, accordingly, increases the interest rate for all future loans.

> The **performance** or the **net income** shows whether the activity of the firm as a whole is profitable, which is normally the main objective of the management team.

The **performance** or the **net income** shows whether the activity of the firm as a whole is profitable, which is normally the main objective of the management team. Here, "profitability" means that the money invested by the owners can make profits and thus increase their wealth. Entrusted by the owners to achieve this objective at any cost, the management of the company has to follow the change in income, using the financial statements, to ensure that the decisions are in accordance with the target fixed by the owners. If this is not the case, the regular monitoring of income enables corrective measures to be taken, before the situation of the company deteriorates.

> The **cash account** includes cash, bank deposits and a number of other monetary elements which the company could liquidate within a very short span of time, usually in less than 3 months.

The **cash account** includes cash, bank deposits and a number of other monetary elements which the company could liquidate within a very short span of time, usually in less than 3 months. The objective here is different from the profit, that is to say it is not to maximize it.[1] However, it is important to have enough cash at all times, to meet financial deadlines, i.e.

---

[1]   *For example, too much liquidity in bank accounts which generates little or no interest, could mean that the management of the company has borrowed too much from banks or asked too much capital from its*

reimburse loans, pay the invoices of suppliers, salaries and taxes, etc. Failure to meet financial deadlines and the inability of the company to meet its commitments may result in insolvency, or even the outright liquidation of the company shortly afterwords. The analysis of the status and evolution of cash flow is therefore of high importance for the survival of the company.

Under the international accounting standards (IAS/IFRS), it is compulsory to publish at least one table dedicated to the analysis of each of these elements. Sections 1.1.1 to 1.1.3 explain the content and format of these tables, as well as the relationships between them.

1.1.1   Balance Sheet

Content

> The **balance sheet** is the basic summary table, which presents the financial situation of a company at a given date.

The **balance sheet** is the basic summary table. It presents the financial situation of a company at a given date. It is measured by the difference between all assets of the company and all its liabilities (obligations to do, to pay) and represents the net value of what belongs to the owners, the "shareholders' equity". The balance sheet therefore presents three main elements: **assets**, **liabilities** (or obligations) of the company and its **shareholders' equity**.

> An **asset** is an item, a resource controlled by the firm from which future economic benefits are expected. It has a positive value for the company.

An **asset** is a resource (controlled by the firm) from which the company expects future economic benefits and has a positive value for it.[2] The future economic benefit is the potential of the asset to contribute directly or indirectly to cash flows for the benefit of the company. The assets of the balance sheet are primarily the "properties" of the company, i.e. what the company is at a given date in purely "physical" terms. It included lands, buildings, industrial equipment, furniture, inventory and cash. There are also intangible assets: either rights (patents or licenses, for example), or financial assets (equity investments, receivables, short-term investments or bank deposits).

> A liability is an **obligation** to do or to pay. It has a negative value for the company.

Liabilities are **obligations** to do or to pay. They have a negative value for the company, since, at maturity, the company will have to reimburse them to third parties. It includes mainly bank

---

owners, and does not know what to do with this excess cash. This can be the sign of mismanagement. However, this analysis would be different if this was done in preparation for the takeover of a competitor.

[2] *Under certain conditions, some items are also included in the assets of the company, even if they do not belong to it (see Chapter 6).*

loans and overdrafts, accounts payables and tax liabilities. We can add other liabilities whose exact timings or amounts are not known, but their existence is sure and certain, such as pension obligations, long-term product warranties or provisions for legal risks.

The **shareholders' equity** is the difference between assets and liabilities. It represents the net value of the firm.

The difference between assets and liabilities results in the **shareholders' equity**. It is the net value of a firm: it represents the value of what owners possess at the time of the establishment of the balance sheet. In normal circumstances, this value must at least include the subscribed capital. It is the initial input of owners, i.e. the capital invested at the creation of the company and the contributions made during each capital increase. Inasmuch as the profits over time are not fully paid as dividends, we should also find the part not distributed under "equity reserves".

The **net income** is the balance between creation and consumption of wealth over a period (revenues – expenses).

The shareholders' equity is also affected by each consumption (expense) or creation of wealth (revenue) in the company. The balance between creation and consumption of wealth over a period is the **net income** (Revenues – Expenses = net Income). If it is positive, the net creation of wealth returns to the owners and the value of their investment increases: this is known as a profit. If negative, it is the opposite: the value of the investment declines and is known as a loss. The net income is therefore the basic indicator of wealth creation for the company.

Format   IAS 1 standard does not impose any compulsory detailed format of presentation. It rather indicates some principles to follow:

- The separate presentation of assets, liabilities and shareholders' equity.
- The distinction between current and non-current assets and current and long-term liabilities. In practice, the threshold is usually of one year: elements with a residual maturity in the company of less than one year are considered to be current items, others as non-current.
- The distinction, among others, between:
    - lands, buildings and equipments
    - intangible assets, such as licenses, patents, software
    - financial assets
    - inventory
    - receivables
    - cash and equivalents
    - accounts payables
    - provisions for contingencies, i.e. those obligations whose exact timings and amounts are not yet known

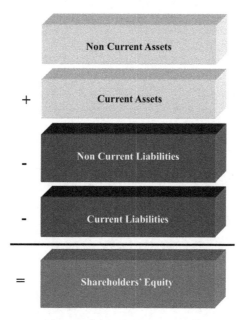

Figure 1.1   Balance sheet structure: "Anglo-Saxon" format.

- – financial debts (especially bonds and bank loans)
- – shareholders' equity, including the initial input by the owner (equity capital), the non-distributed income (reserves) and the net income/loss of the accounting period.
- • The possibility of a finer classification, if it improves the understanding of the financial situation of the company.
- • The presentation of values for at least one comparative year, which allows the reader to compare current values with those of the previous accounting period.

For the actual presentation of the balance sheet, several alternatives are generally used. The choice depends mainly on the accounting tradition of the country in which the company operates (e.g. UK, France, Germany, etc.).

The Anglo-Saxon tradition presents the balance sheet in a list format, which has for "resultant" the shareholders' equity at the bottom of the table. This balance sheet first indicates the assets, from which it deducts the obligations or liabilities. This leads to a balance (Net Assets), which represents the net value of the firm, and corresponds to the value of the shareholders' equity (see Figure 1.1).

In the consolidated balance sheet[3] of BP (British Petroleum) at 12/31/2008 (see Figure 1.2), the amount of Non-Current Assets of $161,854m is clearly distinguished from that of the Current Assets of $66,384m. The total assets are therefore of $228,238m. After deduction of

---

[3] *When a standalone company presents its balance sheet, we speak of an individual balance sheet. The same company can be part of a group of several subsidiaries. The group's financial situation as a whole is presented in the "consolidated balance sheet" (see Chapter 7).*

Financial Reporting under IFRS

At 31 December			$ million
	Note	2008	2007
Non-current assets			
Property, plant and equipment	23	103,200	97,989
Goodwill	24	9,878	11,006
Intangible assets	25	10,260	6,652
Investments in jointly controlled entities	26	23,826	18,113
Investments in associates	27	4,000	4,579
Other investments	29	855	1,830
Fixed assets		152,019	140,169
Loans		995	999
Other receivables	31	710	968
Derivative financial instruments	34	5,054	3,741
Prepayments		1,338	1,083
Defined benefit pension plan surpluses	38	1,738	8,914
		161,854	155,874
Current assets			
Loans		168	165
Inventories	30	16,821	26,554
Trade and other receivables	31	29,261	38,020
Derivative financial instruments	34	8,510	6,321
Prepayments		3,050	3,589
Current tax receivable		377	705
Cash and cash equivalents	32	8,197	3,562
		66,384	78,916
Assets classified as held for sale	4	–	1,286
		66,384	80,202
Total assets		228,238	236,076
Current liabilities			
Trade and other payables	33	33,644	43,152
Derivative financial instruments	34	8,977	6,405
Accruals		6,743	6,640
Finance debt	35	15,740	15,394
Current tax payable		3,144	3,282
Provisions	37	1,545	2,195
		69,793	77,068
Liabilities directly associated with the assets classified as held for sale	4	–	163
		69,793	77,231
Non-current liabilities			
Other payables	33	3,080	1,251
Derivative financial instruments	34	6,271	5,002
Accruals		784	959
Finance debt	35	17,464	15,651
Deferred tax liabilities	20	16,198	19,215
Provisions	37	12,108	12,900
Defined benefit pension plan and other post-retirement benefit plan deficits	38	10,431	9,215
		66,336	64,193
Total liabilities		136,129	141,424
Net assets		92,109	94,652
Equity			
Share capital	39	5,176	5,237
Reserves		86,127	88,453
BP shareholders' equity	40	91,303	93,690
Minority interest	40	806	962
Total equity	40	92,109	94,652

P D Sutherland Chairman
Dr A B Hayward Group Chief Executive

Figure 1.2   Extract of the BP annual report 2007, values in millions of dollars.

Liabilities of $136,129m, the Net Assets amount to $92,109m. This represents the total Equity presented on the bottom line. In the UK, Current Assets and Current Liabilities are generally grouped together, as is the case in this example where they amount to $69,793m. We can thus easily calculate an indicator that measures the Net Current Liabilities of $3,409m (69,793 − 66,384). Bonds maturing in the short term are thus more than covered by liquid assets in the same time frame. This is an important indicator of financial stability in the short term.

According to French tradition, which is also that of most countries of continental Europe, goods and assets possessed by the company are presented in the Assets section, on one side of the balance sheet, and obligations and equity are grouped under the Liabilities section, on

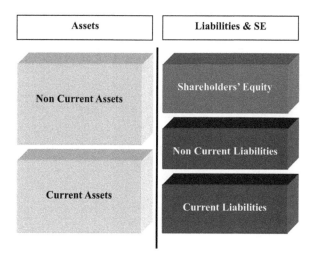

Figure 1.3   Balance sheet structure, French format.

the other side of the balance sheet. The Liabilities therefore represent all funds invested in the company, whether on a limited (debt and provisions) or unlimited period (equity). The Assets represent the form in which financial resources are invested and employed in the business. Of course, it is not always possible to create a direct link between a given resource and a specific application. But originally, any asset had to be financed in one way or another and there was therefore a liability of corresponding value. That is why Total Assets and Total Liabilities are always for the same amount (see Figure 1.3).

In the French balance sheets, the term "Liability" covers two different meanings, which can be confusing. In the meaning mentioned above, "Liability" refers to all the financial resources available to the entity. But "Liabilities" can also designate the obligations of the entity to third parties, whether they are current or non-current. For this reason, the concept does not include equity. These two meanings can be used simultaneously by the same entity in the same balance sheet, as illustrated by the annual balance sheet of Lafarge Group in 2007 (see Figure 1.4).

In Figure 1.4, we can easily identify the basic structure of the balance sheet: Assets at the top and Liabilities below. The two major categories of Assets are Non-current Assets (€21,490m) and Current Assets (€6,818m), giving Total Assets of €28,308m at 12/31/2007. The liability is structured into three sections: first, equity, here called "Shareholders' equity" (€12,077m), then non-current obligations under the designation "Non-current Liabilities" (€10,720m) and current obligations, under the heading "Current Liabilities" (€5,511m). The bottom line of the balance sheet entitled "Total Liabilities" includes both current and non-current liabilities and shareholders' equity (€28,208m).

Like that of BP in the previous example, this presentation enables one to observe easily, for example, whether the values achievable in the short term (€6,818m) are sufficient to cover short-term obligations (€5,511m). The situation of Lafarge seems entirely satisfactory, since there is a surplus (€1,307m).

Consolidated balance sheets

(million euros)	At December 31		
	2007	2006*	2005*
ASSETS			
Non current assets	**21,490**	**20,474**	**20,543**
Goodwill	7,471	7,511	6,646
Intangible assets	472	426	355
Property, plant and equipment	11,904	11,183	12,171
Investments in associates	331	253	376
Other financial assets	1,096	830	626
Derivative instruments – assets	5	70	49
Deferred income tax asset	211	201	320
Current assets	**6,818**	**9,367**	**7,352**
Inventories	1,761	1,619	1,857
Trade receivables	2,515	2,674	2,737
Other receivables	1,061	1,126	925
Derivative instruments – assets	52	60	98
Cash and cash equivalents	1,429	1,155	1,735
Assets classified as held for sale	-	2,733	-
Total Assets	**28,308**	**29,841**	**27,895**
Equity & Liabilities			
Common stock	691	707	704
Additional paid-in capital	6,019	6,420	6,316
Treasury shares	(55)	(72)	(98)
Retained earnings	4,411	3,023	2,025
Other reserves	36	31	(37)
Foreign currency translation	(104)	205	741
Shareholders'equity – parent company	**10,998**	**10,314**	**9,651**
Minority interests	1,079	1,380	2,533
Equity	**12,077**	**11,694**	**12,184**
Non current liabilities	**10,720**	**11,962**	**9,852**
Deferred income tax liability	695	529	515
Pension & other employee benefits liabilities	724	1,057	1,415
Provisions	928	935	984
Long-term debt	8,347	9,421	6,928
Derivative instruments – liabilities	26	20	10
Current liabilities	**5,511**	**6,185**	**5,859**
Pension & other employee benefits liabilities, current portion	79	120	156
Provisions, current portion	201	132	123
Trade payables	1,732	1,598	1,675
Other payables	1,553	1,668	1,575
Income tax payable	148	136	165
Short term debt and current portion of long-term debt	1,762	1,664	2,077
Derivative instruments – liabilities	36	25	88
Liabilities directly associated with assets classified as held for sale	-	842	-
Total equity and liabilities	**28,308**	**29,841**	**27,895**

* Figures have been adjusted after the application by the Group of IAS 19, Employee Benefits, allowing the recognition through equity of the actuarial gains and losses under defined-benefit pension plans

Figure 1.4   Extract of the Lafarge, Balance Sheet, annual report, 2007.

The current/non-current approach goes as far as to separate, *a priori*, within a single homogeneous element, the short-term and the long-term parts. Thus, in the balance sheet of Lafarge, we find in both Non-Current and Current Liabilities, the line "Financial Liabilities", which essentially refers to the financial debt of the group. The part of this debt that matures within one year is allocated to Current Liabilities (€1,762m) and the part that matures in more than one year to Non-Current Liabilities (€8,347m). Reading financial statements therefore requires great vigilance. Most terms are not mandatory and companies can choose others.

1.1.2   Income Statement (or Profit and Loss Account)

One of the two areas of the balance sheet that deserves a very special attention is the change in equity between two fiscal periods. They may increase or decrease as a result of specific operations, such as increases or reductions of capital. The issuance of new shares is an example of a capital increase in a public company. The net income has also an impact on the change in equity. It reflects the amount of net creation or consumption of wealth of the company by its activity or other events between two fiscal periods. It measures the economic performance of the company. All users of financial statements need maximum information on the composition of the result. The second summary table, the profit and loss account (or income statement), gives details about the different elements of expenses and revenues.

A **revenue** is an operation that increases the wealth of the company.

An **expense** is a consumption of resources that impoverishes the company.

According to their call to make the connection between two balance sheets, therefore between two closing dates, the values in the income statement represent only the flows recorded over the period. A transaction that increases the wealth of the company is called a **revenue** and the consumption of resources that impoverishes the company is an **expense**. For example, the revenue that is generally the most important, i.e. the turnover, is not the turnover of the closing date, but the one achieved during the period to which the income statement refers. It is the same for all other revenues and expenses.

The exact content of the income statement is not completely detailed. In all cases, according to the IAS 1 standard, the requirements are to include:

- Financial expenses, representing the cost of financing the entity.
- Revenues from ordinary activities, that is to say, sales and all other revenues that the entity realized in the framework of its activity.
- Income tax.
- Net income of the accounting period.
- Net earnings per share in two variants.[4]

Thus, in the income statement, there is no requirement to give the details of expenses related to the activity. However, the standard strongly recommends that details be provided for one of the following classifications:

---

[4]   *Chapter 8 describes the two types of earnings per share.*

- The classification of expenses according to their nature. On these grounds, we distinguish in particular:
  - consumption of raw materials and other inventory items;
  - wages and salaries (i.e. employee costs);
  - depreciation and amortization of the value of different goods during the period.
- The classification of expenses by function. In this sense, we distinguish:
  - cost of sales, corresponding to the production cost of goods sold or acquisition cost of goods sold;
  - administrative expenses of the entity;
  - distribution expenses;
  - research and development expenses, if the entity has the corresponding activity.

Both patterns lead necessarily to the same net income. The difference lies in the allotment of expenses. For example, employee costs in an industrial company are divided between employees in production, administration and commercial services. In an income statement with a classification of expenses by nature, all these costs are grouped into one item, listed as "wages and salaries". However, in an income statement with a classification of expenses by function, such costs are spread over several items: wages of production staff are included in cost of goods sold; those of administrative staff in administrative expenses; and those of commercial staff in distribution expenses.

The income statement of British Petroleum (see Figure 1.5) is an example of a classification of expenses according to their function in the company. The flexibility of the IAS 1 standard allows the Group to bring together certain items, to detail others and select the most appropriate designations to a specific economic situation.

For example, distribution and administrative expenses are grouped on one line ($15,412m). The group also discloses two intermediate result: the "Profit before interest and taxation. . ." and "Profit for the year".

For the income statement, like the balance sheet, entities may also choose between a single list presentation and a presentation in two columns. Most entities that prepare their accounts according to IFRS standards choose the first presentation. It consists in starting from sales and other ordinary income, and deducting expenses related to business activity. Other expenses are then subtracted, then the financial result and, finally, the tax on profits. The net income of the period is obtained by adding and subtracting different elements listed in Figure 1.5.

The second presentation is similar to that of the balance sheet, opposing assets and liabilities of the entity: it consists in putting side by side the expenses and revenues in two separate columns. It is rarely used today.

1.1.3   Cash-Flow Statement

The **Cash flow statement** details all the operations that generated cash flows during the fiscal period.

Group income statement

For the year ended 31 December				$ million
	Note	2008	2007	2006
Sales and other operating revenues		361,143	284,365	265,906
Earnings from jointly controlled entities – after interest and tax		3,023	3,135	3,553
Earnings from associates – after interest and tax		798	697	442
Interest and other revenues	7	736	754	701
Total revenues	6	365,700	288,951	270,602
Gains on sale of businesses and fixed assets	8	1,353	2,487	3,714
Total revenues and other income		367,053	291,438	274,316
Purchases		266,982	200,766	187,183
Production and manufacturing expenses		29,183	25,915	23,793
Production and similar taxes	9	6,526	4,013	3,621
Depreciation, depletion and amortization	10	10,985	10,579	9,128
Impairment and losses on sale of businesses and fixed assets	11	1,733	1,679	549
Exploration expense	17	882	756	1,045
Distribution and administration expenses	13	15,412	15,371	14,447
Fair value (gain) loss on embedded derivatives	34	111	7	(608)
Profit before interest and taxation from continuing operations		35,239	32,352	35,158
Finance costs	19	1,547	1,393	986
Net finance income relating to pensions and other post-retirement benefits	38	(591)	(652)	(470)
Profit before taxation from continuing operations		34,283	31,611	34,642
Taxation	20	12,617	10,442	12,331
Profit from continuing operations		21,666	21,169	22,311
Loss from Innovene operations	4	–	–	(25)
Profit for the year		21,666	21,169	22,286
Attributable to				
BP shareholders		21,157	20,845	22,000
Minority interest		509	324	286
		21,666	21,169	22,286
Earnings per share – cents				
Profit for the year attributable to BP shareholders				
Basic	22	112.59	108.76	109.84
Diluted	22	111.56	107.84	109.00
Profit from continuing operations attributable to BP shareholders				
Basic		112.59	108.76	109.97
Diluted		111.56	107.84	109.12

Figure 1.5 Income statement 2008, British Petroleum.

It is indeed important to compare the cash position at the date of the balance sheet with that of the previous closing period. But the mere comparison of balances is not enough, because many reasons can explain changes in the balance. The aim of the **Cash flow statement** is to detail all the transactions that generated cash flows during the financial year and thus create a link between the amount of the opening and closing cash balances. As in the income statement, all the values of the cash flow statement are flows for a period and do not represent the operations performed only at the closing date. In the cash-flow statement, the flows are classified into three categories:

- **Cash flows from operating activities.** They are related to transactions in connection with the creation of sales or other ordinary income, and not to flows of investment or financing. They are mostly all flows related to the current activity (cost of sales, administrative and distribution expenses).
- **Cash flows from investing activities.** These are the cash flows related to a movement in non-current assets. Especially, there are the expenditures related to investments (intangible, tangible and financial), including land, buildings, furniture and financial assets. These flows also take into account all operations related to the disposal of non-current assets. These flows are usually not important when it comes to sales of assets at the end of their useful life, such as machinery at the end of its technological life.

Group cash flow statement

For the year ended 31 December	Note	2008	2007	$ million 2006
Operating activities				
Profit before taxation		34,283	31,611	34,642
Adjustments to reconcile profit before taxation to net cash provided by operating activities				
Exploration expenditure written off	17	385	347	624
Depreciation, depletion and amortization	10	10,985	10,579	9,128
Impairment and (gain) loss on sale of businesses and fixed assets	8,11	380	(808)	(3,165)
Earnings from jointly controlled entities and associates		(3,821)	(3,832)	(3,995)
Dividends received from jointly controlled entities and associates		3,728	2,473	4,495
Interest receivable		(407)	(489)	(473)
Interest received		385	500	500
Finance costs	19	1,547	1,393	986
Interest paid		(1,291)	(1,363)	(1,242)
Net finance income relating to pensions and other post-retirement benefits	38	(591)	(652)	(470)
Share-based payments		459	420	416
Net operating charge for pensions and other post-retirement benefits, less contributions and benefit payments for unfunded plans		(173)	(404)	(261)
Net charge for provisions, less payments		(298)	(92)	340
(Increase) decrease in inventories		9,010	(7,255)	995
(Increase) decrease in other current and non-current assets		2,439	5,210	3,596
Increase (decrease) in other current and non-current liabilities		(6,101)	(3,857)	(4,211)
Income taxes paid		(12,824)	(9,072)	(13,733)
Net cash provided by operating activities		**38,095**	**24,709**	**28,172**
Investing activities				
Capital expenditure		(22,658)	(17,830)	(15,125)
Acquisitions, net of cash acquired		(395)	(1,225)	(229)
Investment in jointly controlled entities		(1,009)	(428)	(37)
Investment in associates		(81)	(187)	(570)
Proceeds from disposal of fixed assets	5	918	1,749	5,963
Proceeds from disposal of businesses, net of cash disposed	5	11	2,518	291
Proceeds from loan repayments		647	192	189
Other		(200)	374	–
Net cash used in investing activities		**(22,767)**	**(14,837)**	**(9,518)**
Financing activities				
Net repurchase of shares		(2,567)	(7,113)	(15,151)
Proceeds from long-term financing		7,961	8,109	3,831
Repayments of long-term financing		(3,821)	(3,192)	(3,655)
Net increase (decrease) in short-term debt		(1,315)	1,494	3,873
Dividends paid				
BP shareholders	21	(10,342)	(8,106)	(7,686)
Minority interest		(425)	(227)	(283)
Net cash used in financing activities		**(10,509)**	**(9,035)**	**(19,071)**
Currency translation differences relating to cash and cash equivalents		(184)	135	47
Increase (decrease) in cash and cash equivalents		4,635	972	(370)
Cash and cash equivalents at beginning of year		3,562	2,590	2,960
Cash and cash equivalents at end of year		**8,197**	**3,562**	**2,590**

Figure 1.6   Cash flow statement 2008, Birtish Petroleum.

However, they can be quite significant when the entity disposes of land or financial investments whose value has probably increased significantly since their acquisition.

- **Cash flows from financing activities**. These are all flows associated with movements in equity contributions by the owners or in financial debt. They are mainly increases or reductions of capital, payment of dividends to shareholders, and receipt or repayment of financial loans.

The presentation of the cash flow statement is standardized by the IAS 7. Figure 1.6 shows, for the Britsh Petroleum Group, the three main sections: operating (here called "operating activity"), investing and financing activities.

The cash flow statement for British Petroleum at 12/31/2008 shows as basic information, relatively low in the table, that cash increased by $4,635m during 2008, reaching a level of

$8,197m. This value of $8,197m corresponds to that shown in the balance sheet at 12/31/2008 in the line "Cash and cash equivalent" in the current assets of the balance sheet of the entity.

The increase of $4,635m is divided mainly into three parts:

- An increase of $38,095m related to operating activities. The current activity of the entity is generating cash flow and thus helps to finance at least part of the financial needs elsewhere.
- A cash outflow of $22,767m related to investment operations, mainly due to capital expenditure.
- A cash outflow of $10,509m related to financing activities. This amount is the balance of large movements due to the repayment of loans and the repurchase of shares.

British Petroleum has thus chosen to finance about half of its investments by current flows generated by the activity.

Without the cash flow statement, the analysis of the increase in cash of $4,635m (130% compared to the beginning of the period) would have been much more complicated or even impossible.

1.1.4 Distinction between Income and Cash

The analysis of the income statement and the cash-flow statement of British Petroleum shows that income and cash do not measure the same thing. The net income is a performance measure based on the commitments of the company, while cash flows reflect the cash receipts and disbursements. Thus, although during 2008 the financial performance (the profit) of the BP Group is $21,666m, the changes in its cash show an increase of $4,635m (Figure 1.6).

It is therefore imperative for the understanding of the accounting system to distinguish these two concepts, and that is the goal of Application 1.1. Starting with a statement of cash flows, it introduces, step-by-step information that is necessary to determine the net income of the Rafo Company for the same period. The first three steps are devoted to the calculation and analysis of the change in cash:

1. Status of cash during the year 2008
2. Calculating the change in cash due to only operating activities
3. Analysis of variation in cash.

The following steps add the missing information in order to determine the corresponding revenue or expense, and thus the operating profit:

4. The sales
5. The purchases
6. The consumptions
7. The amortizations.

An eighth step is to determine the net income of the period and analyze it in comparison with the change in cash. This concludes that these two indicators each measure a different aspect of the business situation and are bound together by a common starting point: the balance sheet.

APPLICATION 1.1

Cash Position

M. Ferrara and his partners are owners of the candy shop Rafo, which produces and sells mint and caramel candies. During the night of 12/31/2008 to 01/01/2009 a fire destroys almost all the accounting documents. Only some limited backup data is left. However, a report with 2008 cash inflows and outflows is still available.

Transaction of 2008 (in thousand Euros)

1.	Cash inflow	Sales to supermarket distribution	122,500
2.	Cash inflow	Sales to wholesalers	76,000
3.	Cash inflow	Sales of securities	25,000
4.	Payment	Suppliers of sugar and glucose	60,000
5.	Payment	Suppliers of packaging	25,000
6.	Payment	Transportation services	10,000
7.	Payment	Salaries and social expenses	40,000
8.	Payment	Various incentives	10,000
9.	Payment	Publicity	10,000
10.	Payment	Exterior charges	15,000
11.	Payment	Professional tax	15,300
12.	Payment	Financial expenses	2,500
13.	Payment	Debt repayments	5,000
14.	Payment	Dividends	2,500
15.	Payment	Modernization of the packaging chain	22,500

On 01/01/2008, Rafo had €5,000,000 on its bank account.

What is the Cash Position at the end of the Fiscal Year 2008?   The cash position for 2008 corresponds to the initial cash position plus the sum of cash inflows minus the sum of cash outflows related to the fiscal year.

Cash position on 01/01/2008	5,000
Cash inflows in 2008	+223,500
Cash outflows in 2008	−217,800
Cash position on the 12/31/2008	**10,700**

Cash Generated by the Operating Activity   The objective is to analyze whether the main and recurring business is able to generate enough cash to enable the company to meet its obligations. It can therefore avoid the repeated use of external financing (loans, shares issuance) or even an insolvency situation when new funds are not available (when the current assets can no longer cover outstanding liabilities).

Generally speaking, the movements in operating cash must only include:

- operations related to the reporting period;
- operating activities strictly speaking, excluding financial transactions and investing operations.

APPLICATION 1.2

Which Cash Amount was Generated by 2008 Operating Activities?

Some transactions are not related to the operating activities of Rafo (purchase, transformation, packaging, sale):

- The sale of bonds (transaction 3). This operation is related to non-current financial assets – considering that the securities were not held for speculative reasons. This cash flow is related to the investing activity.
- Transactions 12, 13 and 14 are related to equity (dividends) or long-term debt (debt, financial charges). Those cash flows are related to the financing activity.
- The modernization of the packaging chain (transaction 15). This operation will have an impact on future periods (unlike salaries, this investment will generate economic benefits even after 12/31/2008). This expense represents an investment over 10 years into a non current asset. Therefore the cash flow must be related to the investing activity.

The cash flows generated by operating activities are as follows:

Cash inflows

1. Cash inflow	Sales to supermarket distribution	122,500
2. Cash inflow	Sales to wholesalers	76,000
Total cash inflows from operating activities		198,500

Cash outflows

4. Payment	Suppliers of sugar and glucose	60,000
5. Payment	Suppliers of packaging	25,000
6. Payment	Transportation services	10,000
7. Payment	Salaries and social expenses	40,000
8. Payment	Various incentives	10,000
9. Payment	Publicity	10,000
10. Payment	Exterior charges	15,000
11. Payment	Professional tax	15,300
Total cash outflows from operating activities		185,300
Net cash flows from operating activities		**13,200**

Analysis of Change in Cash   There should be several comparisons: with previous years, with forecasts for 2008, with comparable companies, etc. However, in principle, the business of a company must be widely profitable in cash.

- Otherwise, other specific sources of finance (loans, etc.) must be anticipated. They include constraints (especially payment of dividends and interest on loans).
- It is the cash generated by the operating activities that enables a company to invest (direct payment or indirect financing via loan repayments).

APPLICATION 1.3

Analysis of Cash Flows

Rafo's positions are as follows:

Operating activity		**+13,200**
(See Application 1.2)		
Investing activity		**+2,500**
15. Payment	Modernization of the packaging chain	−22,500
3. Cash inflow	Sales of securities	25,000
Financing activity		**−10,000**
12. Payment	Financial expenses	2,500
13. Payment	Debt repayments	5,000
14. Payment	Dividends	2,500

The investment into the packaging chain is entirely financed by the sale of securities and does not necessitate any debt contracting or other financial resources.

The cash surplus from the operating activity is used, on the one hand, to pay the interests from the debt and to repay debt, and, on the other, to pay a dividend to the shareholders who invested capital in the company.

Determination of the Operating Profit   The universal convention for the recognition of net income is to recognize revenues and expenses when they are realized and not when cash is received or paid. The criteria used for the recognition is the transfer of risks and benefits associated with the ownership of property (see Chapter 2). In practice, that is usually the date of delivery for goods or the completion date for services, and this causes a lag between the cash flow date and that of recognition of income. Whenever a seller grants a settlement period (i.e. sale on credit) – for example, the product is registered for sale prior to payment – the good is therefore delivered to the buyer. The risks and benefits are thus transferred to the latter (the buyer) long before that client receives and pays the corresponding invoice. To determine the net income from cash flows, we must have all the elements related to the time lag of cash.

Regarding sales, at least part of the receipts of year N corresponds to sales during the previous year. Conversely, some of the sales in period N are still to be cash collected (credit sales), because the company provides terms of payments, and that should be taken into account when determining the profit made on sales of N. We must therefore know the amount of receivables at 01/01/N and 12/31/N (see Application 1.4). The amount of receivables at January 1 corresponds to sales made last year and must be deducted from the cash receipts of the period N to get the result. The amount of receivables at December 31 is added to the amount obtained because it corresponds to sales of N; however the cash receipt for that transaction has still not occurred. Thus:

$$\text{Sales}_n = \text{Cash receipt}_n + (\text{Receivables}_n - \text{Receivables}_{n-1})$$

APPLICATION 1.4

Operating Activity (1): Determination of Sales

Let's presume that the accounts receivable were 50,000 on 01/01/2008 and 40,000 on 12/31/2008. The 2008 sales are computed as follows:

Cash inflows 2008	198,500
− Accounts receivable 01/01/2008	50,000
+ Accounts receivable 12/31/2008	40,000
= Sales 2008	**188,500**

The reasoning is similar for purchases of raw materials (see Application 1.5). The company probably has settlement deadlines that must be considered. This time, we must take into account liabilities towards suppliers, which correspond, at the beginning of the year, to purchases made during the previous period and are only paid during the current period. They should therefore be deducted from the disbursements of the period. However, we must add the amount of payables at the end of the period, as they reflect the purchases of the period N for which payment has not yet been made. Thus:

$$\text{Purchases}_n = \text{Cash disbursments}_n + (\text{Payables}_n - \text{Payables}_{n-1})$$

APPLICATION 1.5

Operating Activity (2): Determination of Purchases

On 01/01/2008 the accounts payable were 19,000 and on 12/31/2008 they were 13,000. The purchases of 2008 are computed as follows:

Cash outflows 2008 (transactions 4, 5 and 6)	95,000
− Accounts payable 01/01/2008	19,000
+ Accounts payable 12/31/2008	13,000
= Purchases 2008	**89,000**

This amount corresponds to all the goods and services purchased in 2008. Those expenses are not necessarily equal to the consumptions of the period but are the expenses that have to be listed in the income statement.

Even if it is adjusted with payables at the beginning and end of the period, the amount of disbursements for purchases does not reflect the expense associated with the consumption of materials during the period. The company may have bought materials that have not yet been consumed. Only goods (or materials) consumed, and therefore cleared during the period, represent an expense of the company. Inventories of goods (or materials) still present at the closing date are another embodiment of the same resource: the cash in bank has become a stock, but no consumption has yet occurred.

- The **initial stock** represents the purchases (goods or materials) which were not consumed in the previous period.
- The **final stock** represents the purchases (goods or materials) which were not consumed in the current period.

To properly determine the expense associated with the consumption of materials during the period, we must also know the status of the stock of materials at the beginning and end of the period (see Application 1.6). The **stock at the beginning (initial stock)** of the period represents purchases of the previous period that have generally been consumed during the current period. It is added to purchases of the fiscal period, when determining expenses (of the period). The **stock at the end of the period (final stock)** represents purchases of the period that were probably consumed during the following period. The purchases of period N are not therefore always an expense of period N, but may have an impact on the net income of period $N+1$, when they will be consumed. Thus:

$$\text{Consumptions}_n = \text{Inventory}_{n-1} + \text{Purchases}_n - \text{Inventory}_n$$

APPLICATION 1.6

Operating Activity (3): Determination of Consumption

In addition to the purchases, an initial stock can be consumed. On the other hand it is possible that at the end of the period some purchases will not be consumed and remain as stock. Therefore changes in inventories have to be taken into account.

The initial stock on 01/01/2008 was 16,000 and the year end stock on 12/31/2008 was 12,000. The consumption of the period is computed as follows:

Inventories on 01/01/2008	16,000
+ Purchases of 2008	89,000
− Inventories of 12/31/2008	12,000
= Consumption 2008	**93,000**

Another correction concerns the expenditures for investments (see Application 1.7). Investments are useful to the company for several years, while depreciating in most cases for a period that is quite predictable. Depreciation related to the use or other reasons is a consumption of resource and is an expense for the period (Chapter 5 details the procedures for calculating an expense of amortization and depreciation). The expenditure incurred during the accounting period N does not reflect an expense for the year, but it will have to be estimated on the basis of the useful life of the investment and the rate of consumption.

APPLICATION 1.7

Operating Activity (4): Determination of Depreciations and the Operating Income

Depreciations   To simplify matters, consider that the packaging chain was bought on 01/01/2008 and has a useful life of 10 years. The yearly consumption (transaction 15) is $22,500/10 = 2,250$.

Operating Expenses   Based on what was computed in Applications 1.6 and 1.7 and transactions 7 to 11, it is possible to compute the operating expenses of 2008 without further complications:

Application 1.6	Consumed purchases	93,000
7. Payment	Salaries and social expenses	40,000
8. Payment	Various incentives	10,000
9. Payment	Publicity	10,000
10. Payment	Exterior charges	15,000
11. Payment	Professional tax	15,300
Application 1.7	Depreciation expenses	2,250
	Total	**185,550**

Net Operating Income 2008

Application 1.4	Operating income	188,500
Application 1.7	Operating expenses	185,550
	Net operating income	**2,950**

The operating profit is the profit achieved with the primary business of the company: this is what its "business" or "business model" is able to generate in terms of economic performance. But this is not the whole company performance.

We must add items related to the financing activities of the company, including financial expenses. They are, especially, the interest paid on loans and other bank debt. It is important to note that dividends are not an expense for the company. It is indeed the use of the income which itself is determined by comparing revenues and expenses for the year. After determining all revenues and expenses for the year, we can finally determine the amount to be distributed (dividends) and the part remaining in the company (equity reserves).

APPLICATION 1.8

Computation of the Net Income and its Reconciliation with the Cash Position

Financial Expenses   The cost of debt is 2,500 in 2008 (transaction 14).

Income of 2008

Application 1.7	Net perating income	2,950
Application 1.8	Net financial income	−2,500
Net Income before Taxes		**450**

Reconciliation of the Cash Position and the Net Income

The net income of 450 and the cash surplus of 13,200 are easy to reconcile:

Operating Cash Surplus	**13,200**
Adjustment of cash inflows (198,500 − 188,500)	−10,000
Adjustment of cash outflows (95,000 − 93,000)	+2,000
Recognition of the depreciation expense	−2,250
Net Operating Income	**2,950**
Recognition of the financial expenses	−2,500
Net Income before Taxes	**450**

The two concepts of *operating cash flow* and *operating profit* are often quite distant from each other, which is explained in the case study. They are two indicators with two quite different vocations. The net income measures the economic performance of the company, i.e. its ability to make profits.

The operating cash flow is a financial indicator of the ability of the company to cope with financing needs. It is therefore necessary to identify and follow these two indicators.

1.2   ACCOUNTING PRINCIPLES AND MECHANISMS

1.2.1   Accounting Principles

The financial statements of a company must provide information about its performance, financial situation and its evolution from one year to another. This information should be useful to a wide range of users, although investors are the main target of the financial statements as they provide the capital. The financial statements are based on principles which are composed of two assumptions and a number of qualitative features (IAS 1).

Assumptions   The preparation of financial statements is based on the assumptions of going concern and accrual basis accounting. Under the first assumption, the company should continue its activities in a foreseeable future. Indeed, if the continuation of operations of the company is questioned, one should determine the liquidation values of each asset in the balance sheet because the company would be close to discontinuance of business and therefore to its liquidation. The second assumption, the accrual basis accounting, means that economic events and other business transactions must be recorded when they occur, not when they are paid (receipt or disbursement). Chapter 2 deals with this last point.

Qualitative Features   The objective of the qualitative characteristics underlying the financial statements is to make the information content useful. These characteristics describe a number of attributes that financial statements must possess.

- **Relevance**. Relevant information is information that will affect the decision making of financial statement users. It should thus help users to understand and evaluate past, present or future events related to the company. This attribute (relevance) is a function of the relative importance of information (its *materiality*). For example, a stock of dairy products (yogurts) worth €10,000 is not as important to a retail store as it is for a multinational in agribusiness. The information presented should be of significant importance; that is to say, its presence or absence in the financial statements influences the decision making of investors.
- **Understandability**. Users should immediately understand the information presented in financial statements. This requires three conditions: users have a reasonable knowledge of economic activities of the business and accounting, and are willing to consider the financial statements in a reasonably diligent manner. The complexity of some transactions is not a reason to exclude them from the financial statements.
- **Comparability**. The financial statements must be comparable in time and space. Comparability over time means that we can monitor the financial situation of a company, its performance or changes in its cash flows from one period to another. Thus, the financial statements present not only the figures for the current year but also those of the previous year. The company should strive to use the same accounting methods from one year to

another if the comparison of figures is to be meaningful. However, a change of method is always possible, if sufficiently justified. The comparability in space refers to the need for investors to compare financial statements between companies in the same sector, for example.

- **Reliability**. To be useful, information contained in financial statements must be reliable – that is to say, not contain any error or any bias on what it is supposed to represent. Reliability requires five characteristics:

    - *The substance over form*. This will favour the economic nature of a transaction (or event) when it has to be accounted for and represent it in the financial statements. The legal nature of the transaction is not ignored, but is secondary. Thus, assets rented on financing lease will be present in the balance sheet of the company, among other fixed assets, even though they would not be legally owned.
    - *Neutrality*. This consists in presenting information that is not intended to guide the decision of users in a predetermined direction.
    - *Completeness*. This enjoins to provide all information necessary for making economic decisions, while taking into account the relative importance of each item of data.
    - *Prudence*. This takes into account a certain degree of caution in the exercise of judgements needed in making the estimates. It prevents assets or income from being overstated and liabilities or expenses understated. This principle does not prohibit a positive revaluation of assets, for example, but one should then consider carefully the cost of revaluation.
    - *Faithful representation*. Financial statements should present fairly the financial position and performance of the company. The compliance of all accounting principles shall allow this objective to be achieved.

1.2.2   Accounting Mechanisms

Knowledge of the mechanisms to prepare the financial statements is a necessary step to their understanding. These mechanisms allow the company to deal consistently and rigorously with all associated accounting and financial transactions. Information is collected and synthesized in order to be presented in a understandable way in the financial statements.

Fundamental Identity

> The **fundamental identity** states that the value of assets is equal to the sum of the value of liabilities (obligations) and equity.

The financial statements are based on a relationship of balance called the **fundamental identity** which summarizes all the activities of an enterprise. The latter simply states that the value of assets is equal to the total value of liabilities (obligations) and shareholders' equity. This relationship can be presented as follows:

$$\text{Assets} = \text{Liabilities} + \text{Equity}$$

As stated, it represents the balance sheet of a company. The accounting mechanisms operate in such a manner that this identity is always respected. Failure to respect this relationship means that an error has occurred while processing a transaction, due to an inaccurate estimate of values, a wrong report in the accounts, etc. Conversely, the respect of this identity does not exclude a recording error. The operation of this mechanism is shown in Application 1.9.

APPLICATION 1.9

Recognition of Transactions and the Accounting Equation

In this first part, the objective is to explain the accounting equation through the impact of three transactions: respectively, the balance sheet, the income statement and the statement of cash flows. The Beta company has to recognize its creation, a purchase and a sale.

Hence, the following transaction must be recognized in Beta's accounts:

(1)   At the creation of the Beta company, the owner personally invests €50,000 and borrows €10,000 from the bank. The sum of €60,000 is placed in Beta's bank account.
(2)   The company purchases merchandise for €20,000 and pays in cash.
(3)   The company sells half of its merchandise for €30,000 and is paid on the same date in cash.

The fundamental identity allows the transactions to be recorded, as follows.

First, regarding transaction (1), the initial investment of €50,000 is deposited into the bank account of the company. This bank deposit is an asset because it is a source of future economic benefits. It should not be confused with the loan that will follow. In parallel, we recorded in equity the capital inflow of €50,000 made by the owners. The amount of €10,000 obtained through the loan is recorded as an asset in the bank account. The counterparty liability is a debt of that amount because the loan must be repaid at maturity and thus represents a negative value for shareholders. After this first transaction, the company has assets of €60,000 invested as a deposit in the bank account (Assets) and funded by debt of €10,000 and shareholders' equity of €50,000, i.e. €60,000 in total. The fundamental identity is respected at all times. In the cash-flow statement, this transaction appears in the cash flows from financing activities, because the two flows provide financial resources to the company and are not related to its operational activity.

Transaction (2) involves the purchase of goods in order to sell them, with the hope of making a profit. The purchase was paid by check and there is a simultaneous decrease in cash of €20,000 and an increase in the value of inventory of goods of the same amount. Thus, the amount of total assets does not change because it is only an exchange between different asset items. The debt and equity also remain unchanged. There is thus no impact on the fundamental identity. The cash flow of €−20,000 related to this transaction is a cash flow from an operating activity because it is made in the context of the operational activities of the company.

Finally, transaction (3) corresponds to the sale of 50% of goods, which are sold for €30,000. This operation is analyzed in two stages: first, the increase in assets of €30,000, then the exit from inventory for €10,000 (50% of €20,000). For the first step, no liability can be linked to the increase of the asset: it thus represents an increase in the net value of the company, to be registered in equity. Since this increase is achieved by the company itself (unlike a capital contribution by the owners for example), it is recorded in the net income for the year and generates a movement in the income statement as an income from sales. In the second step, we must record the fact that goods have been exited from the company during the sales

Table 1.1

Transactions	Assets		=	Liabilities	+	Equity	
	Inventory	Cash	=			Equity	Income
(1)		+60,000	=	+10,000	+	+50,000	
(2)	+20,000	−20,000	=		+		
(3)	−10,000	+30,000	=		+		+30,000
							−10,000
Total	**+10,000**	**+70,000**	**=**	**+10,000**	**+**	**+50,000**	**+20,000**

operation. Their value of €10,000, equal to 50% of €20,000 paid for acquiring the initial stock in transaction (2), should no longer appear in the inventory of the company. This loss does not cause a decrease of liabilities and thus represents a reduction of net assets or equity of the company. As it is not a return of capital to owners but a decrease due to the activity of the company, this decrease is recorded as an expense in the income statement. Economically speaking, it is the consumption of inventory in order to generate economic benefits through the sale. The balance of the result at the end of this transaction, and therefore the result of the sale, is a profit of €(30,000 − 10,000) = €20,000. The cash receipt of €30,000 is the only cash flow observed in this transaction. Made in the context of the operational activities of the company, it will appear in the cash flows related to the operational activities in the cash-flow statement.

Following transactions (1), (2) and (3), the total assets are €80,000 (10,000 of inventory + 70,000 in the bank account), while debts are still €10,000 and equity is €70,000 (50,000 of capital inflow + 20,000 of net income). After each transaction, the fundamental identity is respected. Table 1.1 summarizes the movements in the accounts of Beta in relation to these three transactions.

The summaries of these three operations are given in Table 1.2.

Accounts and Ledger The number of transactions that a firm must perform in a year to prepare its financial statements is often very important (thousands or even millions). It is

Table 1.2   Balance Sheet

Assets		Liabilities and equity	
		Capital	50,000
		Net income	20,000
Inventory	10,000		
		Loan	10,000
Cash	70,000		
Total assets	**80,000**	**Total**	**80,000**

Income statement

Sale	30,000
Cost of goods sold (CGS)	−10,000
Net income (i.e. Profit)	20,000

Cash flow statement

Cash flow from operating activities (−20,000 + 30,000)	10,000
Cash flow from investing activities	0
Cash flow from financing activities (50,000 + 10,000)	60,000
Net increase (decrease) in cash	70,000
Cash, beginning of year	0
Cash, end of year	70,000

difficult to follow properly the recording of all transactions using only the fundamental identity. Using accounts not only facilitates the proper monitoring of operations as a whole, but allows the company to rapidly trace all the transactions that have affected a particular account. This bookkeeping system is often schematized by a "T", hence the expression **T-account**.

Account	
Debit	Credit

By convention, the left column of the account is called **Debit**, while the right column is called **Credit**. The logic of these accounts is based on the fundamental identity. It considers that the assets are debit accounts, while the obligations (liabilities) and equity are credit accounts. Any increase in an asset account is thus recorded in the Debit section of this account, while decreases are recorded in the Credit section. The final balance appears on the Debit side. The method is reversed for liabilities and equity accounts: any increase is registered in the Credit side and any reduction in the Debit side. In this instance the final balance appears on the Credit side. Using one side of the account for the registration of an increase and the other for a decrease, means that no negative values are recorded in an account.

$$\text{Assets} = \text{Liabilities} + \text{Equity}$$
$$\text{Debit} = \text{Credit}$$

Applying the concept of "T-account" with its convention of Debit and Credit, like the fundamental identity, leads to the following representation:

Assets		=	Liabilities		+	Equity	
Debit	Credit		Debit	Credit		Debit	Credit

The **ledger** keeps track of transactions that have affected a particular account.

This mechanism permits the recording of various transactions of a company. All accounts are grouped in what is called a **ledger**, which keeps track of transactions that have affected a particular account. Application 1.10 enables us to understand the mechanism of T-accounts.

APPLICATION 1.10

Recognition of Transactions Based on the T-Accounts

In this second part the three transactions of Application 1.9 will be registered in the T-accounts.

Accounts of assets have a debit balance and therefore an increase in the assets value has to be entered in the left column. Liabilities and equity are credit balance accounts and therefore an increase in liabilities must be entered to the right column of the account

The following transaction have to be entered into the T-accounts:

(1) At the creation of the Beta company, the owner invests personally €50,000 and borrows €10,000 from the bank. The sum of €60,000 is placed in Beta's bank account.

(2)   The company purchases merchandise for €20,000 and pays in cash.
(3)   The company sells half of its merchandise for €30,000 and is paid on the same date in cash.

Transaction (1) is an increase of the asset account "cash" and the debit must be entered in the left column. The equity and liabilities accounts are credited. The following accounting entries have to be made:

Cash		Debt		Equity	
60,000			10,000		50,000

The mechanism of T-accounts is to record a decrease in value in the column opposite to that normally used to record an increase in value. Thus, insofar as the assets are "debit accounts", an increase in their value is registered in the left column (Debit). The accounts of debt and equity are usually "Credit accounts". This means that an increase in their value is registered in the right column. Regarding transaction (2), the cash used to acquire stocks of goods, i.e. €20,000, is not registered negatively in the left column of the Cash account, but in the opposite column, in Credit. The €20,000 allow the purchase of stocks of goods. There is therefore an increase in value of the Inventory account. As with all asset accounts, this increase in value is then recorded in the Debit side of the account, as follows:

Cash		Inventory		Debt		Capital	
	20,000 (2)	(2) 20,000					

Transaction (3) is recorded in two steps. First, the sale is recorded. The account *Sales* and other operating revenue accounts operate like the *Equity* account: insofar as a sale increases equity, a revenue is recorded as an increase in equity, that is, in Credit. This means that, for Beta, the amount of €30,000 is recorded in the Credit side of the *Sales* account in the income statement and the same amount is recorded in the Debit side of the *Cash* account, as the value of that asset increases.

The second step is to record the exit of the goods, since they have been sold. Half of the goods have been sold. The cost for the company is €20,000 × 50% = €10,000. In a similar manner to the revenues, expenses are recorded as decreases in equity, that is, in the Debit side of the respective expense accounts. The amount of €10,000 is thus recorded in the Debit of the Cost of goods sold (COGS) account. In return, the Inventory account is credited with the same amount, reflecting the decline in stocks of goods. Movements in the accounts related to Transaction (3) are as follows:

Cash		Inventory		Debt		Capital	
(3) 30,000			10,000 (3)				

COGS		Sales	
(3) 10,000			30,000 (3)

The **closing of accounts** includes operations necessary for determining the net income.

When all transactions have properly been recorded, one should determine the net income at year end. This operation, which is called **accounts closing** is, first, to work out the final value of each account of income (revenues and expenses), then record their respective value in a single account (the income statement) in order to determine whether the company made a loss or a profit (see Application 1.11).

APPLICATION 1.11

Closing of Accounts

After all accounting entries of the period have been made, the general ledger of Beta looks at follows:

Cash		Debt		Equity	
(3) 60,000	20,000 (2)		10,000		50,000 (1)
(3) 30,000					
70,000			10,000		50,000

Inventory		Cost of goods sold		Sales	
(2) 20,000	10,000 (3)	10,000			30,000
10,000		10,000			30,000

The balance of each account is in the bottom line. It is obtained by making the difference of the sums of the debit and credit columns. For example, the cash account has €90,000 on the debit side and €20,000 on the credit side. The balance of €70,000 is written on the debit side since the debits are greater than the credits.

In order to obtain the net income of the company, the revenues and expenses accounts have to be cleared and transferred to the Net income account. Those accounting entries are marked with an (A):

Cash		Debt		Equity	
(3) 60,000	20,000 (2)		10,000		50,000 (1)
(3) 30,000					
70,000			10,000		50,000
					20,000 (B)

Inventory		Cost of goods sold		Sales	
(2) 20,000	10,000 (3)	10,000			30,000
10,000		10,000	10,000 (A)	(A)30,000	30,000

Net income

(A) 10,000	30,000(A)
(B) 20,000	20,000 (A)

The difference of revenues and expenses allows a credit of €20,000 to appear. This means that the revenues are greater than the expenses: there is a profit of €20,000. The next operation consists of transferring the profit to equity, represented here by the (B) entries.

The **trial balance** shows for each account on a single line: the name of the account, movements in Debit and Credit, and the final balance, which is either in Debit or in Credit.

The **trial balance** provides a synthetic view of the movements and balances. This table shows for each account on a single line: the name, movements in Debit and Credit, and the final balance, which is either in Debit or in Credit.

Logically, the total of the Debit and Credit columns must be identical for the movements on the one hand, and balances on the other hand. The trial balance of the Beta company is presented in Table 1.3.

The **journal** records the operations one after the other. All transactions must also be followed chronologically. The journal records the operations, following the same accounting mechanisms as for T-accounts. Transactions are first recorded in the journal, then automatically entered in the **general ledger**. In the journal, a particular transaction is recorded as follows:

	Debit	*Credit*
Date		
Name of "debited" account	Amount	
Name of the "credited" account		Amount

After each transaction is recorded, the total debits must equal the total credits. Thus, this equality will be valid at year-end on all transactions.

Table 1.3

Name of the account	*Movements*		*Balance*	
	Debit	*Credit*	*Debit*	*Credit*
Capital		50,000		50,000
Debt		10,000		10,000
Inventory	20,000	10,000	10,000	
Cash	90,000	20,000	70,000	
COGS	10,000		10,000	
Sales		30,000		30,000
Total	**120,000**	**120,000**	**90,000**	**90,000**

APPLICATION 1.12

Accounting Entries in the Book of Original Entries

This illustration works with the same transactions as previous two (Application 1.10 and 1.11) which have to be entered into the book of original entries:

(1)   At the creation of the Beta company, the owner invests personally €50,000 and borrows €10,000 from the bank. The sum of €60,000 is placed in Beta's bank account.
(2)   The company purchases merchandise for €20,000 and pays in cash.
(3)   The company sells half of its merchandise for €30,000 and is paid on the same date in cash.

The first transaction can be treated as follows: two operations can be entered into the book through one accounting entry:

Cash and cash equivalent (+A)	60,000	
Capital (+E)		50,000
Debt (+L)		10,000

To make the lecture of accounting entries easier, the nature of the affected accounts is put in brackets behind the accounting entry: Assets (±A), Liabilities (±L), Equity (±E), and all accounts with an impact on the net income (±IS for Income Statement). Transactions (2) and (3) are registered as follows:

Inventories (+A)	20,000	
Cash and cash equivalent (−A)		20,000
Cash and cash equivalent (+A)	30,000	
Sales (+IS)		30,000
Cost of goods sold (−IS)	10,000	
Inventories (−A)		10,000

The entries for the closing of account (A and B) are as follows:

Net income	10,000	
Cost of goods sold		10,000
Sales	30,000	
Net income		30,000
Determination of the net income		

Net income	20,000	
Retained earnings		20,000
Transfer of the net income to Equity		

Given that sometimes these are a very large number of accounts in use, companies adopt a numbering system for accounts. The IFRS do not comment on the matter. In France, all companies must use a harmonized and mandatory numbering, called *Plan des comptes*, or **Chart of accounts**. Regarding the balance sheet and income statement, the Chart of accounts distinguishes seven classes of account, which are divided between the balance sheet and income statement (see Figure 1.7).

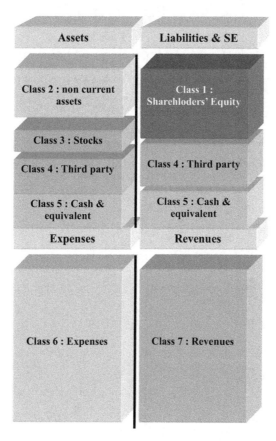

Figure 1.7   Chart of french accounts.

Within classes, numbering becomes increasingly subtle. Thus, within the class 2, for example, category 21 refers to the tangible assets and within this category, No. 211 designates the land and No. 213 the buildings. It is not uncommon to see a company's Charts of accounts with 8- or 9-digit numbers.

There are, of course, other systems of account numbering. In Germany, for example, the system most widely used is *Industriekontenrahmen* (see Figure 1.8).

In this book, examples and exercises are relatively simple and no use of account numbers is required.

1.3   SUMMARY

The three main summary tables published by companies are the balance sheet, the income statement and the cash flow statement. The first shows the financial situation at a specific date, distinguishing assets on the one hand, and equity and liabilities, on the other. The income statement provides information on economic performance expressed by the change in wealth

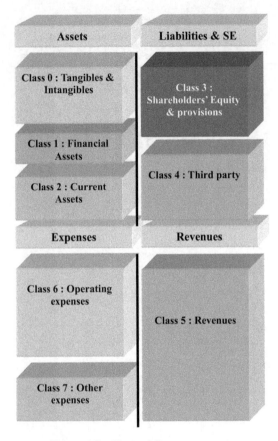

Figure 1.8   Chart of German accounts.

of the owners of an enterprise during a period. Increases in wealth (or revenues) are compared to consumptions (or expenses) and their difference is the income of the period. The cash flow statement allows the company to analyze how it has managed its financial situation during the period. The cash flows are distinguished according to whether they are cash flows from operating, investing or financing activities. There are links between changes in cash and the wealth of the owners, but these indicators are very different, with trends sometimes divergent. One should therefore be able to distinguish between terms such as "expense" and "revenue" and concepts of "cash receipt" and "disbursement".

These tables are the outcome of an extremely rigorous process of recording and processing accounting information. Based on the fundamental identity, any operation within the company generates movements in the accounts at least two different places, so that the total movements in Debit is always equal to that of movements in Credit. Respecting the fundamental identity in each individual transaction, we reach mechanically to balance sheets, income statements and cash-flow statements which are balanced.

1.4 ACTIVITIES

1.4.1 Case Study: Global Ltd

On 01/01/2008, Miss Mayer set up a company for the international trade of cosmetic products, Global Ltd. She personally invested €80,000 in cash, made a studio available in the downtown area valued at €120,000 (which will be used as an office) and which she bought 3 years earlier for €80,000. The bank granted her a line of credit of €50,000. Within the first year, the following transactions took place:

03/15/08 Purchase of merchandise paid in cash from Extra Ltd for €10,000
03/18/08 Purchase of merchandise on credit from Extra Ltd for €30,000
04/01/08 Purchase of a motor truck paid in cash for €30,000
04/18/08 Payment of the invoice from Extra Ltd of 03/18
05/20/08 Purchase of merchandise on credit from Extra Ltd for €20,000
05/25/08 Sale of merchandise on credit for €60,000 (at a cost of €30,000)
05/29/08 Payment of the invoice from Extra Ltd of the 05/20
06/25/08 Settlement of the client's invoice of 05/20
06/30/08 Purchase of merchandise paid in cash from Extra Ltd for €25,000
07/12/08 Return of impaired merchandise to Extra Ltd valued at €7,000
08/15/08 Deposit of €5,000 for an order from the client ABC Enterprise
08/31/08 Sale of merchandise to ABC paid in cash of €30,000 (order from 08/15) (at a cost of €15,000)
10/01/08 Hiring of an assistant
10/20/08 Sale of merchandise on credit to ABC for €20,000 (at a cost of €10,000)
10/31/08 ABC pays the invoice from 10/20
11/23/08 Purchase of merchandise on credit for €50,000
12/20/08 Sale of merchandise on credit of €100,000 (at a cost of €50,000)

On 12/31/08, the salaries and social expenses for 2008 of Miss Mayer and her assistant are €50,000. The depreciation of the transportation vehicle is €4,500 per annum and the depreciation of the office is €5,000 per annum. The income tax rate is 20%.

Make all the accounting entries and adjustments necessary to establish and present the financial statements of Global Ltd. All the transactions will first be entered into the book of original entries and then into the general ledger.

Book of Original entries   First, the capital base needs to be recognized.

01/01/08		
Cash and cash equivalent (+A)	80,000	
Capital (+E)		80,000
Tangible assets (office) (+A)	120,000	
Capital (+E)		120,000

All current transactions of the operating activity are registered chronologically into the book.

03/15/08		
Inventories (+A)	10,000	
Cash and cash equivalent (−A)		10,000

03/18/08		
Inventories (+A)	30,000	
Accounts payable (Extra) (+L)		30,000

01/08		
Transportation vehicle (+A)	30,000	
Cash and cash equivalent (−A)		30,000

04/18/08		
Accounts payable (Extra) (−L)	30,000	
Cash and cash equivalent (−A)		30,000

05/20/08		
Inventories (+A)	20,000	
Accounts payable (Extra) (+L)		20,000

05/25/08		
Accounts receivable (+A)	60,000	
Sales (+IS)		60,000
Cost of sales (−IS)	30,000	
Inventories (−A)		30,000

05/29/08		
Accounts payable (Extra) (−L)	20,000	
Cash and cash equivalent (−A)		20,000

06/25/08		
Cash and cash equivalent (+A)	60,000	
Accounts receivable (−A)		60,000

06/30/08		
Inventories (+A)	25,000	
Cash and cash equivalent (−A)		25,000

07/12/08		
Accounts payable (−L)	7,000	
Inventories (−A)		7,000

08/15/08		
Cash and cash equivalent (+A)	5,000	
Deposit received (+L)		5,000

08/31/08		
Cash and cash equivalent (+A)	25,000	
Deposit received (−L)	5,000	
Sales (+IS)		30,000
Cost of sales (−IS)	15,000	
Inventories (−A)		15,000

10/01/08 No book entry			

10/20/08		
Accounts receivable (ABC) (+A)	20,000	
Sales (+IS)		20,000
Cost of sales (−IS)	10,000	
Inventories (−A)		10,000

10/31/08		
Cash and cash equivalent (+A)	20,000	
Accounts receivable (ABC) (−A)		20,000

11/23/08		
Inventories (+A)	50,000	
Accounts payable (+L)		50,000

12/20/08		
Clients (+A)	100,000	
Sales (+IS)		100,000
Cost of sales (−IS)	50,000	
Inventories (−A)		50,000

At year end, in this example the 12/31/2008, all adjusting book entries have to be made so that the net income of the year comprises all the revenues and expenses of the year (and only from that period). Depreciations represent a consumption of future economic benefits of the company and must therefore be recognised as expenses. The salaries also still need to be recognized.

12/31/08		
Depreciation of transportation material (−IS)	4,500	
Depreciation of buildings (−IS)	5,000	
Accumulated depreciation of transportation material (−A)		4,500
Accumulated depreciation of buildings (−A)		5,000
Salaries and social expenses (−IS)	50,000	
Cash and cash equivalent (−A)		50,000

In order to compute the net income you have to establish first the net income before income tax expense. Therefore you have to make the difference between all the revenue and expenses accounts.

Sales	210,000	
Net income before tax		45,000
Cost of sales		105,000
Depreciation expense		9,500
Salaries		50,000

Then the income tax expense is computed and recognized:

Income tax expense (−IS)	9,100	
Tax liabilities (+L)		9,100

Finally, the income account is divided into tax expense and net income accounts:

Net income before tax	45,000	
Income tax expense		9,100
Net income		36,400

The general ledger re-orders all the book entries in function of the accounts.

General Ledger[5]

Balance Sheet Accounts

Transportation vehicle

30,000	
	30,000

Accumulated depreciation transportation vehicle

	4,500
4,500	

Contributed capital

	80,000
20,000	120,000

Buildings

120,000	
	120,000

Accumulated depreciation buildings

	5,000
5,000	

Tax liabilities

	9,100
9,100	

Inventories

10,000	30,000
30,000	7,000
20,000	15,000
25,000	10,000
50,000	50,000
	23,000

Accounts payable

30,000	30,000
20,000	20,000
7,000	50,000
43,000	

Accounts receivable

60,000	60,000
20,000	20,000
100,000	
	100,000

Deposit received

5,000	5,000

Cash and cash equivalent

80,000	10,000
60,000	30,000
5,000	30,000
25,000	20,000
20,000	25,000
	30,000
	25,000

---

[5]   *in the "T" acount: the last closing entries for the Trial Balance.*

Income Statement Accounts

Cost of goods sold		Depreciation		Sales	
30,000		4,500			60,000
15,000		5,000			30,000
10,000			**9,500**		20,000
50,000					100,000
	105,000			**210,000**	

Salaries		Income tax	
50,000		9,100	
	50,000		**9,100**

Determination of the Net Income

1. First you transfer all revenues and expenses into one account, the net income before tax account: €45,000.
2. Then you establish the amount of the income tax: 20% × €45,000 = €9,100.

Net income before tax		Net income	
105,000	210,000	9,100	45,500
50,000			
9,500			
45,500		**36,400**	

The balance sheet accounts and the net income account are then transferred to the balance sheet, and we finally end up with the following income statement and balance sheet account:

Income statement	
Sales	210,000
– *Cost of goods sold*	(105,00)
Gross margin	*105,000*
Salaries	(50,000)
Depreciation	(9,500)
Net income before tax	*45,500*
Income tax expense	(9,100)
Net income	**36,400**

Balance sheet

Assets			Liabilities and equity	
Cash and cash equivalent		25,000	Accounts payable	43,000
Accounts receivable		100,000	Tax liabilities	9,100
Inventories		23,000		
Total current assets		*148,000*	*Total liabilities*	*52,100*
Transportation vehicle	30,000	25,500	Contributed capital	200,000
(depreciation)	(4,500)		Net income/Retained earnings	36,400
Buildings	120,000	115,000		
(depreciation)	(5,000)		*Total equity*	*236,400*
Total non-current assets		*140,500*		
Total assets		**288,500**	**Total liabilities and equity**	**288,500**

2 INCOME FROM ORDINARY ACTIVITIES

One of the objectives of financial statements is to measure the economic performance of the company, mainly through the income of the year. This indicates the extent to which business activity has increased the wealth of capital providers by comparing revenues and expenses for a period. The income statement presents a number of performance indicators such as net income and income from ordinary activities. The latter is determined by the difference between revenues and expenses from ordinary activities. This chapter discusses the entry in the accounts of these two components. Under the matching principle of costs with revenues, the recording of the former is conditioned by the recording of the latter. The review of conditions of revenue registration is therefore an essential first step. Then comes the recording of ordinary expenses; i.e. expenses needed to achieve the revenues for the year. Indeed, IAS 18 requires, as another condition for the recording of a sale, the ability to measure reliably the cost necessary for its realization.

2.1 REVENUES FROM ORDINARY ACTIVITIES

Ordinary activities are any activities undertaken by a company within its business, and activities that result from it or are its extensions or attachments.

Initially, we must determine the date on which the various operations of the company are recorded, starting with sales, in order to obtain a reliable income of an accounting period. This avoids, for example, the recording of revenues not yet realized and therefore not acquired by the company. In a second step, it is important to determine the correct amount of sales to record. Generally, this is rather simple when you can rely on the net amount of invoices. The examples in this chapter show that several factors can affect this amount and sales transactions are recorded occasionally, even in the absence of invoices. Figure 2.1 shows the structure of this section.

2.1.1 Date of Recognition of Sales

The concept of sales or turnover is vast. IAS 18 uses the generic term of **ordinary revenues** to designate revenues made by the entity as part of its **normal business operations** (sales of goods, services, loans to third parties of property or other assets that generate interest, dividends or royalties).

The first question a company has to answer is: When should it record the sales, or rather, when should it not record them? The press, especially the media and financial analysts, watch closely the evolution of the turnover of companies, because this indicator allows the activities realized to be measured with others. In addition, many employees receive a variable component of their salary based on changes in sales or income. Clear rules for determining the exact date of recognition are essential to prevent the recording of an early or delayed operation.

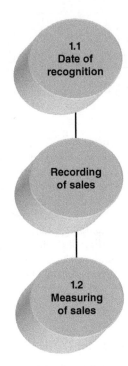

Figure 2.1   Sales and the determinants of their recording.

To answer the above question, we must first state the general principle regarding the sales of goods, which will be illustrated by concrete applications that also apply to other types of sales.

Sale of Goods: General Principle   The sale of a good is realized – and must therefore be recorded in the financial statements – when the company transferred to the buyer the significant risks and benefits incidental to ownership of the good and that the settlement will probably go to the company (see Figure 2.2).

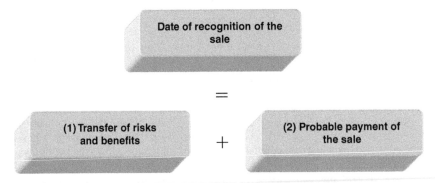

Figure 2.2   The determinants of the date of recognition.

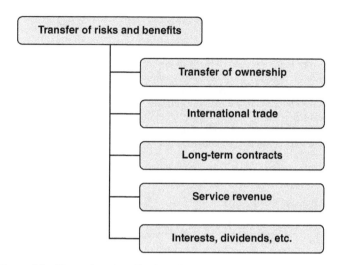

Figure 2.3 Examples of applications for the transfer of risks and benefits.

The recording of a sale does not expect the full or partial payment by the customer, as the latter has commonly variable settlement deadlines. This obviously affects the management of cash in the selling company, but there is no link between payment and sales recognition in the financial statements. In most countries, the seller of a good is its legal owner until full settlement by the client. Leaving aside the payment in determining the date of sale, IFRS do not also take into account the transfer of legal ownership of the good. Goods are thus recorded, sold and taken out of the book inventory of the seller, while the latter is still the legal owner.

The transfer of risks and benefits (Figure 2.3) of a good is, generally, done at its delivery. The signature of the delivery slip by the customer certifies that he has received the good. Therefore:

- The seller has fulfilled its obligations related to the sale.
- The buyer must fulfil its own obligations and pay the agreed settlement.

Revenues and Transfer of Ownership The supply of goods does not automatically mean the transfer of risks and benefits, nor generates the recording of a sale (see Application 2.1).

APPLICATION 2.1

Recognition of a Sale in the Case of a Lease Agreement with Purchase Option

Desirous of buying a new car equipped as he wants it, Mr Yard signs on 03/22/2010 an order for his car in the dealership of Mr Stone. They agree that Mr Yard will finance this purchase of €21,000 through a 3 year credit from the constructor's financial subsidiary. The order form indicates a projected delivery date on 06/15/2010. The car gets to the dealership with one week's delay, on 06/22/2010. Because Mr Yard is on a business trip, he only gets to the dealership on 06/28/2010 and signs the delivery form. The first payment is due on 07/15/2010 and Mr Yard will be the legal owner of his car on 06/15/2013, after the last instalment.

When does the sale occur in a matter of accounting?

Answer   The transfer of risks and economic benefits takes place on the effective date of delivery, 06/28/2010. The order is only a commitment of both parties and projected date of delivery is not taken into account for accounting purposes. Moreover, the delivery of the car at the dealership does not mean that automatically risks and benefits are transferred to the client. The payment conditions have no impact on the date of revenue recognition, but give information on the financial situation of the client. Finally, the economic analysis of the operations leads us to leave aside the legal aspects. The fact that Mr Yard only becomes owner of the car three years later does not prevent the company from recognizing the sale at the date of delivery.

Hence, on 06/28/2010 the following accounting entry is made into the books of the dealership:

Accounts receivable (+A)	21,000	
Sales (+IS)		21,000

A time lag between the transfer of ownership and of risks and benefits does not impact the sales recognition in the financial statements of the seller. Application 2.2 shows that, even when there is a transfer of ownership, a sale is not always achieved and no revenue should then be recognized.

APPLICATION 2.2

Recognition of Sales with Repurchase Agreement

Many car manufacturers have as clients car renting companies which keep the cars only for few months. Such companies, in order to avoid a great stock of used cars, sign contracts with repurchase agreements. The car manufacturer sells new cars to a car lessor and agrees on the date of the sale to repurchase the car 6 months later for a fixed price. On the date of the repurchase the car has still a significant value and the car manufacturer must find a new buyer for the used car.

Thereby, significant risks and benefits related to the car are not being transferred. So no sale can be recognized by the car manufacturer. The car stays within the stock of the manufacturer even though it is at the lessor's place. In economic terms, this type of contract is a lease agreement where the total rent for the car corresponds to the difference between the sale price and the fixed repurchase price.

The extract from the 2009 IFRS annual report of PSA Peugeot Citroën (see Figure 2.4) shows how groups provide information about this phenomenon in their disclosure. During the transition from French GAAP to IFRS, the effect of the restatement of sales with a buyback clause has reduced the turnover of this group to €551m in 2004.

A sale may also be recognized, even without transfer of ownership. For example, many airlines do not own their entire fleet. Some of the aircraft are leased from specialized companies for very long periods, often so long that by the end of a contract the aircraft has reached its age limit of usage and can no longer be rented. The rents (the renter will collect from the airline company during the tenancy) then include almost all the cost of the aircraft.

PSA PEUGEOT CITROËN ▜

In accordance with IAS 18 – Revenue, new vehicle sales are recognised on the date the risks and rewards of ownership are transferred. This generally corresponds to the date when the vehicles are made available to non-group dealers or the delivery date, in the case of direct sales.

Sales at cost of items purchased on behalf of other parties and sales to subcontractors of raw materials, parts and mechanical components that are intended to be bought back at cost are not included in sales and revenue.

Sales of new vehicles with a buyback commitment are not recognised at the time of delivery but accounted for as operating leases when it is probable that the vehicle will be bought back. This principle applies:

* whatever the duration of the buyback commitment;
* for both direct sales and sales financed by Banque PSA Finance and its subsidiaries.

Figure 2.4   Extract from the 2009 IFRS annual report of PSA Peugeot Citroën.

Legally, the owner retains ownership of the aircraft during the contract period. From an economic perspective, the financial risk related to the value of the aircraft, and almost all the benefits of its operations, are transferred to the airline company. At the end of the contract, the aircraft will not be rented again and the company has funded its costs by rents. From an accounting perspective, it is therefore a sale of the aircraft from the renter to the airline company, to be recorded in the accounts of the renter.

APPLICATION 2.3

Requalification of Lease Contracts to Sale Contracts

The company Rentair leases many airplanes to airliner companies for periods from 10 to 20 years. One of its clients is Pogson-Airlines, which rents a plane with 180 seats for 20 years from 01/01/2010 onwards. Due to the very long period over which the plane is leased and the substantial risk that Rentair will not be able to lease the plane again after 20 years, this contract is closes to a purchase contrat on credit than to a rental contract. Therefore, on the date of the transfer of benefits and risks (delivery to Pogson-Airlines), Rentair will enter into its book a sale and an outstanding receivable. The value of the sale will be the discounted yearly rents of €4m at a discount rate of 5%. It is computed in order to correspond to 100% of the price Pogson-Airlines would have to pay in the case of a purchase, here €49.8m.

Accounts receivable * (+A)	49,800,000	
Sales (+IS)		49,800,000
Accounting entry for Rentair on 01/01/10		

Chapter 3 gives details on the accounts receivable. Chapter 6 analyzes the impact of such transactions on the lessor's and lessee's financial statements.

Realization of Sale in International Trade **Incoterms** are international rules governing the sale of goods abroad. These standards define, in particular, the time of transfer of risk of the good from seller to buyer.

The sale of goods abroad is subject to regulations which can be very different from commercial operations in the country of the seller or buyer. The costs and risks of transport and administrative responsibilities to be shared among stakeholders in the transaction (seller, buyer, carriers, etc.) are also taken into account. International rules, known as **incoterms**, (Application 2.4) define this distribution, in particular the transfer of risk of the good from seller to buyer. At this time, the transaction becomes a sale from an accounting point of view and is recorded in the financial statements of the seller.

APPLICATION 2.4

International Sales under Incoterms

The French company Berkane sells electronic components for €240,000 to the Argentinean company Fuentes under the FOB (*Free On Board*) conditions of Incoterms. The seller of the merchandise takes all risks concerning the delivery of the product until the physical transit on board the ship.

The merchandise leaves the factory on 06/03/2010. It arrives in the port of Havre on the 06/05/2010 and is stocked on the quay until the ship *Seastar*, coming from Rotterdam, arrives and takes it on board for Argentina. Due to delay the containers are loaded on the ship only on the 07/04/2010. The accounting entry that needs to be made is:

	07/04/10		
Accounts receivable (+A)		240,000	
	Sales (+IS)		240,000

The accounting entry is made on 04/07/2010 because that is the effective date where the transfer of the risks takes place based on the selling contract. If the company Berkane publishes biannual financial statements, the transaction and the profit related to it can only be recognized in the second semester of 2010.

Long-Term Contracts The achievement of some major projects over several years requires several accounting periods (for instance, the construction of a flyover as the viaduct of Millau in France). The strict application of the principles outlined above would result in recording the sales only at the time of delivery, i.e. at completion of work. The builder of the bridge will not record any revenues for several years before recording an amount and a significant margin in the single delivery period. Such treatment does not properly reflect the economic performance of the building company.

The **percentage-of-completion method** leads to the spread of the turnover and margin throughout the realization period.

The **completed contract method** consists in recording the total margin only upon completion of the project.

IFRS (IAS 11) therefore require the recording of sales in proportion to the progress of the project. Each accounting period is thus endowed with a turnover and a margin corresponding to the percentage of project progress, which then spreads throughout the realization period. This method of recording revenue better reflects the economic performance of the building company and is called the **percentage-of-completion method**, as opposed to the **completed contract method** used in some accounting standards, and consists in recording the margin (in full) only upon completion of the project.

Sale of Services   Services are often provisions whose realization is spread over a more or less long period. In accordance with the principles set out above, the revenue is recorded as the service is realized. Regarding the discrepancy between cash flow generated by the payment and revenue realization, we apply the principles that govern the sale of goods.

APPLICATION 2.5

Recognition of a Sale Concerning a Service Delivery: Rental

The company, Morice-Leasing, gets from the lessee, Trellu, a 3-month rent payment for an apartment in Paris. The monthly rent is €1,000 and the first rent is paid on 12/31/2010 for the period 12/01/2010 to 02/28/2011.

Although the cash inflow is recognized all at once, the revenues from this transaction are recognized over the 3 months at a *pro rata* of one-third a month. The lease consists in the sale of a service which will be executed over the next 3 months. At the end of 2010, only one month can be recognized as revenue since two-thirds of the service will be rendered in 2011. The rent for January and February represents on 12/31/2010 a "debt in nature" to Morice-Leasing. In the balance sheet, those revenues will be recognized in the account "Deferred revenue."

Cash and cash equivalent (+A)		3,000	
Sales (+IS)			1,000
Deferred revenue (+L)			2,000
Accounting entry on 12/31/10			

At the end of January 2011, half of the deferred income must be transferred to income since the service is rendered:

Deferred revenue (−L)		1,000	
Sales (+IS)			1,000
Accounting entry of 01/31/11			

The same accounting entry is reiterated on the 02/28/2011 for the rent of February 2011.

APPLICATION 2.6

Recognition of a Sale for Service Transactions: Travel Tickets

On 12/05/2010, Mr. Black buys a ticket for a flight with his whole family on 02/18/2011, costing him €4,500. The airline company will not be able to recognize this revenue in its accounts of 2010 since the service is only delivered in 2011. Only the cash flow from the payment of the ticket will be recognized and to compensate this accounting entry, a liability will be recognized. In 2011, the airline company will then transfer this liability to the income statement as soon as the service is delivered, corresponding to the beginning of the journey.

Cash and cash equivalent (+A)		4,500	
	Deferred revenue (+L)		4,500
Cash inflow of the sale of tickets on 12/05/2010			
Deferred revenue (−L)		4,500	
	Sales (+IS)		4,500
Recognition of the sale on 02/18/2011			

The example of the German tour operator Tui, which is the leader in this sector in Europe and owns the French company Nouvelles Frontières, reflects the complexity of determining the sales in this activity (see Figure 2.5). The group mentions in particular the principles of recognizing sales of tourism services, "all-inclusive" trips, commissions received, hotel services and flights.

Interest, Royalties and Dividends   The principles are identical to those set for other sales. The turnover is recorded as time passes in regard to interest and royalties. Dividends are recorded when the shareholders get the right to collect them. This results in a mismatch between the accounting period releasing the year's profit of a company (revenue recognition) and the accounting period during which the shareholders of this company will have to record dividends received (receipt).

2.1.2   Measuring of Sales

Section 1.1.1 identified the date on which a sale is recorded. We then have to determine the amount to be recorded. A cash sale is recorded as revenue in *Sales* in the income statement. The counterpart is a *Cash account* in the balance sheet. A credit sale is recorded as revenue in *Sales* in the income statement. The item in the balance sheet is a *Receivable account*

As a matter of principle, turnover and other income was reported upon rendering of the service or delivery of the assets and hence upon transfer of the risk. For tourism services, the turnover was recognised according to the proportion of contract performance within the tourism value chain. The commisson income from package tours of non-Group tour operators sold by the travel agencies was recognised upon payment by the customers; however, upon departure at the latest. Commission income from Group products sold was not recognised until upon departure of the customers. The services of tour operators mainly consisted in the organisation and coordination of package tours. Turnover from the organisation of tours was therefore recognised upon start of the tour. Turnover generated in downstream stages of the tourism value chain such as hotel and flight services was recognised when the customers had used the respective service. Revenue from services in the logistics division was recognised on an accrual basis.

Figure 2.5   Principle of revenue recognition in the IFRS annual report of TUI.

instead of a Cash account. In both cases, the amount is assessed on the basis of the fair value received or receivable from the counterpart (value in cash account of what pays or will pay the customer).

For a product sale amounting to €1,000, the accounting process is one of the following, depending on whether it is a cash or credit sale:

| Cash (+A) | | 1,000 | |
| | Sales (+IS) | | 1,000 |

or

| Receivables (+A) | | 1,000 | |
| | Sales (+IS) | | 1,000 |

In a cash sale, that amount is generally the amount actually received. In a credit sale, we must take into account the time effect of payment, when significant. If a company grants a payment term of 9 months to pay a bill even without explicit interest, the amount to be recorded is less than the nominal value.

APPLICATION 2.7

Measurement of a Sale on Credit without Interest Payments

On 06/20/2010, company Alpha sells an asset to its client Engineer for €105,000 which has one year to pay for it. The interest rate is of 5%. During that year Alpha cannot collect the payment. If it needs cash, it needs to contract a loan at the bank for which it will have to pay interest.

On the other hand, if Alpha immediately gets the money from the sale, it can place it on the money market and gain revenues in form of interest from it. The delay of payment leads to a loss of interest payments.

In both cases, the delay of payment represents a cost for the company. Therefore the real value of this sale must be the discounted cash flow from €105,000, at a rate of 5%. This makes €100,000, which will be recognized in the income statement of Alpha.

Accounts receivable (+L)		100,000	
	Sales (+IS)		100,000
Accounting entry on 06/20/2010			

The real effect of time, 105,000 − 100,000 = €5,000, will be recognized later as a financial income.

The amount in revenue (sales) may differ from the sales price. Indeed, several elements can be added to the price without necessarily being recognized as income (see Figure 2.6).

Value Added Tax   The revenues shall always be exclusive of VAT (Value Added Tax). VAT is paid by the purchaser and collected by the company selling on behalf of the State (i.e. tax authorities). It is neutral to the selling company, who only collects and pays the tax borne by the final consumer. VAT is therefore not a revenue for the firm and should not be included in

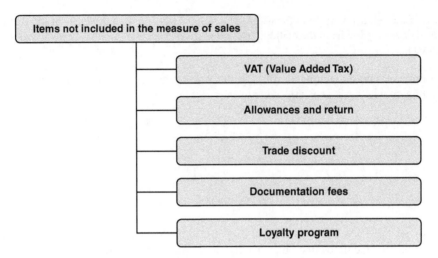

Figure 2.6 Non-included items in the measure of sales.

the income statement. The VAT collected on sales made by the company is directly recorded as a liability towards the State. The total amount collected and recorded in Debit of a Receivables or Cash account is to be divided in Credit of:

- Sales, as a revenue in the income statement; and a
- Debt to the State, as a debt liability (corresponding to the amount of the tax).

Chapter 7 details the mechanisms relating to registration of VAT and other taxes.

Allowances and Returns

> An **allowance** is a reduction in price that is generally given to compensate for a minor defect in a product sold.
>
> A **rebate** is a reduction of price that is given to certain customers or in connection with specific promotions.

Many retailers accept product returns from customers, usually within a certain time. Such a return against reimbursement is not considered an expense *per se* to be recorded in a specific account in the income statement, but rather as the cancellation of sales previously recorded. Although the net income is identical with the two recording types, there is here an effect on the turnover and therefore on the assessment of the business by financial statement users (analysts, financial markets, etc.).

This principle also applies to any **allowance** that retailers give to customers, including compensating for a minor fault on a product sold. These discounts and **rebates** are most often directly on the bills and the amount to be recorded will be the sale price adjusted with the discounts.

Some traders also give **rebates** for commercial reasons (discounts to certain customers or through promotional offers). These are reductions in selling prices, directly taken into account during the initial recording of the sale.

Trade Discount

> **Trade discounts** are granted on the basis of volume of transactions with customers during a given period.

Some retailers give discounts the basis of transactions with customers during a given period. The client then receives no reduction from the first purchase, but only at the end of the period as a credit note on future purchases. These **trade discounts** do not appear on the original bill. However, as they are reductions in the selling price (thus the sales), they must be taken into account when recording the initial sale.

Documentation Fees and Initial Expenses   At the opening of subscriptions in the field of telecommunications or in sports clubs, for example, some retailers require from the customer – in addition to the commitment for a fixed period of several months – a single contribution at the signature under the commissioning of installation expenses or documentation fees.

This single payment could be considered as an isolated service that generates immediate revenue or will be observed during the actual installation of the line. But this benefit is in fact related to the sale of subscriptions and is an increase in its cost during the initial period rather than a supplementary service. Instead of recording it at the signature of the contract as revenue of the exercise, the IAS 18 standard requires, in this case, the spread of this premium on the duration of the realization period (firm initial period).

APPLICATION 2.8

Recognition of Administrative/Handling Fees

On 04/03/2010 Jennifer signs a declaration of accession to a sports club called Fitgym. The monthly fee is £90 for a period of 12 months. In addition, a one-off payment of £180 is asked as a handling fee. For Fitgym this payment of £180 is not an income of April 2010 but must be spread over the next 12 months. The monthly income of Fitgym is therefore $90 + (180/12) = £105$. More precisely, in April Fitgym does not have an income of £270 but an income of £105 and a deferred revenue of £165. In the following months, £15 will always be transferred from the defered income account to the income statement.

Cash and cash equivalent (+A)	270	
Sales (+IS)		105
Deferred revenue (+L)		165
Accounting entry for April 2010		
Cash and cash equivalent (+A)	90	
Deferred revenue (−L)	15	
Sales (+IS)		105
Accounting entry for May 2010		

Loyalty Programs   Many companies launch loyalty programs (Application 2.9). For example, airline companies award points depending on the distance travelled by the customer (i.e. *frequent flyer program*). From a certain threshold, the client may choose to perform a free flight or have other economic benefits.

Although the loyalty points are sold directly with the ticket, it is actually two separate operations. Part of the price paid by the customer is the price of the flight stated on the ticket, and another part is considered as revenue received in advance for a later flight. There is no reason to record a sale, even partially, for this "second flight".

If a certain level of loyalty points is required to obtain a free flight, the customers of the airline will not cross that threshold. Even among those who do, a significant number will not convert their points into flights or other rewards.

In principle, the correction of sales is calculated on the basis of total points earned by customers. An airline company may rely on its statistical analysis on points not converted by its customers to correct its turnover and avoid an excessive reduction of turnover.[1]

APPLICATION 2.9

Recognition of Sales: Customer Loyalty Programs

The new customer loyalty program "Repaid", launched in the beginning of 2010 from the group Roundabout, works as follows: each time a customers spends €1 in the shop, €0.02 is added to her Repaid account. Once the client has more than €20 on her account she can get one product of a Roundabout shop for free corresponding to the amount on her Repaid account. Statistically, based on the data of competitors that have similar loyalty programs, only 80% of the sales generate loyalty points and only 75% of the loyalty points are used by customers, while 25% are added on the Repaid account that never reach the critical level of €20. In January 2010 the group Roundabout generated one billion (€1bn). No one used the Repaid points.

It is very probable that one part of the cash inflows will generate future costs in kind. The amount of the costs in kind can be estimated at:

$$1bn \times 80\% \times 75\% \times 0.02 = €12m.$$

The amount of €12m corresponds to future services that Roundabout has not yet fulfilled and can therefore not be recognized as income but only as deferred revenue. The deferred revenue of €12m will be transferred to income when customers convert their loyalty points into free gifts.

Cash and cash equivalent (+A)	1,000,000,000	
Sales (+IS)		988,000,000
Deferred revenue (+L)		12,000,000
Accounting entry for January 2010 sales		

---

[1] *Loyalty programs illustrate the fact that in the field of financial reporting, all values are not always indisputable and estimates are sometimes necessary. In addition, the interpretation of the facts presented here is not the only one possible. Some consider the cost associated with loyalty points as an increase in the cost of the initial sale and record a corresponding obligation in Liabilities, without correcting the turnover.*

2.2 COSTS OF ORDINARY ACTIVITIES

The correct recording of sales and other ordinary income is subject to rules that have been detailed. To determine the economic performance of a company (its ordinary result), corresponding rules should apply for the recording of expenses. The general principle is to record only the expenses incurred for the realization of revenues of the period, i.e costs are to be associated (or matched) with revenues of the same fiscal period (see Chapter 1). Many expenses are necessary for the realization of ordinary income and are generally presented as one of the following classifications.

- **Classification of expenses by nature**
- **Classification of expenses by function**.

The first **classification** lists expenses by their **nature**, such as materials consumed, external charges, taxes and fees, staff costs.

The second **classification** puts more emphasis on the **function** of expenses in the activity of the company. It distinguishes in particular the cost of sales (expenses incurred for the production of goods or services sold), administration costs, distribution costs and, as appropriate, the costs of research and development.

Both classifications naturally lead to the same net income, as identical expenses are simply grouped differently. Thus, personnel costs of the first classification are spread over several functions when establishing the income statement; according to the second pattern: the charges generated by employees working in the production department are reflected in cost of sales, expenses of administrative staff are allocated to administrative expenses and salaries of sales and marketing employees are included in distribution costs.

After deduction from ordinary income, several major categories of ordinary expenses allow the company to calculate its income from ordinary activities (or operating profit). They will now be detailed.

2.2.1 Consumption of Goods

The sale of goods is part of ordinary business operations of the company and requires previously the purchase of goods. According to the matching of revenues and expenses, this purchase will be treated as an expense only at the time of the sale of the goods. Before the sale, these goods are current assets because economic benefits (the sale) are expected, usually on a short term.

APPLICATION 2.10

Purchase of Merchandise

On 01/01/2010 the company Alpha buys 100 laptops in order to resell them in the short term. The purchase price is €500. The initial accounting entry is:

Stock of merchandise (+A)	50,000	
Cash and cash equivalent (−A)		50,000

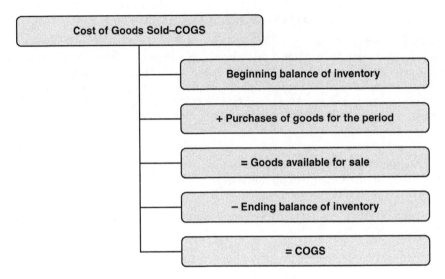

Figure 2.7 Cost of goods sold.

Consumption of goods: according to the matching of revenues and expenses, purchases will only be considered as expenses at the time of their sale.

When the sale is realized, assets (stock of **goods**) are **consumed**. Since it generates its economic benefits, it should be recorded as an expense in the same period as the sale (see Application 2.11).

Thus, the corresponding cost of the sale (cost of goods sold, COGS) corresponds to the costs of purchasing goods that were actually sold during the year, and only these costs. Figure 2.7 breaks down the cost of goods sold.

APPLICATION 2.11

Sale of Merchandise (Permanent Inventory)

In June 2010 Alpha sells 40 laptops for €1,000 (unit price). In September 2010 Alpha sells another 50 at the same price. The accounting entries are as follows:

June 2010		
Cash and cash equivalent (40 × €1,000) (+A)	40,000	
Sales (+IS)		40,000
Cost of goods sold (40 × €500) (−IS)	20,000	
Stock of merchandise (−A)		20,000
September 2010		
Cash and cash equivalent (50 × €1,000) (+A)	50,000	
Sales (+IS)		50,000
Cost of goods sold (50 × €500) (−IS)	25,000	
Stock of merchandise (−A)		25,000

The income statement appears as:

Sales	90,000
COGS	(45,000)
Gross profit*	45,000

*If there are no additional revenues and expenses, the gross profit corresponds to the income from operating activities.

The **perpetual inventory** is to identify assets and liabilities on a daily basis.

The **periodic inventory** is to identify assets and liabilities on a periodic basis.

Many companies do not determine a cost of goods sold after each sale, which corresponds to a **perpetual inventory** monitoring. Instead, they often use **intermittent** or **periodic inventory**, which is to determine periodically (quarterly, annually) their COGS. If during a given year, the company sold all the goods it had purchased during the same period, the COGS is equal to purchases of the period. However, this does not usually occur because unsold items often remain at year end. The company then determines the total purchases of goods that were available for sale (initial inventory + purchases for the year) and subtracts the unsold recorded at year end (ending inventory).

APPLICATION 2.12

Sales of Merchandise (Periodic Inventory)

In June 2010 Alpha sells 40 laptops for €1,000 (unit price). In September 2010 Alpha sells another 50 at the same price. The accounting entries are as follows:

June 2010		
Cash and cash equivalent (40 × €1,000) (+A)	40,000	
Sales (+IS)		40,000
September 2010		
Cash and cash equivalent (50 × €1,000) (+A)	50,000	
Sales (+IS)		50,000

The company establishes the cost of goods sold only at the end of the period:

Beginning of year inventory	=	0
+ Purchases (100 × €500)	=	50,000
− End of year inventory (10 × €500)	=	5,000
COGS	=	45,000

The company must then enter this information into its books. On the one hand, the expense must be recognized and, on the other, the inventories must be adjusted.

12/31/2010		
Cost of goods sold (−IS)	45,000	
Stock of merchandise (−A)		45,000

The income statement appears as:

Sales	90,000
COGS	(45,000)
Gross profit*	45,000

If there are no additional revenues and expenses, the gross profit corresponds to the income from operating activities.

An inventory change reflects the difference found between amounts of inventory between two dates.

In several European countries, most companies present the cost of goods sold using two accounts. They first record the purchase of the exercise as an expense (even if not all consumed) and then an inventory change (initial inventory – ending inventory) at the closing of accounts. This approach uses the same definition of COGS, but expressed differently. Indeed:

$$\text{COGS} = \text{initial inventory} + \text{purchases} - \text{ending inventory}$$
$$= \text{purchases} + [\text{initial inventory} - \text{ending inventory}]$$
$$= \text{purchases} + \Delta° \text{inventory (inventory change).}$$

From an accounting perspective, companies record purchases as expenses as they purchase and make the adjustment for inventory change at the year end (for the case of periodic inventory).

APPLICATION 2.13

Purchases and Sales of Merchandise

On 01/01/2010, Alpha buys 100 laptops in order to resell them in the short them. The purchase price is €500. The initial accounting entry is:

Purchase of merchandise (−IS)		50,000	
Cash and cash equivalent (−A)			50,000

In June 2010 Alpha sells 40 laptops for €1,000 (unit price). In September 2010 Alpha sells another 50 at the same price. The accounting entries are as follows:

June 2010			
Cash and cash equivalent (40 × €1,000) (+A)		40,000	
Sales (+IS)			40,000
September 2010			
Cash and cash equivalent (50 × €1,000) (+A)		50,000	
Sales (+IS)			50,000
31 December 2010			
Stock of merchandise (+A)		5,000	
Changes in inventory (+IS)			5,000

The income statement appears as:

Sales	90,000
Purchases	(50,000)
Changes in inventory	5,000
Gross profit*	45,000

If there are no additional revenues and expenses, the gross profit corresponds to the income from operating activities.

Whatever the approach of the company, the ordinary income is not affected. It is a choice of recording and presentation of accounts.

2.2.2 Consumption of Materials

Materials are items intended for consumption in the production cycle.

Goods are purchases that will be resold.

The company usually buys the materials it needs to carry on business several times during the period. These must be used quickly, either by being consumed in the production cycle (raw **materials**) or sold (**goods**). The following applications adopt the practices generally used.

The accounting technique used here is to consider that the **materials** and purchased goods are resold or consumed immediately. An expense is therefore recorded at the time of purchase of such materials or goods, with an offsetting of a supplier debt or cash account under the terms of settlement (Application 2.14).

APPLICATION 2.14

Purchase of Raw Materials

On 09/28/2009, the company Oward purchases raw materials for €100,000. The payment period negotiated with the supplier, and which Oward will use completely, is of 30 days. The accounting entries are as follows:

Purchase of raw materials (−IS)	100,000	
Accounts payable (+L)		100,000
Purchase of raw materials on 09/28/2009		
Accounts payable (−L)	100,000	
Cash and cash equivalent (−A)		100,000
Payment of the suppliers on 10/28/2009		

The account *Purchase of materials* is an expense account and if no other entry is recorded, the income of 2009 will bear the entire expense. This would be justified if all the material was actually consumed in the production cycle of the year.

However, if, during stocktaking at the end of the year, some of the material is not used, the expense initially recorded will have to be corrected in order to achieve a proper matching of expenses with revenues. Without this correction, the income of the period would bear an expense of consumption of material while actually these materials are not yet used.

APPLICATION 2.15

Recognition of the Consumption of Raw Materials

On the date of the physical inventory, 12/31/2009, Oward has raw materials of €20,000 (see Application 2.14). This amount must be recognized in the balance sheet and, at the same time, the expense of €100,000 must be adjusted in order to fit the real consumption of 2009. The accounting entry that needs to be made is:

Raw material stock (+A)	20,000	
Cost of raw material used (−IS)	80,000	
Purchase of raw material (+IS)		100,000
Accounting entry for the final inventory on the 12/31/2009		

The **consumption of materials** is reflected by a recording of an expense (cost of raw material used), with an offsetting supplier debt or a cash account under the terms of settlement.

If the value of the final inventory of material is less than the initial value of the stock, the company used more than the purchases made during the period and the total value of the expense, commonly referred to the **cost of raw material used**, is greater than the purchase of materials of the period.

APPLICATION 2.16

Consumed Purchases

During 2010, Oward purchases €600,000 of raw materials. The physical inventory at the end of 2010 shows that the final stock of raw materials has a value of €15,000.

The first accounting entry must recognize the consumption of the old stock of 2009. This consumption occurs generally during the first days of the new year. There the initial stock is transferred to the cost of raw material used (an expense in the income statement):

Cost of raw material used (−IS)	20,000	
Stock of raw materials (−A)		20,000
Consumption of the initial stock at 01/01/2010		

During 2010, Oward needs to recognize the purchases that were consumed immediately.

Purchase of raw materials (−IS)	600,000	
Accounts payable (+L)		600,000
Purchase of raw materials during 2010		

The last accounting entry relates to the year end inventory of €15,000.

Stock of raw materials (+A)	15,000	
Cost of raw material used (−IS)	585,000	
Purchase of raw material (+IS)		600,000
Recognition of the final stock at 12/31/2010		

The net expense of 2010 related to raw materials is the sum of the initial raw material stock and the purchases minus the purchases that were not consumed during 2010 and which will be listed in the balance sheet:

Beginning of year inventory 2010	20,000
+ Purchases 2010	600,000
− End of year inventory 2010	15,000
= Cost of raw material used	605,000

Oward's net expense for raw materials in 2010 is €605,000.

The **finished goods** are products manufactured within the company and intended for sale.

The problem of inventory change is also for **finished goods**. Unlike materials and goods, they are not bought from outside, but produced internally from materials purchased with the assistance of other external services, personnel and various machinery and other tangible assets.

It is technically impossible to correct at year end all expense accounts relating to the manufacture of products based on the inventory of finished goods. Nor is this justified in economic terms. Raw materials, for example, are consumed during the production process and no correction of the expense of consumption of material is required.

In contrast, the total consumption recorded during the production cycle does not remain without a counterpart, as the finished products manufactured are sold or are in storage awaiting commercialization. The existence of a final inventory of finished goods thus generates a movement in the accounts, reflecting the value of the stock in the assets. As this is an increase in the value of assets created internally, the counterpart of this inventory change should be a revenue. The most common name of this account is **stored finished goods**: it is a revenue account in the income statement, which offsets the costs of production of goods not yet sold.

APPLICATION 2.17

Finished Goods

During Oward's physical inventory for 2010, a stock of manufactured goods of €60,000 is recognized. This amount comprises eventually a part of the €605,000 of raw materials (Illustration 2.16). But it also comprises production costs:

Stock of manufactured goods (+A)	60,000	
Stored finished goods (+IS)		60,000
Year end stock of finished goods: 12/31/2010		

The net effect of the change in the inventory or finished goods on the income of the company is determined similarly to the recording of changes in the inventory of materials and goods. The initial inventory generates a recording in debit of the *Stored finished goods* account and diminishes the income, while the recording of the final inventory will credit that same account with an opposite effect. The net effect on profit for the period is determined as the balance between changes in the initial inventory and the final inventory.

2.2.3   Other Goods and Services Purchased and Consumed

Besides the materials and goods, the company has many other consumer goods and services purchased from third parties. The determination of a reliable income requires an exhaustive recording of all these services. Here are some examples:

- subcontracting
- rentals
- maintenance and repair
- insurance premiums
- study and research
- external staff
- salaries and fees to intermediaries
- advertising, publications, public relations
- transportation
- travel, missions, receptions
- postage and telecommunications
- banking.

This list is not exhaustive and the company chooses the level of detail that allows it to follow reliably the different types of external expenses. In some European countries (e.g. France or Germany) a standardized list of accounts presents a refined structure of the classification to be followed by companies.

The counterpart of the expense to be recorded is generally a current liability towards a supplier. Even in the case of a cash payment, many companies routinely record all purchase transactions in this type of accounts payable. This will keep track of all transactions with a supplier, which is useful in the case of discounts based on a certain volume of transactions realized during a period. Recording cash payments directly in the credit side of a cash account would not include them in calculations of trade discount.

Application 2.18 illustrates the basic accounting treatment of such an operation.

APPLICATION 2.18

Renting of Commercial Buildings

On 10/25/2010, the accounting department of the company Fast gets an invoice for the rent of a commercial building for October 2010. The amount of €900 is paid on 10/31/2010. The accounting entries are as follows:

Rent expenses (−IS)		900	
	Accounts payable (+L)		900
Invoice for the October rent, 10/25/2010			
Accounts payable (−L)		900	
	Cash and cash equivalent (−A)		900
Payment of the October rent, 10/31/2010			

Companies typically record expenses upon receipt of invoices, but this is not always enough or sometimes requires subsequent corrections.

The matching of expenses with revenues prohibits the recording in the current period of expenses relating to another period. This requires two types of corrections, similar to what has already been shown for the recording of ordinary income:

An **accrued liability** is a liability of the company corresponding to the amount of expense consumed but not yet paid.

- The expenses for the period for which invoices have not yet been received should be accurately estimated and recorded in the period during which they are incurred. The accounting mechanism must ensure that an expense cannot be recorded a second time when the invoice is received by the company.
- We speak in this case of an **accrued liability** (or sometimes accrued expenses).

A **deferred expense** is an asset offsetting an expense recorded but not yet consumed.

- The bills that relate to expenses on future periods are recorded, but the impact on the income of the expense relating to future periods must be transferred to these future periods. The accounting mechanism must ensure that the expense is removed from the income of the current period and is recorded in the proper period in the absence of a new bill.
- We speak in this case of a **deferred expense**.

These two types of correction are part of what are called "adjustments". Application 2.19 presents the accounting process for the first class of corrections.

APPLICATION 2.19

Phone Costs

On 01/04/2011 Fast's accounting department gets a phone bill for December 2010. Usually the December bills are around €400. The exact amount of the bill is €415. The invoice is paid on 01/07/2011.

Fast cannot action this until January 2011 with the recognition of the phone costs. Therefore, the accounting department must recognize the most probable amount of costs for December based on historical data and possible changes of the cost structure. The related accounting entry is:

Telecommunication costs (−IS)		400	
	Accrued liability (+L)		400
Telecommunication costs, 12/31/2010			

Fast does as if it had received the invoice. However, an accrued expense account and not an account payable is credited because a real debt does not exist at that moment.

On the day of the new accounting period this expense is cancelled and the liability disappears. The expense account which is reset with the new period will be credited with the €400 until the invoice arrives.

Accrued liability (−L)		400	
	Telecommunication costs (+IS)		400
Cancelling of the accounting entry, 12/31/2010 – 01/01/2011			

This procedure allows us to recognize any telecommunication invoice without risking the possibility of recording it twice in the accounts:

Telecommunication costs (−IS)		415	
	Accounts payable (+L)		415
Reception of the invoice – 01/04/2011			
Accounts payable (−L)		415	
	Cash and cash equivalent (−A)		415
Payment of the invoice – 01/07/2011			

The net expense of January 2011 is then 415 − 400 = €15. This amount corresponds to the difference between the estimated and the real expense. It is not possible to estimate this difference and usually it is not substantial.

The major part of the telecommunication costs from December 2011 is attached to the right period and through this procedure a risk of taking the invoice into the account twice is avoided.

2.2.4 Taxes

Taxes are of many forms for a company. They represent ordinary consumption recorded in the ordinary result and their recording does not differ from that of other expenses. However, there are often specific accounts of expenses and a specific line of income taxes in the income statement. The amount of taxes due and not paid is reported separately in the balance sheet, or in the notes.

APPLICATION 2.20

Property Tax

On 10/30/2010 the Rosello company receives a tax assessment for the 2010 property tax on its headquarters. The tax amounts to €3,000 and is paid on 11/14/2010. The accounting entries are:

Tax expense (−IS)		3,000	
	Tax liabilities (+L)		3,000
Property tax – 10/30/2010			
Tax liabilities (−L)		3,000	
	Cash and cash equivalent (−A)		3,000
Payment of the property tax – 11/14/2010			

The taxes, which are based on the profit of the year, can be determined with certainty only at the end of the year, according to the difference between revenues and expenses for that year. They are not part of the taxes in line with those addressed here and are on a special line in the income statement just before the net profit of the company.

2.2.5   Personnel Expenses

Personnel expenses represent all of what the company pays to its employees as wages, social security contributions for employees, for employers.

Personnel expenses represent all of what the company pays to its employees. For the recording of most of these expenses (salaries and social contributions), three parts must be identified:

- The net wages and salaries that are paid directly to employees.
- Social contributions by employees that the company retains and pays to social organisms on behalf of employees.
- The employer payroll taxes that the company must pay on its behalf to social organizations.

In most countries, various organisms of social security contribution exist, and obviously different kinds of contributions (health insurance, pension insurance, unemployment insurance, accident insurance, etc.). The financing of the costs incurred by some of these organisms is shared between employees and employers. For example, in France, expenditure for health insurance, unemployment and retirement are financed one-third by the employees and two-thirds by the companies. Other contributions such as accident insurance, for example, are fully borne by firms.

The rates of the various contributions are generally applied to the gross salary of the employee. But the systems are very complex and methods of calculation differ from one system to another or from one contribution to another. The recording pattern for these contributions remains the same, but the company must calculate and monitor its social contributions and those of its employees.

The **gross salary** is the base salary of the employee plus any bonuses, benefits in kind, overtime, etc.

The **net salary** is the gross salary minus social security contributions of employees.

Employer contributions are employer contributions to social organizations and are part of the payroll taxes of the company.

- The **gross salary** is defined as the base salary of the employee, plus any bonuses, benefits in kind, overtime, etc. Different contribution rates then apply to this relatively complete basis for determining the social deductions. They represent a social expense for the employee, but not for the company. This part of social contributions is not recorded in the payroll taxes of the company, but is part of wages and salaries.

- The gross salary minus social deductions generally corresponds to the **net salary** payable to employees. In some countries, including Germany, the company is also responsible for withholding tax on the income of employees and the net amount to pay is reduced accordingly.
- Calculation of **employer's contributions** is also based on gross wages. Unlike the social deductions on behalf of employees, this part of the social contributions is a social expense for the company and is listed as such in the personnel expenses in the income statement.

The payroll or personnel department of the company performs all calculations necessary for the determination of wages and social contributions. The counterpart of the recorded expense is a liability: towards the staff regarding the net amount to pay and towards social organisms regarding the social deductions for employees and employers' contributions. The settlement of these liabilities generally takes place a few days later, when the financial services of the company will trigger the payment process. Application 2.21 shows the accounting process related to the recording of personnel expenses.

APPLICATION 2.21

Recognition of Staff Costs

On 11/27/2010 the human resource department of a company, Marcelo, computes the staff costs of November 2010:

- Gross salaries: €2,600,000
- Payroll deduction (i.e. social expenses paid by the employee): €550,000
- Payroll taxes (i.e. social expenses paid by the employer): €1,000,000.

How should this expense be entered into the accounting books of Marcelo?

Answer   For the accounting entry we have to make a difference between the salaries and expenses paid by the employee on one hand and the social expenses paid by the employer on the other (its contribution). Marcelo has to pay to the employees the net salaries of €2,050,000 (2,600,000 − 550,000). To the social security agencies €1,550,000 (550,000 + 1,000,000). The accounting entries are as follows:

Salaries and social expenses (−IS)	2,600,000	
Salaries payable (+L)		2,050,000
Payroll taxes payable (+L)		550,000
Salaries for November 2010		
Social expenses (−IS)	1,000,000	
Payroll taxes payable (+L)		1,000,000
Welfare state expenses for November 2010		

On 11/30/2010 the financial department of Marcelo pays the salaries to the employees of the company.

Salaries payable (−L)	2,050,000	
Cash and cash equivalent (−A)		2,050,000
Payment of salaries for November 2010		

On 12/10/2010, the finacial department pays the social expenses:

Payroll taxes payable (−L)		1,550,000	
Cash and cash equivalent (−A)			1,550,000
Payment of social expenses for November 2010			

2.2.6   Consumption of Economic Benefits Related to Assets (Depreciation)

Depreciation expenses are expenses that reflect the consumption of economic benefits related to the possession or use of assets with limited useful life.

The consumption of assets used during the period must also be integrated into ordinary expenses. Most of the tangible and intangible assets have a useful life limited in time. Their value will then gradually decline as the economic advantages inherent to them will be consumed. Determining the fair value of the income of the period requires this consumption to be considered in the expenses of the period. This is called **depreciation**.

Chapter 5 details the various parameters that enter the calculation of depreciation expense. Here, only the accounting mechanism is presented.

Amortization expense is recorded in the ordinary expenses of the period under depreciation and, theoretically, the counterpart should be deducted from the corresponding value in the balance sheet. In order not to lose information on the gross value of the property, the depreciation over previous periods is accumulated in a separate account: *Accumulated depreciation*. The net book value of assets is determined as the difference between the gross value of the property and the balance of the *accumulated depreciation* account. Thus, it is not directly visible in the accounts of the company. Application 2.22 illustrates the mechanism for recording depreciation.

APPLICATION 2.22

Accounting Entry for Depreciations

The chief accountant of the company J-Star determines the depreciation of a machine to be €300,000 for the year 2010. The initial value of the asset was €3,000,000. The related accounting entry is:

Depreciation expense (−IS)		300,000	
Accumulated depreciation of the machine (−A)			300,000
Depreciation of a machine for 2010			

This accounting entry does not have an impact on the initial value of the machine. To compute the net value of the machine, you have to make the difference between the initial value of €3,000,000 and the account of depreciation. Since, in this case, we do not know the balance of the accumulated depreciation account, we cannot compute the net value.

2.3   SUMMARY

The net income of the exercise is the most important indicator of the financial performance of the company. It is calculated according to specific rules.

The recording date is determined according to the transfer of benefits and risks of the good or the completion of the service sold. There is no direct link between the transfer of ownership and revenue recognition (turnover), nor between payments by the client and the recognition of revenue. These payments have an impact on the financial performance through the cash flow, while sales impact the economic performance through the movement of the net income.

The turnover is always a net value after deducting any cost associated with the sale transaction. Generally, companies prefer to increase the expenses related to sales rather than reduce the amount of the sale itself, for the reasons mentioned at the beginning of section 2.2. The elimination of all aforementioned elements from the sales make this indicator more stable and comparable, either in time in examining the accounts of a company over several years, or in comparing the economic performance of several companies at a given time.

Expenses are consumptions of assets or external services. According to the principle of matching the revenues and expenses, these consumptions will be treated as an expense only at the realization of the corresponding revenues.

2.4   ACTIVITIES

1.   Rentals and Sales   On 01/01/2010, the jetliner manufacturer, Airjet, signs a trade agreement with the airliner, Airsouth, which contains the following points:

- Sale of five planes for a unit price of €100m. The delivery is planned for 07/01/2010.
- Rental over 30 years of two special aircraft for a yearly rent of €10m per unit. The delivery is planned for 01/01/2011.
- Sale of 10 commercial planes for a unit price of €150m with a repurchase agreement after 5 years for a unit price of €100m. The delivery will take place within July 2010.

How must these sales and rentals be recognized and what accounting entries need to be made in Airjet and Airsouth books?

2.   Application Fees, Discounts and Customer Loyalty Programs   The travel agency Easytravel, established on 07/01/2010, sold, on 09/01/2010 to an enterprise committee, a group trip to China departing on 01/15/2011 with the following conditions:

- The application fees of €500 must be paid cash on the date of order.
- 25% of the total price needs to be paid up front on the date of order.
- The total price of the trip is €80,000; the payment of the balance (75%) is subject to the following conditions: 2/15, *n*/30 (i.e. 2% discount if paid within 15 days, or €80,000 must be paid within 30 days) from the date of departure onwards.
- The customer loyalty program of the travel agency enables customers to get a 10% discount of the actual trip price on the next journey bought within one year.

The enterprise committee decides to pay 30 days after the departure date.

1. *What is Easytravel's sale figure concerning this trip for FY2010? And for FY2011?*
2. *What is the impact of the sale conditions (application fee, discounts and customer loyalty program) on the recognition of Easytravel's sales?*

3. Sales and Rentals   The IFRS consider very long-term rentals to be sales, and sales with repurchase agreements to be leases.

   1. *What were the reasons for this enactment?*
   2. *By taking examples in the automobile and airline industry find reasons for:*

       − *renting an asset for a very long term rather than buying it;*
       − *selling an asset with repurchase agreement rather than renting it.*

4. Rebates and Trade Discounts   Over 2010, the trading group of a chain of supermarkets has the following agreements with its suppliers:

   • A 2% rebate on the catalogue price.
   • An additional discount related to the size of each order based on the following scoring table:

Order	Rebate
Up to €10,000	0%
Up to €50,000	1%
Up to €100,000	1.5%
More than €100,000	2%

   • A year end patronage discount in function of the global sales figures based on the following table:

Total sales	Discount
Up to €200,000	0%
Up to €500,000	0.5%
Up to €1,000,000	1%
More than €1,000,000	3%

   • Purchase history based on the catalogue price of the supplier from the trading group (in € millions):

Month	Amount
January	20
February	80
March	8
April	200
May	150
June	50
July	90
August	70
September	30
October	20
November	42
December	200

What is the 2010 total sales figure of the trading group with this supplier?

3 CURRENT ASSETS

Current assets are economic resources that the company intends to use (or "consume") for the short-term needs of its business. It contains essentially the available cash or cash invested in marketable securities, trade receivables – the result of discrepancies between physical and financial flows – and different inventories (of goods available for resale, raw materials and finished goods). According to industry sectors, these assets are an important part of the balance sheets of companies (see Table 3.1).

Current assets must be given special attention because they are supposed to generate economic benefits in the short term. The solvency of the company depends in part on its ability to meet its financial obligations in the short term. Such obligations derive, for example, from future payments of a portion of wages, taxes and trade payables (credit purchases). One should question the ability of the company to recover the cash arising from credit sales and whose potential amount is represented by the trade receivables, but also on its ability to profitably sell its inventories of goods and products. Understanding the valuation and accounting of these elements is essential. This chapter deals with three main current assets: current financial assets (cash and financial instruments), trade receivables and inventories of goods.

3.1 CURRENT FINANCIAL ASSETS

Firms who have a cash surplus (available in cash, debit bank accounts) may acquire securities in order to receive financial revenues and realize capital gains on sale of securities. Cash, financial securities (stocks, bonds) and other short-term investments are part of what are broadly called the "financial instruments". A financial instrument is cash, *or a contractual right to receive cash or another financial asset from another entity, or a contractual right to exchange financial instruments with another entity under conditions potentially favourable or an equity instrument of another entity* (IAS 32, §11). The company L'Oréal indicates in its annual report the components of its cash account (see Figure 3.1), itself a component of current assets.

> Held-for-trading financial assets are stocks, bonds and other derivatives (options, swaps, futures). They are valued at fair value with changes being recorded in the income statement (upwards or downwards) at the closing of accounts.

There are three main categories of financial instruments in current assets: financial assets at *fair value through profit or loss* (a listed share, for example), the same assets classified as *available for sale* and *derivatives* (futures contract, option to purchase or sell, etc.). Assets at *fair value through profit or loss* represent securities held by the company in the hope of obtaining a gain in the short term (i.e. generally three months) and are more commonly called **held-for-trading financial assets**. The company has acquired these assets in order to generate profits in the

Table 3.1 **Proportion of current assets compared to total asset in some firms**

	Vodafone	BP	Rolls-Royce	AstraZeneca	Unilever
Current assets	6.9%	29.1%	61.8%	34.5%	50.0%
Including:					
Inventories	0.3%	7.4%	17.1%	2.9%	17.4%
Accounts receivables (net)	5.1%	12.8%	25.8%	15.5%	17.1%
Cash and cash equivalents	1.3%	3.6%	15.6%	9.2%	11.5%

Source: Annual reports 2008

short term, benefiting specially from market fluctuations. *Available for sale* financial assets are rather held as cash reserves on a short and medium term (but logically also expected to make profits). They can be classified as current or non-current depending on the objectives of the company during their possession. Other categories of financial assets are financial assets held to maturity, such as bonds held until their maturity date (these assets are described in Chapter 4). Table 3.2 shows the importance of different elements of cash for different companies.

3.1.1　Initial Valuation

Held-for-trading financial assets and financial assets *available-for-sale* are valued at fair value, i.e. the "amount for which an asset could be exchanged or a liability settled, between knowledgeable and willing parties, in an arm's length transaction" (IAS 32). If the financial asset is listed, its fair value is its market value (stock trading price, for example). If not listed, one should use a valuation model, provided that the data used is reliable (derived from an active market). Thus, to determine the fair value of a non-listed obligation, the present value of future cash flows (generated by the bond) will serve as a model for the valuation. Transaction costs (fees and commissions paid to agents, advisers, brokers, costs charged by stock exchanges, transfer taxes and rights, etc.) that are directly attributable to the acquisition of the asset do not increase the value of held-for-trading financial assets: they are recorded directly in the income statement. However, these costs are added to the book value of available-for-sale financial assets.

The fair value is "the amount for which an asset could be exchanged or a liability settled, between knowledgeable, willing parties, in an arm's length transaction".

1.20. Cash and cash equivalents

Cash and cash equivalents consist of cash in bank accounts, units of cash unit trusts and liquid short-term investments with no risk of change in value, and whose maturity date at the date of acquisition is less than three months away.

Figure 3.1　From the Notes of L'Oréal annual report under IFRS, 2008.

Table 3.2   Proportion of cash and cash equivalent in some firms

	Cash + ST deposits/ Total asset	Cash + ST deposits/ Current assets	ST deposits/ ST deposits + Cash
Vodafone	1.3%	19.5%	73.5%
BP	3.6%	12.3%	51.2%
Rolls-Royce	16.2%	26.3%	62.0%
AstraZeneca	9.2%	26.5%	75.8%
Unilever	11.5%	22.9%	77.1%

Source: Annual reports 2008

APPLICATION 3.1

Initial Recording

On May 28, 2010, the firm Opec bought 100 stocks at the cost of €200 each. There were additional transaction fees of €80. Those stocks are considered as trading securities (accounted at fair value through profit or loss).

05/28/2010		
Marketable securities (+A)	20,000	
Transaction fees (−IS)	80	
Cash and cash equivalents (−A)		20,080

3.1.2   Valuation at Closing of the Period

Variations (positive or negative) of fair value of *held-for-trading* financial assets shall be recognized in the income statement, and in equity for (i.e. Other Comprehensive Income - OCI) *available-for-sale* financial assets. The extract from the annual report of AstraZeneca describes the "Cash and cash equivalents" account (see Figure 3.2).

Where there is disposal of held-for-trading financial assets (termination of rights to future cash flows or transfer of these rights, and substantially all the risks and benefits, to a third party and transfer of control), it is necessary to write-off the assets.

13 CASH AND CASH EQUIVALENTS

	2008 $m	2007 $m	2006 $m
Cash at bank and in hand	1,039	1,403	684
Short-term deposits	3,247	4,464	6,419
Cash and cash equivalents	4,286	5,867	7,103
Unsecured bank overdrafts	(163)	(140)	(114)
Cash and cash equivalents in the cash flow statement	4,123	5,727	6,989

The Group's insurance subsidiaries hold cash and short-term investments totalling $400m (2007: $347m; 2006: $320m), of which $278m (2007: $257m; 2006: $220m) is required to meet insurance solvency requirements and which, as a result, is not readily available for the general purposes of the Group.

Figure 3.2   Excerpts from AstraZeneca annual report 2008.

APPLICATION 3.2

How to Recognize Trading Securities while Closing the Accounts

On January 1, 2010, the firm Alpha bought 100 shares of the firm VMS at the price of €300 each (classified as trading securities). The transaction fees represent an additional 1% of the total amount.

- First case: the VMS's share costs €305 on December 31, 2010
- Second case: the VMS's share costs €290 on December 31, 2010

01/01/2010		
Marketable securities (+A)	30,000	
Transaction Fees (−IS)	300	
Cash and cash equivalents (−A)		30,300

First Case

12/31/2010		
Marketable securities (+A)	500	
(305 − 300) × 100		500
Financial gains (+IS)		

Second Case

12/31/2010		
Financial losses (−IS)	1,000	
(300 − 290) × 100		1,000
Marketable securities (−A)		

How to Recognize Available-for-Sale Securities while Closing the Accounts

Assuming VMS's shares were classified as available-for-sale securities, the recording entries would have been:

01/01/2010		
Marketable securities (+A)	30,300	
Cash and cash equivalents (−A)		30,300

First Case

12/31/2010		
Marketable securities (+A)	200	
(305 − 303) × 100		200
Fair value adjustment (+OCI)		

Second Case

12/31/2010		
Fair value adjustment (−OCI)	1,300	
(303 − 290) × 100		1,300
Marketable securities (−A)		

APPLICATION 3.3

Sale of Financial Asset: Trading Securities

On October 30, 2010, the firm Y sells 500 shares of the firm Tital at a price of €110 each. Those shares had been bought for €100 each on January 1, 2009, and had depreciated by €6 by December 31, 2009.

	01/01/2009		
Marketable securities (+A)		50,000	
Cash (−A)			50,000

	12/31/2009		
Financial loss (−IS)		3,000	
6 × 500 shares			
Marketable securities (−A)			3,000

	10/30/2010		
Cash (+A)		55,000	
Marketable securities (−A)			47,000
Financial gain (+IS)			8,000

The final result of this operation is 8,000 − 3,000 = €5,000, but it is split over two fiscal years: in 2009, the firm lost €3,000 and won €8,000 in 2010. Accounting in fair value may result in wide variations in terms of a net result. However, the ordinary profit of the firm is not impacted since losses or gains are of a financial nature.

Sale of Financial Asset: Available-for-Sale Securities

If those instruments are considered as available-for-sale financial assets, the cession must be accounted in this way:

	12/31/2009		
Fair value adjustment (−OCI)		3,000	
6 × 500 shares			
Marketable securities (−A)			3,000

When the firm Y sells the stocks, they have to close the account concerning fair value adjustments within the equity.

	10/30/2010		
Cash (+A)		55,000	
Marketable securities (−A)			47,000
Fair value adjustment (+OCI)			3,000
Financial gain (+IS) [110 − 100] × 500			5,000

3.2 ACCOUNTS RECEIVABLE

Most of the sales of goods or services *are not paid when the revenue is recognized*. There is a time discrepancy between the accounting recording of a revenue and the corresponding cash flow, represented by the payment by the customer for the service provided. This is known as "credit sale", whose payment is deferred. In a credit sale, the company records an account receivable from its client in exchange for a revenue (recorded in the income statement). These receivables derive from the commercial activities of the company and represent the amount the seller is entitled to expect within a specified period at the time of sale. Thus, customers have a debt towards the latter (they will have to settle their debts). The receivables are a specific class of financial instruments, as mentioned by Suez in its accounts (see Figure 3.3a). Indeed, a receivable reflects the amount of credit granted to a client. (See also Figure 3.3b).

(a) B. LOANS AND RECEIVABLES CARRIED AT AMORTIZED COST

This item primarily includes loans and advances to associates or non-consolidated companies, and guarantee deposits.

On initial recognition, these loans and receivables are recorded at fair value plus transaction costs. At each balance sheet date, they are measured at amortized cost using the effective interest rate method.

On initial recognition, trade and other receivables are recorded at fair value, which generally corresponds to their nominal value. Impairment losses are recorded based on the estimated risk of non-recovery. This item includes amounts due from customers under construction contracts (see Section 1.5.13).

(b) **Trade and other current receivables** are measured at the amount the item is initially recognized less any impairment losses using the effective interest method, if applicable. Impairments, which take the form of allowances, make adequate provision for the expected credit risk; concrete cases of default lead to the derecognition of the respective receivables. For allowances, financial assets that may need to be written down are grouped together on the basis of similar credit risk characteristics, tested collectively for impairment and written down, if necessary. When the expected future cash flows of the portfolio are being calculated as required for this, previous cases of default are taken into consideration in addition to the cash flows envisaged in the contract. The cash flows are discounted on the basis of the weighted average of the original effective interest rates of the financial assets contained in the relevant portfolio.

Impairment losses on trade accounts receivable are recognized in some cases using allowance accounts. The decision to account for credit risks using an allowance account or by directly reducing the receivable will depend on the reliability of the risk assessment. As there is a wide variety of operating segments and regional circumstances, this decision is the responsibility of the respective portfolio managers.

Figure 3.3 (a) Excerpts from SUEZ annual report 2008. (b) Excerpts from Deutsche Telekom annual report 2008.

The following bookkeeping entries illustrate the recording of credit sale of goods (1) or services (2).

Sale of Goods (1)

Account receivable (+A)		1,000	
Sales (+IS)			1,000
Sale of five lots of goods (unit price of €200)			

Provision of Services (2)

Account receivable (+A)		4,000	
Fees (+IS)			4,000
Advisory actvities for €4,000			

The payment term of the loan depends on the credit and trade policy of the company and the goods sold. It can be very variable, 30 days, 60 days or even several months. These receivables, however, are generally regarded as current assets because the payment is likely to occur in the time-frame of an accounting period (one year). Therefore, they are part of the current assets of the company. At the settlement date of the debt by customers, the company records entries (1) and (2) in its books:

Sale of Goods (1)

Cash (+A)	1,000	
Accounts receivable (−A)		1,000
Payment for the sale of five lots of goods		

Provision of Services (2)

Cash (+A)	4,000	
Accounts receivable (−A)		4,000
Payment for the advisory activity for €4 000		

The receivables therefore appear in the financial statements only between the time of recognition of a revenue (for a credit sale) and the settlement of the latter. Despite this *a priori* transitional nature, firms providing credit to customers on a regular basis can have quasi-permanently large amounts of receivables in their balance sheets (see Table 3.3).

> The notes receivable derive from sales of goods (for example, fixed assets, vehicles, etc.) whose credit term is often longer than standard customer credit. They appear on the balance sheet at fair value (i.e. present value).

Trade receivables derive from the ordinary business of the company and are equally known as "Receivables", "Trade receivables" or "Clients". However, there are two other categories of receivables: the ***notes receivable*** and *loans* granted to employees and directors of the company.

Table 3.3   Proportion of accounts receivable compared to other assets

	Accounts receivable/ Total asset	Accounts receivable/ Current asset
Vodafone	5.1%	75.1%
BP	12.8%	44.1%
Rolls-Royce	25.8%	41.7%
AstraZeneca	15.5%	45.0%
Unilever	17.1%	34.2%

Source: Annual reports 2008

According to the importance of these items, one should distinguish them in the balance sheet from other trade receivables.

- Notes receivable are claims that are more formalized than usual customer credits. The note is a contract between the seller and the buyer, which must specify the procedures for settlement of the debt and the interest rate applied. These notes derive from sales of goods (for example, fixed assets, vehicles, etc.) whose credit term is often longer than standard customer credit. These notes appear in the balance sheet at fair value (i.e. present value).
- Other receivables, by default, do not come from current operating activities of the company. They include loans to employees and directors of the company (or shareholders), and advances to subsidiaries. Their accounting is similar to the receivables, but may vary as appropriate, particularly in the valuation of loans issued by the company.

3.2.1   Initial Valuation of Receivables

> Net realizable value: Amount of cash that a receivable is supposed to generate at its expiration.

Receivables must be presented in the balance sheet at their **net realizable value**, that is to say the amount (of cash) that a receivable is supposed to generate at its expiration. To the extent that the cash will be collected in the future, one should determine the present value of those cash flows to determine the value of the receivable at the time of its recording (see Application 3.4).

APPLICATION 3.4

Measure and Accounting of a Receivable in the General Case

On January 1, 2010, the company Texto Ltd sells graphic reproduction tools to a German customer, Graphics AG. The tools are purchased under the following conditions: Graphics AG will pay €200,000 at the time the contract is signed, then €300,000 after 12 months and €500,000 after 24 months. Texto Ltd. notes that its customer would have an annual interest rate of 7% if they had wanted a similar credit facility. In such conditions, it is necessary to take into consideration the actualization of the future cash and cash equivalents flows to correctly estimate the value (*fair value*) of the claims.

$$\frac{300{,}000}{1.07} + \frac{500{,}000}{(1.07)^2} = 717.093$$

The sale will appear in the Texto Ltd books as:

	01/01/2010				
Cash and cash equivalent (+A)		200,000		
Accounts receivable (+A)		717,093		
	Sales (+IS)		917,093	

This sale is valued at €917,093, despite the fact that the total payments will be €1,000,000. The customer (Graphics AG) will have to pay more than the actual price of the tools because the seller (Texto Ltd) granted them a credit. The difference between the fair value of the merchandise and the full amount paid represents the cost of the financial service offered by the seller and charged to the customer.

At the end of 2010, Graphics AG makes a second payment of €300,000. The residual value of the receivable at that point is equal to the actualized value of the remaining payment.

$$\frac{500,000}{1.07} = 467,290$$

It is this value of €467,290 that should appear on the balance sheet of Texto Ltd. The firm must be sure that the financial statements mentions not only the payment of €300,000 by the client, but also the new fair value of the remaining receivable (€467,290). The difference between the €300,000 Graphics AG paid and the decrease of €249,803 (717,093 − 467,290) in the receivable accounts corresponds to financial earnings. This gain of €50,197 is due to the interests of the credit Texto Ltd. gave their customers (7% × 717,093) during the year 2010.

	12/31/2010			
Cash and cash equivalent (+A)		300,000		
	Accounts receivable (−A)		249,803	
	Financial revenues (+IS)		50,197	

When the last payment occurs, Texto Ltd. records the following operation:

	12/31/2011			
Cash and cash equivalent (+A)		500,000		
	Accounts receivable (−A)		467,290	
	Financial revenues (+IS)		32,710	

Figure 3.4 shows an example of long-term receivables for the Unilever company. We can see that the receivables are real credits to customers whose maturity sometimes exceeds one year.

For short-term receivables (30 to 60 days of credit), the difference between the nominal value of the debt and its present value is not significant and therefore can be ignored (according to the materiality principle, see Chapter 1). For example, the difference between current €100 and the present value of €100 in 30 days, with an annual interest rate of 5%, is approximately €0.396. The same €100 paid after two years has a present value of €90.7 (with 5% annual interest). The difference is more significant as the credit period lengthens. Short-term receivables are generally recorded at their nominal value.

Ageing of trade receivables	€ million 2008	€ million 2007
Total trade receivables	2 908	3 112
Less impairment provision for trade receivables	(120)	(147)
	2 788	2 965
Of which:		
Not overdue	2 182	2 240
Past due less than three months	499	649
Past due more than three months but less than six months	100	85
Past due more than six months but less than one year	52	57
Past due more than one year	75	81
Impairment provision for trade receivables	(120)	(147)
	2 788	2 965

Impairment provision for trade and other receivables – movements during the year	€ million 2008	€ million 2007
1 January	176	180
Charged to current year income statement	36	39
Reductions/releases	(37)	(40)
Currency retranslation	(10)	(3)
31 December	165	176

Other classes of assets in trade and other receivables do not include any impaired assets.

Figure 3.4   Excerpts from Unilever annual report 2008.

> The net realizable value of a receivable is the estimated selling price in the ordinary course of business activity, less the estimated cost of completion and the estimated costs necessary to make the sale (IAS 2, §6).

A company may adjust the value of its receivables for various reasons. It may be, for example, a return by unsatisfied customers of the goods supplied. Similarly, to encourage clients to settle their bills before maturity, for example 30 days, the company may grant a financial reduction (discount) if advance payment is made. Finally, customers may be unable to pay all or part of their debt. The receivables of the company are then regarded as doubtful. For all these reasons, it is necessary to adjust the amount of receivables recorded, taking into account factors likely to affect their recovery. **Net realizable value** of receivables is a result of adjustments made to their nominal value (see Figure 3.5).

3.2.2   Financial Reductions

The company policy of granting trade credit is designed to facilitate the purchase by its customers and thus increase its sales. However, the company needs cash for its own purchases, to pay its suppliers, employees, taxes, etc. While offering credit, it can encourage its customers to pay their bills as soon as possible. Many businesses offer opportunities for **cash discount** to their clients. Cash discounts are price reductions which are granted on condition that the bill is paid within a short time. This encourages customers to pay quickly and reduces the need for cash by the seller. Most often, it is economically profitable for the customer to take advantage of it, even if it should then take a loan of the invoice amount from a bank. However, the selling company makes an arbitrage between the price reduction granted to the client, because of the discount and the cost inducted by the payment term (monitoring of receivables, cash needs which could cause a recourse to bank loans, etc.). These discounts are expressed as percentage of gross sales.

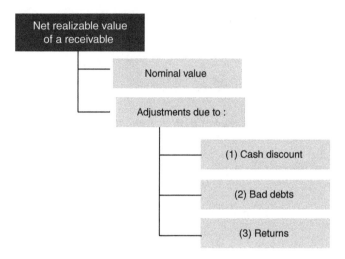

Figure 3.5 Net realizable value of an account receivable.

For example, a company may grant a cash discount of 3% on an amount of €10,000 if the bill is paid within 10 days. This discount is often expressed as "3/10, *n*/60": the company provides 3% discount if payment is made within 10 days (3/10) and a premium will be applied if the price agreed at the sale is not settled within 60 days (*n*/60). Application 3.5 illustrates this principle.

APPLICATION 3.5

How to Record Discount in the Amount of Sales

Alpha-Borneo Spa is an Italian car dealer which also sells agricultural chemistry. The firm sells 10,000 kilograms of chemical fertilizer to an Austrian customer with the following conditions: €5/kg; 2/15; *n*/30 (Alpha-Borneo will gave a discount of 2% if the payment occurs within the 15 coming days). They have the choice of accounting the receivable in two ways:

- The actual price of the merchandise includes the discount.
- The actual price of the merchandise does not include the discount.

First Case: The Receivable is Entered Considering the Discount   The price (€49,000) includes the discount: Alpha-Borneo Spa gives their client a free 15-day credit. At the time of the sale, the entry is:

Accounts receivable (+A)		49,000	
	Sales (+IS)		49,000

If the customer pays 15 days later, he pays €49,000:

Cash (+A)		49,000	
	Accounts receivable (−A)		49,000

If he pays after the 15-day credit, he will pay €50,000. The difference (€1,000) will be recorded as a financial earning in Alpha-Boneo Spa's books:

Cash (+A)		50,000	
Accounts receivable (−A)			49,000
Financial revenue (+IS)			1,000

Second Case: The Receivable is Recorded at its Nominal Value   The price is €50,000 (5 × 10,000). At the time of the sale, Alpha-Borneo Spa enters the operation:

| Accounts receivalbe (+A) | | 50,000 | |
| Sales (+IS) | | | 50,000 |

If the client pays within the 15 coming days, he will benefit from the discount and will pay only €49,000:

Cash (+A)		49,000	
Sales (−IS)		1,000	
Accounts receivable (−A)			50,000

If the client waits 15 days before paying, he will pay €50,000.[1]

3.2.3   Doubtful Accounts (or Bad Debts)

A company that agrees to sell on credit can expect to increase its turnover by facilitating the purchase of its goods and services to customers. But it takes the risk that some customers will not be able to pay their bills. This risk is a cost to the company, which must be reflected in the financial statements. In the balance sheet, receivables should be adjusted to present the most likely amount to be collected. The income of the exercise should incorporate an expense corresponding to the risk incurred by the company. The amount of bad debts is not insignificant: the company should control the collection of its receivables, in case it encounters cash-flow problems of its own (see Table 3.4).

**Table 3.4   Part of Allowances for doubtful accounts
among accounts receivable**

	Allowances for doubtful accounts
Vodafone	10.1%
BP	1.3%
Rolls-Royce	0.0%
AstraZeneca	1.4%
Unilever	3.1%

Source: Annual reports 2008

---

[1] *Be aware of national legislation or local practices where such a discount shall not affect the amount of sales but shall be considered as financial expenses for the firm.*

> **Depreciation is a reduction** in the value of an asset. A receivable is depreciated if one considers that all or part of its amount will not be paid.

The control of receivables and their payment may be very costly for the company. It may resort to debt collection companies to outsource some of these tasks. It can also return to a policy of no credit and require that all sales are paid directly at the time of the transaction, taking the risk of losing some of its customers and seeing its sales decline. Unless you accept these constraints, the uncertain nature of receivables is a cost that the company must manage.

> Allowance for doubtful accounts is an account of depreciation of receivables: a contra account which contains the potential decrease in value that the receivable may undergo.

From an accounting perspective, the risk of bad debts has the direct consequence that the gross receivables no longer represent the amount that can be subsequently generated by these assets. It is therefore necessary to reasonably determine the recoverable amount at maturity of debt. Similarly, losses from bad loans indicate that some credit sales can no longer be included in the financial statements, for all criteria for the recognition of the corresponding revenues are no longer satisfied (reasonable probability of payment). The balance sheet and the income statement are therefore overvalued (respectively current asset and turnover). The amount of receivables and the net income must then be adjusted downward in the same period. These adjustments are made by recording a provision for bad debts, also known as **Allowance for Bad Debts**, Allowance for Doubtful Accounts, or Allowance for Uncollectable Accounts.

Because of the default risk of certain customers, the adjustment of receivables and net income requires three steps (see Application 3.6):

1. The estimation of doubtful accounts.
2. The accounting of allowance for bad debts, whose goal is to simultaneously reduce the value of receivables (recoverable) and recognize a corresponding expense.
3. Write-off of receivables when the default of payment from the customer becomes final.

APPLICATION 3.6

How to Record Bad Debt: General Case

During its first year of existence, the firm Construction Ltd. recorded a €600,000 turnover, €400,000 of them with credit. €100,000 appears in the firm's balance sheet at the end of the year: this means that the other €300,000 has already been collected during the year and that only €100,000 remains to be paid. There are doubts, however, on the ability of Construction Ltd. to collect the whole €100,000.

1. According to other firms durably implemented in the industry, we estimate that 3% of the receivables, namely €3,000 (3% × 100,000) will not be collected.
2. The entry which takes this estimation into consideration is:

| Bad debt expenses (−IS) | 3,000 | |
| Allowances for doubtful accounts (−A) | | 3,000 |

3. Among the clients of the firm that might not be able to pay, the firm Logits, which owes Construction Ltd. €1,000, has gone bankrupt. Construction Ltd will not be paid. Depreciation already happened, so we just have to eliminate both depreciation and receivable from the books.

| Allowance for doubtful accounts (+A) | 1,000 | |
| Accounts receivable (−A) | | 1,000 |

Step 1: Estimation of Doubtful Accounts

> Specific estimation of doubtful accounts: individual estimation of the probability of recovery for each receivable.
>
> Global estimation of doubtful accounts: approximate and arbitrary estimation of receivables which will not be paid, based on historical data or estimations.

Companies can use several methods to estimate the amount of receivables they are unlikely to recover. They can make a **specific estimation** of their receivables, that is to say, estimating the probability of recovery of each of their receivables. However, this process is slow and tedious for large groups with numerous trade receivable accounts.

Without significantly deteriorating the quality of the estimation, companies often resort to a **global estimation** of their doubtful accounts. The company can base its analysis on its past experience of activity. It therefore relies on the actual amounts of claims outstanding from previous years and compares the identified amount with the corresponding turnover or to the gross receivables (receivables prior to estimation of uncertain amounts). Thus, a large number of companies estimate the level of doubtful debts as a percentage of sales or receivables. For example, it may be reasonable to consider that 2% of credit sales will not be settled, or, in the best case, they will be paid with difficulty or delay. A company at the beginning of its operations can refer to other companies in the same industry to make its first estimations. Some companies refine their estimations by applying the percentages obtained (doubtful accounts) to receivables based on their delay in payment. This method consists in classifying the receivables according to the time elapsed since the recognition of the sale and to apply to them a different rate of non-recovery. The rate applied generally increases with the time elapsed since the sale, because the longer the period, the greater is the probability of not being paid (see Application 3.7).

APPLICATION 3.7

Ageing Schedule of Bad Debts

At the end of 2009 (first year of activity), the firm King Cross Pizza recorded €50,000 of receivables. Instead of applying a unique rate of 3% to estimate the proportion of receivables they may not recover, King Cross Pizza uses a table (i.e. an ageing schedule). The firm estimates that only €47,300 of the €50,000 will be paid.

Estimation of bad debt by King Cross Pizza

Age of receivables	Amount (€)	Non-recovery (%)	Estimation
6–12 months	5,000	20%	1,000 (5,000 × 20%)
3–6 months	10,000	10%	1,000 (10,000 × 10%)
Less than 3 months	35,000	2%	700 (35,000 × 2%)
Total	**50,000**		**2,700**

Step 2: Recording of Allowance for Doubtful Accounts According to the *matching* of revenues and expenses, adjustments of receivables are done at the end of each accounting period during which the receivables occurred. Indeed, even if the default of payment is likely to occur during the next fiscal year, revenues (turnover) would have been achieved partly through the credit policy of the company. It is therefore natural to match the corresponding expenses to the risk borne by the company – from credit sales – in the same fiscal period. Before making these adjustments, many companies reclassify potentially uncollectible receivables in a category called *Doubtful accounts*. They then make the necessary adjustments to these accounts. Apart from this reclassification, which adds a step, the rest of the procedure is identical.

It consists in using the *Bad debt expense* account and a balance sheet account, *Allowance for doubtful accounts*, which is nothing other than an account of depreciation of asset value. Although this account appears as an asset, its balance only reduces the value of another item: the receivables. Thus, the estimated amount of bad debts will not directly reduce the amount of account receivables, but shows the amount of net receivables such as: **Net receivables = Gross receivables − Allowance for doubtful accounts**. Allowance for doubtful accounts is an account of depreciation of assets, a **contra account** which contains the potential decrease in value that an asset may undergo.

APPLICATION 3.8

Follow-Up to Bad Debts

The firm King Cross Pizza needs to record in its financial statements the estimation for bad debts (see Application 3.7) of their first fiscal year (2009).

Bad debt expenses (−IS)		2,700	
Allowances for doubtful accounts (−A)			2,700

After this entry, the value of the firm's assets decreases by €2,700. This shows in the balance sheet.

Receivables (gross)	50,000
Allowances for doubtful accounts	(2,700)
Net receivables	47,300

The remaining €47,300 corresponds to the receivables that King Cross Pizza expects to recover.

Adjustments to the amount of allowance for doubtful accounts are often necessary in subsequent years. Indeed, the amount of accounts receivable is rarely identical from one year to the next. A common practice is then to simply adjust the amount of *Allowances* in the balance sheet so that the latter shows an amount of net receivables, which matches the new economic reality of the business (see Application 3.9).

APPLICATION 3.9

Follow-Up to Bad Debts (*continued*)

At the end of the second year of activity (2010), the receivables of King Cross Pizza added up to €70,000. At the beginning of the fiscal year, the situation of the receivables was as follows:

Receivables (gross)	50,000
Allowances for doubtful accounts	(2,700)
Net receivables	47,300

The allowances for doubtful accounts amounted to 5.4% of the gross receivables. There are two different cases:

- Bad debts are considered as definitively lost.
- Managers think that the debts are going to be paid in 2011.

First Case: 2009 Bad Debts are Lost   During the year 2010, receivables have all been collected, except the €2 700 amount of bad debts.

Cash (+A)	47,300	
Allowances for doubtful accounts (+A)	2,700	
Accounts receivable (−A)		50,000

At the end of the second fiscal year, King Cross Pizza computes a new receivables adjustment (€3,780) by applying a 5.4% rate to the €70,000 of current receivables. The operation is as follows:

Bad debt expenses (−IS)	3,780	
Allowances for doubtful accounts (−A)		3,780

Receivables appear in that way in the balance sheet:

Receivables (gross)	70,000
Allowances for doubtful accounts	(3,780)
Net receivables	66,220

The amount of allowances for doubtful accounts only rises by €1,080 but does not truly reflect the situation: the actual costs of credit to customers supported in 2010 totals €3,780.

Second Case: 2009 Bad Debts may be Paid in 2011   Even though the 2009 bad debts have not been collected in 2010, King Cross Pizza's managers think they may be paid in 2011.

Cash (+A)	47,300	
Accounts receivable (−A)		47,300

The amount of receivables at the end of 2010 should be 70,000 + 2,700 (gross amount of bad debts) − (3,780 + 2,700) (bad debt expenses):

Receivables (gross)	72,700
Allowances for doubtful accounts	(6,480)
Net receivables	66,220

Be careful: The total amount of the allowances for doubtful accounts in the balance sheet is €6,480, namely 8.9% of the gross receivables. However, the amount of net receivables is the same because the expense for 2010 only adds up to €3,780.

Bad debt expenses (−IS)	3,780	
Allowances for doubtful accounts (−A)		3,780

Step 3: Write-Off of Doubtful Accounts   When, ultimately, the default of payment of a customer is confirmed, it is necessary to writte-off the accounts receivable and the corresponding allowance for doubtful accounts. The income statement is not affected by this operation (unless the earlier allowance is insufficient) and the impact on the balance sheet is basically zero (see Application 3.10).

APPLICATION 3.10

Cancellation of Bad Debts

The firm Glomerate has €60,000 in receivables at the beginning of 2009. The table below shows an extract of Glomerate's balance sheet on 01/01/2009 (beginning of the fiscal year).

Receivables (gross)	80,000
Allowances for doubtful accounts	(20,000)
Net receivables	60,000

There is a €10,000 allowance for doubtful accounts concerning the client Little, which will not be able to pay.

Allowances for doubtful accounts (+A)	10,000	
Accounts receivable "Little" (−A)		10,000

This entry only decreased the amount of gross receivables by €10,000 because the client, Little, will not pay and is logical to eliminate it from the assets. In addition to the receivable, Glomerate should also suppress the allowances for doubtful accounts which concerned Little's receivable because there is no longer any reason to maintain it (the receivable has already been written off). The balance sheet appears as follow after the correction:

Receivables (gross)	70,000
Allowances for doubtful accounts	(10,000)
Net receivables	60,000

There is no impact on the balance sheet, where the amount of net receivables is still €60,000.

The impact of the write-off of bad loans on the financial statements is not always zero, especially when the estimation of the allowance for doubtful accounts is insufficient or, conversely, too cautious.

APPLICATION 3.11

Cancellation of Bad Debts (*continued*)

The firm Glomerate, which had €60,000 of gross receivables, is told that one of its customer, Little, will not be able to pay the total of its debt, but only €4,000 of the €10,000, it owes.

The following table presents an extract of Glomerate's balance sheet:

Receivables (gross)	80,000
Allowances for doubtful accounts	(20,000)
Net receivables	60,000

Since Glomerate had underestimated the ability of its client to pay, the firm has to cancel the receivable.

Allowances for doubtful accounts (+A)	10,000	
Accounts receivable "Little" (−A)		10,000
Cash (+A)	4,000	
Bad debt expenses (+IS)		4,000

The first entry is nothing but a classic cancellation of the allowances for doubtful accounts. The second one reflects the cash flow and gain coming from the payment. The final operation results in a loss of €6,000 which comes from the bad debt expense of €10,000 (causing a reduced profit in 2009) and the recapture of €4,000 in 2010.

The €4,000 should be recorded as a decrease in "bad debt expenses".

Even after these entries, Glomerate's receivables are still the same:

Receivables (gross)	70,000
Allowances for doubtful accounts	(10,000)
Net receivables	60,000

3.2.4 Returns of Goods

Customers may return goods to the selling firm, usually in a period of 30 to 60 days. The reasons are often a poor functioning of the good, its defective nature, poor quality or any other reason of customer dissatisfaction. From an accounting perspective, these goods have already been recorded in the financial statements. If it was a credit sale, a sale (revenue) in the income statement and a receivable (assets) has been recorded. At the end of each accounting period, the amount of returned goods must be estimated and then deducted from the amount of receivables and sales.

3.2.5   Credit Sales in Foreign Currency

> The local currency is the currency being used in the country where the business is located.

The sales of companies are not restricted to local customers. Products are exported and sales are conducted through subsidiaries. It is likely that customers pay in their own currency, that is to say their **local currency**. If that currency is different from the currency of the selling firm, the seller must convert the amounts relating to the sale in its functional currency (currency used by the company), generally its own local currency.

APPLICATION 3.12

How to Record Receivables in Foreign Currencies

On December 1, 2010, the Belgian firm Salvoy sells $1,000,000 of merchandise to an American retailer with a 60-day credit. At the time the contract is concluded, the exchange rate between euro and the dollar is EUR/USD = 1.25 (1 euro equals 1.25 dollars).

Salvoy enters the following operation:

Accounts receivable (+A) [1,000,000/1.25 = 800,000]		800,000	
	Sales (+IS)		800,000

Exchange rates between currencies may vary considerably in relatively short periods of time. The amount of receivables converted into the currency of the selling firm may not match the amount actually collected, due to changes in exchange rates. One should therefore reflect these changes in the financial statements. Application 3.13 presents a first case with foreign exchange loss and a second case with foreign exchange gain.

APPLICATION 3.13

How to Record Receivables in Foreign Currencies (*continued*)

First Case: Exchange Loss   On December 31, 2010 (when the firm Salvoy closes its accounts), the exchange between euros and dollars is EUR/USD: 1.30. The euro has increased: it is more expensive to buy euros with dollars since the exchange rate was only EUR/USD: 1.25 at the beginning of the month. This variation in terms of exchanges affects the receivable. Actually, if Salvoy's American client pays its receivable on 12/31/2010, Salvoy would only receive $1,000,000/1.30 = €769,231. This must appear in the financial statement.

The receivable must be adjusted to 800,000 − 769,231 = €30,769, and so must the gross profit because of the expense represented by the exchange loss.

Exchange loss (−IS)		30,769	
	Accounts receivable (−A)		30,769

On 01/31/2011, while the receivable expires, 1 euro equals 1.32 dollars. The payment of the receivable generates another loss of €11,655. The entry is as follows:

Cash (+A)	757,576	
Exchange loss (−IS)	11,655	
Accounts receivable (−A)		769,231

(This entry implies that the firm has not adjusted the receivable before its payment).

The adjustments of receivables resulting from sales in foreign currencies are made in any case, the currency rate evolving favourably or unfavourably for the selling firm. The financial statements are intended to reflect the economic and financial situation of the company.

APPLICATION 3.14

How to Record Receivables in Foreign Currencies (*continued*)

Second Case: Exchange Gains   On December 31, 2010 (when the firm Salvoy closes its accounts), the exchange between euros and dollars is EUR/USD: 1.20. This time, the euro has depreciated in front of the dollar (it is now cheaper to buy euros when you have dollars than at the beginning of the month, when 1 euro equalled 1.25 dollars). This variation in terms of exchanges affects the receivable, which has to be re-evaluated to 833,333 − 800,000 = €33,333, while the operating profit increases by the same amount because of an exchange gain.

Accounts receivable (+A)	33,333	
Exchange gain (+IS)		33,333

On 01/31/2011, while the receivable expires, 1 euro equals 1.22 dollars. The payment generates a loss of exchange of 833,333 − 819,672 = €13,661. The value of the receivable in the books is €833,333, recorded at 01/01/2009, but since the euro depreciated in front of the dollar during the month of January 2011, the value of the receivable when paid is only €819,672. When the payment is received, the entry is as follows:

Cash (+A)	819,672	
Exchange loss (−IS)	13,661	
Accounts receivable (−A)		833,333

Salvoy eventually records an exchange gain of 819,672 − 80,000 = €19,672, which is the difference between the amount of receivables at the time of the sale (12/01/2010) and the time of the payment (01/31/2011). However, this gain of exchange is split into a gain of €33,333 in 2010 and a further loss of €13,661 in January.

The variations in the books reflect the variations on the currency exchange.

3.3 INVENTORY

Inventories are assets held for sale in the ordinary course of business.

Figure 3.6 Inventories valuation.

Inventories are assets:

- They are held for sale in the ordinary course of business (for example, goods purchased by a retailer and held for resale, land or other property held for resale by an real-estate company, but may also be finished goods, etc.).
- They may show the work in progress for such sales.
- They may be in the form of raw materials or supplies to be used in the process of production or service delivery (IAS 2, §6).

Inventories sometimes represent large sums in the balance sheet of companies, and this applies to many industrial and commercial companies (Bouygues 8.2%; Essilor 11.2%, Peugeot 10.0%, etc.).[2] The inventory value appears not only in the current assets at year-end accounting, but also impacts the net income of the company through the gross margin and cost of goods sold (see Chapter 2). The appendix to this chapter discusses inventory valuation of raw materials and finished goods. Inventory valuation requires a physical count of goods to be conducted and their respective costs to be identified (Figure 3.6).

3.3.1 Physical Count

To carry out the inventory valuation of goods at year end, it is necessary to know the number of goods to be included in the physical count. This counting requires three steps:

1. One must first count the units in store and in the warehouse of the company. When taking inventory, we operate a physical count of goods in order to establish the number of units on hand at a given date.
2. Some goods may be in transit (units that lie between the premises of the supplier and the company *or* between the premises of the firm and the client). Several cases are possible, including the two most common:
   - If FOB (free on board) shipping point: the buyer bears the cost of transportation and owns the inventories. Goods must be included in the inventory of the buyer.
   - If FOB delivery point: the seller bears the cost of transportation and retains ownership of inventories. Goods should not be included in the inventory of the buyer.
3. Some goods can be consigned. These are goods that a supplier has delivered to a dealer while retaining ownership. The transfer of ownership takes place when the trader sells the goods.

---

[2] *Figures obtained from the consolidated IFRS annual reports, 2007.*

- If the company is the supplier (consignor), then the goods should be included in the inventory.
- If the company is the retailer (consignee), then the goods should not be included in the inventory (if such goods have been counted, they must be deducted).

After this step of precise counting, the determination of the cost of goods is then possible.

3.3.2 Valuation

Initial Valuation

> The acquisition cost is the value used at the entry date, in the company, of goods acquired against payment and is equal to the purchase price plus other expenses necessary to make the goods usable.

The cost of inventories comprises all *costs of acquisition and all other costs* necessary for the availability of goods. The **acquisition costs** mainly include: the purchase price, customs duties and other taxes (other than those recoverable by the entity from the tax authorities), freight and handling costs. Acquisition costs take into account discounts and rebates. The cost of inventories is therefore considered after the application of these subtractive elements. The discounts on cash payments are also deducted from the purchase price of inventories.

APPLICATION 3.15

Acquisition of Goods

In 2010, the firm LochNess Ltd. spent the following amounts for goods acquisition:

• Goods coming from abroad:	€3,635,000
• Customs duties:	€5,000
• Shipping expenses:	€70,000
• Recollection of damaged goods:	€10,000
• Discount on damaged goods:	€10,000
• Cash discount:	€40,000
• Unsold items at December 31:	€350,000

At the beginning of the fiscal year, in January, the value of the inventory was €200,000. The cost of goods in 2010 is as follows:

Inventory at the beginning of the year	€200,000
Plus:	
Purchases	3,635,000
Custom duties	5,000
Shipping expenses	70,000
Minus:	
Recollection and discounts	60,000
Cost of goods available for sale:	3,850,000
Minus: unsold items at the end of the year	350,000
Cost of goods sold (COGS)	**€3,500,000**

Inventory
Inventory and work in progress are valued at the lower of cost and net realisable value on a first-in, first-out basis. Cost comprises direct materials and, where applicable, direct labour costs and those overheads, including depreciation of property, plant and equipment, that have been incurred in bringing the inventories to their present location and condition. Net realisable value represents the estimated selling prices less all estimated costs of completion and costs to be incurred in marketing, selling and distribution.

Figure 3.7   Refers to the method of valuing inventory withdrawal.

Valuation and Cost Flow Assumptions   There are four ways to assign a cost to goods in an inventory:

- Specific identification method;
- Weighted average method (wheat, wine, etc. are mixed: it is impossible to distinguish the units);
- Successive selling out method (FIFO, first in–first out);
- Reverse selling out method (LIFO, last in–first out).

Only two methods are allowed by the IASB to determine the cost of fungible inventories: the "first in–first out" (FIFO) and the weighted average cost method.

The specific identification method attributes to inventory items their actual cost of purchase. However, it only applies to non-homogeneous, high value and identifiable items.

Specific Identification Method   The **specific identification method** consists in assigning to specific inventory items their actual cost of purchase (specific cost at the time of purchase). However it applies only to non-fungible, valuable and identifiable items, such as houses, artwork, etc.

Application 3.16 illustrates the three other methods of inventory valuation that enables us to understand their impact on the income statement through the cost of goods sold.

The question that arises now is: How should we value the consumption of goods (determine their cost), and the final inventory of 12 units left in store?

Weighted Average Cost Method

The weighted average cost method allocates to the inventory items the weighted average cost of purchases for the year and opening inventory, that is to say, all goods that were available for sale.

APPLICATION 3.16

Cost Flow Assumption and Cost of Goods Sold

The firm Fever discloses the following information concerning its purchases and sales of goods:

Data	Number of units	Cost per unit	Total cost
Opening inventory	10	800	8,000
Purchase 1 – 03/01	5	900	4,500
Purchase 2 – 07/01	5	1,000	5,000
Purchase 3 – 10/01	5	1,200	6,000
Purchase 4 – 12/01	5	1,300	6,500
Total for goods to be sold	30		30,000
Goods sold	18		
Unsold goods at 12/31	12		

The **weighted average method** allocates to the inventory items the weighted average cost of purchases for the year and opening inventory, that is to say, all goods that were available for sale. The average cost is thus determined as follows:

$$\frac{\text{Cost of opening inventory} + \text{Cost of purchases during the fiscal period}}{\text{Number of goods in the opening inventory} + \text{Number of goods purchased during the fiscal period}}$$

This method has the advantage of mitigating the effects of price fluctuations during the period. But it has the disadvantage of distorting the value of inventory if prices increased or decreased systematically during the period. If the company uses a perpetual inventory system (inventory valuation after each sale), the average is calculated after each purchase (moving average).

Successive Selling Out Method: FIFO

The FIFO method (First In First Out) states the hypothesis that the first items purchased are sold first, so that the items in inventory at the end of the year are from recent purchases.

The **FIFO** method assumes that items purchased first are sold first, so that the items in inventory at the end of the year are from recent purchases. This approach has the advantage of valuing inventories in the balance sheet at a value close to their replacement cost. However, the cost of goods sold (COGS) is valued to the oldest costs in case of inflation.

Table 3.5   Average cost method (i.e. Application 3.16)

Cost of goods available for sale	30,000
Number of items	30
Average unit cost	1,000
Closing inventory (average cost method)	12,000
Cost of goods to be sold	30,000
Minus: Closing inventory	(12,000)
COGS (Average cost method)	**18,000**

Table 3.6   First in–first out (FIFO) method (i.e. Application 3.16)

Five units bought December 1 (1,300 × 5)	6,500
Five units bought October 1 (1,200 × 5)	6,000
Two units bought July 1 (1,000 × 2)	2,000
Closing inventory (FIFO)	14,500
Cost of goods available for sales	30,000
Minus: Closing inventory	(14,500)
COGS (FIFO method)	**15,500**

Reverse Selling Out Method (LIFO)

> According to the LIFO (Last In First Out) method, we assume that the last items purchased are sold first, so that the items in inventory at the end of the year are the first articles on hand.

The **LIFO** method assumes that the last items purchased are sold first, so that the items in inventory at the end of the year are the first articles on hand. The advantage is to assess the COGS at the latest costs. However, inventories are valued at the oldest costs, therefore even further from the replacement cost.

Once we choose a method of valuation under the consistency principle, we cannot change the method for subsequent years. The impact on the financial statements is not insignificant, as shown in the following summary (Table 3.8).

The turnover of the company Brown is €28,000,000 for the year *N*. The impact on the financial statements of the inventory valuation method is presented.

3.3.3   Depreciation of Inventory

With each new fiscal year, a valuation of the net realizable value of inventories should be conducted. Indeed, some circumstances require a depreciation of the value of inventories, such as their deterioration or loss of market value. One should reflect this information in the financial statements. The *net realizable value* is the estimated selling price in the ordinary course of business, *less* the estimated costs of completion and the costs necessary to make the sale (IAS 2, §6). If inventories are damaged, if they have become obsolete, if their selling price has fallen, if the estimated costs of completion or costs necessary to make the sale have increased, then the cost of inventories may not be recoverable. The net realizable value is estimated on the basis of the most reliable evidence available at the date on which valuations are made. This is the *amount expected from the realization (sale)* of inventories. When the

Table 3.7   Last in–first out (LIFO) method (i.e. Application 3.16)

Ten units in opening inventory (800 × 10)	8,000
Two units bought on March 1 (900 × 2)	1,800
Closing inventory (LIFO)	9,800
Cost of goods available for sales	30,000
Minus: Closing inventory	(9,800)
COGS (LIFO method)	**20,200**

Table 3.8   Summary of financial statement

	Average cost	FIFO	LIFO
Sales	28,000	28,000	28,000
Cost of goods sold:			
Initial inventory	8,000	8,000	8,000
Plus: Purchases	22,000	22,000	22,000
= Cost of goods available for sale	30,000	30,000	30,000
Minus: Closing inventory	(12,000)	(14,500)	(9,800)
= COGS	18,000	15,500	20,200
Gross Margin	**10,000**	**12,500**	**7,800**

entry cost is higher than the net realizable value, it is therefore necessary to depreciate the inventories back to their net realizable value. The company Volkswagen AG points this out in its annual report (see Figure 3.8).

APPLICATION 3.17

Net Realizable Value

The firm Beta produced a good, known as X, the production of which is not completed. Its expected selling price is €800 and the further costs in order to complete the production are estimated at €200. The selling costs are €50. The net realizable value is $800 - 200 - 50 = €550$.

The calculations are per item, unless the inventories relate to the same line of products with similar uses or if they are produced or marketed in the same geographical area and cannot be evaluated separately from other items in the product line. It is thus inappropriate to depreciate a whole inventory using the following criteria: finished products, goods, inventory for the same industry, etc.

If inventories are held to satisfy a sale contract of products or services previously signed, the net realizable value of inventories will depend on the price specified in the contract.

Raw materials and other supplies held for use in the production of inventories are not depreciated below the cost if it is expected that the finished goods in which they will be incorporated will be sold at cost or above. However, when a decline in the price of raw materials indicates

INVENTORIES

Raw materials, consumables and supplies, merchandise, work in progress and self-produced finished goods reported in inventories are carried at the lower of cost or net realizable value. Cost is determined on the basis of the direct and indirect costs that are directly attributable. Borrowing costs are not capitalized. The measurement of same or similar inventories is based on the weighted average cost method.

Figure 3.8   Excerpts of the 2008 annual report, Volkswagen AG.

Consolidated balance sheet
At December 31, 2008

	Notes	2008 £m	2007 £m
ASSETS			
Current assets			
Inventory	10	**2,600**	2,203
Trade and other receivables	11	**3,929**	2,585
Taxation recoverable		**9**	7
Other financial assets	15	**390**	514
Short-term investments		**1**	40
Cash and cash equivalents	12	**2,469**	1,896
Assets held for sale		**12**	7

Figure 3.9   Extract of annual report, Rolls-Royce plc.

that the cost of finished products is higher than the net realizable value, inventories of raw materials or supplies will be depreciated to their net realizable value, which can be measured by the replacement cost.

Depreciation of inventory and release of provision for depreciation of inventory are, according to international accounting standards, recorded as changes in gross values. They are not included in specific accounts providing information on the gross value, depreciation and net values.

The extract of the annual report of Rolls-Royce plc. is an example of the final presentation of main items of the current assets: cash, accounts receivables and inventory (see Figure 3.9). This group has a number of derivative assets (options, swaps, etc.) which are held-for-trading financial assets.

3.4   APPENDIX

3.4.1   Introduction to Cost of Finished Goods

The *costs of conversion* of inventories include:

- costs directly related to the units produced, including direct labour,
- allocation of fixed and variable manufacturing overheads incurred in transforming materials into finished products.

The *fixed manufacturing overheads* are indirect costs of production, and are constant regardless of the volume of production (for example, depreciation and maintenance of buildings and equipment) and management and administration fees. They are allocated to inventories based on the *normal capacity* of the production facilities, which is defined as the average production that may be performed on a number of periods or seasons in normal circumstances. The actual level of production may be withheld if it approximates the normal capacity of production. When production decreases or the production tool is not fully used, the overhead costs that are not allocated are considered expenses for the period: the amount of fixed overheads per unit is not increased.

Variable manufacturing overheads are indirect costs of production, as a function of the volume of production (raw materials and indirect labour). They are allocated to units produced according to the actual utilization of production facilities.

APPLICATION 3.18

Acquisition of Raw Materials

On May 1 the firm Clelisa bought 5,000 kg of raw material (RM) for €500,000. This amount does not include Customs duties of €10,000. The supplier accorded a first price reduction of 4% and a discount of another 3% because Clelisa paid cash. The actual cost of acquisition is computed in this way:

Purchase price	500,000
+ Customs duties	10,000
	510,000
− Discount: 510,000 × 4%	20,400
	489,600
− Discount for paying cash: 489,600 × 3%	14,688
	474,912

The cost of the purchase of this raw material is €474,912. It is this amount that will appear in the firm's books. The cost per unit is obtained by dividing €474,912 by 5,000 units: €95.

Raw material inventory (+A)	474,912	
Cash (−A)		474,912

Clelisa produces a good (*G*) using this raw material. During the month of May, 3,500 units of *G* have been produced using 3,000 kg of raw material. There are additional costs:

- Labour costs: €40,000
- Variable general costs for production: €60,000
- Fixed general costs for production: €20,000
- Plant administration expenses: €30,000
- Transport expenses: €4,000
- Storage expenses (with no link to any new step of production):   €2,000
- Selling expenses: €10,000

The production lines have the capacity to produce 4,000 units of *P* per month.

Production costs are the following:

Raw materials	95 × 3,000	285,000
Labour costs		40,000
Variable general costs for production		60,000
Fixed general costs for production	20,000 × 3,500/4,000 =	17,500
Plant administration expenses	30,000 × 3,500/4,000 =	26,250
Transport expenses		4,000
		432,750

Storage expenses (with no link to any new step of production) and selling expenses cannot be taken into consideration for the stock valuation (€432,750).

Finished goods inventory (+A)	432,750		
Raw material inventory (−A)		285,000	
Cash (or accounts payable) (−A)		147,750	

Inventory costs for service providers are valued at their manufacturing cost, which includes labour and other costs of personnel directly engaged in providing the service, and the corresponding overheads. Profit margins are incorporated into the prices charged by service providers and are not included in inventory costs.

APPLICATION 3.19

Cost of a Service Supply

The firm Friger sells services. Labour cost and general expenses linked to the service supply are valued €28,000. The firm makes a 50% margin on the sell. What is the invoiced price for the service? And what is the cost of the service?

Invoiced price: 28,000 × 1.5 = €42,000
Cost of the service: €28,000

3.5 SUMMARY

Current assets are economic resources intended to generate future economic benefits in the short term.

Companies may acquire financial assets held for trading purposes. These assets are stocks, bonds and other derivatives (options, swaps, futures), valued at fair value. Changes in fair value are then recorded in the income statement (upwards or downwards) at the closing of accounts. When these financial assets are classified as available for sale (holding them on a short and medium term, but not until maturity) changes in fair value affect the equity (i.e. Other Comprehensive Income) without affecting the income statement.

The receivables arise from the mismatch between the timing of recognition of a revenue and its final payment. The value of a receivable must be evaluated each year end and represents the present value of the flows it is expected to generate in the future. In practice, for short-term receivables, the nominal value is used. The company does not always recover the amount of receivables. The estimation of the net realizable value of a receivable is to determine the amount of receivables that could not be paid by clients, whether due to financial concessions granted in the return of goods or simply to insolvent customers.

Inventories are included in the current assets in balance sheets. They correspond to raw materials not consumed during the accounting period, to goods and finished products, semi-finished unsold and work-in-progress. The value of inventories is determined at the end of each accounting period. Arbitration is made between cost and net realizable value, which sometimes gives rise to the recognition of depreciation of inventory, release of depreciation of inventory or even exceptional loss on inventory.

3.6 ACTIVITIES

3.6.1 Financial Assets

1. Valuation of Financial Assets   The holding Holdex bought the following shares during the year 2010:

- 3,000 shares of the firm Financia, for €45,000 on March 15.
- 4,500 shares of the firm Mercury for €260,000 on July 20.
- 3,000 shares of the firm Gadgetex for €150,000 on November 15.

Those prices do not include transaction fees, for an additional 0.5% of the amount.

At the end of the year (12/31/10), prices of stocks are €18, €70 and €40 respectively.

1. *What is the book value of Holdex's financial assets?*
2. *What are the financial losses or gains that Holdex recognized during 2010?*

3.6.2 Accounts Receivable

2. Acounts Payable and Discount   Matbat sells material for construction. During the month of February 2010, Matbat sells:

- €300,000 on the 4th, with 2/15, *n*/60 conditions. The customer chooses to pay in 60 days.
- €100,000 on the 15th, with a discount of 5% and with 1/10, *n*/30 conditions. The client pays cash.
- €200,000 on the 20th, with 5/30, *n*/270 conditions. The client decides to pay in 270 days. The actualization rate is 5%.

1. *What are the operations on the account "accounts payable" in 2010?*
2. *What turnover shall Matbat record for the month of February 2010?*

3. Allowance for Doubtful Accounts   The total amount of the accounts receivables of the Japanese importer Hasan is €300,000 on 12/31/2010. Those receivables are split in this way:

	Amount	*Probability of non-recover*
Receivable aged less than 1 month	€150,000	1%
Receivable aged less than 2 months	€100,000	2%
Receivable aged less than 3 months	€50,000	3%

At the end of 2009, the amount of Hasan's doubtful accounts was €3,000. Hasan estimates that there was no hope of recovering them.

1. *What shall Hasan record on 12/31/2010?*
2. *What are the allowances for doubtful accounts on 12/31/2010?*

4. Returns of Goods Ringo makes MP3 players and sold 100,000 units in 2009, 1,500 of which came back through dysfunction. On 12/31/2009, Ringo's books show €10m for turnover, €2m for accounts payable and €30,000 as an allocation for returns. On 12/31/2010, Ringo's turnover has increased by €2m to €12m and their accounts payable by €1m to €3m.

1. *What should be the amount of returns for 2010 (considering the same return rate as in 2009).*
2. *How should these returns be recorded in books?*

5. Variations on Exchange Rates The Japanese firm Chugai sells pharmaceuticals to Pharmaplus, a Scottish lab, for €130m on 11/01/2010. This transaction is done "free on board" and the pharmaceuticals are sent by plane on 11/10/2010. Payment must be received within 3 months.

The EUR/JPY exchange rate evolves slightly during the period:

Date	EUR/JPY
11/01/2010	125
11/10/2010	130
12/31/2010	127
02/01/2011	115
02/10/2011	118

How do the variations in the Yen exchange rate affect Chugai's books?

3.6.3 Inventories

6. Raw Materials Acquisition Cost Mercury, a firm working in the luxury industry, bought a stock of calfskin for a value of €300,000, with a 3% discount. Their supplier suggested to pay within 15 days and get a 2% discount, or to pay within 60 days. Mercury decided to pay cash.

1. *What is the proper amount to which the stock shall be recorded?*
2. *What is the actual impact of this purchase on Mercury cash account?*

7. Inventory Valuation A refinery observes the following evolutions in its stocks of crude oil:

- On 01/01, there are 1,200,000 cubic metres in stock, at a price of €300 per cubic metres.
- 200,000 cubic metres are refined during the month of January.
- On 02/01, the refinery purchased 300,000 cubic metres at a price of €330 per cubic metres.

- 250,000 cubic metres are refined during February.
- On 03/01, 100,000 cubic metres are bought at the price of €280 per cubic metre.
- 300,000 cubic metres are refined in March.

1. *At the quarter closing, what is the value of the crude oil stock, using the average cost method?*
2. *Would another method have been better for the firm?*

8. Valuation of Finished Goods   Mercury produces 200 handbags a week. The following materials are needed for their production.

- 200 square metres of leather (value in stock: €50 per square metre).
- 600 hours worked. One hour worked by Mercury costs €40.
- Variable general production expenses: €2,000.
- Fix general production expenses: €4,000.
- Storage: €800.
- Marketing expenses: €3,000.

1. *What costs may be taken into account for the valuation of a handbag?*
2. *What is the value of a handbag in Mercury's inventory?*

9. Inventory Depreciation   On 12/31/2010, the firm Gadgetex has 1,000 MP3 players in its stock. They have been recorded at their production cost, namely €150 per unit (Gadgetex sells them for €250). A market study instigated by Gadgetex states that the MP3 players should not be sold for more than €180.

1. *How shall the stocks be re-evaluated on December 31, 2010?*
2. *300 MP3 players remain in stock the following year, but this time, Gadgetex knows they will not be sold. What is the re-evaluation on December 31, 2011?*

4 NON-FINANCIAL LIABILITIES

Ordinary (or current) activities of the company often generate many obligations (liabilities). For example, when a company does not immediately pay its purchases of goods, it records a debt towards its supplier. It therefore has an obligation to pay its bill at a later date. This chapter discusses the various liabilities of a company, except those related to its financing. They are mainly liabilities towards suppliers, staff or the State. They can be classified into three categories:

- **Liabilities** are obligations whose motive, due date and amount payable are known (i.e. all the characteristic features of other liabilities, such as trade payables or accruals).
- **Provisions** are obligations whose motive is known, but not the exact amount nor the due date. The amount to be recorded as liabilities is then determined using reliable estimates.
- **Contingent liabilities** are potential obligations whose existence is confirmed by the occurrence of one or more uncertain future events, which are not totally under the control of the company.

The plan of this chapter follows this classification (see Figure 4.1).

The excerpt of the liabilities section of the balance sheet of the 2008 TOTAL Group highlights the diversity and volume of the liabilities of a large group (see Figure 4.2). We can note that the non-current financial debts amount to €16,191m. The notes to the consolidated accounts state that they are essentially bonds amounting to €13,665m.

Just above appear the other non-current items (provisions and other liabilities) for €17,842m. Finally, the current liabilities appear for €34,327m.

The sum of these liabilities amounts therefore to €68,360m for a total liability and shareholders' equity of €118,310m, which represents nearly 58% of this amount.

The obligations of a financial nature, here amounting to €16,191m + €7,722m, are addressed in Chapter 6 and those related to taxes (€7,973m of deferred taxes) in Chapter 7.

4.1 LIABILITIES

4.1.1 General Case

A liability arises when the risks and benefits of ownership of the good are transferred by a supplier, in the case of delivery of goods. The liability is extinguished upon settlement. In the case of supply of services, the liability is generated at the completion of service by the supplier. These principles are similar to those presented for determining the ordinary income (see Chapter 2). Trade payables and accrued liabilities are presented in the liabilities of the company. However, one should distinguish the accruals and liabilities.

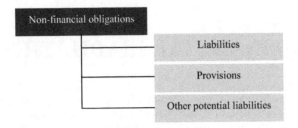

Figure 4.1   Classifications of non-financial obligations.

> **Paid leaves:** The company has the obligation to give its staff time off. Thus, in Europe, employees are entitled to a leave of several weeks. The company must compensate for the leave on the basis of wages normally paid for the same period of activity.

- The notion of **liability** is used for operations already performed and have been charged or have been the object of another formal agreement. A support or justification therefore includes the definitive amounts to be recorded in the accounts of the company. The most common debts are related to the suppliers for amounts to be paid for their deliveries or services provided. Liabilities also exist towards employees, social organisms or the State, for example.

Consolidated balance sheet

TOTAL

As of December 31, (M€)		2008	2007	2006
LIABILITIES & SHAREHOLDERS' EQUITY				
Shareholders' equity				
Common shares		5,930	5,989	6,064
Paid-in surplus and retained earnings		52,947	48,797	41,460
Currency translation adjustment		(4,876)	(4,396)	(1,383)
Treasury shares		(5,009)	(5,532)	(5,820)
Total shareholders' equity – Group share	(Note 17)	48,992	44,858	40,321
Minority interests		958	842	827
Total shareholders' equity		49,950	45,700	41,148
Non-current liabilities				
Deferred income taxes	(Note 9)	7,973	7,933	7,139
Employee benefits	(Note 18)	2,011	2,527	2,773
Provisions and other non-current liabilities	(Note 19)	7,858	6,843	6,467
Total non-current liabilities		17,842	17,303	16,379
Non-current financial debt	(Note 20)	16,191	14,876	14,174
Current liabilities				
Accounts payable		14,815	18,183	15,080
Other creditors and accrued liabilities	(Note 21)	11,632	12,806	12,509
Current borrowings	(Note 20)	7,722	4,613	5,858
Other current financial liabilities	(Note 20)	158	60	75
Total current liabilities		34,327	35,662	33,522
Total liabilities and shareholders' equity		118,310	113,541	105,223

Figure 4.2   Excerpts from TOTAL SA, registration document 2008.

21) Other creditors and accrued liabilities

As of December 31,

(M€)	2008	2007	2006
Accruals and deferred income	151	137	163
Payable to States (including taxes and duties)	6,256	7,860	7,204
Payroll	928	909	879
Other operating liabilities	4,297	3,900	4,263
Total	11,632	12,806	12,509

Figure 4.3   Excerpts from TOTAL SA, registration document 2008.

- Accrued expenses (or accrued liabilities), on the other hand, are operations that have not yet been charged or have not been the object of a formal agreement with a third party. They are obligations towards suppliers for which invoices have not yet been received or are amounts due to staff for **paid leaves**. Although it is sometimes necessary to estimate the amount of the invoice at the date of the financial statements, uncertainty is not commensurate with that which occurs for provisions.

In terms of presentation, accrued expenses (and accounts payable) are most often associated with the Trade Payables item in the liability section of the balance sheet. With few exceptions, they are usually current liabilities. Appendix 21 of the consolidated accounts of TOTAL (see Figure 4.3) presents the various non-financial liabilities other than trade payables. It includes debts towards the State for taxes amounting €6,256m and debts towards social organisms (Payroll) of €928m.

These liabilities added to the trade or accounts payable of €14,815m (see Figure 4.2) represent the non-financial current liabilities of the Group. Applications 4.1 and 4.2 present the accounting of accounts payable and accrued expenses.

APPLICATION 4.1

Invoice from Goods or Services Suppliers

In July 2010, the firm Electrologic ordered components from a German supplier, Bavaria System. The amount of this transaction was €100,000. The reception of the components happened on September 3 and the invoice was received on September 7. According to the contract, Electrologic has to pay Bavaria System within 30 days after reception.

Recording the Invoice on the Reception Date (09/07/2010)   There is no delay between the reception of the goods and the invoicing: both operations happened during the 2010 fiscal year: the expense appears on the P&L with a debt as counterpart on the balance sheet.

Components purchase (–IS)	100,000	
Accounts payable (+L)		100,000
Bavaria System's invoice		

Using the system of permanent inventory (see Chapter 2), the account of Inventories (or stocks) shall be debited in place of Purchases. The components are then considered as current assets.

4.1.2 Accrued Expense: the Case of Paid Leaves

The company must (legal obligation) pay for absences due to leaves of its staff. Thus, in Europe, employees are entitled to a leave of several weeks, and sometimes more under collective agreements. This right is acquired "from month to month", with a reference period which, for example, may run from June 1 to May 31 of the following year. The legal period of use of these rights is from May 1 to October 31, with the possibility of deferral in some cases. The accounts shall, at the end of year, show the amount of paid leaves earned during the year and the related tax and social security expenses. The outflow of economic benefits (payment) is certain and corresponds to the remuneration for services provided by the employees (obligation on the part of the company). The conditions for recognition of a liability are met.

APPLICATION 4.2

How to Record Paid Leaves

The firm Luxcar grants its employees 3 days of paid leave in addition to the 5 weeks legally required. At the end of the 2010 fiscal year, Luxcar evaluates the proportion of paid leave used during the period and also the social charges.

- Paid leave: €80,000
- Social charges: €34,000
- Fiscal charges (a tax computed in link with the number of employees and their salaries): €2,000.

Luxcar books the expense in terms of paid leave throughout the year, any time they are used by the workforce, and also when closing its books, at the end of the year.

At 12/31/2010, the books present the following situation:

Salaries and fringe benefits (–IS)	100,000	
Salaries payable (+L)		100,000
Bavaria System's invoice		

Taxes (–IS)	2,000	
Social security contributions (–IS)	34,000	
State (+L)		2,000
Social organisms (+L)		34,000
Social charges pertaining to paid leave		

When the actual leave occurs, there will be a substitution between the indemnity of paid leave and the salary at the end of the concerned month.

4.2 PROVISIONS

A provision is a liability whose timing or amount is uncertain.

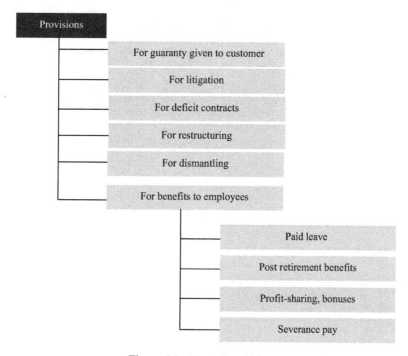

Figure 4.4 Type of provisions.

The financial statements cannot be limited to only recording past operations. According to the prudence and accrual principles, they must also take account of future disbursements, particularly in respect of expenses to come. Recording a **provision** will allow a company to respect the prudence principle, here regarding the liabilities and expenses. In fact, the obligations that existed **prior** to the closing date of the exercise must be taken into account. Operations that have some similarities with those that may be subject to provisions, but do not receive this recognition, are studied in section 4.3. Figure 4.4 presents most common type of provisions.

4.2.1 Definition: Legal or Implicit Obligation

A liability is a present obligation of the company arising from past events whose settlement is expected to result in an outflow of resources embodying economic benefits.

A liability is a **present obligation** arising from past events whose settlement is expected to result in an outflow of resources embodying economic benefits for the company, in general disbursement. The provision is then defined as a liability whose timing or amount is uncertain (IAS 37).

A present obligation may be legal (explicit) or implied. A legal obligation is justified by the law enforcement, regulation, any other source of law or under a contract.

APPLICATION 4.3

Application of a Legal Obligation: Provision for Guaranty Given to Customers

When purchasing household appliances or multimedia devices, the customer receives an invoice that states the general agreements of guaranty. Those agreements may be stated in this way: "the sale remains protected by the legal guaranty of conformity between the sold good and the contract". The period and the geographical limit of the guaranty are then specified, as are the mode of repair (components exchange, technical intervention, loan of equivalent apparel during the repair, etc.).

Shall the seller constitute a provision for guaranty?

Services freely offered to the customer within a guaranty are considered as an outflow of resources embodying economic benefits. They are linked to a legal obligation resulting from a past event (the sale, indeed). The firm will have no choice but to constitute a *provision for guaranty given to customers.*

An implicit obligation arises from the actions of a company when it has reported to third parties, by its past practices, its declared policy or a recent statement sufficiently explicit, that it will assume certain responsibilities.

An obligation is **implicit** when it arises from the actions of a company that reported to third parties – by its past practices, its declared policy or an explicit recent statement – that it will assume certain responsibilities. These third parties therefore expect that it will meet its commitments (see Application 4.4).

A provision should be recognized when the conditions explained in the above definition are met. Appendix 19 of the consolidated financial statements details the Total "Non-current provisions" (see Figure 4.2) and gives an overview of the various provisions that a large group should recognize, in addition to provisions for pension liabilities and taxes. Thus, provisions for restitutions of sites have increased from €3,893m in 2006 to €4,500m in 2008 (see Figure 4.5).

19) Provisions and other non-current liabilities

As of December 31, (M€)	2008	2007	2006
Litigation and accrued penalty claims	546	601	497
Provisions for environmental contingencies	558	552	574
Asset retirement obligations	4,500	4,206	3,893
Other non-current provisions	1,804	1,188	1,215
Other non-current liabilities	450	296	288
Total	7,858	6,843	6,467

Figure 4.5 Excerpt from Total SA, registration document 2008.

APPLICATION 4.4

Constructive Obligations and Provisions

The firm Northampton Grabbing & Co. (NGC) exploits a quarry not far from a small touristic town. The activity of NGC indubitably creates severe damage to the environment. However, no legal obligation exists in the State that may oblige NGC to restitute the land after closing the quarry. However, NGC promised to an association of local residents, shortly after beginning its activity in 2010, to take action at the end of its exploitation period (5 years from now).

Shall NGC constitute a provision for land restitution?

As far as the environment is concerned, a firm may have to constitute several kinds of provisions: asbestos suppression, depolluting or land restitution (in the case of NGC). Even if there is no legal obligation, as soon as a firm publicly indicated to a third party (an association of local residents, for instance) that it will assure its responsibilities, we can speak of a constructive obligation. A provision should be recorded. At the 2010 closing, NGC shall compute the provision for the part already exploited. If there is any part of the site that has not yet been exploited, there is no obligation concerning it.

4.2.2 Measurement

Method of expected value: when the provision includes a large number of items, the obligation is estimated by weighting all possible outcomes by their probability.

The amount of the obligation must be estimated reliably: we must make an estimate of expenditure required to settle the present obligation at the balance sheet date. It is rare enough not to obtain a reliable estimate. The company takes an appraisal on the operation, supplemented by experience of similar transactions and, possibly, by reports of independent experts. When provision to be measured includes a large number of items, the obligation is estimated by weighting all possible outcomes by their probability. This statistical method is called the **method of expected value**. The provision is therefore different depending on whether the probability of losing a given amount is 70% or 95%.

APPLICATION 4.5

Provision Evaluation: Method of Expected Value

Electrologic sells device for high-precision measurement, especially for aeronautical purposes. A legal guaranty is included in each contract in case of manufacturing defect. In 2010, an internal study proved that, if minor manufacturing defects were detected on sold products, the total amount of repairs to be paid by Electrologic would be €500,000.

If major manufacturing defects were to be found, the amount would top €2m. Historical data within the firm make the management think that 80% of the products will have no defects, 8% will present minor defects and 12% major ones.

What amount shall be recorded as a provision for guaranty given to customers?

Electrologic shall evaluate the probability of disbursement for the totality of its guaranty obligations. The expected value of those repairs is determined as follows:

$$(80\% \times 0) + (8\% \times 500,000) + (12\% \times 2,000,000) = €280,000.$$

This amount shall be recorded as a provision for guaranty given to customers at the close of the 2010 fiscal year.

For provisions with maturities exceeding one year, their value must be discounted if it is significant.[1] For this, we must consider not only the amount of payment envisaged, but also foresee the date of disbursement. The IAS/IFRS do not provide any guidance on how to fix the maturity of the provision and, therefore, on the need for discounting. However, discounting is required for all provisions with maturities exceeding one year. The discount rate should be a pre-tax rate, reflecting current market assessments of time value of money and risks specific to the liability. When provisions are discounted, the book value of the provision increases each year to reflect the time elapsed. This increase in provision is recorded in financial expenses.

APPLICATION 4.6

Evaluation of Provisions: Discounting

The firm Electrologic is in contention with a customer, Sheffield Steels, concerning two devices delivered by Electrologic on September 25, 2010. Sheffield Steels considers that both devices are not working properly, which caused side effects in the production of its own products, and, finally, complaints from its own clients of the aeronautical industry.

Electrologic contested the situation but Sheffield Steels decided to ask for a Court decision (Sheffield Steels expects €150,000 as damages). On 12/31/2010, while closing its books, Electrologic decided to record a provision of €100,000 concerning this contention. With the delays likely with this procedure, the Court is unlikely to make a decision before 2013.

How should you analyze and book this case for the 2010, 2011 and 2012 closing?

Constitution of the Provision in 2010   First, we have to establish that the case meets the conditions needed for the constitution of a provision. A generating event did occur (the sales), creating a legal obligation of guaranty. This means an expected outflow of resources embodying economic benefits (disbursement of damages) but whose date and amount cannot be known yet (those events are linked to the Court decision).

Second, we have to take into consideration the time and expected disbursed amount in 3 years, namely €100,000, to compute the 2010 endowment, with a discount rate of 5% (the rate a bank would give to Electrologic for a 2-year borrowing):

$$\frac{100,000}{(1 + 0.05)} = €90.703$$

---

[1]   *The discount can express the value, at today's date, of an amount payable (or cash) in the future.*

This amount is recorded on 12/31/2010 as an operating expense, with a provision account on counterpart (balance sheet)

Other operating expenses (–IS)	90,703	
Provisions (+L)		90,703
Constitution of the provision in 2010		

Evolution of the Provision in 2011 At the 2011 closing, the Court has not yet made its decision. Electrologic shall record another expense for 5% of €90,703, namely €4,535. This is a financial expense, and the counterpart is still the account provision (balance sheet), which evolves to 90,703 + 4,535 = €95,238.

Financial expenses (–IS)	4,535	
Provisions (+L)		4,535
Adjustment of the provision in 2011		

Evolution of the Provision in 2012 At the 2012 closing, the Court has not yet made its decision. Electrologic uses the same computing method as in 2011 and obtains a €4,762 financial expense (95,238 × 5%). At the end of the day, the provision is equal to 90,703 + 4,535 + 4,762 = €100,000, the amount of the provision initially planned.

Financial expenses (–IS)	4,762	
Provisions (+L)		4,762
Adjustment of the provision in 2012		

In 2013, the Court will have to pronounce its judgement. The provision will be cancelled (see Application 4.7 for booking).

During the fiscal period events may occur that challenge the analysis of a related transaction that gave rise to the recording of a provision (e.g. the new analysis may lead to a decrease of the provision). Provisions should be reviewed at each balance sheet date and adjusted to reflect the best estimate at that time. If an outflow of resources (payment) is no longer likely to occur, the provision must be "reversed", that is to say cancelled.

APPLICATION 4.7

Changes Affecting a Provision and Write-Off

On September 15, 2011, several employees of Textilex receive a letter telling them they will be fired because of the strong difficulties of the division "jackets". A severance pay of €60,000 is offered to them, but the employees contest the decision, demanding a severance pay of €150,000. They engage in a legal procedure. Textilex's lawyer estimates that the firm may have to pay €100,000 per person.

The Court decision happens at the end of 2011, and Textilex is ordered to pay €120,000 to employees as damages. Following the advice of its lawyer, Textilex lodges an appeal. No payment occurs, since a final decision has not been made. However, in 2012, Textilex is ultimately ordered to pay €160,000 per employee.

Analysis and Journal Entries in 2010   At the 2010 closing, there is a legal obligation resulting from past events (the firing of employees in September) but both its date of payment and amount are unknown. A disbursement will occur in the future if the firm is condemned, for an amount likely to be €100,000 according to Textilex's lawyer. A provision shall be constituted (it will affect the performance of the firm since it is a charge, appearing in the P&L).

Other operating expenses (–IS)		100,000	
	Provisions (+L)		100,000
Constitution of the provision in 2010			

Analysis and Journal Entries in 2011   At the 2011 closing, the firm has been sentenced in the first Court case to pay €120,000 per person. The provision shall be adjusted to reflect this new situation (the expected disbursement is bigger than before, even if Textilex waits for a second judgement). Despite this, no payment occurs in 2011.

Other operating expenses (–IS)		20,000	
	Provisions (+L)		20,000
Adjustment of the provision in 2011			

Analysis and Journal Entries in 2012   In 2012, Textilex is ultimately sentenced to pay €160,000 per employee. The obligation will be honoured by the payment of severance pay to the employees. The provision shall be written-off in the balance sheet.

Provisions (–L)		120,000	
Other operational expenses (–IS)		40,000	
	Cash and cash equivalents (–A)		160,000
Payment of the severance pay and provisions written-off			

In this case, the provision has not been properly estimated at the beginning. One of the limits of this obligation is the difficulties to easily state the future amount to be paid, even if the sincerity of managers and lawyers cannot be discussed.

4.2.3   Different types of provisions

Several reasons can justify the establishment of provisions. Some are explicitly mentioned in IAS 37 (Provisions, Contingent Liabilities and Contingent Assets) and IAS 19 (Employee Benefits), others are to be established under the general principles of constitution of provisions (see section 4.2). The list of provisions that follows is not exhaustive, but contains the most common provisions in the life of a company.

Provision for Warranties   These provisions are recognized when there is a manufacturing defect of goods sold or when such products require repairs as part of customer service, or even a pure and simple exchange (for products of low value). This is particularly the case of car manufacturers that provide a warranty of 3 years "parts and labour or 100,000 km". The conditions of establishment of the provision require the achievement of sales before the year end, accompanied by a guarantee obligation towards customers. It may be a legal or contractual obligation, or simple business practices that create an expectation from the customer.

Once the product is sold, a "potential" default is supposed to exist under the exercise, even if the failure or manufacturing defect is found during the following year. It is therefore "probable" on the closing date, that this obligation will result in an outflow of economic benefits (cash resources). The company expects no return, including monetary returns, from the repairs relating to the guarantee. It will only execute its obligation. This outflow of resources is mainly constituted by the repair costs (spare parts and labour). The amount is often determined on the basis of statistics, namely the number of defects found in previous years (company history) and evaluation of the expenditures incurred. This solution is particularly used for mass production. Finally, when the provision includes many elements, the obligation is estimated by weighting all possible outcomes by their probability (see Application 4.5).

Provision for Litigations   These provisions are intended to cover the financial risks involved in litigation in which the company is involved. An outflow of resources is likely due to compensation of damages and external costs of trial.

Provision for onerous contract

An onerous contract is a contract for which the unavoidable costs of meeting the contractual obligations exceed the economic benefits expected.

If a company has an **onerous contract** – that is to say, that the unavoidable costs of meeting the contractual obligations exceed the economic benefits expected from the contract (product to be invoiced) – the present obligation arising from this contract must be recorded and evaluated as a provision. The unavoidable cost of a contract is the net cost of exit of the contract, or the lowest amount of the two following:

- Cost of contract performance;
- Compensation or penalties arising from failure of performance.

Some contracts may be cancelled without compensating the client. They therefore involve no obligation. Other contracts show the rights and obligations for both contracting parties. When such a contract is in deficit due to certain events, there is a liability to be recognized.

APPLICATION 4.8

Provision for Onerous Contract

In February 2010 the Royal Construction Society (RCS) signed a contract for a bridge construction in Eastern Europe. They plan to complete the bridge in November 2011. The expected revenue from this operation is €25m.

On 12/31/2010, the management control department presents to the RCS management the sum of expenditures already spent (or to be spent, as far as 2011 is concerned):

- 2010 fiscal year : €9m
- 2011 fiscal year : €18m

The increase in these expenses primarily results from an increase in the labour and energy costs. The contract shows a deficit (€27m of expenses for €25m invoiced). The expected loss is €2m.

At the end of 2010, only a third of the construction is achieved (9/27). The turnover to be recognized in 2010 is $25 \times 1/3 = €8.3m$ for the 2010 exercise, the loss recognized by RCS shall be $9 - 8.3 = €0.7m$ (amounts are rounded). Since the expected loss for this contract is €2m, RCS shall record a provision for onerous contract of $2 - 0.7 = €1.3m$.

Other operating expenses (–IS)	1,300,000	
Provisions (+L)		1,300,000
Constitution of the provision in 2010		

Provision for Restructuring

> A restructuring is a planned program controlled by the management, which significantly changes the scope of a business or how this activity is managed.
>
> Closure of a division is reflected by the sale of one of the components of the company in a single transaction or by stopping the operation of a business.

Restructuring is defined as a planned program controlled by the company management, which significantly changes the scope of the activity (its business) or how this activity is managed by improving productivity, for example. It may be the sale or the **closure of a division or line of business**, site closure following a decision to relocate, etc.

The provision for restructuring should include only costs incurred by this operation, as the penalties for termination of operating leases for production equipment that will not be used or the redundancy of staff. Expenditures related to the activities of the company shall in no way be provisioned, for example:

- the cost of retraining or relocation of staff retained;
- marketing expenditures;
- change or modification of a computer system;
- changes in trade names, etc.

Indeed, these expenditures can be considered to be related to the future activity and are not liabilities for restructuring at the reporting date. They would have been recorded in the same way if they had been recognized out of the restructuring operation.

APPLICATION 4.9

Restructuring: Constructive Obligation and Constitution of a Provision

In November 2010, the Board of Filigrane, an Italian firm specializing in fabrics, encounters too many difficulties coming from China and decides to stop producing shirts. Its costs, especially as far as the workforce is concerned, far exceeds those in China.

On 12/01/2010, the President presents the administrative board with a report highlighting the main points relating to the closure of the Shirts workshop. Filigrane has informed its customers, mainly specialized retailers and supermarkets, of its decision by a letter. 30 of the 40 employees of the workshop also received a registered letter telling them that they were going to be fired. The other 10 employees will receive information that they will be employed in another division of the firm.

Since the situation is extremely critical, Filigrane will close its workshop as soon as possible, and not later than February 2011. No new orders will be taken, but past orders will be fulfilled, which should last until April.

This restructuring operation has the following impacts on the expenses:

- Severance pay for the employees leaving Filigrane: €500,000
- Training expenses for the 10 people kept in the firm: €40,000
- Expenses for restructuring the distribution network: €30,000

What shall be the amount to be provisioned?

If we take into consideration the list of criteria needed to be met to determine the amount of the provision: everything that is linked to employee trainings or restructuring of the distribution network cannot be provisioned.

The amount of provision will be limited to the amount of the severance pay for the workers that are leaving.

Other expenses (–IS)	500,000	
Provisions (+L)		500,000
Constitution of the provision		

Provisions for Dismantling

> Provision for dismantling: provision for the rehabilitation of a site at the cessation of activity of the company.

The costs of **dismantling**, removal and restoration of a site on which the main asset is located (structure) are included in the costs of acquiring the asset (see Chapter 5). The company conducts an initial evaluation of these costs by discounting the estimated amount.

These costs correspond to a specific component and have, as a counterpart, a provision in the Liability section. These expenditures have not yet been initiated and their settlement will apply only at the end of the exploitation of the site. The *Dismantling* component will be depreciated with a specific schedule (method and duration).

APPLICATION 4.10

Factory Dismantling: Provision, Actualization and Recording

When it started its new factory in the suburbs of Galway in January 2010, Electrologic took into consideration its future obligation to dismantle the workshop 10 years later as contracted with the municipality.

The cost of this future operation has been estimated as €800,000 by two reports coming from different experts.

How shall this operation be analyzed, considering that the firm uses a 7% discount rate?

Electrologic shall record a provision at the beginning of 2010 for an amount equal to the discounted future cost of the factory closing.

$$\frac{800,000}{(1+0,07)^{10}} = €406,640$$

At the recording time, on 01/04/2010 (at the factory opening), all the costs concerning the dismantling of the firm shall be integrated in the Balance Sheet as an asset. The account provision is credited and an account of non-current asset is debited.

Non-current asset (factory) (+A)		406,640	
	Provisions (+L)		406,640
Constitution of the provision in 2010			

On 12/31/2010, at the closing, the value of the provision shall be re-evaluated according to that time at 406,640 × 7% = €28,465. The new amount, 406,640 + 28,465 = €435,105, represents the discounted value of the dismantling operation.

Financial expenses (–IS)		28,465	
	Provisions (+L)		28,465
Financial charge representing the actualization			

The same process shall be implemented for 2009: 435,105 × 7% = €30,457. After years, the account will be credited by €800,000, namely the expected amount of the dismantling expense.

Employee Benefits   The field of employee benefits is important and complex. Labour costs include wages, but also paid leave, payroll taxes and fringe benefits, including retirement allowances. These benefits are paid by an entity (company) to the staff members during their period of employment, at the time of cessation of employment or after employment. Previously, many companies did not account the debts of many social obligations as liabilities. Now, the IFRS requires that obligation (IAS 19).

These benefits are provided under arrangements or formal agreements between a company and staff or their representatives. They can also result from laws or industry agreements (collective agreements, for example). Overall, the company must recognize a liability due, when a staff member has "rendered services in exchange for benefits that will be paid at a future date", and an expense in the income statement when the entity uses the "economic benefit arising from services rendered by an employee in exchange for employee benefits". One must therefore identify and recognize a provision for "past" rights by employees, insofar as these rights are for services (the work done) already made to the entity. If the company has committed on **post-employment benefit**, it often pays the contributions to a specialized mutual fund. It may also cover itself by buying assets, and its net liability is therefore equal to the difference between commitments and the investments made.

Compensated Absences The company may compensate absences for various reasons: paid leave, sick leave, short-term disability, employee's marriage, maternity (or paternity) leave, death, relocation, military service, etc. It should recognize the expected cost of these benefits in the short term for cumulative or non-cumulative compensated absences. Cumulative compensated absences are rights to absences that can be carried forward and can be used in future years if they have not been fully utilized under the current period. They are acquired rights: if they leave the company, employees are entitled to the settlement of unused benefits (holidays). The company must assess "the expected cost of cumulative compensated absences" according to the unused rights to the closing date. The recognition of these rights occurs when they are "acquired" by employees.

APPLICATION 4.11

How to Sum and Record Paid Leave

The firm Textilex grants each of its 1,000 employees 3 days of illness leave per annum. As it was agreed between the management and unions, that employees have the opportunity to keep these days for the next year if they do not use them in first place. Applying the "Last in, first out" principle, illness leaves are imputed primarily on the current year stock, then on the reported sold of the previous year (if any).

At 12/31/2010, the books show that employees have used only one of their 3 days on average. Using historical statistics, Textilex estimates for 2011 that 900 employees will not take more than the contractual 3 days of illness. The remaining 100 will take 4 days on average. Textilex estimates that they will have to pay $1 \times 100 = 100$ days of illness, accordingly to the agreements with unions (namely one extra day for each of the 100 people). The firm will therefore report liabilities equalling 100 days of illness leave. One day of illness leave is evaluated at €120.

The records are as follows at 12/31/2010:

employee expenses (–IS)		12,000	
	Employees (+L)		12,000
Paid leave			

The rights to non-cumulative compensated absences are not carried forward if the rights of the exercise are not fully utilized. They are lost and when employees leave the company, they cannot collect a settlement of unused rights. This is the case, for example, with maternity leave or absences for military service. As long as the absence does not happen, the company recognizes no expense nor liability, as the length of employee service does not increase the amount of benefit involved.

Post-Employment Benefits

> The cost of services rendered during the year is the increase of the current value of the obligation in accordance to defined services rendered during the year.

These benefits are recorded in expenses throughout the employment period and are payable after the cessation of activity, which is usually at retirement. For an extra year of work, the employee acquires additional rights that must be valued. IAS 19 refers to **costs of services**, which include pensions, annuities or other equivalent benefit as a result of formal agreements (or not). They are classified as defined contribution plans or defined benefit plans, depending on the economic terms and conditions of the transaction. The risk borne by the company is very different, depending on the nature of the obligation.

A pension scheme can be based on the distribution. There is then a general and compulsory system administered by the Social Security[2] and complementary pension funds. The contributions in 2010 allow for payment of pensions to former employees in 2010. The amount of the pension varies according to years of activity. The company (including the employee) contributes to the financing of retirement by making defined contributions.

Defined Contribution

> In a defined contribution plan, the obligation of the company is limited to the payment of contributions without worrying about the amount of benefits paid by the fund or financial difficulties faced by this organization.

In this **scheme**, the employer pays fixed contributions to a separate entity (a private or public fund). Social security schemes and pension funds operate according to these rules. There is no legal or implicit obligation to pay complementary contributions if the fund cannot meet its obligations related to payment of pensions. The commitment of the employer is limited to the payment of contributions at regular intervals (monthly or annually), whose amount is fixed at the outset but can be readjusted, for example, each year. The amount of post-employment benefits received by an employee upon retirement is determined by the amount of contributions paid by the company or by a number of points acquired and the value of the points.

For the employee, the amount of benefits is not known in advance. It will depend on the demographic evolution of the concerned population and the performance achieved by the fund that receives contributions and invests them on financial supports chosen on the basis of expected performance. The employee bears the actuarial risk when the benefits are less than expected or the invested assets are insufficient to meet expected benefits.

The recognition of these schemes is straightforward, because the obligation of the company presenting its financial statements is determined by the amounts payable for the year. Actuarial gains and losses therefore do not exist. The payable contribution must be recorded as liabilities (e.g. accrued expenses) and expenses in the income statement in the year it is due.

---

[2] *Generally through a National retirement pension fund.*

APPLICATION 4.12

Payments to Defined Contribution Plans

In addition to the general social contributions and mandatory payments to the national Retirement Plan, Textilex pays extra benefits for managers who retire. The annual allocation represents €50,000 and is to be paid before 01/15/2011 to Sodeep, a bank's subsidiary. The cost of these benefits must be recorded as expenses during the years when the manager works by Textilex (once Textilex has paid Sodeep, they are free of any obligation). The cost of this expense equals the exact amount of the period's payment.

Employee expenses (–IS)	50,000	
Cash and cash equivalents (+L)		50,000

Since the payment is due within 12 month, there is no need to discount the amount.

Defined Benefit Plan

In a defined benefit plan, the company undertakes to pay the benefits agreed to retirees.

The analysis and accounting operations that are related to defined benefits are complex. Indeed, one should evaluate the commitments undertaken under future benefits. Only the basic elements necessary for the understanding of the system are presented here.

In this scheme, the company must pay the benefits provided to active employees and retirees. It bears the actuarial risk (higher benefits than anticipated or risk associated with investments made). Its obligation may be revised upwards. The recognition of these plans is complex because of the assumptions necessary to measure the obligation or expense. In addition, benefits may be settled many years after the departure of employees from the company. These schemes are funded by contributions from the company. They are paid to funds, legally independent from the company.

Accounting for defined benefit plans requires the use of reliable actuarial techniques. The company must take into account the demographic (mortality and departure of staff) and financial (future increases in salaries and medical costs) variables that may have significant influence on benefits. In the balance sheet, the amount recorded as liabilities under defined benefit is the present value of the accrued defined benefit to the closing date. In the income statement, the company must record as expenses the total cost of services rendered during the year, and the financial cost.

Projected unit credit method: each year of employment gives entitlement to an additional unit of benefit. Each unit is assessed separately to obtain the total amount of the final obligation.

To determine the present value of its obligation, the cost for services rendered and possibly the cost of past services, the company must distribute benefits in proportion to years of service.

According to this **projected unit credit method**, one considers that each year's work gives entitlement to one additional unit of benefit. Each unit is assessed separately to obtain the total amount of the final obligation.

Accounting for Pension Liabilities In the balance sheet, the amount of defined benefits to be recorded as liabilities is the present value of the obligation at the balance sheet date:

- plus any actuarial gains (or minus losses) not recognized;
- minus past service cost not yet recognized;
- minus the fair value at the balance sheet date of assets of the plan that will be used to secure the obligation to pay benefits.

In the income statement, the amount that must be recorded as expense (or revenue) corresponds to the following elements:

- cost of services rendered during the year (increase of the obligation);
- financial cost resulting from the nearing of the date of settlement of benefits;
- expected gross profitability of all assets of the plan;
- actuarial gaps, if they are recorded;
- past service cost;
- effects of any curtailment or settlement of the plan.

APPLICATION 4.13

Projected Unit Credit Method[3]

When an employee retires, Textilex grants them a set amount equals to $x\%$ of the last years salary, x being the number of years during which the employee has been with Textilex. For a top manager hired on 01/01/2010, the starting annual salary was €100,000: this salary will increase by 5% (compound) each year. The discount rate used is 4.5% per year.

If this manager quits after 5 years, at the end of 2014, we may present a table containing the computing of the obligation (for simplicity, we assume that the actuarial rate will not have changed and that the employee will not have left the entity at an earlier or later date).

The 2010 record is as follows:

Workforce expenses (–IS)		1,019
	Pension liabilities (+L)	1,019

The 2011 record is as follows:

Workforce expenses (–IS)		1,065
Financial expenses (–IS)		46
	Pension liabilities (+L)	1,111
Financial expenses representing the discounting		

---

[3] *Adapted from §65 of IAS 19.*

Data for the 5 coming years

Year	Annual pay (1)	Payment for the precedent years (2)	Payment for the current year (3)	Sum (4)	Opening obligation (5)	Interest at the beginning (6)	Costs of services during the exercise (7)	Closing obligation (8)
2010	100,000	0	1,216	1,216	0	0	1,019	1,019
2011	105,000	1,216	1,216	2,432	1,019	46	1,065	2,130
2012	110,250	2,432	1,216	3,648	2,130	96	1,113	3,339
2013	115,753	3,648	1,216	4,864	3,339	150	1,163	4,653
2014	121,551	4,864	1,216	6,080	4,653	209	1,216	6,078

Details of the computing:

(1) In 2011, $100,000 \times 1.05 = 105,000$. In 2012, $100,000 \times 1.05^2 = 110,250$. In 2014, $100,000 \times (1.05)^4 = 121,551$. We need to take into consideration the annual contractual increase

(2) In 2010, there is no allowance for the precedent year (=0). In 2011, we sum up $0 + 1,216 = 1,216$. In 2012, $0 + 1,216 + 1,216 = 2,432$, etc.

(3) Namely 1% of the last year's salary (€121,551 in 2014)

(4) Sum $(2) + (3)$

(5) The opening obligation is the present value of benefits attributed to current and prior years. In 2014, $4,864 \times (1.1)^{-1} = €4,653$. In 2013, $3,648 \times (1.1)^{-2} = 3,339$, etc.

(6) The interests are computed using a discount rate of 4.5%. As far as 2011 is concerned, the opening obligation, namely 1,019, to which an interest rate of 4.5% is applied: $1,019 \times 4.5\% = 46$. In 2012, $2,130 \times 4.5\% = 96$, etc.

(7) Let us observe the increase of the present value of the obligation due to the activity during the exercise.

$$2010: 1,216 \times (1.045)^{-4} = €1,019$$
$$2011: 1,216 \times (1.045)^{-3} = €1,065$$
$$2012: 1,216 \times (1.045)^{-2} = €1,113$$
$$2013: 1,216 \times (1.045)^{-1} = €1,163$$

(8) The closing obligation is the present value of benefits attributed to current and prior years.

$$2010: 121,551 \text{(end of career salary)} \times 1\% \times (1.045)^{-4} = €1,019$$
$$2011: 121,551 \times 1\% \times (1.045)^{-3} = €2,130$$
$$2012: 121,551 \times 1\% \times (1.045)^{-2} = €3,339$$
$$2013: 121,551 \times 1\% \times 1.045 = €4,653$$
$$2014: 121,551 \times 5\% = €6,078.$$

We may also find the amount of the closing obligation by summing up column (7) and interests in column (6). For instance, in 2012: $(1,019 + 1,065 + 1,113) + (0 + 46 + 96) = €3,339$.

Conclusion This application denotes the fact that the cost of post-employment benefit alleged to a defined year, equals the difference between the closing obligation and the opening obligation. This change in present value comprises:

- On the one hand, the increase in the present value of the obligation due to the current service of the salary in the firm.
- On the other hand, the financial cost due to the fact that the retirement date (and so, the date at which the allowance is supposed to be paid) gets closer.

Profit-Sharing, Bonuses and Deferred Compensation

> The profit-sharing plan is an extra payment that has a collective and random character and results from a formula linked to the performance of the company.

A company should recognize the expected cost of payments under the profit-sharing plan and bonus if and only if:

- it has a present obligation,[4] legal or implied, to make these payments in accordance with past events;
- a reliable estimate of the obligation can be made.

In certain profit-sharing plans, employees are entitled to their part only if they stay several years in the company. There is therefore an implied obligation (not present), since employees provide a service that increases the amount to be paid if they remain active until the end of the year specified in the plan.

The evaluation of this implied obligation takes into account the possibility that some employees of the company will depart without receiving any incentive. This is regarded as an expense rather than a distribution of net income. Indeed, it is related to the activities of employees and not to a transaction with the owners of the company.

Finally, if full payments under profit sharing and bonus are not due in the 12 months following the end of the year in which the employees worked, these payments then become long-term benefits.

APPLICATION 4.14

Profit-Sharing: An Explicit Obligation

Textilex signed an agreement with unions concerning a profit-sharing plan: 3% of gross margin are attributed to employees who have been in the firm during the whole year. If no employee leaves the firm during the exercise, the total amount of payment will be 3%, as planned. The firm expects voluntary leaving to lower this rate to 2.8%.

The 2010 financial statements, established in February 2011, present a gross margin of €500,000. The General Assembly takes place on 05/03/2011. The payment shall be made on 07/13/2011 by electronic transfer.

How to Compute and Record the Profit-Sharing Textilex has a legal obligation (contractual agreement), but other firms may only have a constructive obligation (for instance, if the bonus is historically granted). Textilex's plan sets the amount of the benefit (3% of gross margin), which is computed in February, before approval of the financial statements, which only takes place in May. The payment occurs within 12 months. All the conditions required by the standard are met.

---

[4] *The present obligation exists if and only if the company has no realistic alternative but to pay the amount.*

Taking into consideration the turnover in labour force, the applicable rate is 2.8% of the gross margin, namely 500,000 × 2.8 = €14,000. Since this expense is certain and shall be attached to the 2010 period, an accrued liabiltiy account shall be credited on 12/31/2010:

Workforce expenses (–IS)	14,000	
Accrued liability (+L)		14,000
Constitution of the profit-sharing		

Following the transfer linked to the payment of profit-sharing, the account is debited on counterpart of the cash.

Accrued liability (–L)	14,000	
Cash and cash equivalents (–A)		14,000
Payment		

Termination Benefits   These are employee benefits payable as a result of the termination by the entity (company) of the employment contract of one or more employees before the normal age of retirement or to encourage voluntary departures. The company must have a detailed and formal plan for termination, without a real chance to withdraw. This plan should indicate the date at which it will be applied, the function and approximate number of employees involved and the termination benefits for each job classification. The implementation of the plan should begin as soon as possible and not be too long to avoid any significant change in its application. All of these arrangements are intended to ensure that companies do not recognize an excessive amount under future severance payments.

In the case of an offer made to encourage voluntary departures, the assessment of compensation for termination of the work must be done on the basis of the number of employees likely to accept the offer. An employee may also agree to leave voluntarily (resignation) in exchange for compensation. These benefits are generally lump sums, but they may also include an improved pension benefits or a salary payment until the end of the notice. They are recorded as liabilities and expenses in the income statement, if and only if the company is committed to ending the employment contract conclusively for the reasons just mentioned.

The compensation for contract termination due more than 12 months after the closing date must be discounted. The applicable rate is determined by reference to market rates at the closing date for corporate obligations of first category. IAS 19 does not state whether to report separately the changes of acquired rights from the time effect, namely the cost of services rendered from the financial cost that arises with discounting. A recording of the effects of discounting the financial expenses seems more relevant.

4.2.4   Information about Provisions in the Financial Statements

For each class of provision, the company must submit, to the users of financial statements, information on:

- its book value at the beginning and end of year;
- the increase in existing provisions;

- the new provisions made;
- the amounts used during the exercise;
- the increase during the exercise in the discounted amount, which results from the passage of time and the consequences of changes that may affect the discount rate.

It must also indicate:

- a brief description of the nature of the obligation (type of operation involved);
- the expected maturity date;
- relative uncertainties;
- if possible, the amount of any expected refund.

The company may refuse to disclose all or part of this information to the extent that, in a dispute with third parties, some elements could cause serious prejudice. It must then merely indicate the nature of the litigation and why this information was not provided. However, under IAS, such a situation should occur only in extremely rare cases.

In terms of presentation of financial information in the balance sheet, the recurring elements must be distinguished from non-recurring elements, except "when a presentation according to the criterion of liquidity provides reliable and more relevant information", according to IAS 1 (Presentation of Financial Statements, §51). For liabilities, recurring elements include trade payables and the short-term part of long-term financial debts.[5] The non-current liabilities consist essentially of the fraction of more than a year of financial debts and provisions.

This requirement needs the company to analyze the maturity of the obligation, taking into account the criterion of the reference period, generally 12 months. Thus, for a provision of guarantee to customers, the portion that covers the period of less than one year is reflected in current liabilities, and amounts provisioned for the guarantee period of more than 12 months are in non-current liabilities. This leads to a presentation in the appendices similar to that of the Vodafone Group in its 2008 accounts (see Figure 4.6). The current provisions of £356m are clearly separated from the non-current amount of £306m. For each class of provision, the movements of the period (allocation and reversals) are reported.

4.3   CONTINGENT LIABILITIES

> A contingent liability is a potential obligation whose existence will be confirmed only by future events not wholly within the control of the company.

Contingent liabilities are risks that are not provisioned, but the company wishes to inform users of financial statements of their existence by a statement in the Notes. These are potential obligations arising from past events and whose existence will be confirmed only by the

---

[5] *The standard gives a list of three criteria for current liabilities: settlement during the normal operating cycle, a liability held for the purpose of being traded, or settlement of the liability within 12 months after closing.*

26. Provisions

	Asset retirement obligations £m	Legal £m	Other provisions £m	Total £m
1 April 2006	148	99	157	404
Exchange movements	(4)	(2)	(6)	(12)
Amounts capitalised in the year	17	–	–	17
Amounts charged to the income statement	–	34	186	220
Utilised in the year – payments	(2)	(11)	(45)	(58)
Amounts released to the income statement	–	(4)	(4)	(8)
31 March 2007	159	116	288	563
Exchange movements	27	21	15	63
Arising on acquisition	11	–	2	13
Amounts capitalised in the year	27	–	–	27
Amounts charged to the income statement	–	57	167	224
Utilised in the year – payments	(6)	(5)	(72)	(83)
Amounts released to the income statement	–	(11)	(106)	(117)
Other	(10)	–	(18)	(28)
31 March 2008	208	178	276	662

Provisions have been analysed between current and non-current as follows:

	2008 £m	2007 £m
Current liabilities	356	267
Non-current liabilities	306	296
	662	563

Figure 4.6 Excerpt from Vodafone annual report 2008 – Note 26.

occurrence (or not) of one or more uncertain future events not wholly within the control of the company.

For example, it may be the deposit granted by a company to another entity as collateral for a loan, the unexpired discount bills, etc. Contingent liabilities are not systematically recorded, but a note is required, however, that is more descriptive than quantitative (see Figures 4.7 and 4.8). For the company, and a class of events, there is a margin of appreciation in recognition between the liabilities and the mere production of information in the Notes to financial statements.

18.3 - Contingent liabilities

Management is confident that balance sheet provisions for known disputes in which the Group is involved are sufficient to ensure that these disputes do not have a material impact on its financial position or profit. This is notably the case for the potential consequences of a current dispute in Belgium involving former senior executives and managers of the Group.

The Group has also signed an agreement concerning statutory employee training rights in France (DIF). In accordance with French national accounting board (CNC) opinion 2004-F, the related costs are treated as an expense for the period when the training is received and no provision is set aside in the periods when the training rights accrue. As of December 31, 2008, accrued rights corresponded to around 900,000 hours.

Figure 4.7 Excerpt from Schneider Electric annual report 2008, Note 18.3.

Contingent liabilities

The Group is the subject of legal proceedings and tax issues covering a range of matters, which are pending in various jurisdictions. Due to the uncertainty inherent in such matters, it is difficult to predict the final outcome of such matters. The cases and claims against the Group often raise difficult and complex factual and legal issues, which are subject to many uncertainties and complexities, including but not limited to the facts and circumstances of each particular case and claim, the jurisdiction and the differences in applicable law. In the normal course of business management consults with legal counsel and certain other experts on matter related to litigation and taxes. The Group accrues a liability when it is determined that an adverse outcome is probable and the amount of the loss can be reasonably estimated. In the event an adverse outcome is possible or an estimate is not determinable, the matter is disclosed.

Figure 4.8   Excerpt from FIAT Spa annual report 2008.

Figure 4.9 shows a decision tree that can classify an event, previously recorded as a provision in the liabilities, into a contingent liability to be listed in the Notes to financial statements or as an element that does not require specific information.

4.4 SUMMARY

The non-financial liabilities of the company consist of liabilities (i.e. accrued expenses, payables), provisions and contingent liabilities. For a liability, all significant elements (motive, maturity, amount due) are known.

Provisions are liabilities whose maturity and/or amount are uncertain. They are subject to strict conditions:

- A provision can be recorded only if at the end of the year, the company, in respect of a third party, has a present obligation, legal or implied, resulting from a past event. Moreover, to settle this obligation, the company will make a disbursement, whose amount can be reliably estimated.
- When the "time value" is significant, the amount of the provision should be discounted.
- For each class of provision, the company must give, to the users of financial documents, information in the Notes on many issues such as book value at the beginning and end of the year, additional provisions, or amounts used during the exercise.
- Major repairs are recorded as assets in the form of a specific component, and are not provisions.

Employee benefits are all the considerations given by the company (wages, paid leaves, pensions, etc.) for the activities performed by its employees. Pension liabilities are often substantial amounts. For the accounting treatment, it is necessary to distinguish two types of scheme:

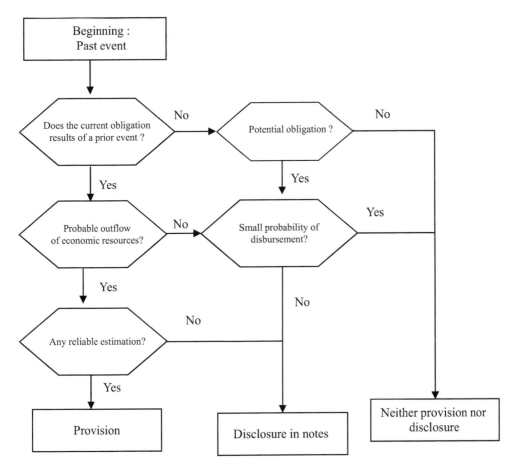

Figure 4.9 Decision process in case of contingent liabilities.

- **The defined contribution plans.** The obligation of the company is limited to the payment of contributions, regardless of the amount of benefits paid by the fund or the financial difficulties faced by this organization.
- **The defined benefit plans.** The company undertakes to pay benefits to retirees and agrees to bear the actuarial risk and investment risk.

Contingent liabilities are not systematically included in the balance sheet but are disclosed in the Notes. The attributes of an obligation are then fulfilled only in the occurrence of an event not controllable by the company.

4.5 ACTIVITIES

1. Provision for Rehabilitation Sheffield Steels owns a factory that polluted the land on which it is built. Sheffield Steels estimates that its factory will cease to work around 2020, a date at which it will be too old to sustain. An exterior consulting cabinet stated in 11/10/2010 that the future cost will be €10m. We will use an 3% discount rate.

1. *On 12/31/2010, what provision should appear in Sheffield Steels' books?*
2. *What provision should appear on 12/31/2012? How should the difference be recorded?*

2.   Provision for Guaranty Given to Customers   The computer firm Axer sells notebooks. In 2010, it granted to its customers a 12-month guaranty on 100,000 computers (for both parts and labour). Axer's after-sales service estimates that there is a 94% chance that no incident will happen, a 4% chance that Axer will need to do a €100 repair and a 2% chance of a €500 repair.

On 12/31/2010, what provision should be recorded in Axer's books?

3.   Provision for Litigation   The Italian editor Delicioso publishes culinary books everywhere in Europe. A customer had to stay 3 months in hospital after having very badly executed one of the recipes. He brought an action against Delicioso and asked for €1m in damages. At the closing, Delicioso's lawyer estimates that there is a 90% chance that the judge will reject the complaint.

What should the amount of provision that Delicioso records in its books?

4.   Provision for Litigation   The Royal Construction Society (RCS) just finished the restoration of a bridge. However, the client, Southampton City, considers that the bridge still has several grave defects, and brings an action against RCS. According to its lawyer, RCS might have to pay £300,000 in damages. Because of the delay, the court might not give its decision until 2011. The discount rate is 3%.

1. *What provision should RCS record?*
2. *Why may managers refuse to record the provision?*

5.   Provision for Deficit Contract   Nuclys is a subcontractor of an international conglomerate of the electric industry that intends to build a nuclear plant in China. In January 2007, they signed a €100m contract that shall last 5 years (until 12/31/2011).

On 12/31/2010, the controlling department by Nuclys estimates that the firm has engaged expenses of €89m since January 2007 and that they will need to spend a further €18m to finish the contract. The increase in expenses compared to 2010 is primarily due to the increase in wages and materials in China.

1. *What is the percentage of completion by 12/31/2010?*
2. *What is the accounted turnover at this date?*
3. *What loss is expected in 2011?*
4. *What provision should be booked on 12/31/2010?*

6.   How to Manipulate Provisions   There has been a change in the car renting society Hearts management in November 2010. Concerning the 2010 fiscal year, the firm presents books to its Accounts Commissioner that include provisions for litigation four times larger than in 2010 and provisions for vehicle repair three times larger.

What may be the new management's reasons for presenting such provisions?

7. Paid Leave The traditional biscuit maker, The Welsh Scone (TWS), has 200 employees to whom it grants 25 days of paid leave per year. On 12/31/2010, the average non-used credit is 3 days per employee. According to TWS data over the past 10 years, the employees only take 24 days of paid leave per year. The rights to use those days are cumulative for 2 years, and each day of paid leave is valued at €140.

What should the provision in TWS's books be on 12/31/2010?

8. Profit-Sharing for the Employees Fullsix, a marketing agency, historically divides 5% of its net margin to its employes. On 12/31/2010, the firm counts 200 employees and expects a net margin of €500,000.

How should the profit-sharing be booked for employees at Fullsix?

9. Post-Employment Benefits In 1936, the firm Gloucestershire Mechanicals (GM) signed an agreement with its employees which grants an extra pension for the employees who worked more than 20 years for GM, representing 20% of the final year salary. Every year, in December, an actuarial study is made by an independent cabinet.

What information should be included in this study? How should this the operation be entered?

4.5.1 Case Study: Biogas

Biogas, a gas producer since 1964, employs 10,000 people in its main production centre, near Aberdeen, Scotland, where it treats liquid nitrogen, natural gas and ozone. Biogas has been in conflict since 2007 with the small town of Dheathain, which is the closest town to the plant and has accused Biogas of pollution. Biogas recorded a €100m provision for litigation in 2007, in case there was an unfavourable court decision.

In 2008, the Court ordered Biogas to pay €80m to Dheathain and to completely restitute the land after it closed down its activities. Biogas plans to close its production centre in 2038 and the cost of land restitution has been estimated to be €300m. Neither Biogas nor Dheathain lodged appeals concerning this decision.

Seeing an opportunity in this decision, several inhabitants of Dheathain also decide to sue Biogas. Biogas's lawyer thinks that, since Biogas has already paid damages to the municipality, there is an 80% chance that the Court will turn down the demand from those people. However, in another case, Biogas might have to pay €1m per person in 2010. This second trial causes a scandal which leads to the resignation of the Biogas management. Biogas's shareholders quickly elect a new management, who consider quitting the industry of liquid nitrogen and ozone to concentrate on the core activity, namely natural gas. A €100m provision has been recorded. The actualized rate used by Biogas is 3%.

1. *What are the consequences of the Court decision on Biogas 2008 results?*
2. *What amount of provision for land restitution should be booked by Biogas in 2008?*
3. *What should be the amount of provision for litigation to record, following the action for Dheathain's inhabitants?*
4. *Is the provision for restructuring acceptable? What may be the reasons for the management recording a provision?*

In 2009, Biogas decides to stop its activity in liquid nitrogen. The firm fires 1,000 employees and offers them a paid severance of €50,000. The employees reject this plan and take Biogas to Court. Biogas's lawyer thinks that the firm might have to pay €80,000 per employee in 2011.

In 2009, negotiations occur between the Biogas managers and the unions, leading to several agreements:

- Biogas managers grant its 9,000 employees a profit-sharing plan representing 8% of the net margin, namely €50m in 2009.
- Biogas's employees will now have 4 days of paid leave in case of a wedding, child birth or death of a parent.
- Any employee who retires will receive a bonus representing 1% of their salary by year of seniority (for instance, an employee paid €40,000 a year who leaves after 25 years of working for Biogas will get a €10,000 bonus).

200 Biogas employees with 29 years of seniority and an average annual pay of €50,000 shall retire in 2010.

5. *What amount of provision for litigation should be recorded 2009?*
6. *What are the consequences of the profit-sharing plan on Biogas's 2009 results?*
7. *What are the consequences of the increase in paid leaves rights on Biogas's accounts in 2009?*
8. *What is the amount of the provision for paid relevance to be recorded in 2009?*

5 NON-CURRENT ASSETS

This chapter discusses the treatment of assets that will generate economic benefits for the entity for a period beyond the duration of a single operating cycle and are called "non-current assets". It is mainly this duration criteria that distinguishes them from current assets such as inventory and receivables covered in Chapter 3.

Non-current assets can be analyzed according to various criteria. The nature of assets is usually the first criterion used in both the balance sheet presentation and in accounting standards. Thus we can distinguish:

- Intangible assets, which are assets without physical substance and non-monetary (software, development expenditures, trademarks, licenses, etc.).
- Tangible assets, which are physical assets (land, buildings, machinery, furniture, computer equipment, etc.).
- Non-current financial assets, which are monetary values (shares in other companies, long-term loans, etc.).

The period during which the company can expect to obtain economic benefits from the use of the asset is the second criterion of classification of non-current assets. We distinguish:

- Assets with limited useful life (software, machines, buildings, etc.).
- Assets with unlimited useful life (land).
- Assets with undefined useful life (trademarks).

This chapter mainly follows the classification by nature and presents, first, the intangible and tangible assets and, second, the financial assets (see Figure 5.1). The criterion of useful life is addressed in each of the two sections.

5.1 TANGIBLE AND INTANGIBLE ASSETS

Tangible assets are physical assets: land, buildings, machinery, furniture...

Intangible assets are assets without physical substance and are non-monetary: software, development expenditures, trademarks, license...

The useful life of an asset is the period during which the company expects to use it.

The residual value of an asset is the net amount a firm expects to obtain at the end of its useful life after deducting the expected costs of disposal.

Depreciation is the systematic allocation of the depreciable amount of an asset over its useful life. It reflects the rate of consumption of economic benefits of the asset, and it is irreversible.

The fair value is the amount for which an asset could be exchanged between knowledgeable and willing parties and acting in normal conditions of competition.

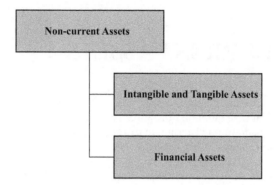

Figure 5.1   Classification of non-current assets.

Tangible assets and **intangible assets** are of various natures. The rules for recording in the accounts should reflect this diversity and present for each asset an appropriate answer to a set of questions (When to record the asset? Which value? etc.). Initially, one should identify the date on which the asset is recorded for the first time in the accounts of the company. In other words, when can we consider that an asset exists and can generate economic benefits for the company? In a second step, one should determine the value of the asset at the moment of its recording in the accounts. As such, we distinguish mainly the acquisition and the manufacturing of an asset by the company. The initial value must be monitored in subsequent years. The method of monitoring depends on the useful life of the asset:

- For assets whose useful life is defined (machine, production line, etc.), their economic value will one day be zero or equal to a **residual value** at which the company believes it can sell them to others. The challenge is to reliably estimate the timing and duration of consumption of economic benefits generated by the asset during its use, i.e. to determine the method and duration of **depreciation**. Similarly, loss of asset value should ideally be recorded in real time in the books of the company.
- For assets whose useful life is undefined or unlimited, a close monitoring must be established to check if the book value of the asset at the date of closing is still economically justified or if the recording of impairment is necessary. Impairment may also involve assets with a limited useful life.

The economic value of an asset may exceptionally increase over time. This is particularly true for certain lands and other properties whose market value has appreciated significantly since their acquisition. The question of revaluation of these properties arises. Ignoring the increase in value is certainly prudent, although the net book value of these assets does not then reflect their economic value. Balancing the two objectives of prudence and fair presentation of the economic **fair value** is difficult.

The last thing to be analyzed is the exit of the asset from the accounts of a company. An asset is written-off the balance sheet when it is sold or has is of no further use to the enterprise (for example, it is discarded or destroyed). Figure 5.2 presents all these different steps.

5.1.1   Recording Date

An asset is recorded in the accounts of the company if it is probable that economic benefits associated with the asset will flow to the company and that the latter is able to reliably estimate

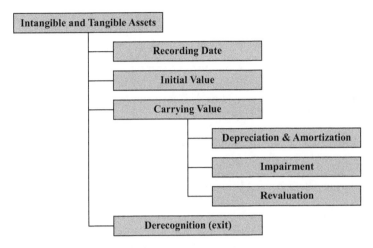

Figure 5.2 Recording criterion for intangibles and tangible assets.

the cost of that asset. This relatively abstract principle has significant practical consequences, some of which will be presented below. The simplest situation is the purchase of the asset with a cash settlement. Application 5.1 illustrates the movements that are then recorded in the accounts.

APPLICATION 5.1

Purchase of a Computer Paid Cash

On 01/03/2008, the manager of the firm W purchased a laptop from a retailer. He paid €1,200 by check.

01/03/2010		
Non current assets (+A)	1,200	
Cash and Cash equivalents (−A)		1,200

The economic approach to sales (see Chapter 2) also applies for the recording of assets in the balance sheet. The date of first recording does not depend on the transfer of legal ownership, but on the takeover of the asset (see Application 5.2). A company can thus register assets, which are at its disposal and are used, although it is not the owner and/or it has not paid for them in full.

APPLICATION 5.2

Credit Purchase of a Computer

On 01/03/2010, the manager of the firm W purchased a laptop from a retailer. The supplier grants him a 30 day delay for payment.

	01/03/2010		
	Non current assets (+A)	1,200	
	Accounts payable (+L)		1,200

In the case of assets acquired, the recording date can usually be easily identified. It is the date on which the risks and benefits of ownership of the property are transferred (see Chapter 2).

However, for assets that the company develops itself, it is more difficult. The development period can take several years. During this phase, the value of assets in progress is generally monitored on a separate line in the assets section. At this stage, the asset is appreciating in value at each closing date but is not yet used and does not generate future economic benefits.

The recording of assets in progress is particularly delicate when it comes to intangible assets. Indeed, because of the lack of physical substance, the precise time of the creation of an intangible asset is difficult to determine. Its pure and simple existence and its evaluation are even harder to understand. IFRS (IAS 38) define a list of criteria which, when they are all filled, require the recording of the intangible asset created. The company should thus cumulatively show:

1. The technical feasibility of completing the intangible asset so that it will be available for use or sale.
2. Its intention to complete the production of the intangible asset in order to sell or use it.
3. Its ability to sell or use the intangible asset.
4. The ability of the asset to generate future economic benefits either by sale on an active market, or by internal use.
5. The existence of sufficient resources to complete the project.
6. Its ability to measure reliably the costs attributable to the project.

If at least one of these six criteria is not met, it is not an asset within the meaning of IAS 38 and the corresponding expenditures are recorded in the year's expenses of the company.

In practice, this demonstration is often difficult to conduct (see Application 5.3 relative to the development expenditures in the automotive industry).

APPLICATION 5.3

Estimate of Future Economic Benefits Given by the Project of a Vehicle

The demonstration of criteria No. 4 in the above list is not easy to compute. It implies that the automobile industry has to evaluate the whole economic advantages. Those advantages happen during the whole commercial period of the car (between 6 and 8 years most of the time) and during the following years, when the sales of spare parts contributes to the economic value. The standard, however, implies that the car manufacturer is able to evaluate economic advantage that might last 12 or 15 years, and possibly more.

(a) Automobile Division

Development expenditure on vehicles and mechanical assemblies (engines and gearboxes) incurred between the project launch (corresponding to the styling decision for vehicles) and the start-up of pre-series production is recognised in intangible assets. It is amortised from the start-of-production date over the asset's useful life, representing up to seven years for vehicles and ten years for mechanical assemblies. The capitalized amount mainly comprises payroll costs of personnel directly assigned to the project, the cost of prototypes and the cost of external services related to the project. No overheads or indirect costs are included, such as rent, building depreciation and information system utilisation costs. The capitalized amount also includes the portion of qualifying development expenditure incurred by the Group under cooperation agreements that is not billed to the partner. All development expenditure billed to the Group by its partners under cooperation agreements is also capitalized. As from 2007, all development expenditure incurred to develop mechanical assemblies compliant with new emissions standards is monitored on a project-by-project basis and is also capitalized.

PSA PEUGEOT CITROËN

Figure 5.3 PSA Peugeot Citroën, registration document 2008, p. 201.

The complexity of the problem becomes even more apparent from reading the excerpt from the 2008 reference document of PSA Peugeot Citroën Group (see Figure 5.3).

The types of project whose development expenditures are recorded as assets (vehicles and mechanical components) are specified. The choice of the style sets the stage in the development of a vehicle from which all six criteria are met. The costs incurred during the previous stages are immediately recorded as expense in the income statement. The development ends with the transition from a pre-production vehicle to a vehicle on the production line. This passage also mentions the perimeter of the costs of the project with a special mention of the methodology used for projects done in cooperation with other manufacturers. The cost of development thus identified and evaluated on 12/31/2008 amounts to €8,293m for a net book value at the same time of €3,793m.

5.1.2 Initial Value

Initial value: Value of an asset or a liability at its first recording in the accounts of the company.

The initial value of an asset is its cost, whose composition does not change whether it is an acquired asset or has been developed by the company. The general principle adopted by the IFRS for determining the cost is to retain only the costs directly attributable to the asset, that is to say:

- The purchase price of assets after deduction of any discounts and rebates.
- Any other costs directly attributable to the transportation of the asset to its place of use and to putting it in working order:
    - personnel costs,
    - the costs of preparing the site;
    - shipping and initial handling costs;
    - assembly and installation costs;
    - the costs of testing that the good functions properly;
    - professional fees.
- The initial estimate of the costs of dismantling, removal of the asset and restoring the site on which it is located.
- The borrowing costs incurred during the production period of the asset (IAS 23). They are considered as an element contributing to the initial value of the asset, because we consider that their existence is directly related to the acquisition or production of the non-current asset.

All these costs are included in the initial value until the asset is in the right place and in the necessary condition to be used according to the objectives of the management of the company. Another element may affect the book value of the asset, according to the result of the analysis conducted by the company: the subsidies.

> Government grants are assistance in the form of transfers of resources to a company in exchange for the fact that the latter has complied or will comply with certain conditions relating to its operational activities.

- **Subsidies** in connection with the acquisition of a particular asset can be considered (IAS 20) as:
    - Sources of additional financing. They then appear in equity and, where appropriate, are released progressively, as depreciation of the funded asset is recorded.
    - A decrease in fair value of the funded asset if we consider that the company would not have acquired the asset without the subsidy. Subsequent evaluations will be made on this reduced cost.

Figure 5.4 shows the choice of the Renault Group in relation to this option.

K – Property, plant and equipment

Investment subsidies received are deducted from the gross value of the assets concerned.

Figure 5.4   Renault, registration document, 2008, p. 207.

Costs not directly related to the asset or to the preparation phase, as has just been defined, are excluded from its initial value. These are:

- costs of opening a new facility;
- costs of introducing a new product or service;
- operating costs of an activity in a new location or with a new class of customers;
- administrative costs or overheads;
- costs incurred between the completion of the asset and its actual implementation;
- costs of under-activity;
- costs of relocating or restructuring;
- borrowing costs related to the period after the completion of the asset.

The expenditures incurred in connection with maintenance, for example, are systematically recorded as an expense. However, if these expenses are likely to create additional economic benefits associated with the asset, then they meet the definition of an asset and are recorded as assets on the same basis as other non-current assets. They are thus expenditures that can increase the useful life of an asset or quality of the products of a production line. Occurring at a date subsequent to the date of acquisition, these costs will still be added to the value of the asset.

Where appropriate, the initial value must also take into account the spread of disbursements over time. For example, the disbursement associated with costs of demolition and restoration of the site after its useful life, will take place with a lag of several years. In order to ascertain the fair value of such expenditures at the posting date, it is necessary to estimate these future costs when acquiring assets and determining their present value – that is, to discount the future cash flows. Subsequent changes of these estimated future expenditures will remain without impact on the acquisition cost or net book value of the asset.

APPLICATION 5.4

How to Discount Deferred Payment: Allocation for Reparation

In 02/15/2010, the firm Wong puts a blast furnace (value: €5,600,000) into operation. This value does not include the expenses due as land reparation when the furnace will no longer be used. Those expenses are estimated to €400,000. the discount rate is 5%. Rather than booking a value of €6,000,000 (5,600,000 + 400,000), the part of the value that corresponds to the future land reparation shall be discount to a rate of 5%. Actually, expenses of €400,000 in 20 years equal $400,000 \times 1.05^{-20}$ today, namely €151,000. The booking value of the blast furnace is so evaluated to $5,600,000 + 151,000 = €5,751,000$.

The cost of land repair is not to be paid to a supplier when the blast furnace is put in service. It is an obligation to have the land reparation done in 20 years time, which requires a provision as liabilities (IAS 37)

	02/15/2010			
	Non-current assets (+A)	5,751,000		
	Accounts payable (+L)		5,600,000	
	provisions (+L)		151,000	

5.1.3 Carrying Value

The carrying valuation of assets should aim at the consistency between their book value in the balance sheet and their fair value, to ensure that the balance sheet reflects the financial position of the company. One should particularly avoid any overstatement of assets in the balance sheet compared to its fair value, with the risk of violating the prudence principle. This section therefore describes the various accounting issues related to asset impairment. There are two types of impairment:

- the regular impairment, called depreciation (or amortization);
- the occasional impairment, unplanned at the acquisition of the assets, generally known as losses of value.

It also discusses the gains in value of an asset over its use in the company.

Depreciation

> Depreciation of an asset is the value consumed or used by a business during a given period.
>
> The net book value of an asset at a given moment is determined as the difference between, on the one hand, its initial value and, on the other hand, the accumulated depreciation and losses of value.

Depreciation of an asset is the value consumed or used by a business during a given period. Indeed, by definition, an asset generates future economic benefits that will result in revenues for the company. In many cases, these are hardly identifiable. However, because of matching the expenses with revenues (see Chapter 2), it is necessary to identify the expenses (depreciation) to be matched with the corresponding revenues. The use of the asset – quantified by the annual depreciation expense – leads to a depreciation, which is recorded during the accounting years in the *accumulated depreciation* and allows the **net book value** to be determined. The net book value of an asset at a given moment is determined as the difference between its initial value and the related accumulated depreciation (assuming the absence of losses of value).

Given the diversity of assets that may appear in company accounts, accounting standards generally impose no precise methodology for calculating depreciation by category of asset. Upon entry of the asset in the books, companies establish what is called a **depreciation schedule**, which must take into account the following parameters:

- The duration during which the asset will provide economic benefits to the company.
- The rate at which the asset value will decrease from one year to another.
- A possible residual value that the company expects to achieve at the end of the useful life, at the disposal of the asset.

Apart from the initial value, all other elements of the depreciation schedule are subject to estimates that sometimes commit the company for very long periods. It must therefore be guided by the method used for assets of a comparable nature and/or use in order to establish a schedule that best reflects the consumption of economic benefits related to the asset, both as regards the duration and method of depreciation.

Duration of Depreciation The duration of depreciation affects the financial statements. Thus, a company may seek to submit a higher net income by spreading more than necessary on the duration of depreciation of certain assets. The annual depreciation expense is reduced by a (supposedly) longer useful life of the asset. The duration of depreciation should therefore be estimated as reliably as possible. IAS/IFRS do not mention any indicative duration for each asset class and the company must thus find the most appropriate duration by taking into account all information in its possession. In addition to the reference to common practice, the actual use of an asset has certainly an impact on the useful life. Thus, an industrial robot which is used at a rate of 3×8 hours daily will wear out more quickly than a robot of the same model used only 8 hours a day.

Component: identifiable part of an asset that can be treated separately and will be depreciated over a period different from the period of other component(s).

If an asset has several **components** that individually have a significant cost and their useful lives different from each other, each one is depreciated separately. The homogeneous depreciation on the longest useful life of these elements would violate the prudence principle, because the elements that have a short useful life would still be depreciating when they are already unusable. The implementation of this approach, may lead to a significant reduction in the depreciation period. Figure 5.5 shows that for Air France KLM, the latter cannot exceed 30 years for certain aircraft equipment.

This approach sometimes leads to isolating major maintenance costs and treating them as a standalone asset, even if they are not individual assets. This technique is used for all major maintenance and planned work (see Figure 5.6).

Aircraft are depreciated using the straight-line method over their average estimated useful life of 20 years, assuming no residual value.

During the operating cycle, in developing fleet replacement plans, the Group reviews whether the amortizable base or the useful life should be adjusted and, if necessary, determines whether a residual value should be recognized.

Any major airframes and engines (excluding parts with limited useful lives) are treated as a separate asset component with the cost capitalized and depreciated over the period between the date of acquisition and the next major overhaul.

Aircraft components that allow to insure the use of the fleet are recorded as fixed assets and are amortized on a straight-line basis on the estimated residual life time of the aircraft/engine type on the world market. The useful lives is 30 years as a maximum.

Figure 5.5 Air France KLM, reference document 2008–2009, p. 132.

(xiv) Property, Plant and Equipment and Depreciation
Property, plant and equipment comprises assets acquired or constructed by the Group. Property, plant and equipment (other than assets in the course of construction) are stated in the consolidated balance sheet at cost less accumulated depreciation. The fair value of property, plant and equipment acquired as a result of the Restructuring was deemed to be the cost amount recognised at that date. Cost includes expenditure that is directly attributable to the acquisition of the items. Accumulated depreciation includes additional charges made where necessary to reflect impairment in value.

Assets in the course of construction are stated at cost and not depreciated until commissioned.

The charge for depreciation of property, plant and equipment is based on the straight line method so as to write off the costs of assets, after taking into account provisions for diminution in value, over their estimated useful lives. The asset lives adopted are reviewed annually and for the year ended 31 March 2008 were:

AGR power stations	6 – 15 years
PWR power station	27 years
Eggborough power station	8 years
Other buildings	30 years
Other plant and equipment	18 months – 5 years

Expenditure incurred to replace a component of an item of property, plant and equipment that is accounted for separately, or to improve its operational performance is included in the asset's carrying amount or recognised as a separate asset as appropriate when it is probable that future economic benefits in excess of the originally assessed standard of performance of the existing asset will flow to the Group and the cost of the item can be measured reliably. Expenditure to improve safety or in order to meet increased regulatory standards is also capitalised. Expenditure on major inspection and overhauls of production plant is capitalised, within other plant and equipment, when it meets the asset recognition criteria and is depreciated over the period until the next Outage. For AGR power stations, this depreciation period is two to three years, for the PWR power station it is 18 months and for Eggborough it is four years.

Major spare parts are classified as property, plant and equipment and assigned to individual stations when they are expected to be utilised over more than one period. They are depreciated using the applicable station lifetime estimate.

Gains and losses on the disposal of property, plant and equipment are included in operating profit.

Figure 5.6   British Energy, annual report 2008.

The organization of systematic reviews requires the separation of the maintenance component of the remaining parts of the asset upon initial recording in the accounts of the company. The planned revision is an indicator for the fact that some elements of the asset have a useful life well below that of some of the remaining elements. The fact of not knowing exactly in advance the assets that need to be replaced does not prevent the company from taking the rapid wear of a portion of the asset into account. Application 5.5 describes the accounting of an asset with a maintenance component.

APPLICATION 5.5

Approach with the Component "Maintenance"

In the aim of producing its products, the firm Brooks uses very complex installations that have to be regularly stopped to undergo "heavy maintenance".

On 01/02/2010, Brooks puts new machinery into service, with an entry value of €1,600,000. Its utility period is estimated to be 15 years. This installation shall be stopped during one month every 3 years for the heavy maintenance. Using the reparations of other machines as examples, the cost of the first maintenance is estimated to be €100,000.

The planned realization of an important maintenance shall not be booked separately in Brooks' balance sheet. Within the installation valued at €1,600,000, there may be significant components that have a utility life shorter than other parts of the installation. This may lead to a split booking, as follows:

01/02/2010			
Technical installations (+A)	1,500,000		
Technical installations – repair (+A)	100,000		
Accounts payable (+L)		1,600,000	

The technical installations will be depreciated over 15 years, but the maintenance component, only over 3 years. Then, it will be replaced by another maintenance component booked to the actual value of the first maintenance, that will also be depreciated over 3 years, and so on. During the whole life of the installation, five maintenance components will succeed one another.

To determine the amount of depreciation expense, we must estimate the useful life of the asset to be depreciated. Three cases have to be distinguished:

- Some assets have an unlimited useful life. It is mostly land that cannot physically disappear and is therefore a potential source of unlimited economic benefits.
- Other assets have a limited useful life, which remains difficult to estimate because it is undefined or unknown. This is the case of certain rights or goodwill.[1] It is also impossible to apply one of the methods of depreciation shown below.
- The last category of assets includes all those for whom a reasonably certain estimate of the useful life is possible. We also speak of a "defined useful life". For these assets, depreciation schedules are established.

It is sometimes difficult to choose between a defined and an undefined useful life. Figure 5.7 details the criteria considered by the LVMH Group when assessing the useful life of brands. It is a fine economic analysis that takes into account the individual circumstances of each brand.

The most durable assets among depreciable assets are usually buildings with, according to their nature, useful lives of between 20 and 50 years, and sometimes even 100 years. Figure 5.8 presents the depreciation periods of the Implats Group.

In the case of Accor (see Figure 5.9), the useful life of assets of a similar nature depends on the type of use. Thus, the choice of different depreciation periods for constructions is justified whether they are economy hotels, on the one hand, or hotels in the middle or high scale on the other.

The Depreciable Amount The depreciation expense, or depreciation allowance, aims to apportion the total consumption of the asset over its useful life. This use represents an impairment that does not always match the initial value of the asset. For certain assets, it is possible to know their residual values upon commissioning. This corresponds to the value that the company will be able to recover by selling the asset, after a few years. If this value is quite significant compared to the initial value, the depreciable amount is calculated as the difference between the initial value and residual value.

---

[1] *Goodwill is an intangible asset. When a company is acquired by another, the price paid may differ from the fair value of net assets of the acquired business (fair value of equity). If this difference is positive, it is called "goodwill" (see Chapter 8).*

1.8. Brands, trade names and other intangible assets

Only acquired brands and trade names that are well known and individually identifiable are recorded as assets at their values calculated on their dates of acquisition.

Costs incurred in creating a new brand or developing an existing brand are expensed.

Brands, trade names and other intangible assets with finite useful lives are amortized over their useful lives. The classification of a brand or trade name as an asset of definite or indefinite useful life is generally based on the following criteria:

- the brand or trade name's positioning in its market expressed in terms of volume of activity, international presence and notoriety;
- its expected long term profitability;
- its degree of exposure to changes in the economic environment;
- any major event within its business segment liable to compromise its future development;
- its age.

Figure 5.7   LVMH, reference document 2008.

1. Summary of significant accounting policies (continued)
1.5 Property, plant and equipment (continued)
Other assets
These assets are depreciated using the straight line method over the useful life of the asset limited to life of mine as follows:

Asset type	Estimated useful life
– Information technology	3 years
– Vehicles	5 and 10 years
– Other assets	1 – 5 years

Amortisation rates are reassessed annually.

Figure 5.8   Implats, annual report 2008.

Property, plant and equipment are depreciated on a straight-line basis over their estimated useful lives, determined by the components method, from the date when they are put in service. The main depreciation periods applied are as follows:

	Upscale and Midscale Hotels	Economy Hotels
Buildings	50 years	35 years
Building improvements, fixtures and fittings	7 to 25 years	7 to 25 years
Capitalized construction-related costs	50 years	35 years
Equipment	5 to 15 years	5 to 15 years

Figure 5.9   Accor Group, reference document 2008.

Depreciation Methods   Several methods of depreciation are used and if the accounting standards generally impose no particular method, they however require the economic justification of the chosen method. The depreciation expense for a period must match the proportion of economic benefits consumed in the period compared to the estimated total. Figure 5.10 shows the four methods of depreciation most commonly used.

> **Straight-line method:** the amount of depreciation is equal in each period. The depreciation expense for a period is equal to the depreciable amount divided by the number of periods.

The **straight-line** method is the simplest. It is often used by default if no other is imposed, and assumes that the depreciation of an asset occurs linearly in time. This means that the amount of depreciation for the period n is equal to the period $n + 1, n + 2$, etc. To find the depreciation

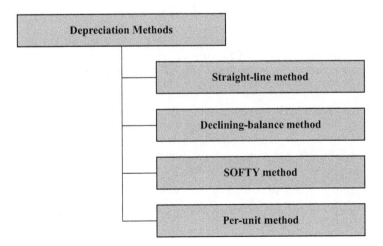

Figure 5.10   The four depreciation methods.

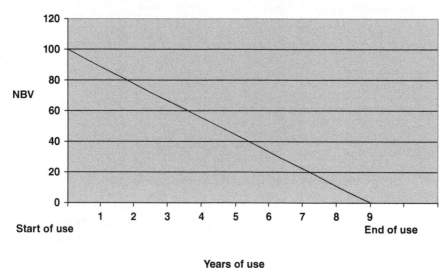

Figure 5.11   Change in the NBV with the straight-line method.

expense for a period (D_n), simply divide the depreciable amount by the number of periods.

$$D_n = (\text{Initial value} - \text{Residual value})/\text{Number of years}$$

Figure 5.11 describes how the evolution of the net book value (NBV) can be reflected. Application 5.6 illustrates the implementation of this method.

APPLICATION 5.6

Straight-Line Method

On 01/03/2011, the firm Pech buys, for €20,000, a vehicle that shall be used by commercial services. The utility period is estimated to be 5 years and Pech does not expect any residual value after that date. Straight-line depreciation seems to be the best solution.

The allocation to depreciation linked to the consumption of the economic benefits coming from the use of the car represents €20,000/5, namely €4,000. This results in the following depreciation plan:

Year	Opening value	Depreciation expense	Net book value
2011	20,000	4,000	16,000
2012	16,000	4,000	12,000
2013	12,000	4,000	8,000
2014	8,000	4,000	4,000
2015	4,000	4,000	0

The allocation for depreciation is recorded as an ordinary expense at the end of the year. On counterpart, an account Accumulated depreciation of non-current asset sums up those allocations as a contra-asset account. This method presents the advantage of not being required to impute the allocation for depreciation directly to the entry value (and to conserve this value, which is an important element of the life of the asset). The net book value is computed as the difference between the intial value and the ending balance of the account accumulated depreciation. The record in 2011 shall be as follows:

	12/31/2010			
Depreciation expense (−IS)		4,000		
Accumulated depreciation (−A)			4,000	

Declining-balance method: the depreciation expense for a period varies, allocating a greater expense on the first periods.

Certain assets are not depreciated linearly. For example, vehicles undergo a fairly rapid depreciation during the first months of use, and much slower thereafter. This has no impact on the total amount to be depreciated over the depreciation period (= useful life). However, this affects the amount of depreciation expense for a given period, by charging a higher expense on the first periods and "relieving" all subsequent periods. This method is called a **declining-balance method** or "accelerated depreciation" due to the declining depreciation expenses from one period to another. Two techniques are commonly used. According to the first one, the depreciation expense of the period is calculated by multiplying the net book value at the end of the previous period (NBV_{n-1}) by the same percentage rate each year. As the net book value drops every year, the annual depreciation also decreases, resulting in a declining effect in the annual expense.

$$D_n = NBV_{n-1} \times R_d$$

where R_d is the rate of depreciation and D_n is the depreciation expense for the year n.

Figure 5.12 shows the evolution of the net book value with this method.

The application of this method requires, after a few years, an intervention in the calculation of the depreciation expense. Otherwise, the depreciation period would exceed by far the period chosen for the asset. Based on the net book value of the previous year, a zero net book value would almost never be reached. To meet the useful life initially chosen and independent of the depreciation method, the most common solution is to switch at some point to the straight-line method. For this, one has to calculate, for each year, the linear rate resulting from the switching to the straight-line method for the residual period and compare it with the decreasing rate (see Application 5.7). Once the linear rate exceeds the decreasing rate, one should switch methods.

APPLICATION 5.7

Declining-Balance Method

The initial situation is the same as in Application 5.6. However, this time, the chief accounting officer of Pech considers that the declining balance is the best solution, with an appropriate rate of 40%. The allocation for depreciation shall reflect the consumption of economic benefits linked to the use of the vehicle, namely €8,000 (40% × €20,000) in 2011.

The method of depreciation changes after 2014 due to the comparison between the declining balance rate of 40% and the straight-line rate that would have been applicable this year. Only two years remain, with a straight-line rate of 50%: this means that, applied to the value at the beginning of 2014 (€4,320), the resulting allocation is greater than the allocation obtained with the declining-balance method.

It would have been premature to use the straight-line method from 2013. There would have remained 3 years of utility for the vehicle, which implies a rate of 33%. If applied to the value at the beginning of 2013 (€7,200), the resulting allocation would have been smaller than the one obtained with the declining-balance (with a rate of 40%).

The resulting depreciation plan is as follows:

Year	Beginning value	Depreciation expense	Net book value
2011	20,000	8,000 (40%)	12,000
2012	12,000	4,800 (40%)	7,200
2013	7,200	2,880 (40%)	4,320
2014	4,320	2,160 (50%)	2,160
2015	2,160	2,160 (50%)	0

The record in 2011 shall be as follows:

	12/31/2011		
Depreciation expense (−IS)		8,000	
Accumulated depreciation (−A)			8,000

The depreciation expense using the declining-balance method (€8,000) is twice as big as the one computed with the straight-line method (€4,000). This effect will progressively reverse itself in the coming years since the total depreciation amount is identical, no matter the method.

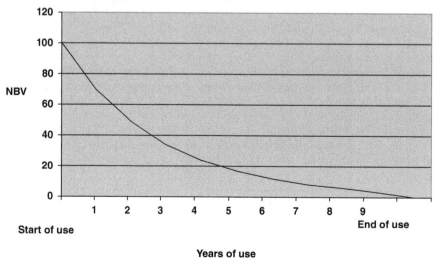

Figure 5.12   Change in the NBV with the declining-balance method.

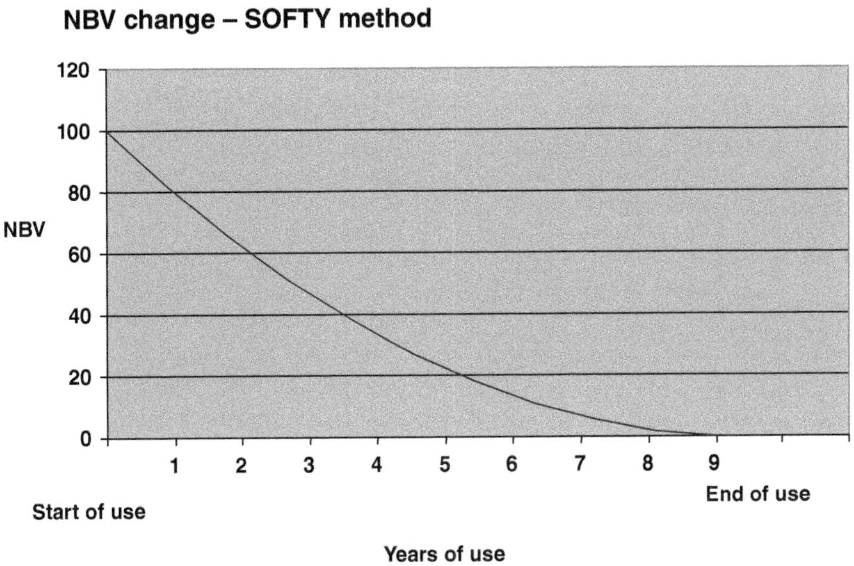

NBV change – SOFTY method

Figure 5.13 Change in the NBV and SOFTY method.

A second technique that leads to a declining evolution of depreciation is to add the numbers of years, to divide the depreciable amount by this sum and multiply the result of the division by the number of remaining years of useful life.

$$D_n = \frac{\text{(Initial value} - \text{Residual value)}}{\text{Number of years}} \times \text{Numbers of years remaining}$$

As the number of years remaining decreases every year, an effect of declining depreciation expense will occur over time. This method is sometimes called the "SOFTY method" (Sum OF The Year). Figure 5.13 illustrates the evolution of the NBV. This technique does not require a change of method towards the end of useful life, as is the case for the technique presented above.

Application 5.8 illustrates this calculation.

APPLICATION 5.8

SOFTY (Sum OF The Year) Method

The beginning situation is the same as in Application 5.6, but Pech's chief accounting officer considers that the SOFTY variation of the declining-balance is the most appropriate. The total number of digits is $15 (= 1 + 2 + 3 + 4 + 5)$. The allocation for depreciation reflecting the consumption of economic benefits linked to the use of the vehicle in 2011, $5/15 \times$ €20,000, namely €6,660 in 2011. In 2012, it will be of $4/15 \times$ €20,000 = €5,330, etc. The resulting depreciation plan is as follows:

Year	Beginning value	Depreciation expense	Net book value
2011	20,000	6,600	13,340
2012	13,340	5,330	8,010
2013	8,010	4,000	4,010
2014	4,010	2,670	1,340
2015	1,340	1,340	0

The record in 2011 shall be as follows:

12/31/2011		
Depreciation expense (−IS)	6,600	
Acumulated depreciation (−A)		6,600

For some assets, the useful life can be estimated on the basis of the volume of production. A machine A is able to manufacture total of X parts before being replaced. If the company expects a production volume that varies from one period to another, it is preferable to compute the depreciation expense on the basis of the production during the period compared to the total capacity X. This method is called the **per-unit method** and applies mainly to assets used directly in manufacturing, and have a significant value (see Application 5.9).

APPLICATION 5.9

Per unit method

The initial situation is the same as in Application 5.6, but Pech's chief accounting officer wants to take into account the effective use of the vehicle to justify the annual depreciation since the use of the vehicle may be variable from one year to another.

It estimates the use of the vehicle as follows:

2011	40,000 km
2012	50,000 km
2013	50,000 km
2014	40,000 km
2015	20,000 km

In summary, the vehicle will have been used for 200,000 km.

The allocation for depreciation reflecting the use of the economic benefits linked to the use of the vehicle represents $(40,000/200,000) \times €20,000 = €4,000$ in 2011. In 2012, it will be $(50,000/200,000) \times 20,000 = €5,000$. The resulting amortization plan is as follows:

Year	Beginning value	Depreciation expense	Net book value
2011	20,000	4,000	16,000
2012	16,000	5,000	11,000
2013	11,000	5,000	6,000
2014	6,000	4,000	2,000
2015	2,000	2,000	0

The record in 2011 shall be as follows:

12/31/2011		
Depreciation expense (−IS)	4,000	
Accumulated depreciation (−A)		4,000

Pro rata   A *pro rata* principle applies to all methods of depreciation: the depreciation of the first year must take into account the date of commissioning the assets (the per unit depreciation is, in fact, based on a pro rata). For example, it is economically unreasonable to charge a depreciation expense corresponding to the use for a whole year to an asset put into service only 3 months before the closing date. It is necessary to allocate a proportion to this first annual expense and add the residue to the end of the last useful period in order to approximate, at maximum, the useful accounting life with the useful physical estimated life. This proportion may be close to the day, or even the month or semester. In the latter case, the assets placed in service during the first semester are depreciated at the rate of total annuity depreciation, and those placed in service during the second semester at half of an annuity.

Impairment   All assets can be depreciated unexpectedly and financial statements must reflect this impairment. The risk of such depreciation is less for depreciable assets, although they may also be affected. However, it strongly affects the non-depreciable assets which, without specific interventions, would always appear with their initial value in the accounts of the firm, especially intangible assets.

A procedure called an **impairment test** allows a company to face the risk of impairment of assets (IAS 36). Its objective is to verify whether, at a given date, the future cash flows generated by an asset at least match the net book value recorded in the company's balance sheet at that date. This implies that cash flows can be directly assigned to a specific asset. If this is impossible, the company must gather as many assets as needed to directly assign the cash flows to this group. Such a group of assets is called a **Cash-generating unit** (CGU). Figure 5.14 illustrates the approach of the Accor Group which identifies both individual assets and CGUs as elements that can be tested for impairment.

Generally, the impairment test is performed only if there is evidence of a specific impairment of the asset (or CGU). Some evidence comes from within the company (for example, physical obsolescence of the asset, declining economic performance), but others are external (for example, changes in economic conditions or interest rates). In the absence of such evidence, no calculation to determine a possible impairment is to be done. The Accor Group has chosen two indicators, turnover and earnings before interest depreciation and amortization (EBITDA) (see Chapter 9) to determine whether to proceed to the second step of the impairment test, which consists in determining the recoverable value of the asset and comparing it to its book value (see Figure 5.15). Both indicators are calculated for each of the four businesses of the Group.

For some assets, the test must be compulsorily carried out each year, even in the absence of evidence of impairment. This is the case of intangible assets with undefined useful lives, intangible assets in progress and goodwill.

The impairment test is held only once a year. No date is imposed, especially not a date close to the financial year end. But whichever date is chosen, it should be the same from year to

Cash-generating unit

Impairment tests are performed individually for each asset except when an asset does not generate cash inflows that are largely independent of those from other assets or groups of assets. In this case, it is included in a cash-generating unit (CGU) and impairment tests are performed at the level of the cash-generating unit.

In the hotel business, all the property, plant and equipment incorporated to a hotel are grouped together to create a cash-generating unit.

Goodwill is tested for impairment at the level of the cash-generating unit (CGU) to which it belongs. CGUs correspond to specific businesses and countries; they include not only goodwill but also all the related property, plant and equipment and intangible assets.

Other assets, and in particular intangible assets, are tested individually.

Figure 5.14   Accor Group, reference document, 2008.

year. The test consists in comparing the net book value of the asset or the CGU with its recoverable value. The recoverable value is the estimated amount of cash that the asset or CGU may generate for the company. An asset or a CGU can generate cash for the company in two ways:

- Whether by its use in business, which generates cash through the turnover related to the sale of its products. This is called **value in use** (or **use value**).
- Whether from its sale. The cash generated is determined in this case as its sale value after deducting the necessary expenses until the sale. This is called **fair value less costs to sell**.

Criteria used for impairment tests

For impairment testing purposes, the criteria considered as indicators of a possible impairment in value are the same for all businesses:

- 15% drop in revenue, based on a comparable consolidation scope; or

- 30% drop in EBITDA, based on a comparable consolidation scope.

Figure 5.15   Accor Group, reference document, 2008.

1. Valuation by the EBITDA multiples method

Accor operates in a capital-intensive industry (involving significant investment in real estate) and the EBITDA multiples method is therefore considered to be the best method of calculating the assets' fair value less costs to sell, representing the best estimate of the price at which the assets could be sold on the market on the valuation date.

For impairment tests performed by hotel, the multiples method consists of calculating each hotel's average EBITDA for the last two years and applying a multiple based on the hotel's location and category. The multiples applied by the Group correspond to the average prices observed on the market for transactions and are as follows:

Segment	Coefficient
Upscale and Midscale Hotels	$7.5 < x < 10.5$
Economy Hotels	$6.5 < x < 8$
Economy Hotels United States	$6.5 < x < 8$

For impairment tests performed by country, recoverable amount is determined by applying to the country's average EBITDA for the last two years a multiple based on its geographic location and a country coefficient.

If the recoverable amount is less than the carrying amount, the asset's recoverable amount will be recalculated according the discounted cash flows method.

2. Valuation by the discounted cash flows method

The projection period is limited to five years. Cash flows are discounted at a rate corresponding to the year end weighted average cost of capital. The projected long-term rate of revenue growth reflects each country's economic outlook. For 2008, a long-term growth rate of 2% was used for developed countries.

Figure 5.16   Accor Group, reference document, 2008.

The company which wants to maximize its profit chooses the use that gives the maximum of these two values, and this maximum is called the recoverable value. If it is below the net book value, the asset must be depreciated by the difference.

IAS/IFRS do not specify the method of calculating the value in use. Generally, companies take as reference the present value of a multiple of a performance indicator. The Accor Group, for example, chose a methodology in two phases, the first based on a multiple of EBITDA, and the second on a test of future cash flows. Figure 5.16 illustrates the difficulty of establishing a methodology adapted to the economic reality of a company.

When a CGU is impaired, it raises the question of the allocation of this loss of value to various assets of the CGU. The only guidance provided by IAS/IFRS is to require, first, the impairment

At 31 December 2008 Trademarks and other intangible assets with indefinite useful lives, attributable for €167 million (€158 million at 31 December 2007) to the CNH – Case New Holland, consist of trademarks and similar rights from which, based on the competitive environment, the Group expects to be able to obtain a positive contribution to its cash flows for an indefinite period of time. For the purposes of impairment testing, those assets were attributed to the respective cash-generating units without the need for any recognition of impairment.

In particular the vast majority of goodwill, representing approximately 93% of the total, is allocated to cash-generating units in the Agricultural and Construction equipment, Ferrari and Comau Sectors. The cash-generating units considered for the testing of the recoverability of the goodwill are generally the product lines of the Sectors themselves.

PSA PEUGEOT CITROËN

Figure 5.17   PSA, reference document, 2008.

of goodwill when it is part of a CGU that has to be depreciated. Otherwise, the company is free to attribute the impairment loss on a *pro rata* basis to all of the assets comprising the CGU, or certain assets in priority before affecting others. The methodology chosen by the PSA Group should reflect a practice (Figure 5.17).

After recording an impairment, the company checks every year if there are indicators for a recovery of the asset value and the write-off of depreciation. In this case, there should be a reversal of depreciation in the accounting records, except for goodwill.

Application 5.10 shows the process for the accounting of impairment.

APPLICATION 5.10

Impairment Test

On 01/01/2011, the firm Ragnar puts into service a new machine, the acquisition cost of which is €200,000. This machine has a useful life of 5 years according to Ragnar. The society considers that the straight-line depreciation reflects the correct depreciation of the value of the machine during the 5 years and estimates that the machine may be sold at the end of the period for €20,000. This new machine will allow an increase in Ragnar's turnover, estimated as follows:

Year	Additional turnover
2011	€200,000
2012	€240,000
2013	€280,000
2014	€320,000
2015	€360,000

Ragnar's margin before depreciation and taxes is 15%. For instance, the machine allows an additional margin of $15\% \times 240,000 = €36,000$ in 2012. The discount rate, which also takes into consideration the risks imputable to the activity, is 10%.

Should Ragnar record a loss in value on 12/31/2011?

First Step: Depreciation and Net Book Value

- Depreciation for the year 2011: $(200,000 - 20,000)/5 = €36,000$
- Net book value: $200,000 - 36,000 = €164,000$

Second Step: Comparison between the Net Book Value and the Recoverable Value The value in use of the machine equals the present value of future cash flows. These cash flows include the margin due to additional turnover that the machine allows and the present value of its cession price (€20,000 at the end of 2015).

$$(240,000 \times 15\% \times 1.10^{-1}) + (280,000 \times 15\% \times 1.10^{-2})$$
$$+ (320,000 \times 15\% \times 1.10^{-3}) + (360,000 \times 15\% \times 1.10^{-4}) = €154,044$$

Conclusion

The net book value of €164,000 is greater than the recoverable value of €154,044. That means that Ragnar has to record a depreciation of the machine, for the difference, namely €9,956.

The corrected net book value is €154,044. If the residual value does not change at €20,000, the depreciation plan shall be modified in order to add an additional depreciation of (154,044 − 20,000)/ 4 = €33,511 for each of the 4 remaining years.

The record of 2011 includes the allocation for depreciation due for 2011 plus the impairment depreciation. Both elements are recorded as ordinary expenses for the 2011 exercise. The record is as follows:

	12/31/2011		
Depreciation expense (−IS)		36,000	
Impairment loss (−IS)		9,956	
Accumulated depreciation (−A)			45,956

Revaluation

Revaluation: new estimate of the value of an asset or liability.

All future valuations of assets in the financial statements of the company are generally determined by recording the initial value, which is equal to the cost of acquisition or production cost. Most accounting standards focus on the evaluation on the basis of cost. However, the values of assets with an unlimited useful life or a very long useful life (land, buildings) may significantly increase over the years. A valuation based on historical cost generates a growing undervaluation of this type of asset. Until an actual transaction on an asset does not occur, the capital gain remains an unrealized gain and is therefore subject to the general risks of its estimate. Some accounting standards settle the conflict between the presentation of the economic value and the prudence principle by prohibiting any **revaluation**. IAS/IFRS allow two methods of revaluation, each subject to a number of conditions: the general revaluation and fair value.

General revaluation The general method of revaluation (IAS 16) may apply to all tangible and intangible assets, and represents an alternative to maintaining historical cost. The company has to decide whether or not it wishes to conduct revaluations. All elements of the same class of assets should, where appropriate, be revalued, the revaluation of individual assets being prohibited. Other features of this method are as follows:

- The revaluation is not required every year, particularly for assets with a long useful life that are not subject to significant fluctuations in value between two balance sheet dates. It may be reasonable to revalue them, for example, every 3 to 5 years. Between these two dates of revaluation, the asset continues to be depreciated on the basis of the last recorded value.
- Initially, the revaluation has no impact on the net income of the period. Rather than recording it as a revenue for the year, this method provides for the recording of the counterpart (increase in assets) in the reserves, in a separate *Revaluation reserve* account.
- As the depreciation base increases, the depreciation expenses for years to come will be greater, with a corresponding impact on incomes for years to come.
- For assets with a limited useful life, the revaluation has no direct impact on the useful life, but it may be an indication for its extension and shall encourage the company to reflect on this question. If the useful life is maintained, annual allocations are adapted and then increased so that the net book value reaches the residual value at the end of the useful life.
- In the assets of the balance sheet, the net book value will equal the revalued amount and we must restore the consistency between the initial value, accumulated depreciation and net book value. This can be done either by increasing the gross amount and the depreciation by the same percentage as the net book value, or by choosing the revalued amount as the new initial value and resetting the accumulated depreciation.

Application 5.11 shows the procedures for applying the method of revaluation.

APPLICATION 5.11

Assets Revaluation

Even though Estelle is not public, the group decides to apply IAS/IFRS standards, starting in 2011. Estelle owns a building on a prestigious avenue of London. The building is almost entirely depreciated when the firm decides to adopt IFRS. The group decides to revaluate the building and to proceed to new revaluations in the coming 3 to 5 years. The historical book value was £15m, the net book value of the building on 12/31/2010 was £2m.

An independent realtor valorizes the building to £30m at the opening balance sheet, on 01/01/2011. The usefeul life is estimated to be 30 years. There are two possible methods of depreciation:

- The first option consists in multiplying all the values already booked by 15. The previous gross value would be $15 \times 15 = £255$m; the sum of past depreciation would be $13 \times 15 = £195$m; and the net book value estimated by the realtor results in the difference of the two : $225 - 195 = £30$m.

	01/01/2011			
Buildings (225 − 15) (+A)		210		
Accumulated depreciation (195 − 13) (−A)			182	
Revaluation reserve (+SE)			28	

- The second option needs to write off the values presently recorded in the accounts and to start a new economic life for the building. The previous value is replaced by the estimation for the realtor. The sum of past amortizations is set to zero. The new book value is £30m.

01/01/2011		
Buildings (30 − 15) (+A)	15	
Accumulated depreciation (0 − 13) (+A)	13	
Revaluation reserve (+SE)		28

Those two options come to the same result: the same net book value and the same revaluation reserve. Allocation for depreciation and potential depreciation for the coming years shall be computed according to this new valuation. The 2011 record will be identical, no matter which option is chosen.

12/31/2011		
Depreciation expense (£30m/30 years) (+A)	1	
Accumulated depreciation (−A)		1

Revaluation reserve: an equity account in which changes in value due to revaluation are recorded.

Figure 5.18 shows the case of an annual revaluation. Any increase in value is recorded in the revaluation reserve account in equity. An impairment loss is first offset against the revaluation reserve and will have an impact on the income of the period only if the revaluation reserve has been fully consumed.

1.11. Property, plant and equipment

With the exception of vineyard land, the gross value of property, plant and equipment is stated at acquisition cost. Any borrowing costs incurred prior to use of assets are expensed.

Vineyard land is recognized at the market value at the balance sheet date. This valuation is based on official published data for recent transactions in the same region, or on independent appraisals. Any difference compared to historical cost is recognized within equity in "Revaluation reserves". If market value falls below acquisition cost the resulting impairment is charged to the income statement.

Vines for champagnes, cognacs and other wines produced by the Group, are considered as biological assets as defined in IAS 41 Agriculture. As their valuation at market value differs little from that recognized at historical cost, no revaluation is undertaken for these assets.

Figure 5.18 LVMH, reference document, 2008.

Measurement of certain tangible assets at fair value as deemed cost

Publicis opted to revalue its building at 133, avenue des Champs Elysées in Paris at its fair value and to consider this value as being the deemed cost at the transition date.

The fair value of this building at the transition date amounts to 164 million euros, which represents an adjustment of 159 million euros compared to its carrying amount under previous accounting standards. The valuation was performed by an independent expert using the rent capitalization method.

PUBLICIS GROUPE

Figure 5.19   Publicis Group, Reference document, 2008.

A particular application of the method of revaluation is the time of the first application of IAS/IFRS. IFRS 1 (*First-adoption of IFRS*) in fact exceptionally allows the revaluation of individual assets instead of an application to an entire asset class. As in the case of general revaluation, the new book value is the basis for evaluations in subsequent years, particularly the depreciation expenses. The Publicis Group has chosen this method for the evaluation of its building on the Champs-Elysees in Paris, whose value increases from €5m to €164m (see Figure 5.19). The difficulty is then to estimate in the most reliable and objective way this new value in the absence of an actual transaction.

Fair value   Like the general revaluation, this method is an alternative to historical cost and it is the company that chooses the method to be adopted (IAS 40). Its scope of application is very limited, because only a part of properties of the company are concerned. They are buildings and/or land called "investment": the company wants to rent them, and not occupy or use them in its industrial, commercial or administrative activity. In that matter they are close to financial instruments and IAS/IFRS therefore allow their evaluation at fair value (see below the evaluation principles of non-current financial assets). The method of fair value only applies to all real estate investment, and not to individual assets. Unlike assets valued by the method of revaluation, these assets are no longer depreciated. At each balance sheet date, the new fair value is determined and any deviation from the book value at that date is recorded as income or expense in the period.

The group Unibail-Rodamco applies the method of fair value for its investment buildings and details are given in Figure 5.20 about the methodology used. The effect on the profit for the year was of €1.67 billion in 2007.

5.1.4   Derecognition

An asset is derecognized either during its sale or disposal, or when no economic benefit can be expected from its use. The difference between a possible net revenue and the net book value of the non-current asset is the net result of the derecognition, which is included in the income for the year. If it is a revenue, it should not be classified as income from ordinary activities.

1.5. Asset valuation methods

Investment property (IAS 40)

Investment property is defined as property held for the purpose of receiving a rental income or capital appreciation or both.

Nearly all properties in Unibail-Rodamco's portfolio (94.9% in value terms) are recorded as investment properties. Properties undergoing refurbishment, to be re-let once works are complete, are also categorised as investment property.

Under the benchmark treatment recommended by IAS 40, investment properties are shown at their market value.

The market value adopted by Unibail-Rodamco is determined on the basis of appraisals by independent external experts, who value the Group's portfolio as at June 30 and December 31 of each year. A discount is applied to the gross value in order to reflect disposal costs and transfer taxes[1]. The discount rate varies by country and by the tax situation of the property.

Figure 5.20 Unibail-Rodamco, reference document, 2008.

5.2 FINANCIAL ASSETS

> Financial assets are investments in the short or long term expected to generate future benefits to the company by the mere fact of their possession (for example, dividends received) and/or their resale (for example, capital gains).

Like assets whose direct use by the company is necessary to its regular activities, financial assets are investments that, in the short or long term, are expected to generate future benefits to the company by the mere fact of their possession (for example, dividends received) and/or resale (for example, capital gains). Short-term financial assets or investments have been discussed in Chapter 3 with the current assets. This section deals with financial assets in the long term, whatever their nature (stocks, bonds). However, acquiring a number of shares of a company for takeover, for example, is considered as "equity investment" and is discussed in Chapter 8 on consolidation.

Long-term financial assets (or financial instruments) are cash reserves that the company wants to maintain over several years in anticipation of a subsequent resale, while acquiring dividends and other interest income during their possession. Thus, when new investment opportunities emerge, the company will use these funds to make the investment. From an accounting perspective, one should however distinguish financial assets available for sale from assets held to maturity. Indeed, the evaluation and recognition of these financial assets differ according to their classification. Moreover, the transfer of financial assets from one category to another is either prohibited or highly regulated and may be subject to penalties.

5.2.1 Financial Assets Held to Maturity

> **Assets held to maturity:** assets that the company wishes to keep or must keep throughout their useful life (bonds, for example).

Financial assets held to maturity are, by definition, generally held for a long term. These are assets with fixed or determinable payments with a fixed term (for example, a fixed-rate bond). Unlike financial assets in the short term – "speculative" cash reserves – it would be inconsistent if changes in fair value of assets at maturity affected the financial statements over the years. Thus, in the case of an acquisition of a bond of a nominal value of €1,000, if the company intends to hold it up to its recovery by the issuer, there is no reason to show the potential capital gain or loss on that asset in the financial statements. The company is not affected by changes in fair value of the bond. It will receive at maturity €1,000, the nominal value of the bond. The evaluation and subsequent recognition of that bond (assets held to maturity) will be at **amortized cost** using the method of **effective interest rate**. However, the intention of the company to hold the assets (to maturity) is not sufficient: it must also have the ability. Indeed, it seems ironic that a company classifies a large number of assets in bonds held to maturity, when it is already experiencing cash flow problems.

> **Transaction cost:** additional cost of a transaction.

During the initial recognition (at acquisition), assets held to maturity are valued at fair value plus transaction costs directly attributable to the acquisition or issuance of the instrument.

> # APPLICATION 5.12
>
> ## Amortized Cost Method
>
> On 01/01/2011, the firm Omega bought 500 obligations (financial asset considered as held-to-maturity) issued at the price of €980 for a nominal of €1,000 each, with a fixed interest rate of 5%. Those are reimbursable on 12/31/2018. Transaction fees were €4,000. While buying the obligations, Omega booked the following recording:
>
> | | | |
> |---|---|---|
> | *01/01/2011* | | |
> | Financial asset (held to maturity) (+A) | 494,000 | |
> | Cash and cash equivalents (980 × 500 + 4,000) (−A) | | 494,000 |

> **Effective interest rate:** real annual interest rate recalculated taking into consideration all transaction fees and costs.

At the closing of each of the following financial statements, financial assets held to maturity are accounted at amortized cost using the effective interest rate. "The amortized cost of an asset or financial liability is the amount to which the asset or liability was assessed at initial recognition minus principal repayments and any reduction for depreciation" (IAS 39, §9).

If a bond is issued at a value less than its nominal value, it is called a **discount**. If it is repaid to a value greater than its nominal value, it is called **redemption premium**. These premiums are not included in the initial cost of a financial asset, but in the calculation of the amortized cost. They will be gradually reintegrated to the book value of the asset over the terms of the loan. The book value of the financial asset is determined by the amortized cost method, with a particular depreciation method, the method of effective interest rate.

APPLICATION 5.13

Amortized Cost Method (*continued*)

The different type of flows (cash inflows and outflows) would be used to determine the effective interest rate. "the effective interest rate is the rate such that the present value of the cash flows generated by the financial instrument is equal to zero" (IAS 39, §9).

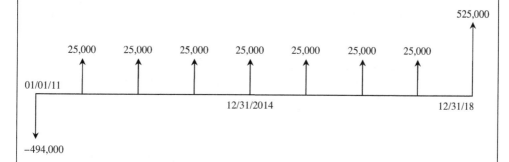

$$-494,000 + \sum_{t=1}^{7} 25,000(1 + \text{rate})^{-t} + 525,000(1 + \text{rate})^{-8} = 0$$

$$\text{Rate} = 0.05187 \approx 5.19\%$$

The function IRR (Internal Return Rate), available in most financial calculators, might help to realize the computing of the effective interest rate. In our example, it is 5.19%.

The amortized cost of this asset is computed using the effective interest rate (computing has been done with every numbers after the comma of the IRR).

Dates	Effective interests	Interests paid	Amortization	Amortized cost
01/01/2011				494,000
12/31/2011	25,624[a]	25,000[b]	624[c]	494,624[d]
12/31/2012	25,656	25,000	656	495,280
12/31/2013	25,691	25,000	691	495,971
12/31/2014	25,726	25,000	726	496,697
12/31/2015	25,764	25,000	764	497,461
12/31/2016	25,804	25,000	804	498,265
12/31/2017	25,845	25,000	845	499,110
12/31/2018	25,890	25,000	890	500,000
		6,000		

(a) 25,624 = 494,000 × IRR; (b) 25,000 = 500 obligations × 1,000; (c) 624 = 25,624 − 25,000; (d) 494,624 = 494,000 + 624.

The records are as follows:

01/01/2011		
Financial asset (held to maturity) (+A)	494,000	
Cash and cash equivalents (980 × 500 + 4,000) (−A)		494,000
12/31/2011		
Cash and cash equivalents (+A)	25,000	
Financial asset (held to maturity) (+A)	624	
Interest revenue (+IS)		25,624
12/31/2012		
Cash and cash equivalents (+A)	25,000	
Financial asset (held to maturity) (+A)	656	
Interest revenue (+IS)		25,656

Notes The sum of the "amortization", 6,000, equals the difference between the initial value of the assets and their final value (500,000 − 494,000). This difference is "amortized" over the period of the asset.

The net book value of the asset increases each year. The same record is to be recorded in 2012, 2013, 2014, 2015, 2016, 2017 and 2018 (with different amounts according to the evolution of the amortized cost). The amount that the firm will perceive on 12/31/2018 remains €500,000 (amortized cost, in the last column of the table).

Unlike financial assets held for trading (i.e. *fair value through profit or loss*), financial assets held to maturity are tested for impairment and are impaired if necessary. As for non-financial assets, objective indicators of impairment are needed. A mere drop in stock or bond prices is insufficient to establish an impairment. The depreciation expense is adjusted in subsequent years, depending on changes in the fair value of bonds. If it increases, a revenue must be recognized. The reversal in profit (directly or indirectly) does not lead to an amount of assets recorded greater than the amount at amortized cost that would have been recorded at the date of reversal of depreciation, if no impairment loss had been recognized.

APPLICATION 5.14

Different Assumption for 2016

On 12/31/2016, Omega happens to know that the firm that issued the obligation has entered financial troubles and that it may be unable to reimburse the whole borrowing at the end of the period, but only 70% (namely €350,000)

The effective rate remains 5.19% since it shall be computed at the acquisition of the obligations. At this date, Omega had no idea that the firm issuing the obligation would not be able to repay it in totality. The amortized cost of this asset is determined in the same way until 12/31/2016. At this point, the book value of the asset is €498,265. Despite this, Omega will only get €350,000.

Dates	Effective interests	Interests	Amortization	Amortized cost
01/01/2011				494,000
12/31/2011	25,624	25,000	624	494,624
12/31/2012	25,656	25,000	656	495,280
12/31/2013	25,691	25,000	691	495,971
12/31/2014	25,726	25,000	726	496,697
12/31/2015	25,764	25,000	764	497,461
12/31/2016	25,804	25,000	804	498,265

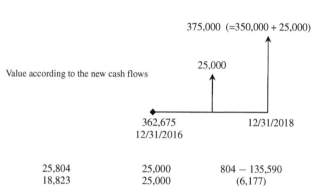

12/31/2016	25,804	25,000	804 − 135,590	362,675
12/31/2017	18,823	25,000	(6,177)	356,498
12/31/2018	18,502	25,000	(6,498)	350,000
			(144,000)	

On 12/31/2016, the amortized cost is €498,265 in spite of €362,675 (new value determined by discouting of future cash flows to the initial effective interest rate). The value in books shall be depreciated by the difference, namely 498,265 − 362,675 = €135,590. The record on 12/31/2016 is as follows:

12/31/2016		
Financial expense (−IS)	135,590	
Financial asset – Held to maturity (−A)		135,590

During the following exercise, the method of amortized cost continues to be applied. This time, the collected interest is significantly greater than the product of interest to be recorded (25,000 − 18,823), which is logical since there has been a loss in value on the obligation (depreciation). The record in 2017 will be as follows:

12/31/2017		
Cash and cash equivalents (+A)	25,000	
Financial asset – Held to maturity (−A)		6,177
Interest revenue (+IS)		18,823

Notes The sum of all the amortization, including the depreciation of 144,000, equals the difference between the initial and final value of the assets (494,000 − 350,000).

5.2.2 Available-for-Sale Financial Assets

> **Assets available for sale:** assets which the company wants and expects to be separated from during the current financial year.

The **assets available for sale** are financial assets held in order to generate capital gains in the medium or long term, in addition to dividends or interest earned during their possession. These assets are securities with fixed or variable revenue, which are not classified in any other categories of financial assets (held-for-trading assets, loans and receivables or assets held to maturity). Unlike assets held to maturity, only the intention of the company is sufficient for their classification. Insofar as the company may at any time sell these cash reserves, capital gains or losses must be reflected in the financial statements.

As for assets held to maturity, financial assets available for sale are, at initial recognition, measured at fair value plus transaction costs that are directly attributable to the acquisition or issuance of the asset. The equity instruments, such as shares not listed on an active market, are exceptions. Their fair value cannot be reliably determined; they are valued at cost and are tested for impairment. Changes in fair value of assets available for sale are recognized in Other Comprehensive income (equity).

APPLICATION 5.15

Available for Sale (Financial Assets)

The firm Momi bought stocks of the firm Bêta and classified them as available for sale on 12/15/2010 for €2,000. On 12/31/2010, the stocks have a fair value of €2,020.

12/15/2010		
Financial asset (available for sale) (+A)	2,000	
Cash and cash equivalents (−A)		2,000
12/31/2011		
Financial asset (available for sale) (+A)	20	
Fair value adjustment (+OCI)		20
The potential profit is accounted as equity		

On 12/31/2011, the fair value of the financial asset of Bêta decreases to €2,015.

12/31/2016		
Fair value adjustment (−OCI)	5	
Financial asset (available for sale) (−A)		5

Similar to the assets held to maturity, assets available for sale may be subject to impairment. "A financial asset is impaired if its book value exceeds its estimated recoverable amount" (IAS 39, §58). However, the only decline in stock prices is not enough to consider impairment. Objective indicators of impairment must exist, such as significant financial difficulty of the issuer of securities, breach of loan agreement such as an actual default of payment of interest or principal, a high probability of bankruptcy of the issuer, etc.

APPLICATION 5.16

Available for Sale (*continued*)

On 12/31/2011, the firm Bêta goes bankrupt and only €1,200 may be recoverable. The adjustment record is as follows:

12/31/2011		
Fair value adjustment (+OCI)	15	
Impairment loss (−IS)	800	
Financial assets (available for sale) (−A)		815

The fair value of financial assets available for sale may increase after impairment. A reversal is possible if an objective indicator of improvement exists. It does, however, apply only to the instruments of interest rates, and shares are therefore excluded. In this case, "the loss should be reversed and the amount of reversal included in the net income for the year" (IAS 39, §67). The reversal recognized in income cannot exceed the previously recorded impairment.

APPLICATION 5.17

Available for Sale (*continued*)

It appears that, on 12/31/2012, €1,300 of Bêta's securities will be recoverable.

12/31/2012		
Financial assets (available for sale) (+A)	100	
Recover on depreciations (+IS)		100

(We will assume that these securities were not stocks, just for this example.)

When assets available for sale are sold, the amounts recorded in Other Comprehensive Income are reversed in the net income (as for the impairment of these assets). The difference between the fair value of the asset, its acquisition cost (reduced, if necessary, of reimbursements and depreciation) and depreciation is recorded as an expense.

APPLICATION 5.18

Available for Sale (*end*)

Assuming there has been no depreciation; consider that the stocks are sold on 05/28/2012 for €2,018.

12/31/2012		
Cash and cash equivalents (+A)	2,018	
Fair value adjustment (−OCI)	15	
Financial assets (available for sale) (−A)		2,015
Financial gains (+IS)		18

5.3   APPENDIX: HEDGE ACCOUNTING

Financial instruments, especially derivatives, can be used to hedge diverse risks (interest rate risk, prices, etc.). IAS/IFRS (IAS 39) allow a specific accounting procedure in order that the financial statements properly reflect the hedging policy the company has implemented. It should be pointed out that hedge accounting is neither compulsory nor a right for companies. Thus, a company may have an effective hedging policy, without using the option of the hedge accounting procedure. Hedge accounting is not a right in the sense where firms must fulfil a number of criteria to be eligible. For example, the hedging is recognized only if all the following criteria are met (IAS 39, §88).

- There is a formal designation and documentation of the hedging relationship: the entity's risk management objective and strategy for undertaking the hedge.
- The hedge is expected to be highly effective in achieving offsetting changes in fair value or cash flows attributable to the hedge risk. The actual results of the hedge are within 80% and 125% (IAS 39, AG 105–113).
- For cash flow hedges, a forecast transaction that is the subject of the hedge must be highly probable.
- The hedge effectiveness can be reliably measured.
- The hedging policy has been assessed on an ongoing basis.

There are three types of hedge relationships according to IAS 39 (§86). The *fair value hedge* focuses on risks that may affect the income statement of the value change of a particular financial instrument already recorded in the balance sheet of the hedged company. For example, it can be willing to protect a fixed rate bond against interest rate changes.

A *Cash flow hedge* focuses on the hedge of change in cash flows steming from a financial instrument already recorded or from anticipated transactions. Theses cash flow changes may impact the net income of the entity eventually. For example, it can be a policy to:

- hedge future interest payments of a bond,
- hedge price risk changes of a planified purchase (or sale),
- hedge a future transaction against exchange risk.

The *hedge of a net investment in a foreign entity*, as defined by IAS 21, is not covered in this book (its accounting treatment is similar to the case of a cash flow hedge).

The recording of hedging will depend upon the type of hedging. Thus, for a *fair value hedge*, the gain (or the loss) stemming from the re-evaluation of the hedging instrument at its fair value is recorded in the income statement. The gain (or loss) associated with hedged risk and stemming from the value adjustment of the hedged item has to be recorded in the income statement (IAS 39, §89). Application 5.19 illustrates, in a simplified manner, the accounting treatment.

APPLICATION 5.19

Fair Value Hedge

The firm Hedge bought on 10/01/2010 fixed rate bonds for €100,000 (including transaction fees) in order to invest a portion of its cash. Those bonds belong to the "available for sales" category. Hedge's management fears an increase in interest rates, which would depreciate the value of this investment. They decide to hedge this risk with a future on interest rate, maturity October 2011, for a nominal value of €100,000. At the end of the 2010 exercise, both contracts and bonds were valuated at €98,000. The 2010 records are as follows:

10/01/2010			
Bonds (+A)		100,000	
Cash and cash equivalents (−A)			100,000
12/31/2008			
Hedging derivatives (+A)		2,000	
Fair value adjustment (+IS)			2,000
Fair value adjustment (−IS)		2,000	
Bonds (−A)			2,000

On 12/31/2010, the fair value of the future is 100,000 − 98,000 = €2,000. Since it allows the firm to sell its bonds for €100,000 while those contracts sold on 12/31/2010 would only cost €98,000, the firm shall expect to sell this derivative for €2,000. This value is the fair value of the derivatives that the firm shall present as an asset and include in its income statement. The revenue which appears in the income statement is levered by the diminution in fair value of the obligations (due to changes in interest rates). Thus, the net income of the firm is not impacted by the change, which is the purpose of the hedge accounting. If the firm has not chosen to implement a hedge policy, it would have to record a loss of value of €2,000 on its bonds and, irremediably, a similar decrease in its net income.

In the case of a ***cash flow hedge,*** the gain (or loss) associated with the hedging instrument is recorded in Other Comprehensive Income (equity), for the effective part of the hedging. The ineffective part of the hedging is recorded in the income statement (IAS 39, §95). In the case of hedging an anticipated transaction: *at the date when the anticipated transaction is recorded, all associated profits or losses recorded in equity have to be then recorded in the initial value of the instrument considered* (IAS 39, §96–98). In all other cases, values recorded in Other Comprehensive Income (equity) have to be recorded in the income statement in the same period where the hedged transaction affects net income (IAS 39, §96–98). Application 5.20 illustrates this accounting treatment in a simplified version.

APPLICATION 5.20

Cash flow hedge

On 11/01/2010, the firm Hedge thinks that it will have to purchase 100 tons of raw material 4 months ahead, on 02/01/2011. As the managers fear an increase in the cost of raw materials, they decide to buy as a hedge a 4-month future concerning the material for a cost of €1,200 per ton. On 12/31/2010, while closing the accounts, the 1-month future is valuated €1,400 per ton. On 02/01/2011, the firm buys the 100 tons it requires for a cash price of €1,350.

Since the price of the future has increased from €1,200 to €1,400 between 11/01/2010 and 12/31/2010, the value of the contract has increased from €200 × 100 tons = €20,000.

12/31/2010			
Hedging derivatives (+A)		20,000	
Fair value adustment (+OCI)			20,000

When the period is ended, on 02/01/2011, the price of raw material has decreased from €1,400 to €1,350. The first time, the firm has to record the change in fair value concerning the hedging derivative.

	02/01/2011		
Fair value adjustment (−OCI)		5,000	
Hedging derivatives (−A)			5,000

The firm has then to close the account. At the end of the contract, the firm receives €15,000.

	02/01/2011		
Cash and cash equivalents (+A)		15,000	
Hedging derivatives (−A)			15,000

At the same time, the firm buys, for €135,000, raw material that only cost €120,000 if we take into consideration all the operations above. It clearly was the objective of the hedging: setting in advance the price of the raw material.

	02/01/2011		
Raw materials (+A)		120,000	
Fair value adjustment (−OCI)		15,000	
Cash and cash equivalents (−A)			135,000

5.4 SUMMARY

Non-current assets may be **tangible**, **intangible** or **financial**.

Tangible assets are physical assets (land, buildings, machinery, furniture, computer equipment, etc.). Intangible assets are assets whose value is mainly without physical substance (software, development expenditures, trademarks, licenses, etc.). Financial assets are monetary values (shares in other companies, long term loans, etc.).

The use of non-current assets (other than financial assets) is a regular annual expense recorded under the item *Depreciation expense*. This use may be linear (straight-line) or accelerated (declining-balance). For non-current assets with unlimited or undefined useful life (for example, land, goodwill), there is no depreciation expense.

All non-current assets (including financial assets) are likely to be the object of an impairment test (once a year for intangible assets without a defined useful life). This test consists in comparing the net book value of the asset with its recoverable value to determine if the impairment of its present value in financial statements is required.

The non-current financial assets are initially measured at fair value plus transaction costs directly required for their acquisition. They are classified into two categories: assets held to maturity or assets available for sale. Financial assets held to maturity are subsequently measured using the amortized cost method. Financial assets available for sale are subsequently measured at fair value, which is recorded in return in equity, in reserve for value adjustment. It is only at the sale of the title that the reserve (positive or negative) will affect the net income.

5.5 ACTIVITIES

1. Depreciation Plan On 09/01/2011, the firm Helmsey buys machinery for its factory. The entry value is €200,000 and the utility period is estimated as 6 years. Helmsey expects a residual value of €20,000 at the end of this period. They plan to use the straight-line method to depreciate this machine.

1. *Prepare the depreciation plan using an appropriate pro rata and taking into consideration the expected residual value.*
2. *Record the depreciation expense for the 2011 exercise.*

2. Entry Value Using the data of the first activity, what is the impact of a credit period of 2 years granted by the supplier?

1. *Prepare the depreciation plan using an appropriate pro rata and taking into consideration the expected residual value.*
2. *Record the depreciation expense for the 2011 exercise.*

3. Subsidies Using the data of the first activity, what is the impact of a €30,000 subsidy given by the county for that type of acquisition?

1. *Prepare the modified depreciation plan.*
2. *Record the depreciation expense for the 2011 exercise.*

4. Component "Maintenance" Using the data of the first activity, what is the impact of a technical control to be made every other year? The security manager of the factory justifies this intervention because of security regulations that must be enforced. Each intervention costs €26,000.

1. *Prepare the modified depreciation plan.*
2. *Record the depreciation expense for the 2011 exercise.*

5. Revaluation The firm FAST Ltd is an industrial society that owns units of production in several European states, in which they produce automobile sport materials. The firm has a solid reputation as a supplier of standardized products for famous car manufacturers. On 01/01/2010, a new production unit (producing sports seats) is set in the Spanish factory. Its acquisition value is €1,680,000 and its utility period is estimated as 6 years during which the installation shall be depreciated in totality using a straight-line method. Since FAST Ltd products are easily sold (because of standardized), every machine is valuated at its fair value. Here are the estimations for the said production unit:

- 01/01/2011 : €1,500,000
- 01/01/2012 : €1,000,000
- 01/01/2013 : €900,000
- 01/01/2014 : €500,000

1. *Specify how the sport seats production unit may be recorded using fair value, regarding IAS 16, between 01/01/2010 and 01/01/2014.*

2. *Proceed to records according to the different following variations:*

    *   *A new evaluation is made every 3 years, namely on 01/01/2011 and 01/01/2014.*
    *   *A new evaluation is made once a year.*

6. Amortized Cost and Effective Interest Rate   On January 1st, a firm purchased 4,000 bonds (when issued) with the following characteristics:

*   *Face value: €50*
*   *Reimbursement at maturity date (i.e. 4 years later)*
*   *Issued price after issuance fees : 95%*
*   *6% stated interest rate, paid annually every 01/01.*

The firm wants to hold these bonds to maturity.

1. *Determine future cash flows asociated with this asset.*
2. *What is the effective interest rate?*
3. *Record all necessary information that result from the ownership of this asset.*

7. Purchase and Cession of an Available-for-Sale Asset   During January 2010, a firm sells 10,000 stocks previously considered as available-for-sale for a price of €625,000. When bought, those stocks were €59.8 per unit plus transaction fees of €3,000. On 12/31/2010, the stocks' value was €61 per unit. Record the booking of the following operations:

1. *Purchase of the stocks.*
2. *Closing adjustment.*
3. *Sale.*

8. Depreciation of an Available-for-Sale Asset   Some bonds that had been bought by the firm Agia for €2,000,000 (available-for-sales) have been evaluated at the 2010 closing, to €1,800,000. At the beginning of February 2011, Agia happens to know that the firm that issued the obligations is in a difficult financial situation and will be unable to reimburse more than €500,000.

1. *Book the appropriate records.*
2. *Presuming in April 2011 that the firm will be able to reimburse €600,000, what record should you book?*

6 FINANCING

The financial resources, or assets, required for a business to operate are not always paid immediately in cash from available funds generated by its activities. Very often they must be financed. Several options are possible. Raw materials and merchandises, for example, are often purchased on credit, so that suppliers temporarily finance the business through their credit authorization. Reliance on **debt** in the form of undivided traditional loans is a common solution. The company can call upon a bank or public savings fund for an **organized market** loan (section 6.1). Since acquiring an asset outright is not always desirable, the company may choose to finance an item and use it for its operations without formally owning it, as is the case for rented material (section 6.2). Finally, financing can be directly supplied by the owners of the entity (section 6.3).

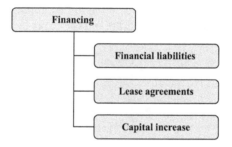

Figure 6.1   Options available for financing.

A **financial liability** is a loan or obligation (an ownership title in the form of a share or title deed, action, contribution, or debt security) contracted by the business, accounts payable, or a financial derivative product.

6.1   FINANCIAL LIABILITIES

A **financial liability** is a loan or obligation (an ownership title in the form of a share or title deed, action, contribution, or debt security) issued by the entity, accounts payable, or a derivative financial instrument. As for any liability, it represents a contractual obligation to pay another company either in cash or with another financial asset, or to exchange financial instruments with another company in potentially unfavourable conditions. Financial liabilities are entered on the balance sheet at their cost, transaction fees included.

APPLICATION 6.1

Booking of a "Classic" Loan with a Reimbursement in Fine

A firm issues 1,000 obligations on 01/01/2008. Those obligations are issued to a nominal value of €1,000 (per unit) with a fixed interest rate of 6%. They are reimbursable on 12/31/2011. Transaction fees are negligible. The firm books the following records:

01/01/2008		
Cash and cash equivalents (+A)	1,000,000	
Loan (+L)		1,000,000
12/31/2008, 12/31/2008, 12/31/2010		
Financial expenses (−IS)	60,000	
Cash and cash equivalents (−A)		60,000
12/31/2011		
Loan (−L)	1,000,000	
Financial expenses (−IS)	60,000	
Cash and cash equivalents (−A)		1,060,000

The **amortized cost** is the amount of future cash flows payable adjusted to the initial purchase cost interest rate.

Financial liabilities are subsequently valued at their **amortized cost**.[1] The amortized cost (AC) is the amount of future cash flows payable adjusted to the initial purchase interest rate. This rate (i) levels out future cash flows (CF) to the initial value, net of issue costs as follows:

$$AC_{i,\delta-\alpha} = \sum_{\delta=1}^{n} CF_{i,\delta} (1+i)^{-\delta}$$

The interest rate attained this way is charged to profit or loss. The difference between the amount actually paid out by the company and the amortized cost either increases or decreases the amount borrowed.

Entering the amortized cost on the books takes into account the fact that loans can be issued and/or reimbursed at amounts greater or lesser than their nominal or face value (which serves as the reference value to which interest rate payments are applied). When the amount *received* is respectively less than or greater than the nominal value of the loan, we refer to a positive or negative **bond premium**. When the amount *reimbursed* is respectively greater than or less than the nominal value of the loan, it is termed a **call premium**. The interest rate set by the company is adjusted according to market interest rates at the time of issue, and the existence of a bond and/or call premium, so that the effective rate for the loan is equal to the rate dictated by the market, given the level of risk for the company.

APPLICATION 6.2

Booking of a "Classic" Loan with Constant Annuities

On 01/01/2008, a firm borrows €1,000,000 at an interest rate of 5%, reimbursable in three equal annuities. Fees are negligible. The annuity of this loan is computed as follows:

$$a = 1,000,000 \times \frac{0.05}{1 - (1+0.05)^{-3}} = €367,208$$

---

[1]　*Liabilities at "fair value through profit and loss" and derivatives should be measured at fair value. They are not discussed in this book.*

Using this formula:

$$a = V_0 \times \frac{r}{1 - (1 + r)^{-n}}$$

Where:

$V_0 =$ borrowed amount
$r =$ interest rate
$n =$ number of periods

Date	(1) Outstanding capital	(2) Interests (1) × 5%	(3) Reimbursement (4) – (2)	(4) Annuities
12/31/2008	1,000,000	50,000	317,208	367,208
12/31/2009	682,792	34,139	333,068	367,208
12/31/2010	349,724	17,486	359,724*	367,208
	0		1,000,000	

Rounded data

The records are as follows:

01/01/2008		
Cash and cash equivalents (+A)	1,000,000	
Loan (+L)		1,000,000
12/31/2008		
Financial expenses (−IS)	50,000	
Loan (−L)	317,208	
Cash and cash equivalents (−A)		367,208
12/31/2009		
Financial expenses (−IS)	34,139	
Loan (−L)	333,068	
Cash and cash equivalents (−A)		367,208
12/31/2010		
Financial expenses (−IS)	17,486	
Loan (−L)	349,724	
Cash and cash equivalents (−A)		367,208

APPLICATION 6.3

Booking a Loan with a Premium

A firm issues 1,000 obligations on 01/01/2008. Those obligations are issued at a price of €950 for a nominal value of €1,000 and with a fixed interest rate of 6%. They are reimbursable on 12/31/2011. Issuing fees, for an amount of €47,000, are cut out of the obtained amount. While issuing the loan, the firm books the following record:

01/01/2008		
Cash and cash equivalents (+A)	903,000	
Loan (+L)		903,000

The total cost of this borrowing for the firm consists in three parts:

- The interest expense, representing 6% of the outstanding liability.
- Issuing fees of €47,000, to be paid when the loan is obtained.
- The €50,000 premium, which is the difference between the amount obtained on 01/01/2008 and the amount to pay back on 12/31/2011.

The effective interest rate takes into consideration all those elements. This allows an equilibrium to be found between inflows and outflows.

$$903,000 = \sum_{t=1}^{4} \frac{60,000}{(1 + \text{rate})^t} + \frac{1,000,000}{(1 + \text{rate})^4}$$

For this case, the effective interest rate is of 9% (8.9937% precisely)

The cost of this borrowing is estimated using the effective interest rate or Internal Interest Rate (IRR). The difference between the effective interest rates and the nominal interests paid is added one period after another to the borrowed amount. This regularly increases the liability until it is equal to the reimbursable amount at term.

Date	Effective interests	Interests	"Amortization"	Amortized cost
01/10/2008				903,000
12/31/2008	81,213[a]	60,000[b]	21,213[c]	924,213[d]
12/31/2009	83,121	60,000	23,121	947,334
12/31/2010	85,200	60,000	25,600	972,534
12/31/2011	87,466	60,000	27,466	1,000,000
			97,000	

[a] $81,213 = 903,000 \times IRR$
[b] $60,000 = 1,000 \text{ obligations} \times €1,000 \times 6\%$
[c] $21,213 = 81,213 - 60,000$
[d] $924,213 = 903,000 + 21,213$

Book entries for the subsequent years are as follows:

12/31/2008			
Financial expenses (−IS)		81,213	
Loan (+L)			21,213
Cash and cash equivalents (−A)			60,000
12/31/2009			
Financial expenses (−IS)		83,121	
Loan (+L)			23,121
Cash and cash equivalents (−A)			60,000
12/31/2010			
Financial expenses (−IS)		85,200	
Loan (+L)			25,200
Cash and cash equivalents (−A)			60,000
12/31/2011			
Financial expenses (−IS)		87,466	
Loan (+L)			27,466
Cash and cash equivalents (−A)			60,000
Loan (−L)		1,000,000	
Cash and cash equivalents (−A)			1,000,000

35. Finance debt

	Within 1 year [a]	After 1 year	2008 Total	Within 1 year [a]	After 1 year	$ million 2007 Total
Borrowings	15,647	16,937	32,584	15,149	15,004	30,153
Net obligations under finance leases	93	527	620	245	647	892
	15,740	17,464	33,204	15,394	15,651	31,045

[a] Amounts due within one year include current maturities of long-term debt and borrowings that are expected to be repaid later than the earliest contractual repayment dates of within one year. US Industrial Revenue/Municipal Bonds of $3,166 million (2007 $2,880 million) with earliest contractual repayment dates within one year have expected repayment dates ranging from 1 to 40 years (2007 1 to 35 years). The bondholders typically have the option to tender these bonds for repayment on interest reset dates; however, any bonds that are tendered are usually remarketed and BP has not experienced any significant repurchases. BP considers these bonds to represent long-term funding when internally assessing the maturity profile of its finance debt. Similar treatment is applied for loans associated with long-term gas supply contracts totalling $1,806 million (2007 $1,899 million) that mature within nine years.

bp

Figure 6.2 Excerpt from the 2008 annual report, BP.

Financial liabilities can represent significant amounts (see Figure 6.2). BP relies on leasing to finance its activities. Leasing contracts are one long-term financing option.

6.2 LEASE AGREEMENTS

This section deals with accounting practices for leasing agreements. Leasing equipment usually does not pose any particular problems. According to the principles outlined in Chapter 2, the rent is recognized on the lessee's income statement as an expense charged to profit or loss for the lease period.

Chapter 5 defined the scope of assets to recognize on the company's balance sheet and explains the concept of economic ownership. According to this concept, all assets for which the company assumes all or nearly all of the risks and benefits associated with ownership appear on the balance sheet, regardless of whether it is the legal owner or not. Thus, some leasing agreements more closely resemble sales contracts and are referred to as **finance lease agreements,** as opposed to genuine lease agreements often called **operating leases**.

The distinction between these two types of agreement is very important. In the case of a finance lease agreement, the leased item is considered as an acquisition by the lessee. However, it is not yet paid for when it is first entered on the balance sheet since payment will be made in instalments over the lease period. Consequently, a financial debt is recorded on the lessee's

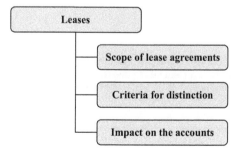

Figure 6.3 Lease agreements.

balance sheet. The lessor, on the other hand, must consider the item as sold, remove it from his balance sheet, and recognize a sale on his income statement, all the while maintaining legal ownership of the item in question. Since the sale has not yet been paid by the lessee, it is recorded as a receivable on the lessor's balance sheet.

After we present the scope of lease agreements, we will look at the criteria used to differentiate operating leases from finance-lease agreements. Finally, we will examine the effects on the balance sheet and income statement of restating an operating lease as a finance-lease agreement (IAS 17).

6.2.1   The Scope of Lease Agreements

> A **lease agreement** transfers the right of use for an asset from the lessor to the lessee for a given amount of time in exchange for payment.

A **lease agreement** involves the following elements (IAS 17):

- The lessor transfers the right of use for an asset to the lessee.
- This right is granted for a set period of time.
- In exchange, the lessee pays the lessor an agreed amount.

During the lease period, the lessee assumes the same financial rights and obligations for the rented item as an owner, except that these rights are limited in time. The agreement does not need to be in the form of a standardized legal contract. Chapter 2 mentions an example of a sales agreement with a buyback clause that, financially speaking, more closely resembles a lease agreement than a sale. Service contracts are another example of this since they often include lease agreements as an important component.

APPLICATION 6.4

Service Contract

The firm Albi On concluded a service arrangement with the firm Rodier for a term period of 5 years. Albi On pays an inclusive annual fee split into four quarterly payments. According to the contract, Rodier sets 17 photocopiers by Albi On and provides them with maintenance and, if necessary, exchange. The annual fee also includes the repair of the photocopiers within 2 days after Albi On signals an incident to Rodier's technical centre.

To what extent is this contract a lease?

Answer   The contract includes several elements. It grants Albi On the right to use the photocopiers for a 5-year period. Albi On pays an annual fee that includes compensation for this right of use. The part of the contract relative to the use of the photocopier can be assimilated to a lease.

The value of the photocopiers and the part of the fee regarding their location are to be determined and analyzed according to the criteria specified in this chapter. The payments corresponding to the other elements included in the contract are to be considered as services and shall be booked as expenses of the income statement in the adequate period.

Lease agreements can apply to all kinds of assets (real estate and property, machines, vehicles and other means of transportation, furniture, office and computer supplies, telecommunications, etc.).

When an agreement pertains to different kinds of goods, it can sometimes be divided into sections that deal with each type of asset separately. This is the case in particular for real estate leases that include both use of land and buildings. A land lease agreement can be considered as an operating lease, while the building lease component may meet the criteria for a finance lease agreement.

APPLICATION 6.5

Property Location

The firm Davis signed with the real estate firm Rubini a lease contract of a commercial site in a commercial area near Birmingham. In addition to the store, the contract includes 3,000 square metres of land with parking space for 80 vehicles.

How should this contract be analyzed?

Answer   The contract includes two different elements that are to be analyzed separately: the land and the construction. We have to confer on them a respective value and a part of the rent (which would be useless if the value of the land was negligible regarding the value of the building). If we take into consideration the fact that the land is located in a commercial area close to a major city, then its value is probably significant and there will be no choice other than to divide the contract in two parts.

The **inception of the lease is** the date the lease agreement is signed, or when it is to take effect, and the marks the two parties' reciprocal commitment to the terms of the agreement.

However, when several agreements deal with the lease of the same item or property, they must be examined together so that the company's financial "lease situation" can be analyzed as a whole, not just one component. It can happen (especially for major elements such as real estate, large-scale technical equipment, fleets of vehicles, computers, etc.) that the transaction can involve several different legally-binding contracts, including, for example:

- The lease agreement itself;
- A maintenance contract for one or more of the rented items;
- A financing agreement that may involve an external bank or financial institution.

An analysis of all of the relationships established by the lease agreements determines how they will be entered in the lessor's and lessee's annual financial statements.

The starting point for this analysis is the **inception of the lease**, usually when the lease agreement is signed. Its terms apply for the entire **lease term**. Thus an operating lease cannot be later restated as a finance lease agreement, and vice-versa. The agreement must clearly specify its effective date, which is the start of the lease term. There can be a long delay between the date the agreement is signed and its effective date.

> The **lease term** designates the time period that the lessee is contractually obliged to rent the asset, and the subsequent time period(s) for which the lease agreement can be extended under bargain terms.

APPLICATION 6.6

Lease of a Property: The Bid-O Case

This example will be used in further applications of this chapter in order to present the comprehensiveness of the reflexion while analyzing a location contract.

The firm Bid-O negotiated with the firm Bailexpert a lease contract covering a property (land and building) for a commercial use and with the following characteristics:

- Construction of a building following Bid-O's recommendations within 15 months after the signature of the contract
- Signature of the contract: 10/06/2007
- Beginning of the contract (occupation of the place by Bid-O): 01/01/2009
- No property transfer or bargain purchase option
- Expected value of the property at the beginning of the contract: €10,000,000 (land: €4,000,000 and building €6,000,000)

Question 1: What contract shall you analyze?

Answer   There is only one contract which concerns two elements that are economically different:

- The land
- The construction.

The land (evaluated at €4,000,000) represents 40% of the whole value of the property and therefore cannot be considered negligible. The value of the land cannot be considered as an addition to the building's value.

Both land and building are significant components of the contract and will be analyzed separately as if they were two different contracts.

Question 2: At what date shall the analysis be made?

Answer   In the case of an operating lease or a finance lease, the date to which the decision is taken is the inception of the lease contract (at the latest, the date of signature). In this case, the date of signature is 10/06/2007. The analysis should be based on the situation at that date.

Bid-O occupies the place starting on 01/01/2009, once the construction is achieved. After this date, the leased property enters in the lessee's balance sheet in the case of a finance leasing.

6.2.2   How to Differentiate a Operating Lease from a Finance Lease Agreement

The purpose of analyzing leasing agreements is to determine if the primary benefits and risks inherent to owning the asset have been transferred to the lessee. It is impossible to give an exhaustive list of criteria for this but IAS 17 cites a few that help to set guidelines for determining if a lease does indeed qualify as a finance lease:

(a) **Automatic transfer of ownership.** At the end of the lease term, the asset is automatically transferred to the lessee. The lessee is then the sole party that can benefit from the use of the good. In exchange, the lessor usually charges the lessee for at least the good's full value. The lessee is considered as the economic owner from the start of the lease term.

(b) **Bargain purchase option.** At the end of the lease term, the lessee is offered preferential terms for purchasing the leased asset at such a low price that in most cases, the lessee will choose this option at the end of the lease term. The underlying logic is comparable to the concept of automatic transfer of ownership. However, the existence of a purchase option alone does not qualify the agreement as a finance lease; for that, the probability that the lessee will take this option at the end of the lease term must be "almost certain".

(c) **Uncancellable lease term.** The length of the agreement cannot be changed and covers the **major part** of the asset's useful life. This criterion is based on the idea that in a situation like this, no other lessee, nor the lessor, can benefit from significant financial benefits related to the leased asset at the end of the term. The useful life usually corresponds to the length of time applied for the depreciation of similar assets when they are acquired. There is no official value for what constitutes the "major part" of the asset's useful life, but the US standard guideline of 75% of the estimated useful life can be used as a reference. However, if the rate is set at 74.5%, for example, it does not mean that the criterion is not met and that the agreement is considered an operating lease (this would be the case according to the US GAAP, which recommends a more mathematical approach to this issue).

(d) **Minimum lease payments.** This criterion considers the financial risks associated with ownership of the asset, in other words the payment due, to determine its economic owner. If the present value of the minimum payments represents at least **substantially** the fair value of the leased asset, it is considered as an acquisition for the lessee. Like the concept of the "major part" of the useful life for the lease term, there is no "official" guideline for calculating the value of "substantially". Often, the US standard of 90% is used as a reference, but this is only to be used as a guideline, as for the estimated useful life percentage mentioned above. A rate of 89.9% does not guarantee that an agreement will be considered an operating lease.

The discount rate used has a significant impact on how the agreement is categorized since the payments to take into account are often spread over a very long period of time. Several situations can occur:

- If a rate is specified in the lease agreement, it is this **contractual rate** that is used to calculate the present value.
- If this is not the case, sometimes it is possible to determine an **implicit rate**, but only when there is automatic transfer of ownership or a bargain purchase option. In these situations, the present value for all of the payments to be made by the lessee equals its acquisition cost. It is therefore possible to determine the implicit discount rate by comparing it with the asset's fair value at the start of the lease term.

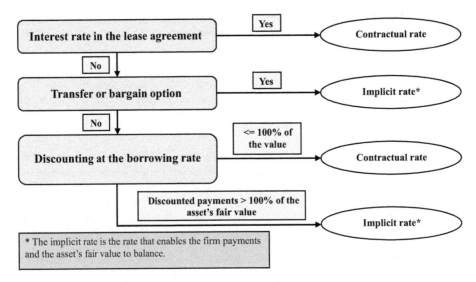

Figure 6.4 How to determine the discount rate.

- If there is no contractual rate, automatic transfer of ownership, or bargain purchase option, the lessee applies the rate it would probably have been paid if it had financed the acquisition of the leased asset through a bank or external financial institution. If the lessee has access to advantageous financing options with low interest rates, the present value calculated this way may be greater than the fair value at the start of the lease term. In this case, the implicit rate calculated on the basis of the payments and the item's fair value is used as the discount rate.

Figure 6.4 summarizes the criteria used to determine the discount rate.

(e) **The specificity of the leased asset.** If the leased asset is so specialized that only the lessee can use it without significant modifications, he is considered the sole user of the item during its entire useful life. The lessor will inevitably make the lessee assume all of the risks and rewards and the lessee is considered the economic owner.

The lease agreement needs to meet only one of these criteria for it to be considered as a finance lease, though other criteria also exist. However, it is the economic substance of the transaction that ultimately determines its classification: financially speaking, is it an acquisition financed by the lessor, or not? If the answer is yes, the agreement is indeed a finance lease, and if not, it is just an operating lease.

The list of criteria is more limited for land leases. The fact that land has an unlimited useful life makes it impossible to transfer the major part of the benefits or substantially all risks associated with ownership without outright transfer of the ownership title itself. In other words, if there is neither automatic transfer of ownership, nor a bargain purchase option, a land lease is always considered as an operating lease.

In the list above, with the exception of automatic transfer of ownership, all of the other criteria include elements that are subject to interpretation (bargain, major part of useful life, substantially all, and specificity). This approach of the standardsetter (IASB) is a voluntary option to avoid the temptation to circumvent set guidelines.

APPLICATION 6.7

How to Distinguish an Operating Lease from a Finance Lease

The firm Freddy is about to sign a lease contract for a new factory. The CFO wants to prevent the location being qualified as a finance lease in order to protect the firm's debt ratios. He manages to negotiate a 20-year lease term (50% of the useful life of comparable assets). Negotiations with the lessor are pretty difficult because the present value of future payments only represents 89.9% of the factory's value.

Is this an operating lease or a finance lease?

Answer As far as US GAAP are concerned, the answer would be easy: since the present value of the cash flows does not exceed 90% of the factory value, it is an operating lease. IFRS provide another answer: the difference of 0.1% between the actual present value and the unofficial step of 90% does not change the economic substance of the contract, which would have to be treated as a finance lease. However, if it is impossible to conclude using the five criteria above, the comprehensive reading of the contract may provide additional elements.

Many lease agreements include renewal options. In certain cases, penalties apply when the lessee does not choose to renew. When applicable, both elements should be examined.

APPLICATION 6.8

How to Distinguish an Operating Lease from a Finance Lease (*continued*)

Since there are high chances that the contract would be qualified as a finance lease, Freddy's CFO has put new propositions to the lessor.

- A 20-year lease period (present value of future payments: 65% of the plant's value
- An option for a 10-year second lease period (present value of future payments: 30% of the factory's value)
- If Freddy's does not exercise its option, it will pay the lessor a penalty, the present value of which equals 25% of the plant's value.

Is this an operating lease or a finance lease?

Answer The first lease period is an operating lease, but there clearly will occur additional payments, no matter what Freddy's management decide. *Either* Freddy exercises the option, the lease period equals $20 + 10 = 30$ years (75% of the useful life of the plant) and with lease payments representing 95% of the value, in which case it is a finance lease; *or* they do not, in this case the payments represent 90% of the value of the plant: it is also a finance lease.

No matter what Freddy does, the criteria qualify this lease as a finance lease.

APPLICATION 6.9

The contract between Bid-O and Bailexpert includes the following elements:

- − Annual rent: €1,200,000; charges: €100,000.
- − Uncancellable length of the contract: 10 years.
- − Length of depreciation of the building if purchased by Bid-O: 20 years
- − Average debt interest rate of Bid-O during 2006 last quarter: 4.6%

Question 3: How should the land component be analyzed?

Answer   The contract does not come with a property transfer, nor with an option of bargain purchase, although Bid-O does not obtain substantially all of the benefits provided by the land. The lease of the land is an operating lease.

Question 4: How should the building component be analyzed?

Answer   Criteria (a) and (b): The contract does not imply the automatic transfer of property nor offer a bargain purchase option.

Criteria (c): The initial outright period is 10 years, there is no bargain renewal option. 10 years equals 50% of the depreciation period of 20 years, which is less than the unofficial 75% step.

Criteria (d): the lease is computed proportionally to the fair value of the building within the property (6,000/10,000 = 60%; 60% × 1,200 = €720,000). As there is no implicit interest rate mentioned in the contract, present value of future payments is calculated using the 4.6% rate (using the Excel formula VP).

- • Rate: 4.6%
- • Number of payments: 10
- • Annual disbursement: €720,000.

We obtain a present value of lease payments of €5,669,000, which represents 94.5% of the initial fair value of the building (€6,000,000). It is more than the unofficial step of 90%. Since this step has been crossed, the lease of the building is a finance lease. The decision is taken on 10/06/2007, but the building is recognized in Bid-O's assets starting on 01/01/2009 (when starting to exercise its right to use).

6.2.3   The Effects of Finance Lease Agreements on Accounting

The Lessee's Accounts   Qualifying an agreement as a finance lease results in certain movements on both the balance sheet and the income statement.

Recognizing and Measuring the Asset on the Balance Sheet   The leased asset is considered as an acquisition by the lessee and appears as an asset on its balance sheet. It is treated like any other asset of similar nature, especially in terms of the methods used for estimating the asset's useful life and depreciation. The value of the asset in the balance sheet at inception depends on the lessee's intentions.

- • If the lessee becomes the owner of the asset at the end of the lease term, it is depreciated over the period corresponding to the asset's useful life that is usually applied for similar acquired assets.

D.4. Leases and sale and leaseback transactions

Leases are analysed based on IAS 17 "Leases".

Leases that transfer substantially all the risks and rewards incidental to ownership of an asset to the lessee are qualified as finance leases and accounted for as follows:

- the leased item is recognized as an asset at an amount equal to its fair value or, if lower, the present value of the minimum lease payments, each determined at the inception of the lease;

- a liability is recognized for the same amount, under "Finance lease liabilities";

- minimum lease payments are allocated between interest expense and reduction of the lease liability;

- the finance charge is allocated to each period during the lease term so as to produce a constant periodic rate of interest on the remaining balance of the liability.

Figure 6.5 Excerpt of reference document 2007, Accor.

- However if ownership is not transferred, the depreciation covers the shortest length of time within the non-cancellable lease term, including bargain renewal periods if there are any and the estimation of the useful life for other similar assets. The gross value used for calculating the depreciation is the present value of the payments for the course of the lease term.

Recognizing and Measuring the Liability on the Balance Sheet At inception of the lease, the liability corresponds to the value of the leased asset. It is reimbursed over time through the lessee's payments. The amount reimbursed equals the difference between the payments and the interest expense. The interest is calculated by applying the discount rate to the debt amount.

Recognizing and Measuring the Lease Payments Lease payments do not appear on the income statement because, financially speaking, it is not a question of leasing, but of acquisition of the asset by the legally-authorized lessee. However, the income statement is affected through the depreciation expense and the interests calculated according to the methods indicated above. The result is an improvement in the operating income since the interest is recognized as financial expense and the depreciation expense is usually much less than the leasing cost. Some groups, such as Accor, describe their accounting methods for finance leases in their annual report (see Figure 6.5).

Application 6.10 illustrates the entire analysis of a lease project, as well as how the transactions are recognized and measured in the lessee's and lessor's financial statements.

APPLICATION 6.10

Lease of a Property: The Bid-O Case (*continued*)

Question 5: What is the depreciation period of the asset in Bid-O's balance sheet?

Answer   There is no transfer of property at the end of the contract (neither automatic transfer nor bargain purchase option). The actual period is the shorter of the following two: the outright period of the contract (10 years) or the depreciation period used by the company for the same kind of asset (20 years).

In conclusion, the depreciation period in Bid-O's balance sheet is 10 years.

Question 6: What are the impacts in Bid-O's balance sheet and income statement after 10/06/2007?

Answer   There is clearly no impact on the financial statements until 01/01/2009. However, the disclosure of this off-balance sheet committment is mandatory by IAS 17 on 10/06/2007. Those disclosures shall be updated until the end of the lease term on 12/31/2018.

Question 7: What are the impacts in Bid-O's balance sheet and income statement after 01/01/2009?

Answer   At inception of the lease, the building is recognized as if it had been purchased. The value of the asset is the lesser of either the present value of future lease payments (€5,669,000) or the cost (€6,000,000).

As counterpart, a financial debt appears as a new liability, divided into two parts:

- The reimbursment for the present year (2009, €459,000) as current liability
- The reimbursments for the coming years (€5,210,000 in 2009) as non-current liability.

Non current assets (+A)	5,669,000
Current financial liability (+L)	459,000
Non current financial liability (+L)	5,210,000

Question 8: What are the effects in Bid-O's balance sheet and income statement at the end of 2009?

Answer   The lease of the land does not generate any special treatment. Payments are considered as operational expenses with a debt or treasury account as counterpart.

As far as the building is concerned, the following table presents the evolution of its value in the balance sheet and income statement of Bid-O during the whole lease period:

- Payments are stable during the whole period with €270,000 per year. Their present value decreases automatically with time.
- The reimbursment of the debt is computed as a difference between the annual lease payment (€720,000) and the interests of the period. Interests are computed using an interest rate of 4.6% and a debt amount of €5,669,000 in 2009. The relative weight of interests decreases with successive reimbursements.

- The depreciation of the building is computed using the straight line depreciation method, namely one-tenth of the entry value of each year (€567,000).

At each closing, the part of the loan that is reimbursable on the following year is reclassified as current liabilities. All amounts in the following table are in thousands of €.

Year	Leases			Financial debt				Life of the asset		
	Nom. val.	*Year*	*Pres. val.*	*Opening*	*Reimb.*	*Final expense*	*Closing*	*Opening*	*Allocation*	*Closing*
2009	720	1	688	5,669	459	261	5,210	5,669	567	5,102
2010	720	2	658	5,210	480	240	4,730	5,102	567	4,535
2011	720	3	629	4,730	502	218	4,227	4,535	567	3,968
2012	720	4	601	4,227	526	194	3,702	3,968	567	3,402
2013	720	5	575	3,702	550	170	3,152	3,402	567	2,835
2014	720	6	550	4,152	575	145	2,577	2,835	567	2,268
2015	720	7	526	2,577	601	119	1,976	2,268	567	1,701
2016	720	8	502	1,976	629	91	1,346	1,701	567	1,134
2017	720	9	480	1,346	658	62	688	1,134	567	567
2018	720	10	459	688	688	32	0	567	567	0
Total	**7,200**		**5,669**		**5,669**	**1,531**			**5,669**	

The following records shall be booked at the end of 2009.

Lease expense (−IS)		480,000	
	Cash and cash equivalents (−A)		480,000
Rent of the land			
Interest expense (−IS)		261,000	
Current financial debt (−L)		459,000	
	Cash and cash equivalents (−A)		720,000
Rent of the building			
Depreciation expense (−IS)		567,000	
	Depreciation (−A)		567,000
Depreciation of the building			
Non current financial debt (−IS)		480,000	
	Current financial debt (+L)		480,000
Reclassification of the 2010 debt as current liabilities			

The Lessor's Accounts The lessor is considered to have sold the leased product as of the transfer date of its associated risks and benefits, which corresponds to the beginning of the lease term. The lease asset disappears from its balance sheet, and a *cost of goods sold* expense for the same amount is recorded in the income statement. In addition, a sale is entered on the income statement for the present value of the minimum payments with a receivable for the same amount as on the asset side on the balance sheet.

APPLICATION 6.11

Lease of a Property: The Bid-O Case (*continued*)

The cost of the building and the land for Bailexpert were respectively of €5,172,000 and €3,452,000.

Question 9: What are the impacts in Bailexpert's balance sheet and income statement on 01/01/2009?

Answer When the lessee takes possession of the lease, the building, previously booked at its cost, is sold and shall be derecognized in the balance sheet. A revenue corresponding to the sales price is recognized in the income statement. That way, the total impact on profit or loss of the lease contract is immediately recognized in the income statement of Bailexpert.

The lease of the land does not generate any book records for now.

Derecognition of the building in the BS		
Cost of sales (−IS)	5,172,000	
Non-current asset (−A)		5,172,000
Recognition of the sale		
Financial asset – Receivable (+A)	5,669,000	
Sales (+IS)		5,669,000
Reclassification of the current part of the receivable as current asset		
Current assets – Receivable (+A)	459,000	
Non-current financial asset – Receivable (−A)		459,000

Question 10: What are the impacts in Bailexpert's balance sheet and income statement at the end of 2009?

Answer The €480,000 inflows corresponding to the lease of the land generate an operating income.

The lease payment of the building (€720,000) is to be split between financial income for the interests (€261,000) and the payment of the current receivable (€459,000).

The part of the receivable to be paid in 2010 (€480,000) is then reclassified from a non-current financial asset to a current asset.

Payment of the lease of the land		
Cash and cash equivalents (+A)	480,000	
Lease revenue (+IS)		480,000
Payment of the rent of the building		
Cash and cash equivalents (+A)	720,000	
Interests income (+IS)		261,000
Receivables – Current (−A)		459,000
Reclassification of the short-term part of the receivable as current asset		
Receivables – Current (+A)	480,000	
Receivables – Non current (−A)		480,000

6.3 EQUITY TRANSACTIONS

For many different reasons, a company may want to increase (or reduce) its equity. There are several ways of increasing equity, but they are not without consequences on the company's financial structure. Before we address the accounting entries required for these transactions, it is important to understand the effects that each of these transactions can have on the company's financial statements and structure.

6.3.1 Increasing Shareholders' Equity

Cash contributions simultaneously increase the company's **shareholders' equity** and **cash assets.** They can therefore help to improve its financial structure. Indeed, ultimately, cash assets are used to acquire new assets without using external capital sources, namely liabilities. However, cash contributions are not the only form of contributions possible. For example, contributions of land or buildings simultaneously increase the equity and value of non-current assets. This increase in capital can also result from bond issue conversion. When a company issues convertible bonds, an increase in equity can occur at any time as conversion requests are made. Debt conversion results in an increase in equity and a reduction in financial liability. The impact on the company's financial structure is clear, and its financial dependence (on creditors) is reduced.

Finally, the conversion of reserves into capital does not constitute an equity increase in so far as the total amount of equity does not change. It results in an increase in share capital and a decrease in reserves (or a reduction in reported earnings). Such a conversion of reserves into share capital does not impact the company's financial structure. A summary of accounting entries according to equity increase method appears below:

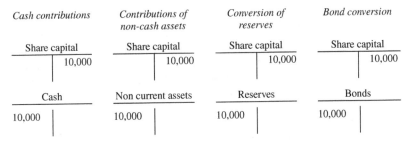

When a company increases its capital, it issues a certain number of shares without any certitude regarding the total amount it will receive in return (the number of shares acquired by investors). The procedure usually involves issuing shares with a nominal value even though in several countries, including Canada and the United States, it is possible to issue actions without a nominal value.

There are two reasons for using the nominal value for shares. First, to protect creditors, as some countries do not allow the dividend payments above nominal value. Second, setting a nominal value lower than the issue price also prevents the current shareholders from unfair losses. In fact, the corporate profits earned over previous years that contributed to increased shareholders' equity usually have not been entirely distributed as dividends; a portion of the profits is kept as reserves. The current shareholders have a right to the dividends. However, when the equity is increased, new external shareholders have the same rights to the reserves as the current shareholders, even if they did not bear any level of risk. Therefore, two elements can help to avoid penalizing current shareholders:

- Setting a new share issue price greater than the nominal value.
- Offering preemptive rights to current stockholders.

The issue price is the price that a shareholder (current or new) must pay for a new share. It is usually greater than the nominal value to compensate for the portion of reserves that will be available from now on to new shareholders without having contributed to it. At most, it is equal to the fair value of the company's shares after the equity increase:

$$\text{Nominal value} \leq \text{Issue price} \leq \text{Fair value of shares after equity increase}$$

When the issue price is the same as the nominal value, the issue is said to be **at par**. The difference between the issue price and the nominal value is the share premium (Issue price − Nominal value = Share premium). To avoid subverting the position of current shareholders, they are given priority to subscribe for the equity increase in proportion to their share ownership. They therefore are granted **preemptive rights** (PR) for purchasing securities so that they can maintain their proportionate ownership interest in the company, if they so desire.

$$\text{Issue price} + n \times \text{PR} = \text{Fair value of shares after equity increase}$$
$$n \times \text{PR} = [\text{Fair value after equity increase} - \text{Issue price}]$$

where n = number of PR needed to purchase a new share.

Thus, a shareholder detaining 30% of the company's equity has the first option to purchase new shares at 30% of the equity increase. However, current shareholders are not obliged to subscribe for equity increase. They can sell their rights so that other investors who want to participate, but lack the rights to do so (either current or new shareholders who want to buy more shares beyond their current ownership), can purchase shares. The fair value of shares after the equity increase is equivalent to the weighted average of the old market price and the issue price of the new shares calculated as follows:

Fair value of shares after equity increase
$$= \frac{(\text{Average old market price} \times \text{Number of old shares}) + (\text{Issue price} \times \text{Number of new shares})}{\text{Total number of shares after equity increase}}$$

The issue price and the preemptive rights are a way to maintain fair and proportionate ownership terms between current and new shareholders. Application 6.12 describes the adjustment mechanisms for preemptive rights and the issue price.

APPLICATION 6.12

Nominal Value and Preemptive Rights

In order to finance future investments of €2,000,000, company WhiteWise wants to implement a capital increase. Present equity is as follows:

Capital	5,000,000 (100,000 shares, nominal value €50)
Reserves	10,000,000
	15,000,000

The first step consists in determining the fair value of the existing shares. Some assets are under valued at €1,000,000. The fair value of the stocks is computed as follows:

$$\frac{5,000,000 + 10,000,000 + 1,000,000}{100,000} = €160$$

if the price of the new shares is set to €100, for instance, the number of new stocks shall be 2,000,000/100,000 = €100, namely 20,000. The fair value of the shares after the capital increase is computed as follows:

$$\frac{(5,000,000 + 10,000,000 + 1,000,000) + 2,000,000}{100,000 + 20,000} = €150$$

In theory, the value of a preemptive right is 150 − 100 = €50. Since the 100,000 old shares represent 100,000 preemptive rights for 20,000 new shares, namely 5 preemptive rights for one new share, it means that a preemptive right is valued at 50/5 = €10.

However, a new shareholder who will want to subscribe to the capital increase will have to pay €100 plus the price of 5 preemptive rights, namely €150 or the fair value of a share right after the capital increase. He gets his share at its fair value and buys preemptive rights to former shareholders who do not want to subscribe to the capital increase but who get compensation by selling their preemptive rights.

Accounting procedures for shareholders' equity increases involve raising the subscribed capital by the shares' nominal value. The difference between the issue price and the nominal value is recognized in equity as the **share premium**.

Cash assets (+A)		*Issue price*		
	Subscribed capital (+SE)		*Nominal value*	
	Share premium (+SE)		*Difference*	

APPLICATION 6.13

The company WhiteWise proceeded to the €2,000,000 capital increase as planned (see application 6.12). In the case of a nominal value for the new shares of €50 (as for the old shares), the book entries are the following:

Cash and cash equivalents (+A)		2,000,000	
	Subscribed capital (+E)		1,000,000
	Share premium (+E)		1,000,000

After the capital increase, WhiteWise's equity is as follows:

Capital	6,000,000	(120,000 shares, nominal value of €50)
Reserves	10,000,000	
Share premium	1,000,000	
	17,000,000	

The share premium usually appears within the reserves:

Share emission premium (−E)		1,000,000	
	Reserves (+E)		1,000,000

Equity appears as follows:

Capital	6,000,000	(120,000 shares, nominal value €50)
Reserves	11,000,000	
	17,000,000	

If the nominal value of the new shares was €100 (as the issuing price), there would not have been any share premium.

Capital	7,000,000	(100,000 shares, nominal value €50 plus 20,000 shares, nominal value €100)
Reserves	10,000,000	
	17,000,000	

6.3.2 Reducing Shareholders' Equity

Reduced shareholders' equity is usually the result of loss absorption or repurchasing shares.

Reduced equity is usually the consequence of loss absorption, or of repurchasing shares. Share repurchasing, or buyback, can be for two purposes: either to permanently retire the shares, or to resell or redistribute them at a later date.

- **Loss absorption.** When a company records significant losses, it can absorb part of the amount by reducing the shareholders' equity without additional expenditure. This is the opposite of an equity increase by conversion of reserves.

APPLICATION 6.14

Loss Absorption

The firm BlueBad has been experiencing financial difficulties for a few years. One year after another, the losses went bigger and bigger. Bluebad's equity is as follows:

Capital	1,500,000	(1,000 shares, nominal value €150)
Reported losses	−200,000	
	1,300,000	

The managers would like to absorp the losses and will book the following record:

Capital (−E)		200,000	
	Reported losses (+E)		200,000

Since the capital has been reduced without changing the number of shares, this operation results in a decrease of the nominal share value. For BlueBad, the nominal value of the share is reduced by 200,000/1,000, namely €20. The new nominal value of the share is €130.

- **Share repurchasing.** Many companies initiate a buyback of their own shares. The goal can be to maintain or increase the share market price, or to compensate shareholders by repurchasing their securities at advantageous rates. Another objective may be for the company to hold its own shares with the perspective of reselling or redistributing them as part of an employee profit-sharing or compensation plan. If the company does not want to keep the shares, the accounting procedure for share repurchasing involves reducing the share capital.

APPLICATION 6.15

The company Grey decides to buy 100,000 of its own shares at their end month value, namely €60 (total amount: €6,000,000). These shares had been issued for €3,000,000 with a nominal value of €10. The book entry of the repurchase is as follows:

Capital (100,000 shares × €10) (−E)	1,000,000	
Share premium (−E)	2,000,000	
Reserves (−E)	3,000,000	
Cash and cash equivalents (−A)		6,000,000

The nominal value of capital is reduced by €1,000,000. The remaining €5,000,000 is deducted from the reserves or from the share premium if the share premium had not previously been converted into reserves. This operation leads to a reduction of the firm value of Grey of €6,000,000 − €3,000,000 = €3,000,000 as the shares had been repurchased at a market value twice as high as the (historical) issuing price. If the market price had been lower than the issuing price, Grey's firm value would have increased. This kind of gains or losses related to operations on equity are not recognized in the profit or loss of the income statement, but are directly recorded in equity.

On the other hand, if the company prefers to keep its shares, the equity subscribed as such is not affected, and *a treasury share* account appears in the statement of shareholders' equity. However, the balance of the *own share* (treasury share) account reduces the total equity.

APPLICATION 6.16

The firm Red decides to buy 100,000 of its own shares at their end of month value, namely €60 (total amount: €6,000,000). These shares had been issued for €6,000,000 with a nominal value of €10. The firm needs these shares in order to comply to some top management's compensation rules (stock-options). The acquisition of the shares is recorded as follows:

Capital (−E)	6,000,000	
Cash and cash equivalents (−A)		6,000,000

If these shares are sold later for a unit price of €70 (a price *higher* than the repurchase price), the book entry will be as follows:

Cash and cash equivalents (100,000 × €70) (+A)	7,000,000	
Share premium (+E)		1,000,000
Capital (100,000 shares × €60) (+E)		6,000,000

If these shares are sold later for a unit price of €50 (a price *lower* than the repurchase price), the book entry will be as follows:

Cash and cash equivalents (100,000 × €50) (+A)	5,000,000	
Share premium (−E)	1,000,000	
Capital (100,000 shares × €60) (+E)		6,000,000

6.3.3   Statement of Shareholders' Equity

> The **statement of shareholders' equity** is a required financial statement indicating all transactions affecting the company's total shareholders' equity for a given year.

The growth or diminution of shareholder wealth is measured by changes in shareholder's equity observed over the course of a given year. However, this variation can stem from various types of transaction, such as equity increases, that may not generate additional wealth. The **statement of shareholders' equity** indicates all of the transactions that affect the total shareholders' equity for a given year. This statement (which is required along with the three other financial statements) shows the actual and/or potential wealth available to shareholders. The balance sheet equation helps to explain the factors that affect changes in shareholder wealth:

$$\text{Equity} = \text{Assets} - \text{Liabilities} \Leftrightarrow \Delta\,\text{Equity} = \Delta\,\text{Assets} - \Delta\,\text{Liabilities}$$

Three main sources impact the total equity:

- The total comprehensive income – composed of net income as it appears on the income statement and of some other elements[2] – is the primary source of variations in stockholder wealth and is entered in the statement of shareholders' equity. Wealth increases with profits, and decreases when losses are reported.
- The second source comes from shareholder compensation. Dividends based on the net income or reserves effectively distribute wealth to shareholders. Once distributed, this wealth is no longer available at the company level.
- Capital transactions have a clear impact on the total amount of equity. However, it is important to distinguish between equity increases and share repurchasing. Equity increases do not affect shareholder wealth since there is no value creation. Share repurchases are to be treated like dividends since they are a form of shareholder compensation and reduce the amount of wealth available to the remaining shareholders.

All of these elements are taken into account on the statement of shareholders' equity. Figure 6.6 shows Astra Zeneca statement of shareholders' equity. A more detailed analysis of this statement can help to better understand the accounting procedures that determine the figures that appear on it.

Astra Zeneca's shareholders' equity does not vary only because of the net income and the dividends paid.

- The amount of shareholders' equity at the beginning of 2008 was $14,915m.
- The increase in net income for 2008 of $4,224m was partially compensated by the payment of dividends on the 2007 income of $2,767m.
- The company issued new shares during the year generating $159m, which included $1m in subscribed capital at a nominal value and $158m in share premiums. We can

---

[2] *For more detailed information about the elements of the total comprehensive income, see Chapter 9.*

19 CAPITAL AND RESERVES

	Share capital $m	Share premium account $m	Capital redemption reserve $m	Merger reserve $m	Other reserves $m	Retained earnings $m	Total $m	Minority equity interests $m	Total equity $m
At 1 January 2006	395	692	53	433	1,345	10,679	13,597	94	13,691
Total recognised income and expense	–	–	–	–	–	6,970	6,970	24	6,994
Transfer to other reserves¹	–	–	–	–	53	(53)	–	–	–
Dividends	–	–	–	–	–	(2,217)	(2,217)	–	(2,217)
Issue of Ordinary Shares	6	979	–	–	–	–	985	–	985
Re-purchase of Ordinary Shares	(18)	–	18	–	–	(4,147)	(4,147)	–	(4,147)
Share-based payments	–	–	–	–	–	129	129	–	129
Treasury shares	–	–	–	–	–	(13)	(13)	–	(13)
Transfer from minority interests to payables	–	–	–	–	–	–	–	(6)	(6)
Net movement	(12)	979	18	–	53	669	1,707	18	1,725
At 31 December 2006	383	1,671	71	433	1,398	11,348	15,304	112	15,416
Total recognised income and expense	–	–	–	–	–	5,934	5,934	35	5,969
Transfer to other reserves¹	–	–	–	–	(20)	20	–	–	–
Dividends	–	–	–	–	–	(2,658)	(2,658)	–	(2,658)
Issue of Ordinary Shares	1	217	–	–	–	–	218	–	218
Re-purchase of Ordinary Shares	(20)	–	20	–	–	(4,170)	(4,170)	–	(4,170)
Share-based payments	–	–	–	–	–	150	150	–	150
Transfer from minority interests to payables	–	–	–	–	–	–	–	(10)	(10)
Net movement	(19)	217	20	–	(20)	(724)	(526)	25	(501)
At 31 December 2007	364	1,888	91	433	1,378	10,624	14,778	137	14,915
Total recognised income and expense	–	–	–	–	–	4,176	4,176	48	4,224
Transfer to other reserves¹	–	–	–	–	27	(27)	–	–	–
Dividends	–	–	–	–	–	(2,767)	(2,767)	–	(2,767)
Issue of Ordinary Shares	1	158	–	–	–	–	159	–	159
Re-purchase of Ordinary Shares	(3)	–	3	–	–	(610)	(610)	–	(610)
Share-based payments	–	–	–	–	–	176	176	–	176
Transfer from minority interests to payables	–	–	–	–	–	–	–	(11)	(11)
Dividend paid by subsidiary to minority interest	–	–	–	–	–	–	–	(26)	(26)
Net movement	(2)	158	3	–	27	948	1,134	11	1,145
At 31 December 2008	362	2,046	94	433	1,405	11,572	15,912	148	16,060

¹ Amounts charged to other reserves relate to exchange adjustments arising on goodwill.

Figure 6.6 Financial report AstraZeneca 2008.

suppose that the following entries were required to obtain these amounts:

Cash assets (+A)	159,000,000	
Subscribed capital (+E)		1,000,000
Share premium (+E)		158,000,000

- The group initiated share repurchasing totalling $610m, which reduced the total shareholders' equity.

Own Shares (−E)	610,000,000	
Cash assets (−A)		610,000,000

Foreign currency translation differences also have an impact on shareholders' equity (see Chapter 8).

6.4 SUMMARY

Three financing methods have been presented in this chapter: financial liabilities, lease agreements, and operations with shareholders.

Financial liabilities are recognized and measured on the balance sheet at their amortized cost according to the initial purchase interest rate. Derivatives are measured at their fair value according to the income statement.

Financially speaking, lease agreements often more closely resemble sales contracts than to classic leases. The criteria used to differentiate genuine operating lease agreements from finance leases are often difficult to pin down. No offical list exists, though five basic criteria can be identified for reference. Restating an agreement as a finance lease has major consequences for both the lessor's and the lessee's balance sheet.

The lessor enters a sale and immediately records an increase in income equal to the revenue generated over the entire lease term. In parallel, the asset disappears from the balance sheet and is replaced by a receivable.

The lessee becomes the asset's economic owner. On financial statements, it is treated like any other asset of similar nature, especially in terms of the methods used for estimating the asset's useful life and depreciation method. In addition, a liability of the same value as the asset is recognized and is reimbursed over time through the lessee's lease payments after the interest on the debt is deducted.

The statement of shareholders' equity presents all of the transactions that affect the total shareholders' equity for a given year. The changes in equity that appear can be attributed to various transactions, some of which, such as equity increases, do not result in increased wealth. The balance sheet equation helps the factors that affect changes in shareholder wealth to be understood.

Reduced equity is usually the consequence of loss absorption, or of repurchasing shares. Share repurchasing, or buyback, can be for two purposes: either to permanently retire the shares, or to resell or redistribute them at a later date.

6.5 ACTIVITIES

1. Date of Analysis of a lease contract   A lease contract is signed between the firm Davis and Rubini on 10/02/2008. At this point, the land is only a wasteland but Rubini is planning to build a store based on Davis's requirements within 16 months. The lease term starts on 02/01/2010 and covers an outright period of 12 years.

When should the contract be analyzed in order to treat it in financial statements of the lessor (Rubini) and the lessee (Davis)?

2. Definitions

1. *Explain the concept of economic ownership.*

2. *Explain the difference between the commencement of a lease contract and the inception of the lease.*

3. Accounting of a Loan   A firm borrows €500,000 at an interest rate of 4%. Transactions fees are negligible and the loan is to be reimbursed in five constant annuities.

1. *Compute the amount of an annuity.*
2. *Prepare the reimbursement table (closing capital, annuity, repartition between interests and payments).*
3. *Indicate the book entries regarding the payment of the first annuity.*

4. Lease of a Building   The company Senguillot seeks to rent offices for a long term. It contracts with the firm Bilout which has just built a new €5m building on a €3m land. The contract specifies that:

- Sentguillot will pay a €1m annual rent and additional charges of €100,000.
- Sentguillot will not cancel the contract during the 10 coming years.

Senguillot usually depreciates its real estate property over 25 years. Its average debt interest rate is 5% at the commencement of the contract.

1. *Is the rent an operational lease or a finance lease?*
2. *Shall the building be recognized in Senguillot's balance sheet? If yes, what should be the useful life?*
3. *What is the impact of this lease in Bilout's financial statements?*
4. *What are the book entries in Bilout's accounts at the end of the first year of lease?*

5. Capital Increase   *Enumerate all the different ways to increase equity.*

6. Issuing New Shares   Coldcat's equity appears to be €20m on its balance sheet. Half of this amount consists of shares (100,000 shares of €100 nominal value), the other half consists of reserves. The firm wants to finance its future projects by a capital increase of €10m.

1. *Assuming that assets and liabilities are correctly evaluated, what, from an accounting point of view, is the fair value of the shares?*
2. *If the company decides to issue 100,000 new shares at the price of €100 each, what is the fair value of shares after the capital increase?*
3. *What, in theory, is the value of the preemptive right?*
4. *Will former shareholders be subverted compared to the new ones?*

7. Deficit   The firm FishnChips is closing the current financial year with a loss, for the third consecutive year. Its equity consists of 100,000 shares of a nominal value of €100 and €2m of accumulated losses.

If the management wants to eliminate the losses, what will be the new nominal value of a share?

8. Shares Repurchase   The firm Roks want to buy 100,000 of its own shares (at €20 each) in order to comply to its obligations to its top management in terms of stock options. Those shares have a nominal value of €10 in Roks' books.

1. *What are the book entries recorded by Roks?*
2. *Shares are finally sold at the price of €18. Please indicate the appropriate records.*

7 TAXATION

Companies can take advantage of a range of public services, many of which are free of charge. However, they are not really "free" in the true sense of the word since the State uses tax revenue to finance them. First and foremost, in accounting terms, taxes represent a liability. Further, the sole purpose of the taxation system is to determine the tax base and collect the taxes due. In France[1] since 1917, to this end, taxation has officially been based on accounting records. To determine corporate income tax rates, the French tax system offers a compromise between two different approaches:

- Applying specific income assessment and determination guidelines,
- Accepting standardized accounting procedures as a basis for determining income.

Instead of having to issue both a balance sheet and a taxable income statement, French companies' taxable income is indirectly based on their accrual-based income. Accounting, therefore, partly determines this amount and provides an essential tax auditing tool. This connection between accounting and taxation is common to all countries, even if it is not always respected. In most countries in Europe, they are usually interdependent. Thus a solid knowledge of accounting is necessary for understanding taxation, which, as an area of study, is the logical and necessary extension of accounting.

First of all, it's important to identify which taxes are imposed on businesses (section 7.1). There are various types of tax with different names (direct taxes, indirect taxes, duties, etc.), and while terms may differ, the collection concept remains the same. This chapter addresses payable and deferred income tax (sections 7.2 and 7.3), and sales and value added tax (section 7.4).

IAS 12 is the only international taxation standards that deal with financial statement income tax reporting, assessment and presentation. It has been first applied in 1981 and then revised in 1996 and 2000 and deal with federal and international taxation based on taxable earnings.

7.1 INCOME TAX AND OTHER TAXES

Every company's primary objective is to create value, which is then distributed among its various stakeholders. According to a conception of businesses as partnerships, as a supplier of public goods and services, the State is a stakeholder. Tax authorities can thus be considered a business partner; albeit one that occupies a very particular role in the company's operations. As a recipient of accounting information for tax assessment and collection, the government acts as an uninvited third party whose presence is felt in all contracts with provisions for common, non-negotiable "contract clauses", meaning taxation procedures. This situation is justified

---

[1] *Tax systems are quite different for one country to another. In this chapter, the autors often refer to the French tax environment in order to be concrete. The outcome of the analysis, and especially the accounting treatment of tax issues according to IFRS, is comparable for environments in other countries.*

by the particular requirements of tax imposition: tax laws are primarily aimed at procuring financial resources for the State, which then redistributes them. With this goal in mind, it is obligated to assess a company's contribution capacity at a given moment in time as accurately as possible and facilitate the job for the tax authorities. The relationship between the businesses and the State tax authorities is based on the existence of known tax declaration procedures. Companies produce the documents required for calculating their taxes and the tax authorities verify that the taxpaying company complies with the underlying rules and procedures.

Companies are taxpaying entities subject to a variety of different taxes. They have to be very familiar with the "nature" of these taxes in order to manage them better, especially since it's businesses that usually fill the coffers of the State treasury (for example, by paying the VAT). It's important to distinguish income tax from sales and value added tax, payroll tax, and other types of tax.

7.1.1   Income Tax

Taxation of earnings (taxable, and not accounting income) varies according to the legal structure of the company in question, but is based on a general principle: the government collects a portion of corporate revenues when there are any. In France, this collection takes the form of **individual income tax** (*impôt sur le revenue*, IR) and the **corporate income tax** (*impôt sur les societes*, IS) on legal entities.

Thus, for a sole proprietorship, the income earned by the business owner is not taxed as for a company, but is added (or deducted if there is a deficit) to his or her other earnings. The tax is calculated according to the amount of total income revenue, and also the person's family situation according to a progressive scale that varies from 0% to 40% (IR 2008, not including additional social charges). It is an overall individual income tax that does not appear on the business's balance sheets. The tax owed is considered a personal expense for the business owner, not the legal entity. Income earned by the sole proprietorship is therefore always pre-tax. The same applies to business partnerships, which are transparent in terms of taxation. Here again the income earned by these businesses is not taxed on a corporate level, but as individual income for the partners involved according to their own profiles. Assuming the associates in the partnership are physical persons, the same reasoning as above applies.

For corporate structures, the approach is different. As opposed to a sole proprietorship, or a partnership where only the business owner or partner is considered a taxpayer in his or her own right, the designated "business corporation" is accorded a separate fiscal identity. As is the case for corporations and limited liability partnerships (SA and SARL structures in France), income taxes are determined for these structures and paid at proportional rates. The partners are not taxed individually unless the company distributes dividends.

7.1.2   Sales Tax or Value-Added Tax

Sales taxes are taxes based on the sale of goods and services. Two approaches exist:

- The 'traditional' sales tax approach consists of perceiving the tax at each time a good is sold. If the good is resold, the selling company will include the paid sales tax in the sales price, and it will be again subject to sales tax. This cumulative process ends when the good is finally sold to the ultimate customer.
- According to the "value-added-approach", companies are totally exempted from the tax (which then is commonly called Value-added tax (VAT). Companies will recover the

paid VAT by offsetting it to perceived VAT from their customers. Only the difference between both amounts will be the VAT payable to tax administration. The perceived amount is generally higher than the paid amount as it includes the tax on the value added by the company itself and its margin. Each share of the value of a good or service is taxed only once, and there is no cumulative effect of succeeding taxations in the case of re-sales between companies. This also explains why the tax rates in countries adopting the VAT approach are generally higher than in the ones adopting the first approach. Both the paid and the perceived VAT are not recognized in the income statement. The payable amount is not an expense of the company but the payment collected upon the customers on behalf of the tax administration. Perceived amounts represent a liability, paid VAT represents a receivable for the company. Booking mechanisms for the VAT model are detailed in the appendix to this chapter.

The paid sales tax according to the first model is recognized as an expense by the paying company, while the perceived sales tax has to be reversed to the tax administration and therefore does not qualify as a revenue. Instead it is recognized as a liability. Booking mechanisms for the VAT model are detailed in the appendix to this chapter.

7.1.3 Other taxes

There is a huge variety of other taxes to pay by companies in France. The following (non-exhaustive) list gives an idea of this variety. Other countries, and sometimes within countries, regions, cities, etc., may require more or other taxes.

- The **apprenticeship tax**, which is now mainly used to finance student internships and work-study programs. It is calculated at a rate of 0.50% of the total gross payroll (0.60% in certain cases).
- **Contributions to continuing education and training**. All employers, regardless of the number of employees in a company, are required to contribute in order to further professional training development. For companies with over 20 employees, the contribution rate is equal to 1.6% of the total gross payroll.
- The **housing tax** is an annual tax that employers with at least 10 employees must pay to help to finance the construction of new housing units or similar projects. It is paid at a rate of 0.45% of the total gross payroll for the previous calendar year.
- **Salary tax** refers to a payroll tax that is owed by employers who are exempt from VAT, but pay taxable salaries and wages to their employees (employers subject to paying VAT are exempt). The tax rate is on a progressive basis (4.25%, 8.5% or 13.60%) depending on the total gross payroll.
- **Professional tax.** The "*taxe professionnelle*" is one of four local direct taxes whose proceeds are designed to finance the municipality in which the business is based.
- **Land tax.** The "*taxe foncière*" applies to all buildings and constructions owned by the business. It also contributes to local government financing.
- **Corporate vehicle tax.** The "*taxe sur les véhicules*" applies to vehicles owned by businesses as opposed to those owned by individuals. The amount of this annual tax varies according to the vehicle's excise tax, its CO_2 emissions rate, and how old it is.
- **Registration fees.** "*Droits d'enregistrement*" refer to both a procedure and a tax on corporate transactions (business creation, mergers, restructuring, capital growth, dissolution, etc.). An administrative procedure results in a tax amount owed depending on the type of transaction in question and can take the form of a set fee, or progressive or proportional charges.

As mentioned above, this list of taxes that businesses are subject to in France is far from exhaustive, but gives an idea of the wide range of applicable taxes. The accounting system must take them into account in two ways:

- On the balance sheet, as indicated above for the VAT.
- On the income statement as charges, like the company's other expenses (that are not considered capital or permanent assets). These charges apply to the year or period when the company's **payability** for the taxes in question was first established. This is the case for all taxes other than corporate income tax. These taxes represent all of the services and infrastructure the government makes available to businesses. In return, these expenses are expressed on the income statement a liability that disappears once they are paid. Liability can be immediate or deferred. Corporate income tax is the most classic example.

The particular procedures for taking these taxes into account are intimately linked to the specificities of each country's tax laws and depend on budgetary considerations.

Tax payability: The government revenue authority's recognized right to require a taxpayer to pay a particular tax at a given moment.

7.2   CORPORATE INCOME TAX

7.2.1   Determining Taxable Income

The government claims a portion of corporate earnings. The amount of the corporate income tax (IS in France) is not actually directly calculated using accounting income, strictly speaking, but on taxable income, which is based on accounting income. The difference is due to adjustments not reflected in the accounts, which explain the distinction so that:

$$\text{Taxable income} = \text{Accounting income} \pm \text{Adjustments}$$

The scale of the adjustments varies from country to country and depends on specific objectives, taxation constraints, and of course the connection between the accounting and taxation procedures. In theory, they do not have any impact on the bookkeeping per se, and are taken into account only for income tax determination. However, taxation still does influence accounting practices. Indeed, taxation laws can impose rules that lead companies to prefer particular accounting methods over others for tax-related reasons.

In many Continental European countries, tax valuation rules rules are strongly linked to accounting rules. For example, according French tax law: "Businesses must comply with the definitions set forth in the *Plan Comptable Général* [official French accounting guidelines] on condition that they are not incompatible with the rules governing the tax base" (Article 38.4, Annex 3). It is specified that, in theory, an expense can only be considered deductible from the income tax calculation if it has been recorded in the accounting system. Nevertheless, adjustments are required which increase or reduce the taxable income compared to the net income in the accounting system.

Thus an expense entered as such on the books, but not recognized for tax purposes is added back. This expense may reduce the accounting income, but does not reduce the taxable income.

It is not a tax-deductible expense and therefore cannot be taken into account as such. This happens quite frequently.

It may concern some types of expenses in their entirety, such as, in France for example, expenses that tax authorities consider as "extravagant", even if they were contracted in the interest of the company (a client who is invited on vacation on a yacht will surely be more inclined to do business with the company and will therefore generate more taxable income!). All expenses of this nature are added back to determine the total taxable income. The same applies to fines and late fees charged to companies (only contractual penalties incurred as part of contractual relations are deductible), as well as certain taxes such as corporate income tax.

Other expenses may be tax deductible by nature, but the amount fiscally accepted is different from the one accounted for in the book of the company. A quite common example is the amount for depreciation and amortization expenses, as the relevant methods and durations of useful life differ between those identified by the entity and those accepted by tax authorities. In these cases, the total amount of the depreciation expense during the whole useful life of the asset would be the same in both systems, accounting and taxation, but the distribution over time of these expenses would differ from one system to the other.

In the same vein, while it may occur only rarely, proceeds that were not entered on the books as such can be added back when they are considered as taxable for the tax period in question. These adjustments will result in total taxable income that is higher than the accounting income.

Even less frequently, deductions can apply to products that were entered on the balance sheet, but were not entirely taxable for all or part of the tax period. They can also apply to expenses not entered during the period in question (but often were already entered at an earlier date), when they are in fact deductible from the taxable income. Expenses that are unrecorded, but deductible nonetheless can include incentives paid by the government to encourage certain types of expenditures – anti-pollution efforts, for example. They result in total taxable income that is less than the accounting income.

This chapter does not cover all of the adjustments of this nature. Figure 7.1 shows the general scheme for reconciliation of net income before tax to taxable income.

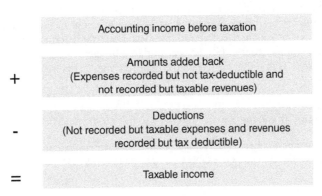

Figure 7.1 Reconciliation of net income and taxable income.

Note 16.2. Effective tax rate

(in million of euros)	2006 [1]	2007	2008
OPERATING PROFIT BEFORE TAX (A)	688	1,146	885
Non deductible impairment losses	18	53	(18)
Elimination of intercompany capital gains	2	417	298
Tax on share of profit (loss) of associates	7	10	7
Other	21	25	7
TOTAL PERMANENT DIFFERENCES (NON-DEDUCTIBLE EXPENSES) (B)	48	505	294
UNTAXED PROFIT AND PROFIT TAXED AT A REDUCED RATE (C)	(182) [*]	(905) [**]	(422) [***]
PROFIT TAXED AT STANDARD RATE (D) = (A) + (B) + (C)	554	746	757
STANDARD TAX RATE IN FRANCE (E)	34.43%	34.43%	34.43%
TAX AT STANDARD FRENCH TAX RATE (F) = (D) X (E)	(191)	(257)	(261)
Effects on tax at standard French tax rate of:			
Differences in foreign tax rates	17	40	39
Unrecognized tax losses for the period	(32)	(21)	(31)
Utilization of tax loss carryforwards	32	14	7
Changes in deferred tax rates	9	5	1
Share of profit (loss) of associates	7	10	7
Net charges to/reversals of provisions for tax risks	(46)	15	(6)
Other items	(24)	(31)	1
TOTAL EFFECTS ON TAX AT STANDARD FRENCH TAX RATE (G)	(37)	32	18
TAX AT STANDARD RATE (H) = (F) + (G)	(228)	(225)	(243)
TAX AT REDUCED RATE (I)	(30) [*]	(9) [**]	(29) [***]
INCOME TAX EXPENSE (J) = (H) + (I)	(258)	(234)	(272)
Pre-tax operating profit taxed at standard rate	554	746	757
Income tax expense	(174)	(217)	(222)
GROUP EFFECTIVE TAX RATE	31.4%	29.1%	29.3%

Figure 7.2 Excerpt from the Accor 2008 annual report.

Taxable income therefore represents the difference between taxable revenues and deductible expenses. Adjustments are often numerous, as is shown below in the example of Accor. In addition, Accor determines an effective tax rate based on the difference between the payable and deferred tax amounts observed in the consolidated financial statement and the accounting income before taxes. This financial indicator measures the company's ability to optimize its tax expenses (see Figure 7.2).

7.2.2 Determining Tax Expense

Tax expense: The amount of taxes on taxable earnings owed to the government for a given accounting year or period.

Businesses are required to submit a tax statement within 3 months following the end of the accounting year or period. The **tax expense** is calculated by applying a rate to the taxable

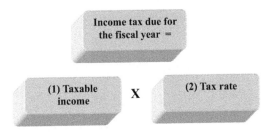

Figure 7.3   Computation of the tax expense.

income (see Figure 7.3). Though this rate may vary depending on the type of business structure (15% for small and medium-sized companies within certain limits), or for specific kinds of product, it is usually set at 33.33%. This is the rate in effect at the end of the fiscal year or period.

7.2.3   Recording Taxes on the Balance Sheet

Taxes are recorded as set expenses for the year or period in which they were incurred, and for which they are owed to the government.

APPLICATION 7.1

Book Entry for the Income Tax Expense and Instalments

The taxable income of 2007 of copany Loopie was €120,000. The tax rate is 33.33%, and there are four instalments to pay, in March, June, September and December. The book entry for the tax expense of FY 2007 and for each instalment for the profit of FY 2008 (not known until the end of FY 2008) are as follows:

Tax expense 2007:

December 31, 2007			
Tax expense (−IS)		40,000	
Tax liability (+L)			40,000

Instalment for income tax 2008:

15 of March/June/September/December			
Tax liabilities (−L)		10,000	
Cash and cash equivalent (−A)			10,000
Instalments for income tax 2008			
(120,000 × 33.33% × 0.25 = 10,000)			

In many countries, the amount is determined (all expenses and products entered), and corporate income tax is not paid all at once, but in advance in **instalments** based on the previous year's taxable income. The first instalment is paid immediately following the end of the fiscal year. The amount of each payment is calculated so that the total equals the tax amount paid for the previous year's taxable income. These payments constitute a debt on behalf of the government to the company by crediting a cash account; they do not constitute a tax expense at that stage.

At the time the instalments are paid, the company does not yet know what its taxable income situation will be at the end of the year and, consequently, if it will record taxable earnings or not.

APPLICATION 7.2

Payment of the Year End Difference

The sum of the instalments is $10,000 \times 4 = €40,000$. The taxable income of the company Loupie for 2008 is €300,000. The income tax for 2008 is $300,000/3 = €100,000$. Therefore, the company must pay on 04/15/2009 the difference of $100,000 - 40,000 = €60,000$. The book entry is:

15 of April 2009		
Tax liabilities (−L)	60,000	
Cash and cash equivalent (−A)		60,000
Payment of the balance of income tax 2008		

The balance is due by the 15th of the fourth month following the end of the fiscal year. In most countries, the fiscal year-end is December 31 and the balance due on April 15. Businesses normally take the initiative to pay the balance without waiting for the tax authorities' request for payment.

APPLICATION 7.3

Carrying Back Deficits

The company Vivi loses €90,000 in 2008, after it made up to €150,000 profit in the three previous years. It is possible to impute the whole deficit and to get a credit of $90,000/3 = €30,000$.

04/15/2009		
Tax liabilities (+A)	30,000	
Deficit carried back (+IS; +E)		30,000
Accounting entry related to the deficit of 2008		

If the instalments paid exceed the amount of the taxes due (zero in the case of net loss), the company has a credit with the government, which must pay it back. It is possible for the credit to be applied to new liable accounts.

The net accounting income that appears on the company's balance sheet is therefore equal to the difference between the accounting income before taxes and the corporate tax due for the fiscal year (see Figure 7.4).

If the company does not record earnings, but a net operating loss, it has two options:

- It can "carry forward" the tax credit and apply it to subsequent years.
- It can opt to "carry back" the losses to a previous year or years with taxable income.

Normally, recording a net loss for one fiscal year is applied to subsequent years. This is referred to as a **tax loss carry-forward** and must be applied to the fiscal years immediately following the loss, for an unlimited length of time. However, if the company has earned taxable income

Figure 7.4   Net profit for the year.

in previous years, it can opt for a **tax loss carry-back**, where it applies the current year's loss to its earnings recorded over the three previous years. Thus it can recover part of the taxes it was liable for and paid in previous years in the form of a refund. In concrete terms, the tax credit is entered as an asset and is calculated according to the tax rate in effect when the carry-back is applied, which effectively increases the year's accounting income by the same amount. This credit can be applied to future IS payments (instalments, balance payments or reminders). If it has not been entirely applied within 5 years, the remaining balance is refunded (companies facing legal proceedings for restructuring, liquidation or bankruptcy can request an immediate refund). Any shortfall that was not able to be carried back can still be applied to taxable income in subsequent years.

Tax loss carry-forward involves applying a net operating loss to earnings in subsequent years.

Tax loss carry-back involves retroactively applying a net operating loss to income from a previous year or years.

APPLICATION 7.4

Carrying Back Deficits

The company Vivi loses €90,000 in 2008, after it made up to €150,000 profit in the three previous years. It is possible to impute the whole deficit and get a credit of 90,000/3 = €30,000.

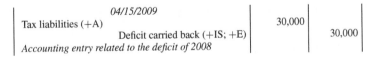

	04/15/2009		
Tax liabilities (+A)		30,000	
	Deficit carried back (+IS; +E)		30,000
Accounting entry related to the deficit of 2008			

Application 7.5 summarizes the income tax balance sheet book entry procedure.

APPLICATION 7.5

Recognition Procedure for Income Tax

The company Besac made an accounting profit of €125,500 in 2007. Expenses as high as €24,500 are considered to be non-deductible on a tax basis. To simplify matters, the company did not make any interim tax payments in 2007. The accounting profit in 2008 is €634,800. €34,800 of the revenues are not taxable income for 2008 and will only be subject to taxes in 2009. For 2008 all the expenses are deductible.

First, it is necessary to compute the taxable income for 2007 which follows from the accounting profit of 2007 (€125,500) and some adjustments due to tax rules. Actually, the expenses of €24,500 have to be reintegrated because they are not deductible. The taxable income for 2007 is therefore €150,000. The income tax is one-third of the taxable income, that is €50,000. On the 12/31/2007 the following accounting entry is made:

12/31/2007		
Income tax expense (−IS; −E)	50,000	
Tax liabilities (+L)		50,000
Income tax 2007		

Finally, the net income of Besac is 125,500 − 50,000 = €75,500 in 2007. This tax liability must be paid before 04/15/2008. Under the hypothesis that no interim payment was made, the accounting entry is:

04/14/2008		
Tax liabilities (−L)	50,000	
Cash and cash equivalent (−A)		50,000
Payment of the income tax 2007		

However, usually it is necessary to make interim payments for the income tax of the current year although the profit is not known. Those payments must be made before the (15th) of March/June/September/December. The interim payments are computed on the basis of the previous year's (here 2007, which makes €150,000) taxable income. One interim payment corresponds to 8.33% of the previous year's taxable income (that is, €12,500).

15 March/June/September/December 2008		
Tax liabilities (−L)	12,500	
Cash and cash equivalent (−A)		12,500
Interim payments of the income tax 2008		

The taxable income for 2007 might not be known on the date of the first interim payment (03/15/2008). Therefore this deposit can be computed on the basis of the taxable income of the previous year (here 2006). Then, on the date of the second interim payment (06/15/2008) an adjustment will take place so that the two first interim payments correspond to 8.33% × 2 of the taxable income for 2007.

At fiscal year end 2008, the income tax for 2008 must be recognized. The accounting income is €634,800. The non-taxable income of €34,800 must be deducted so that the taxable income amounts to €200,000. On 12/31/2008 the following accounting entry is made:

12/31/2008		
Income tax(−IS)	200,000	
Tax liabilities (+L)		200,000
Income tax 2008		

For 2008, the net income after tax of Besac is 634,800 − 200,000 = €434,800.

The balance of the income tax minus the interim payments must be paid before 04/15/2009. This is $200,000 - (4 \times 12,500) = €150,000$. The corresponding accounting entry is:

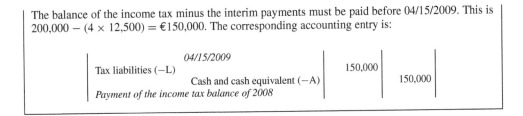

7.3 DEFERRED TAX

Tax expenses are not limited to current liabilities, but include **deferred tax** creating future assets or liabilities. This occurs when the accounting value for assets or liabilities differs from their values according to tax rules. The expense may not be fiscally deductible for a given year, but it can be for subsequent years. It is therefore necessary to distinguish the concepts:

- Tax liability, i.e. the effective amount to pay to tax administration.
- Total tax liability for a particular period, i.e. the amount of tax liability which would occur if the tax expense had been calculated according to accounting rules. Only temporary differences between accounting and tax, which will be balanced in the future, will be taken into account.

The difference creates a deferred tax (asset or liability).

Figure 7.5 gives an overview of potential sources of differences between current income tax and total income tax. This example of British Airways shows not only sources of differences but also highlights the dimension of these differences. The total tax credit amounts to £43m, more than four times the current tax credit of £9m.

In addition to the impact on the tax expense in the income statement, deferred taxes may also arise directly in the balance sheet, and be charged to equity. This happens if the underlying expense or revenue had also been booked directly in equity, or some other comprehensive income. Figure 7.6 illustrates some of these elements in the case of Britsh Airways.

Another type of information provided by companies is the reconciliation between the theoretical tax amount based on the tax rate applied to the (accounting) profit or loss before tax, and the effective tax expense/credit including deferred elements as recognized in the (accounting) income statement. Figure 7.7 shows the details of such reconciliation for British Airways 2008/2009, explaining the difference between a theoretical tax credit of £112m and the recognized tax credit of £43m.

Other companies go a step ahead and indicate the effective tax rate, to be compared with the nominal tax rate. Figure 7.8 concerns Deutsche Telekom. While the nominal tax rate is 30.5% in 2008, the effective tax rate for the same year is 41%.

The regular practice of deferred tax operations is motivated by an interest in considering that tax in the context of the full range of transactions can eventually generate tax savings or liabilities, not just during the period in question, but in subsequent years as well. The future consequences of tax collection on assets and liabilities that appear on the balance statement can then be taken into account to minimize discrepancies between accounting income and

a Tax on (loss)/profit on ordinary activities
Tax (credit)/charge in the income statement

	Group	
£ million	2009	2008 Restated
Current income tax		
UK corporation tax	(37)	72
Relief for foreign tax paid	(3)	(2)
Advance corporation tax reversal	26	(47)
UK tax	(14)	23
Foreign tax	2	1
Adjustments in respect of prior years – UK corporation tax	(18)	(8)
Adjustments in respect of prior years – advance corporation tax	21	
Total current income tax (credit)/charge	(9)	16
Deferred tax		
Effect of the change in the rate of UK corporation tax on opening balances		(70)
Property, plant and equipment related temporary differences	(65)	(57)
Effect of abolition of industrial buildings allowances	79	
Pensions	41	237
Unremitted earnings of associate companies	11	5
Advance corporation tax	(26)	47
Tax losses carried forward	(56)	
Exchange differences	(3)	
Share option deductions written back	1	5
Other temporary differences	(3)	(1)
Adjustments in respect of prior years – deferred tax	8	12
Adjustments in respect of prior years – advance corporation tax	(21)	
Total deferred tax (credit)/charge	(34)	178
Total tax (credit)/charge in the income statement	(43)	194

Figure 7.5   Excerpt from the British Airways annual report 2008/09.

taxable income (see Figure 7.8). This helps to prevent tax considerations from distorting the company's apparent financial situation.

7.3.1   Recognition of Deferred Tax on the Balance Sheet

Deferred tax corresponds to the business' tax liability over subsequent years. It must be paid or refunded at a later date as either:

- differences between the accounting and taxable income for an asset or liability, or
- losses carried forward (or delayed tax credits).

Tax (credit)/charge directly to equity

	Group	
£ million	2009	2008
Deferred tax		
Deferred tax on net movement on revaluation of cash flow hedges	(251)	67
Deferred tax on foreign exchange in reserves	(133)	(21)
Deferred tax on share options in issue		7
Corporation tax rate change for items credited directly to reserves		(6)
Deferred tax on Iberia unremitted earnings	(6)	
Tax (credit)/charge taken directly to equity	(390)	47

Figure 7.6   Excerpt from the British Airways annual report 2008/09.

b Reconciliation of the total tax (credit)/charge

The tax (credit)/charge for the year on the (loss)/profit from continuing operations is less than the notional tax credit on those (losses)/profits calculated at the UK corporation tax rate of 28 per cent (2008: 30 per cent). The differences are explained below:

£ million	2009	2008 Restated
Accounting (loss)/profit before tax	(401)	922
Accounting (loss)/profit multiplied by standard rate of corporation tax in the UK of 28 per cent (2008: 30 per cent)	(112)	277
Effects of:		
Non-deductible expenses	7	7
Foreign exchange and unwind of discount on competition investigation provisions	9	2
Share option deductions written back	1	5
Deductions available on aircraft refinancing surpluses	(4)	(5)
Disposals and write-down of investments	3	(1)
Tax on associates' profits and dividends		(5)
Tax on subsidiary unremitted earnings	(2)	
Overseas tax in relation to branches	(1)	
Euro preferred securities accounted for as minority interest	(5)	(4)
Tax on revaluation of intra-group foreign currency loans	(4)	(5)
Effect of pension fund accounting under IFRIC 14	(5)	(11)
Effect of abolition of industrial buildings allowances	79	
Unrecognised deferred tax asset on pension deficit	2	
Other permanent differences		(2)
Current year losses not recognised	2	
Adjustments in respect of prior years	(10)	4
Rate benefit of trading loss carry back	(3)	
Effect of UK corporation tax rate reduction from 30 per cent to 28 per cent		(68)
Tax (credit)/charge in the income statement (note 12a)	**(43)**	**194**

Figure 7.7 Excerpt from the British Airways annual report 2008/09.

Indeed, the tax value of an asset or liability may not be the same as its accounting value. Tax liability is then determined on the basis of the calculated value which is based on tax rules to determine future taxable income. Thus, for a payable expense entered as such in year N, but deductible in year $N+1$, the tax value for this liability at the end of the fiscal year is zero since it does not yet exist as a liable expense (see Figure 7.9).

> **Temporary differences:** Differences between the accounting value of an asset or liability on the books and value for tax purposes.
>
> **Deferred tax liability:** Tax on earnings paid over future periods due to temporary differences in tax value vs. accounting value.

Temporary differences arise from completed transactions with positive or negative tax consequences other than those that are accounted for in calculating the tax liability and are expressed as a difference between the company's accounting income and taxable income in the future. If deferred tax is not taken into account, the situation will be distorted insofar as the deduction will actually be made in the future. The excerpt from the annual report for Accor (Figure 7.10) shows the company's amount of deferred tax.

Deferred tax liability is therefore recognized on the balance sheet for all taxable temporary differences, except under particular conditions. It concerns differences that generate amounts that will be liable in the future, and will therefore represent a future tax expense. On the other hand,

Reconciliation of the effective tax rate. Income taxes of EUR 1,428 million in the reporting year (2007: EUR 1,373 million; 2006: EUR (970) million) are derived as follows from the expected income tax expense that would have arisen had the statutory income tax rate of the parent company (combined income tax rate) been applied to profit before income taxes:

millions of €	2008	2007*	2006*
Profit before income taxes	**3,452**	**2,453**	**2,612**
Expected income tax expense (income tax rate applicable to Deutsche Telekom AG: 2008: 30.5%; 2007: 39%; 2006: 39%)	1,053	957	1,019
Adjustments to expected tax expense			
Effect of changes in statutory tax rates	3	734	(8)
Tax effects from prior years	29	65	(517)
Tax effects from other income taxes	115	42	7
Non-taxable income	(86)	(217)	(151)
Tax effects from equity investments	124	(23)	(63)
Non-deductible expenses	110	63	78
Permanent differences	(47)	28	(270)
Impairment of goodwill or negative excess from capital consolidation	71	130	4
Tax effects from loss carryforwards	(34)	(306)	(975)
Tax effects from additions to and reductions of local tax	86	92	109
Adjustment of taxes to different foreign tax rates	3	(182)	(190)
Other tax effects	1	(10)	(13)
Income tax expense (benefit) according to the consolidated income statement	**1,428**	**1,373**	**(970)**
Effective income tax rate (%)	41	56	(37)

Figure 7.8　Excerpt from the Deutsche Telekom annual report 2008.

permanent differences between net income and taxable income do not generate deferred taxes. For example, differences arising from goodwill recognition and impairment will not be recognized as business combinations in general and also related goodwill are not subject to taxation

---

APPLICATION 7.6

Recognition of a Deferred Tax Liability

During 2008 the company Lelo recorded a depreciation expense of €8,000 for an item purchased at €20,000 by using a special method for tax purposes. Had Lelo used the straight line depreciation method, the depreciation expense would only have been €5,000.

Under IFRS, depreciation methods used only for tax purposes are not admitted and depreciation differences must be nullified. Under certain national accounting standards, however, it is possible to maintain the differences.

A greater depreciation expense enables the company to have a smaller profit and to reduce the actual tax payments. Since, however, the depreciation cannot exceed the purchase price, those differences will be nullified later. If the depreciation is greater today, then it will be smaller tomorrow since the total amount of depreciation must be the same independently from the depreciation methods used. The tax savings of this period will generate additional tax expenses of later periods.

The fact of cancelling the depreciation difference of $8,000 - 5,000 = €3,000$ allows us to recognize a deferred tax liability of $3,000 \times 1/3 = €1,000$.

	12/31/2008		
Non-current assets (+A)		3,000	
Depreciation expense (+IS; +E)			2,000
Deferred tax liability (+L)			1,000
Recognition of a deferred tax liability			

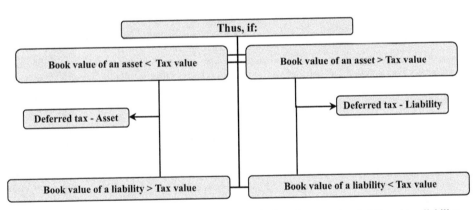

Figure 7.9 Criteria of acknowledgement between Deferred tax asset and deferred tax liability.

Note 16.3 Details of deferred tax (Balance Sheet)

(in million of euros)	2006	2007	2008
Timing differences between company profit and taxable profit	137	137	164
Timing differences between consolidated profit and company profit	78	40	53
Recognized tax losses	82	22	5
SUB-TOTAL, DEFERRED TAX ASSETS	**297**	**199**	**222**
Timing differences between company profit and taxable profit	66	25	40
Timing differences between consolidated profit and company profit	179	145	159
SUB-TOTAL, DEFERRED TAX LIABILITIES	**245**	**170**	**199**
DEFERRED TAX ASSETS, NET (LIABILITIES)	52	29	23

Figure 7.10 Excerpt from the Accor 2008 annual report.

> **Deferred tax assets:** Tax on earnings payable in subsequent years in the form of deductible temporary differences, tax loss carry-forward, or unused tax credit.
>
> **Deductible temporary differences:** Temporary differences that generate amounts deductible from taxable income in subsequent years.

Deferred tax assets must be entered for all **deductible temporary differences** since there will probably be taxable earnings to which these differences can be charged in the future. This is the case for tax loss carry-forward since there will surely be taxable earnings in the future to which it can be applied. These differences generate amounts that are deductible from the determination of taxable income, resulting in a reduction in future taxes owed.

As it is the case for payable tax, deferred tax is recognized in the income statement as either income or an expense and is included in the net income for the year. The corresponding amount is recognized on the balance sheet as an asset or a liability.

APPLICATION 7.7

Recognition of a Deferred Tax Asset

Tinane has made a great loss of €90,000 in 2008. The company will be able to carry this loss forward and lower taxes on future benefits. Hence, the company can recognize a deferred tax asset of $90,000 \times 1/3 = €30,000$.

	12/31/2008		
Deferred tax asset (+A)		30,000	
Deferred tax revenue (+IS; +E)			30,000
Recognition of a future tax credit			

7.3.2 Allocation

> The **liability method** involves allocating tax liability and credit at the tax rate expected to be in effect at the time of payment.

Using the **liability method**, deferred tax liability and credit is calculated and allocated at the tax rate applicable for the period when the asset is created, or the liability is paid. This takes into account how the asset or liability was generated or paid for at the amount expected to be paid or owed. At each year-end, if there has been a change in the tax rate or tax laws (the potential impact of a rate change is entered as equity), the amount of the deferred tax initially calculated is adjusted.

7.3.3 Reporting

Deferred tax liability and credit is reported separately from other liabilities and receivables on the balance sheet of the business, and is also entered separately from current income tax liabilities. Settlement of tax liabilities and credits on the balance sheet is only done if it is legally authorized. In addition, for tax liability, it is only carried out if the company has the intention of earning the income in the same time period, and for deferred tax liability, settlement only occurs if the tax is due to the same tax authority. When a business distinguishes current assets and liabilities from deferred assets and liabilities on its financial statement, the different tax credit and liability are included under deferred assets and liabilities.

7.4   APPENDIX: VALUE-ADDED TAX

Value-added tax is an indirect tax levied on (end) consumers of goods and services.

Value-added tax (VAT) is tax levied on end-consumers of goods and services. In most countries, it represents a significant source of tax revenue for the government. First conceived of by Maurice Lauré in France, VAT is now applied in many countries around the world. In the European Union, it is the only tax common to all member states since the adoption of the Sixth VAT Directive in 1977, which established its application throughout the EU. This directive was actually repealed and replaced by the VAT Directive 2006/112 adopted on November 28, 2006. The revised version is based on established laws and includes the successive revisions and changes made to the initial text.

VAT is generated as added value and is created through a system of instalment payments made by each business participant in the economic circuit, which explains why it is called **value-added tax**. Thus, in a sense, the tax is only paid at the end of the circuit and the overall tax expenditure is equal to the tax calculated on the final value of goods or services.

Transactions subject to the TVA include those carried out for business, industrial, agricultural operations and corporations, as well as by shopkeepers, merchants, craftspeople and self-employed individuals.

7.4.1   VAT Accounting Principles

In theory, this tax does not represent an expense for businesses, which are only intermediary consumers and play a tax collection role. Most transactions carried out by businesses are subject to this tax, except for exports and deliveries made within the European Union, which are exempt in the interest of encouraging international trade (the supplier issues invoices without tax added). Also exempt are post office expenses, insurance premiums, which are subject to a different tax, and financial expenses associated with business loans (bank fees for other banking services are subject to VAT, which the company can claim back).

In most countries, different tax rates exist; the main rate in European countries is between 15% and 25%, with the majority of countries adopting rates close to 20%. Very often, reduced rates are adopted on sales of specific goods and services, such as food, medical services and medicines, books and press, etc. The precise scope of these reduced rates varies from country to country, such as the rates themselves. In France, for example, there are two reduced rates (5.5% or 2.1%), while in Germany there is only one (7%). The VAT is calculated by adding the mandated tax rate to the net sales price including discounts, so that:

$$\text{Before tax value} + \text{VAT} = \text{Tax} - \text{included value}$$

This mechanism triggers simple treasury operations that the company must recognize in its accounting. The VAT amount collected by the company equals what it invoices its customers in addition to the sales price of the services or merchandise provided. The company receives the tax when the invoice is paid. It is then transferred to the government after deduction of any VAT that the company has itself paid through purchases made from its own suppliers. This **deductible VAT** is the VAT amount that a business is invoiced and has to pay to its suppliers; it is then subtracted from the **VAT collected** from its customers.

VAT collection can nonetheless be financially costly for companies due to payment delays. Since according to the VAT tax laws in effect, the company can be obliged to pay back the VAT that it has already been invoiced, but not yet collected in cash by its customers. Significant amounts can therefore be mobilized. More rarely, the VAT can provide the company with a practically constant financial resource, depending on the type of business structure and its sector of activity. Indeed, these transactions pass from liabilities and expense accounts, but do not ever effect the income statement, which should not ever be influenced by the VAT (except in the case where VAT deduction is not allowed by law, expenses are recorded as tax included).

$$\text{VAT payable to the government} = \text{VAT collected} - \text{Deductible VAT}$$

7.4.2 Recording VAT Collected

Only amounts corresponding to the pre-tax amounts for goods and services appear on the income statement. The VAT collected is in no circumstances considered as income, but rather as a debt to the government.

APPLICATION 7.8

Recognition of the Collected VAT from a Sale of Goods

The company LT delivers on 05/15/2009 goods to one of its French clients. The invoice amounts to €100,000 (VAT not included). The VAT rate is 19.6% and the customer must pay within 60 days.

05/15/2009			
Accounts receivable (+A)		119,600	
	VAT collected (+L)		19,600
	Sales of goods (+IS; +E)		100,000
Sale of goods			

The sale or transfer of capital assets is recognized on the balance sheet according to the same logic. The company was able to deduct the VAT when it acquired the assets being resold, but then must add the VAT to the resale price. However, this is not the case if the VAT was not initially deductible.

APPLICATION 7.9

Recognition of the Collected VAT from a Sale of a Non-current Asset

On 04/04/2009, the company LT sells a tangible asset for €50,000 in cash (the VAT is 19.6%).

	04/04/2009		
Cash and cash equivalent (+A)		59,800	
	Collected VAT (+L)		9,800
	Revenues from the disposal of assets (+IS; +E)		50,000
	Disposal of non-current asset paid in cash		

In theory, companies recognize the VAT they collect in their accounting system according to the specific country's liability laws and guidelines. Liability is defined as the tax authority's recognized right to require taxpayers to pay the tax at a given moment. Businesses submit a declaration for the total value of their liable transactions that have been completed within a set time period specified by the tax authority (generally monthly, and within a few days after the month end). The payment is joined to the declaration. There can also be a claim to a refund or credit for the use of goods or services acquired, imported or delivered to the company itself.

> A buyer has the right to VAT deduction from the moment the seller is subject to VAT payment.

Liability rules often vary according to the type of transaction – in France, for example, the following rules apply:

- For **goods**, the VAT is applicable from the delivery of the goods sold. It is therefore the delivery of the goods (when it is physically handed over to the buyer) that triggers this liability. In practice, liability more often corresponds to the invoicing date since the invoice is usually issued at the time of delivery. The date the invoice is paid is never taken into account in determining liability.
- For **services**, the VAT applies from the moment payment (partial or in full) is received for the service, regardless of when the service was provided, or the invoicing date. This system involves the government assuming the credit accorded to the customers. Instalment payments made before the service is provided results in VAT liability. This concerns all types of payment. The buyer is liable (deductible) to VAT from the moment the price is paid. The seller is liable (collected) from the moment the buyer receives payment. An alternative system exists to simplify the process where the VAT is paid when the invoice is issued. Indicating this option on the invoice itself is not strictly required, but it is important that customers should know. The company therefore becomes liable for VAT when the customer's account is debited (when the sum owed is entered on its books) when the invoice is issued. If advance payments have already been made before invoicing, the tax is still owed on the amount.

These rules do not entirely correspond to those of the IFRS regarding revenue recognition. There might therefore be gaps between operations recognized in an IFRS balance sheet, and the VAT amounts relating to these transactions.

7.4.3 Recording Deductible VAT

Only pre-tax amounts for expenses are recognized on the income statement and balance sheet. The VAT paid to suppliers is never, in any circumstances, considered as part of the value of an asset or of an expense, but a receivable towards the government. Only companies that carry out transactions subject to VAT have the right to recover the VAT paid to suppliers as long as the tax paid concerns goods used for the company's operation and they have an invoice from the supplier that specifically indicates the amount of VAT tax paid. The invoice is considered proof of the book entry and the right to deduction. In addition, deduction is only possible once the supplier has paid the tax. Thus it is only once the supplier becomes liable to the tax that the customer can claim the right to the deduction.

APPLICATION 7.10

Recognition of the Deductible VAT from a Purchase of Merchandise

The company Basti bought on credit goods for €100,000 delivered on 05/15/2009.

05/15/2009			
Purchase of goods (−IS; −E)		100,000	
Deductible VAT (+A)		19,600	
	Suppliers (+L)		119,600
Purchase on credit of goods			

However, this kind of entry is not valid if VAT is not deductible by law, even if it appears on the invoice. In this case, the expense amount is entered as a liability tax included. If the item is a capital asset, the amount appears on the balance statement as tax-included, and it is this amount that will be used as a basis for calculating its depreciation, if it can be depreciated. This concerns only specific expenses detailed in the French tax code, including private passenger vehicles and related services such as repairs, and also company expenses on accommodation for executives and their staff (this exclusion is not applicable to expenses related to lodging provided at no cost at construction sites, or at company facilities for security guards and surveillance staff). The fact that the VAT that increased the expense in question is not deductible naturally renders in effect the concept of neutrality, which normally applies to the VAT process, null and void.

APPLICATION 7.11

Purchase of Assets that are Not Tax Deductible

On 08/17/2009 the company Pouli purchases on credit two vehicles: one commercial vehicle for €19,136 (of which 3,136 VAT) and one leisure travel vehicle for €21,528 (of which 3,528 is VAT). Both vehicles are subject to the VAT of 19.6%.

08/17/2009			
Leisure travel vehicle (+A)		21,528	
Commercial vehicle (+A)		16,000	
Deductible VAT (+A)		3,136	
	Suppliers (+L)		40,664
Purchase of vehicles on credit			

On 01/17/2010, both vehicles are repaired for €200 each (VAT not included). Only the tax related to the commercial vehicle is tax deductible. Therefore a global expense of $200 + (200 \times 1.196) = €439.20$ is recognized.

01/17/2010			
Reparation costs (−IS; −E)	439.20		
Deductible VAT (+A)	39.20		
Cash and cash equivalent (−A)		478.40	
Invoice of reparations paid in cash			

Of course, these are only the general accounting mechanisms, and there may be a many special situations depending on the respective national VAT laws.

7.4.4 Recording for the Monthly VAT Declaration

The VAT amount owed to the government minus the deductible VAT is normally declared and paid on a monthly basis. The declaration includes:

- The VAT collected from all sales and services provided for the month in question.
- The deductible VAT for non-current assets acquired during the month.
- The deductible VAT for other goods and services purchased during the month.

This declaration summarizes the company's position in relation to the State. The book entries are made by balancing the corresponding accounts to show the total tax debt or credit.

APPLICATION 7.12

VAT Declaration

In January 2009, the company Marie collects €100,000 of VAT on its sales, a VAT of €20,000 is deductible because of asset purchases and €35,000 is deductible because of purchases of goods and services. At the end of January the company makes the following book entry:

01/31/2009		
Collected VAT (−L)	100,000	
Deductible VAT from non-current asset acquisitions (−A)		20,000
Deductible VAT from operating activities (−A)		35,000
Payable VAT(+L)		45,000
Accounting entries for the VAT declaration for January 2009		

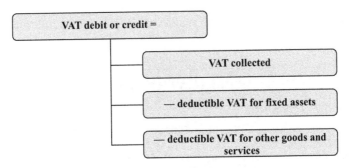

Figure 7.11   VAT determination.

If the VAT collected exceeds the total amount of deductible VAT, the company owes a debt to the government. In this case, the VAT declaration is accompanied by the corresponding payment, which must arrive no later than the 25th of the following month. The payment thus settles the company's payable VAT with a cash account credit.

APPLICATION 7.13

Payment of the Tax Liabilities

The company Marie must pay the €45,000 to the State no later than 02/25/2009.

02/25/2009		
Payable VAT (−L)	45,000	
Cash and cash equivalent (−A)		45,000
Payment of the payable VAT for January 2009		

Conversely, if the amount of deductible VAT is greater than the amount of VAT collected, the company will have a VAT credit. In this case, the government owes the company the difference.

APPLICATION 7.14

VAT Declaration

In January 2009, the company Cali collects €50,000 of VAT on its sales, a VAT of €20,000 is deductible because of asset acquisitions and €35,000 is deductible because of purchases of goods and services. At the end of January the company makes the following accounting entry:

01/31/2009		
Collected VAT (−L)	50,000	
VAT credit (+A)	5,000	
Deductible VAT from asset acquisitions (−A)		20,000
Deductible VAT from operating activities (−A)		35,000
Recognition of a VAT credit in January 2009		

This VAT credit can be used to reduce the amount of VAT due for the following month.

APPLICATION 7.15

Statement of VAT (*continued*)

In February 2009, the company Cali collects €90,000 of VAT on its sales, a VAT of €45,000 is deductible because of purchases of goods and services. No asset purchase takes place. Nonetheless, the company can use the VAT credit of January 2009 of €5,000.

	02/28/2009		
Output VAT (−L)		90,000	
	Input VAT from operating activities (−A)		45,000
	VAT credit (−A)		5,000
	Due VAT (+L)		40,000
	Accounting entries for the statement of VAT for February 2009		

7.5 SUMMARY

Businesses are taxpaying entities subject to a variety of different taxes. They must be familiar with their nature in order to manage them better, especially since they play a major tax collection role on behalf of the government (in particular for VAT). It is important to differentiate income tax from turnover tax, payroll tax and other taxes.

Taxes represent an accounting expense to record. There is currently only one international set of tax standards: IAS 12. These standards apply specifically to income tax accounting, assessment and reporting on financial statements. They were first established in 1981, and then revised in 1996 and 2000 and deal with domestic and international taxes based on taxable earnings.

Corporate income tax (IS in France) is not calculated on the basis of the company's accounting income, strictly speaking, but on its taxable income, which is derived from the accounting income. The difference between the two stems from corrective adjustment not entered on the balance sheet. These modifications either add back value that increases the taxable income, or represent deductions that reduce it.

An expense entered as such, but not recognized for tax purposes, is then added back. This expense, which reduces the accounting income, cannot reduce the taxable income. It is not a tax-deductible expense and cannot be taken into account as such. Deductions can apply to income that would have been entered on the books, but that are not entirely or partially taxable for the tax period in question, and also to expenses not included in the accounting for the period in question, but that are in fact deductible from the taxable income.

Taxable income thus represents the difference between taxable income and deductible expenses. Even if an expense is not tax-deductible, it is still considered an accounting liability and must be entered as such so that the bookkeeping reflects the company's financial situation as accurately as possible.

Tax liability represents an expense for the year and is calculated by applying a tax rate to the taxable income. Though this rate may vary depending on the type of business structure (15% for small and medium-sized companies within certain limits), or for specific kinds of products, it is usually set at 33.33%.

However, according to the IAS 12, tax expenses are not limited to current liabilities, but also include deferred tax. The common practice of taking into account deferred tax is motivated by an interest in considering the taxes due for the year's transactions that may generate savings or tax credit over time, and not just for the period of time in question. This technique makes it possible to enter all of the future tax collection consequences for assets and liabilities on the balance sheet, and to eliminate discrepancies between accounting and taxable income. This helps to prevent tax considerations from distorting the company's apparent financial situation. Deferred tax corresponds to fluctuations in the business's tax liability over subsequent years due to:

- differences between the accounting and taxable income for an asset or liability, or
- losses carried forward (or delayed tax credits).

These temporary differences result from completed transactions with positive or negative tax consequences other than those accounted for in calculating the tax liability, and that are expressed as a difference between the company's accounting income and taxable income in the future.

Deferred tax liability is therefore entered on the balance sheet for all taxable temporary differences, except under particular conditions. It concerns differences that generate amounts that will be liable in the future, and that will therefore represent a future tax expense.

In contrast, deferred tax assets must be entered for all deductible temporary differences as long there will likely be taxable earnings in the near future that they can be applied to. These differences generate amounts that are deductible from the determination of taxable income, resulting in a reduction in future taxes owed.

Sales are taxed according to the "Sales-tax approach" or according to the "Value-added approach". According to the latter, the VAT is not a tax addressed to companies as such, except in special circumstances. Instead, companies play the role of tax collector for a duty that is ultimately paid by end-consumers. They charge VAT on sales of goods and services and then deduct the TVA they have paid for non-current assets and other goods and services (unless the deduction is prohibited by law) from the amount collected. If the difference is positive, the company pays it to the tax administration. If not, it is a debt owed by this administration. Booking mechanisms related to VAT do not affect corporate income statements, only third-party accounts. This system thus results in basic cash account transactions that the company must record in its accounting.

7.6 ACTIVITIES

1.   Recognition of income Tax   Loupie Ltd made a profit of €53,400 in 2008. During the accounting period, the following transactions have to be taken into account:

- Expenses for hunting permits, bought for Loupie's best customer, amounting to €1,500.
- Fines which add up to €100.

Besides, the company recognized revenues of €10,000 which will only be taxable in the next period.

Compute and make the book entries concerning the taxes of those transactions for fiscal year 2008.

2. Recognition of Interim Tax Payments The company Tinane made a taxable income of €3,000,000 in 2007 and €4,500,000 in 2008. The company always closes accounts on December, 31.

    1. *Compute the interim tax payments for 2009, and consider two hypotheses:*

        The taxable income 2009 is €6,000,000.
        Tinane makes a loss in 2009.

    2. *Indicate the corresponding accounting entries.*

3. Determination of Taxable Income 2008 figures of the company BT are as follows:

- An accounting income before taxes of €250,000.
- A tax deposit paid in 2008 for the income tax expense 2008 of €100,000.
- A taxable income of €390,000.

Determine the taxable income of 2007 and BT's tax liabilities at the end of 2008.

4. Computation of the Collected VAT for Sale of Goods Vivi Ltd is a company that purchases goods in order to resell them. For March 2009, it has:

- received a receipt for a delivery of €400,000 (VAT not included);
- delivered goods for €300,000 (VAT not included);
- invoiced a sale of goods for €600,000 (VAT not included);
- received a cash inflow of €598,000.

What is the amount on which the company will compute its output VAT for March 2009 (of 19.6%)?

5. Computation of the Collected VAT for Service Transactions The company Lolo provides services. In March 2009, it has:

- established an estimate of €400,000 (VAT not included);
- carried out a service for an amount of €300,000 (VAT not included);
- invoiced a service for €600,000 (VAT not included);
- received a cash inflow of €598,000 (VAT not included).

What is the amount on which the company will compute its collected VAT for March 2009 (of 19.6%)?

6. Computation of Payable VAT During December 2008, Coco Ltd has delivered goods for €100,000 (VAT not included) and purchased goods and services for €150,000 (VAT not included) of which €20,000 are not tax deductible.

Determine the deductible VAT for December 2008 and write down the corresponding accounting entries.

7. VAT Reimbursement The tax return for the VAT of the company Lelo states for the months January, February and March 2009 the following credits:

- January 2009: €334,000.
- February 2009: €75,000.
- March 2009: €654,000.

Specify if the company can ask for a refund of each credit and, if this is the case, indicate the book entry for the refund.

8 GROUP ACCOUNTS

Many companies maintain close ties to one another through commercial, contractual, or other kinds of agreements. These relationships can create what is referred to as a **group**. In this case, the annual financial statements for each individual company can prove to be frustratingly insufficient as sources of financial information. Usually the transactions carried out between companies within a business group are not subject to the same market conditions as for economically independent companies. In this situation, documenting the financial activities, financial status, and performance for the group as a whole is indispensable for investors and other business partners to assess the value of their investment.

The purpose of **consolidated financial statements** is therefore to give an idea of the financial situation and the transactions carried out by the entire corporate entity composed of legally independent companies. These statements consider the parent company and all the subsidiaries as one single economic entity, even if it is not legally recognized as such. Therefore, they feature only purchases, sales, accounts receivable, debt, investments, and all other transactions with legal entities outside the group.

The transactions completed between companies which are part of the group are therefore removed. It is not enough to just add up the values from each of their balance sheets, income statements and other financial statements or charts to arrive at the consolidated statement. To present an accurate picture of the group's situation as a whole, a process referred to as "consolidation" is required to purge the accounts of any transactions between subsidiaries.

This chapter first describes the different types of relationship that can exist between companies. It then explains in detail the different steps involved in moving from individual subsidiary company accounts to the financial statements for the entire business group in the order shown Figure 8.1.

Group: A parent company and all of its subsidiaries.

Consolidated financial statements: The financial statements of a group presented as those of a single economic entity.

8.1 TYPES OF FINANCIAL RELATIONSHIPS BETWEEN COMPANIES

The requirement to establish **consolidated financial statements** and how accounts are consolidated depend on the level of control or influence that the companies exert on each other. Three types of financial relationships can exist between companies:

- Control (IAS 27)
- Joint control (IAS 31)
- Significant influence (IAS 28).

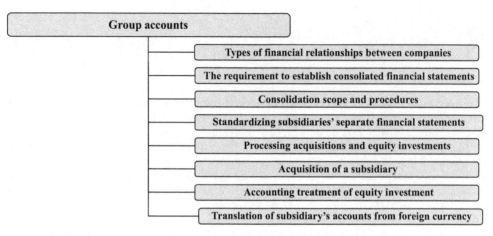

Figure 8.1   From subsidiary's accounts to business group accounts.

8.1.1   Control

Control refers to the power to govern the financial and operating policies of an entity so as to obtain benefits from its activities. The controlling company is called the **parent**, and the entity controlled is the **subsidiary**. This is the strongest connection that can exist between two companies since the subsidiary is completely dominated by the parent company and blends in with the **group**, losing all of its management autonomy.

The power that the parent company has over its subsidiaries can assume different forms depending on the type of control:

- De jure control
- De facto control

De Jure Control   De jure control occurs when the parent company controls directly or indirectly the majority of the subsidiary's voting rights. The number of voting rights does not necessarily correspond to the number of shares controlled by the parent company. Differences between number of shares and number of voting rights may occur in the following circumstances:

- Shares with double or multiple voting rights accorded to, for example, investors demonstrating their interest in participating in the company's management.
- Shares without voting rights.
- Conditional voting rights, related for example to convertible bonds which might be converted into shares.

The parent company's either indirect or direct acquisition of voting rights helps to determine its percentage of control. However, the percentage of equity reflects one company's share ownership in another, and therefore its rights to dividends, and is therefore different from the percentage of control, especially in cases of indirect holding.

Direct control: When one company controls a second company through holding a majority of its votings rights for example.

Indirect control: When one company controls a company indirectly through controlling a third company third company.

APPLICATION 8.1

Percentage of Control

Figure 8.2 discloses participation links between Max, Nick and Sam. Values point out voting rights.

Max directly controls 70% of Nick and so controls Nick's operating and financial strategies. Max also directly controls 20% of Sam but does not have the direct control of the firm.

Nick directly controls 60% of Sam and so controls Sam's operating and financial strategies. Since Max controls Nick, Max controls indirectly Nick's shares in Sam. If we add it to the 20% of direct control of max, the latter controls 80% of Sam's voting rights.

Although the percentage of control of Max in Sam is up to 80%, its percentage of (financial) interest is lower: it corresponds to the addition of 20% (direct control of Max) and 70% $\times$ 60% = 42% through indirect participation. Total interest of Max in Sam is 62%.

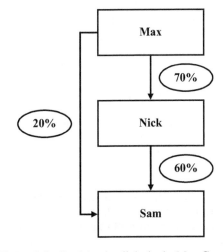

Figure 8.2   Participation links in the Max Group.

De Facto Control   A company that does not own the majority of voting rights in another can still exert **de facto control**. The diversification of the shareholders and the behaviour of certain types of investor (pension funds, venture capital companies, etc.) can grant it:

- Power over more than half of the voting rights according to the terms of an agreement with other investors.
- The power to participate in the entity's financial and operating policy decisions.

Companies of which the Group holds, whether directly or indirectly, the majority of voting rights enabling control to be exercised, are fully consolidated. Companies that are less than 50 % owned but in which VINCI exercises *de facto* control – i.e. has the power to govern the financial and operating policies of an entity so as to obtain benefits from its activities – are consolidated using this same method. This relates mainly to CFE, a Belgium construction group quoted on the Brussels stock market, of which VINCI owns 46.84% and over which it has *de facto* control in view in particular of the widely-held nature of the Company's shareholder register.

Figure 8.3   Excerpt from the 2008 annual report, Vinci.

- The right to appoint or remove a majority of the members of the Board of Directors (or the equivalent administrative body) if it exercises control over the company.
- The power to cast the majority of votes at meetings of the Board of Directors (or the equivalent administrative body) if that body controls the company.

The example of Vinci (see Figure 8.3) and its subsidiary CFE clearly illustrates control in a situation with less than 50% of voting rights.[1] The power to participate in the entity's financial and operating policy decisions is called **in-substance control**.

Special Purpose Entities (or Vehicles)   In some cases, the parent company is granted control by virtue of an agreement even without holding any voting rights and/or capital investment. Controlling another company does not require to be one of its shareholders.

The criteria used to implement the IFRS stress the substance of transactions over their (legal) appearance. Indeed, some business groups remove equipment, property, receivables, and more often debt from their balance sheets and transfer their management to less transparent so-called special purpose entities (SPE). In substance, the company's intention is less the transfer of management of these elements to another entity but rather to derecognize these elements in its own financial statements and to improve by that its financial position as disclosed in its balance sheet. In these cases, control can be revealed through in-depth analysis of the contract clauses. If this analysis confirms the control over the SPE, it will be considered as an entity of the group, and all its, assets and liabilities, revenues and expenses will consolidated in the group accounts, even though there is no apparent legal relationship between the SPE and the parent company.

The reliance on SPEs and the criteria that apply in this context to identify financial control is a good illustration of the underlying principles of the IFRS. Clearly, it is important to understand the standards' ultimate objective in order to better grasp the concept of control.

APPLICATION 8.2

Control and Special Purpose Entities

At the end of 2001, Enron declared dropping economic results. That triggered in particular the reimbursement of all the SPE loans right away, whose existences were not known by the investors. Several thousand SPE blew up bringing out billions of dollars of debts for the group that had been

---

[1]   *More details on full consolidation shown in Figure 8.3 are provided later on in this chapter.*

invisible until then. The Enron case had been the starting point for a fundamental evolution of SPE reporting: Accounting and financial authorities issued new accounting and reporting standards requiring the consolidation of that kind of entities.

SPE's are created for a limited and specific purpose. They can take the form of a legal entity or the form of an organization without its own legal status.

As mentioned above, control may be established even without any investment of the parent company in the SPE. SIC 12 identifies the following types of circumstances that should be considered in evaluating the relationship between a reporting company and a SPE:

- If the SPE engages in predefined activities dictated in its statutes or articles of incorporation. It can therefore neither add nor refuse to comply with these activities.
- If the SPE's activities are carried out on behalf of the company to fulfill specific operating needs in the interest of benefiting from the SPE's advantages.
  - The aim of the SPE is primarily intended to provide the company with long-term financing, or financing for operations that are current or essential to the company.
  - The SPE provides goods and services that are consistent with the company's main operations. Without it, the company would have to provide these goods and services itself.
- In substance, the company holds the decision-making authority needed to take advantage of the majority of the SPE's benefits by implementing a "financial strategy" procedure to delegate decision-making powers.

Examples:

  - The power to unilaterally dissolve a SPE.
  - The power to revise the SPE's charter or bylaws.
  - The power to veto suggested changes to the SPE's charter or bylaws.

- The company has the right to take advantage of the majority of the SPE's benefits and, consequently, is exposed to the risks associated with its business activities.

Examples:

  - The right to the majority of financial benefits offered by an entity in the form of future net cash flow, earnings, net assets or other economic benefits.
  - The right to the majority residual interests in a planned residual distribution or in a liquidation of the SPE.

- In substance, the company assumes the residual or inherent risks associated with ownership of the SPE and its assets.

Examples:

  - The contributors have not a significant interest in the SPE's basic net assets.
  - The contributors do not have any rights to the SPE's future economic benefits.
  - The contributors are not substantively exposed to the inherent risks associated with the SPE's net assets or operations.
  - In substance, the contributors receive compensation equivalent to a lender's return through a debt or equity interest.

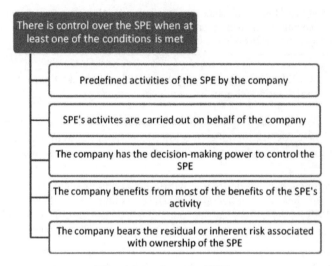

Figure 8.4   Control of SPEs.

When one of these five conditions is met, this might be an indicator for a control-relationship, and the reporting company should consolidate the SPE. Further, this list is not exhaustive and other situations may exist that qualify the relationship as control. Figure 8.4 summarizes the criteria used to identify a company's control over a SPE.

8.1.2   Joint Control

When two or more companies control together another entity, the relationship is qualified as **joint control**. Decisions cannot be made by only one or some of the partners, and no one partner is permitted to impose decisions on the others. Joint control exists only when it is agreed that strategic, financial and operating decisions are to be made unanimously by all involved partners. This sharing of power is not necessarily tied to the distribution of financing, or of the entity's operations among the partners. This situation is relatively rare, and the number of entities that share joint control is usually limited to two or three.

Partners that exert joint control do not always invest financially at the same level or have equal voting rights. Vinci's two-thirds investment in the "Consortium Stade de France" is a good example (see Figure 8.5).[2] Since this investment percentage is significantly greater than 50%, it could be concluded that Vinci is the controlling company. Nevertheless, existing contractual agreements dictate that all decisions related to financial policies and operations must be made jointly with Vinci's partner, Bouygues. It is therefore a case of joint control.

> **Joint control** refers to the shared control of a business activity according to a contractual agreement.

---

[2]   *More details on how to consolidate jointly controlled entities and on proportionate consolidation in Figure 8.5 are provided later on in this chapter.*

Proportionate consolidation is used for jointly controlled entities. This relates in particular to joint venture agreements *(sociétés en participation)* in the construction division, various companies in the concessions division, and Consortium Stade de France, of which VINCI owns 66.67% and where there is a shareholders' agreement with Bouygues, which owns 33.33%. This agreement organises the joint control by this Company's two sole shareholders.

Figure 8.5   Excerpt from the 2008 annual report, Vinci.

8.1.3   Significant Influence

Significant influence refers to the power to participate in the financial and operating policy decisions of an entity, but without control over those policies. A company that is subjected to significant influence is often called the "associated company", especially if the investor holds, directly or indirectly, a substantial investment without the authority to exercise shareholder or partnership rights in managing the company. Thus significant influence is presumed if the investing company holds directly or indirectly at least 20% of the voting rights, unless it can be proven otherwise. If the contribution is less than 20%, the investing company may prove its influence. Voting rights include those that may become available following bond conversion into shares, or bond warrants.

Significant influence over a company can be demonstrated in other ways than through voting rights including, for example:

- Representation on the board of directors or equivalent governing body of the investee;
- Participation in the policy-making process, including participation in decisions about dividends or other distributions;
- Material transactions between the investor and the investee;
- Interchange of management staff;
- Provision of essential technical knowledge.

The distinction between significant influence and control can sometimes be hazy. According to the principles discussed in the section above on control, an investment rate of less than 50%, as in the case of Renault's alliance with Nissan, does not rule out the existence of control. A complete analysis of the financial relationship between the two companies is necessary before making any final conclusions. Figure 8.6 illustrates Renault's representation on Nissan's supervisory board, the role of a subsidiary common to Renault and Nissan, and Renault's position in terms of assets (representing future financial benefits) and debts (representing risks) incurred by Nissan. An analysis of the overall situation leads to the conclusion that Renault does not have outright control, but (only) significant influence over the Japanese auto manufacturer.

> **Significant interest** is the power to participate in the financial and operating decisions of an entity, but not control over those policies.

8.2   THE REQUIREMENT TO ESTABLISH CONSOLIDATED FINANCIAL STATEMENTS

As soon as one company controls at least one other, a parent company-subsidiary relationship exists, and consequently, consolidated financial statements for the group in question are required.

Renault holds 44.3% ownership in Nissan. Renault and Nissan have chosen to develop a unique type of alliance between two distinct companies with common interests, uniting forces to achieve optimum performance. The Alliance is organised so as to preserve individual brand identities and respect each company's corporate culture.

Consequently:

- Renault does not hold the majority of Nissan voting rights.
- The terms of the Renault-Nissan agreements do not entitle Renault to appoint the majority of Nissan directors, nor to hold the majority of voting rights at meetings of Nissan's Board of Directors; at December 31, 2008 as in 2007 and 2006, Renault supplied 4 of the total 9 members of Nissan's Board of Directors
- Renault Nissan BV, owned 50% by Renault and 50% by Nissan, is the Alliance's joint decision-making body for strategic issues concerning either group individually. Its decisions are applicable to both Renault and Nissan. This entity does not enable Renault to direct Nissan's financial and operating strategies, and cannot therefore be considered to represent contractual control by Renault over Nissan. The matters examined by Renault Nissan BV since it was formed have remained strictly within this contractual framework, and are not an indication that Renault exercises control over Nissan.
- Renault can neither use nor influence the use of Nissan's assets in the same way as its own assets.
- Renault provides no guarantees in respect of Nissan's debt.

In view of this situation, Renault is considered to exercise significant influence in Nissan, and therefore uses the equity method to include its investment in Nissan in the consolidation.

Figure 8.6   Excerpt from the Renault annual report, 2008.

A subsidiary can itself be a parent to another company. The subgroup may be exempt from presenting consolidated financial statements if three conditions are met:

- The parent company of the subgroup has informed its other shareholders and business partners of the intention to exercise the exemption and they are not opposed to it.
- The company's securities are not listed on a stock exchange.
- The parent company publishes its consolidated financial statements in compliance with the IFRS and makes them publicly available.

The fact alone of exerting joint control over a company managed with one or more partners, or manifesting significant influence over one or several companies does not alone qualify as forming a group. In these cases, establishing consolidated financial statements is not required.

8.3   CONSOLIDATION SCOPE AND METHODS

8.3.1   Guiding Principle

A group consists of the parent company and its subsidiaries. Holding companies are those that possess stock in subsidiaries with the right of direct intervention in their management. These holdings are purely financial in nature if they are not doing any commercial or industrial activity. Otherwise, they are sometimes called "mixed holdings".

The **scope of consolidation** therefore includes financial statements for the parent company and all of its direct and indirect subsidiaries with information on all business activities in all countries concerned. The consolidated financial statements also show the relationships between the parent company or its subsidiaries and jointly controlled and associated companies. The accounting methods used for each type of company are appropriate to the parent company's level of control or influence: full consolidation, proportionate consolidation, or the equity method.

> **Scope of consolidation:** The financial statements for the parent company and all of its direct and indirect subsidiaries with information on all business activities in all countries concerned.

Full Consolidation   **Full consolidation** refers to the accounting procedure used for subsidiaries. A subsidiary's financial statements are included in their totality in the consolidated statements. This includes all assets and liabilities, income, and expenses, even if the parent company and other subsidiaries' investment in the subsidiary in question is less than 100%. The consolidated balance sheet therefore complies with the essential requirement for the balance sheet, which is to present all elements controlled by the group. However, if the level of investment is less than 100% of the equity, this means that shareholders outside the group have an interest in this subsidiary. They have a right to their share of the subsidiary's assets, liabilities and profits. Their share falls under the heading of **non-controlling interest** on the group's financial statements.

> **Full consolidation:** A consolidation method where a subsidiary's financial statements are included in their totality in the consolidated statements: all assets and liabilities, income, and expenses, even if the parent company and other subsidiaries' investment in the subsidiary in question is less than 100%.

Equity Method   Establishing the existence of significant influence is not enough on its own to justify using the full consolidation method since the target company's assets, liabilities and other aspects are not controlled by the parent company. In this case, the method of consolidation used is called the **equity method** (IAS 28). It involves constantly reevaluating the interest in the business group's equity so that the value of the group's investment in the target company is measured at its share in equity at any given moment. The variations in this value from one year-end to the next are recorded as income for the year in question.

> **Equity method:** Constant re-evaluation of the interest in the group's accounts so that the value of the associate's investment in the group balance sheet corresponds to the group's share in the associate's equity at the closing date.

Proportionate Consolidation   For jointly controlled entities (IAS 31), two consolidation methods are possible: the equity method (described above) and **proportionate consolidation**. The latter is a true consolidation method since all elements appearing on the balance sheet and income statement of the jointly controlled entity are included in the consolidated financial statement, and intercompany transactions are removed. However, these eliminations are only performed at the parent company's rate of investment in the jointly controlled entity.

Disclosure of Consolidation Scope and Methods   The number of companies to be integrated in group accounts can sometimes be very important.

Figure 8.7 shows the number of companies that are included in the scope of consolidation for Vinci (2196 companies as of December 31, 2008). All three consolidation methods are represented.

Number of companies by reporting method

	31/12/2008			31/12/2007		
(number of companies)	Total	France	Foreign	Total	France	Foreign
Full consolidation	1,676	1,069	607	1,610	1,025	585
Proportionate consolidation	433	202	231	404	187	217
Equity method	87	42	45	76	35	41
Total	2,196	1,313	883	2,090	1,247	843

Figure 8.7   Excerpt from the 2008 annual report, Vinci.

A. *Number of Companies Consolidated at Year-End*

	Dec. 31, 2008	Dec. 31, 2007	Dec. 31, 2007
Fully-consolidated companies			
Manufacturing and sales companies	287	290	288
Finance companies	37	36	34
	324	326	322
Companies at equity			
Manufacturing and sales companies	37	37	33
Finance companies	1	1	1
	38	38	34
CONSOLIDATED COMPANIES AT DECEMBER 31	362	364	356

Figure 8.8   Registration document 2008, PSA Peugeot-Citroën.

PSA Peugeot Citroën has chosen to use the equity method for jointly controlled companies. Thus, only full consolidation (324 companies), and the equity method (38 companies) are used (see Figure 8.8).

Figure 8.9 summarizes the relationship between the degree of influence over a company and the consolidation method to use for the consolidated financial statements.

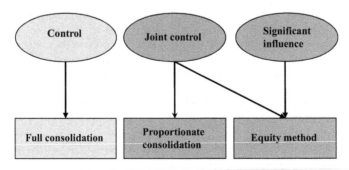

Figure 8.9   Type of control and consolidation method.

> **Proportionate consolidation:** A method of accounting whereby only the venturer's share of each of the assets, liabilities, income and expenses of a jointly controlled entity is included in the consolidated financial statement.

APPLICATION 8.3

Definition of the Scope of Consolidation

SAS Corp. owns equity investments which are detailed in Figure 8.10.

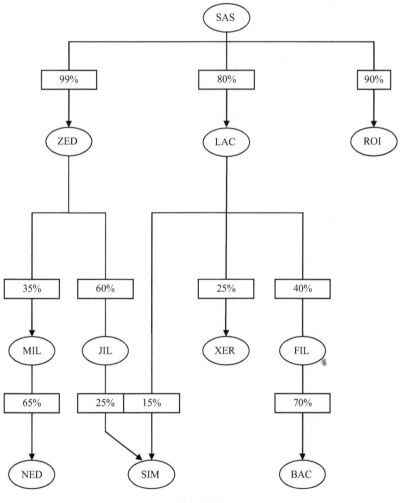

Figure 8.10

Lac appointed the majority of the members of the board of directors of Fil.

Jil owns Sim's shares with double voting rights. Here is an extract of Sim's status: "Every shareholder, whatever his nationality is, whose shares have been nominatives for three years at least, can benefit from a double voting right." No other kind of shareholders benefits from that measure.

What are the level of control and influence that SAS has on other firms?

Answer   First of all, there are three firms of which SAS owns direct equity investments. The percentage of control is the same as the percentage of interest. In these three cases, the percentage is higher than 50%. So, SAS controls all these companies, and therefore they all are fully consolidated.

Firm	Nature of the link	Consolidation method	Percentage of control
Zed	Control (direct)	Full consolidation	99%
Lac	Control (direct)	Full consolidation	80%
Roi	Control (direct)	Full consolidation	90%

Through the control of Zed, SAS controls indirectly Zed's equity investment in Mil and Jil. So, SAS has a significant influence on Mil with 35% of control and controls Jil with 60%. Trough the control of Lac, SAS controls indirectly Lac's equity investment in Xer and Fil. So, SAS has a significant influence on Xer with 25%. The percentage of control of SAS in Fil is only 40%. However, SAS controls the latter through the appointment of the majority of the members of the board of directors.

Firm	Nature of the link	Consolidation method	Percentage of control
Mil	Significant influence (indirect)	Equity method	35% (through Zed)
Jil	Control (indirect)	Full consolidation	60% (through Zed)
Xer	Significant influence (indirect)	Equity method	25% (through Lac)
Fil	Control (indirect)	Full consolidation	40% (through Lac)

Ned is a subsidiary of Mil but SAS does not control Mil. So, SAS does not control either Ned and the percentage of control is 0%. However, SAS deserves a part of the dividends of Ned. Its percentage of interest is: $65\% \times 35\% \times 99\% = 22.5\%$

SAS indirectly controls Jil's and Lac's investments in Sim. Shares of Jil have a double voting right. So SAS controls 2×25 (Jil) $+ 15$ (Lac) $= 65$ parts out of a total of $100 + 25 = 125$. This represents a percentage of control of 52% and means that SAS controls Sim.

SAS also controls Bac through its subsidiary Fil.

Firm	Nature of the link	Consolidation method	Percentage of control
Ned	Control chain broken	No consolidation	0%
Sim	Control (indirect)	Full consolidation	$(25 \times 2 + 15)/125 = 52\%$
Bac	Control (indirect)	Full consolidation	70% (through Fil)

8.3.2   Exclusion from the Scope of Consolidation

IFRS are designed to provide a complete representation of the group as a whole, and only allow exclusions from the scope of consolidation in two situations:

- When the parent company's control is questioned. This can be caused by drastic and long-lasting restrictions on fund transfers. Such restrictions can occur in countries that have instituted foreign exchange controls. Control can also be limited due to legal proceedings or financial legislation in a particular country.
- When the securities held are to be transferred in the immediate future (within 12 months), they cannot be included in calculating the number of voting rights.

However, the lack of a connection between two businesses does not constitute in and of itself a right to exclusion. This is the case for example for industrial multinationals controlling financial institutions. The financial business cannot be excluded from the scope of consolidation merely because this activity is different from the one of the rest of the group.

8.4 HARMONIZING SUBSIDIARIES' SEPARATE FINANCIAL STATEMENTS

Consolidation involves integrating all of the separate financial statements for companies included in the scope. It gives a **true and fair view of the group's net assets, financial structure and income**. The consolidating company must therefore adopt standardized accounting principles that describe guidelines and methods appropriate to its specific characteristics. The subsidiaries' separate financial statements do not always use the group's guidelines and methods since they are established in compliance with local economic, financial, legal and/or tax requirements, which may be different from those for the consolidated statements. In addition, the financial statements for foreign subsidiaries are often established in the local currency. It is therefore necessary to set a common restatement procedure for the financial statements for all subsidiaries in order to present the group's statements in the same currency.

This section first presents an overview of the restatement process in terms of balance sheet dates, presentation and valuation. It then details the restatement procedures for subsidiary statements in foreign currencies.

8.4.1 Guiding Principles

First of all, the closing date for accounting statements must be the same for all of the subsidiaries within the scope of consolidation. However, an exception is possible if the closing date of the subsidiary is not earlier than 3 months before the group closing date, and if adjustments are made for the main transactions. This exception is only justified when it is impossible, or at an excessive cost to establish the financial statements of the subsidiary at the closing date of the consolidated financial statements. If there is a difference in the closing dates, an explanation is provided in the notes. Harmonization also applies to the recognition and measurement of assets, liabilities, expenses and revenues, as well as to the notes. It affects, for example:

- Reclassifying transactions: Some accounting systems include a category for exceptional or extraordinary transactions in the income statement, even though IFRS guidelines for income statement do not allow this presentation. The transactions in question therefore must be redistributed to other categories.
- Depreciation: Several parameters influence which depreciation method a company chooses to use. In particular, tax effects can have a major impact on depreciation expenses. If the method used is not financially justifiable, the transactions in question may need to be restated.

- Provisions: Recognition and measurement principles vary from one country to another.
- Leases: IFRS consider some lease agreements as acquisitions, so they must be restated.
- Income tax: In some countries, the tax liability is only the amount that is owed to the tax authorities for the current accounting period. However, the IFRS recommend the use of the deferred tax method (see Chapter 7).
- Retirement obligations: Some sets of accounting standards, including IFRS, require the recognition of retirement provisions while others do not so and only require disclosure about these obligations in the notes. Differences also exist in the measurement methods used for these provisions (projected units credit method, etc.)
- Debts and accounts receivable denominated in foreign currency: They are measured on the balance sheet at the closing date rate. Some sets of accounting standards do not allow the recognition of unrealized gains in the income statement, but others including the IFRS require their recognition.

8.4.2 Translation of Subsidiary Accounts Denominated in a Foreign Currency

Restating subsidiaries' separate statements that are denominated in different foreign currencies is an important part of harmonization and consolidation procedures. Since the consolidated financial statements are expressed in a single currency, an appropriate method is needed to translate the subsidiaries' accounts into the reporting currency used on the consolidated financial statements.

Companies implement their international strategies through their operations in foreign companies. Above and beyond basic import–export transactions, companies can establish subsidiaries in the countries where they do business, or acquire existing local companies in order to distribute their products in the local or regional market, manufacture products, or conduct research. This legal autonomy affects accounting since the subsidiary must comply with the accounting standards specific to the country where it is located. However, it must also report financial information according to the harmonized accounting guidelines that the parent company has decided to use for its consolidated financial statements.

Foreign currency translation of subsidiaries' annual financial statements into the reporting currency used in the group's consolidated financial statements is therefore a tricky matter. Sometimes dramatic differences in the exchange rates between the different currencies can have a major impact on the group's financial situation and/or net profit. The translation method used must reflect both the group's economic functioning and the relationship between the parent company and subsidiary as accurately as possible.

> **Foreign currency translation:** The conversion of subsidiaries' financial statements in a foreign currency into the reporting currency used in the group's consolidated financial statements.

Types of Currency used by a Group   Three currency concepts are important in the consolidation process: the local currency, the functional currency, and the reporting currency. For a given subsidiary, these can refer to three different currencies, though there may be only one or two involved for the same company. It all depends on the economic context of the subsidiary's business.

Local Currency   The **local currency** refers to the currency used in the country where the parent company or a subsidiary is located. Most often, the company's annual financial statements are presented in this currency to comply with national laws and regulations in the country in question. Annual financial statements in local currency are the basis for the translation process.

Local currency is the legal tender used in the country where the company in question is located.

Functional Currency   The **functional or operating currency** is the currency used in the business environment in which the company's primary activities take place. The local subsidiary therefore must take into account the impact of exchange rate fluctuations on its financial situation and net profit. The functional currency is determined according to several criteria.

In most cases, the currency used for the company's operating transactions is used. This is the currency used, for example, for denominating and paying the sales price for goods and services, or for invoicing and paying expenses (purchases, payroll, etc.). The currency that funds from financing activities are generated in (for issuing equity securities, loans, etc.), and also the currency that is used for managing cash flow for operating activities can also be checked. All of these transactions are carried out in what is referred to as the functional currency.

If several currencies are used for these transactions, additional criteria based on the relationship between the parent company and the subsidiary can be applied. The functional currency is that of the parent company, or a subgroup when the local company is acting as an extension of it. This is the case, for example, for a local company that only distributes goods imported from its parent company and then transfers the funds back to the parent company when the goods are sold. The local company is then referred to as a "non-autonomous entity" as opposed to an "autonomous entity" that carries out its own activities in the local currency. Its expenses, sales and debts are denominated in the local currency, which is also the functional currency in this case. The scale of the transactions between the local company and its parent can also help to assess the degree of autonomy.

In sum, the guiding principle for determining the functional currency is to choose the currency that most accurately represents the substance of the transactions.

Functional currency: The currency that the company in question uses on a daily basis.

APPLICATION 8.4

Functional Currency

The functional currency of all Melt Group subsidiaries in the Eurozone is the euro. Thus, the functional currency is the same as the local currency and so, there is no conversion to do. However, the euro may also be the functional currency outside the Eurozone when main supplying, sale and financial operations are realized in euro. The functional currency is in this case different from the local currency and variations of exchange rate are recognized and measured in the subsidiary accounts in its local currency.

If Melt has several subsidiaries in the USA or in other American countries, their functional currency is probably the US dollar. It will be all the more likely that there are manufacturing sites in that geographic area, that allow a higher level of independence. Their annual accounts must be converted (apart from those in the USA) from their local currency to their functional currency (i.e. US dollar). What is important is the economic substance of the business and not the link between the parent company and its subsidiaries. In the example of Melt, there are two functional currencies but it is common to have many more.

Reporting Currency   The reporting currency is the currency that the group uses for its consolidated financial statements. Most often, it is the same as the parent company's functional currency, but this is not mandatory. Subsidiaries that use a reporting currency other than their functional currency must translate their financial statements. This can represent a second translation procedure if the subsidiary's local currency is not the functional currency.

Reporting currency: The currency used to present the company's financial statements.

APPLICATION 8.5

Reporting Currency

The Melt Group (see Application 8.4) is likely to choose the euro as the reporting currency. In that case, the financial statements of subsidiaries situated in America must be translated into euros. For the subsidiaries on the American continent for which the US dollar is not the local currency, it means that they'll have to translate their accounts twice, a first time from their local currency to their functional currency (US dollar), and a second time from the functional currency (US dollar) to the reporting currency (euro).

Melt could also declare the US dollar as the reporting currency. Indeed, if the group is listed on the stock exchange in the USA but not in Europe, it would be more relevant to publish the accounts in US dollars because the main users of the financial statements would probably prefer them to be published in the local currency.

In contrast to the translation into the functional currency, the main objective of the translation into the reporting currency is not to represent the company's economic situation or assess the performance of the subsidiaries, but to draft the group's consolidated statements in a single currency. This translation method is therefore designed to have as little impact as possible on the relative importance of the various items on the balance sheet and income statement.

Translation into the Functional Currency: The Historical Rate Method

Historical rate method: A translation method aiming at presenting a subsidiary's financial statements as if they had been directly entered in the group's functional currency.

Given that companies generally conduct business in their functional currency, the historical rate method of translation attempts to present a subsidiary's financial statements as if they had

For the purpose of presenting Consolidated Financial Statements, the assets and liabilities of entities with a functional currency other than sterling are expressed in sterling using exchange rates prevailing on the balance sheet date. Income and expense items and cash flows are translated at the average exchange rates for the period and exchange differences arising are recognised directly in equity. Such translation differences are recognised in the income statement in the period in which a foreign operation is disposed of.

Figure 8.11 Excerpt from the 2008 annual report, Vodafone.

been directly entered in the group's functional currency. Thus equipment acquired a few years prior to a given closing date is converted and depreciated according to the exchange rate in effect on the date of acquisition, while cash assets and other elements resulting in monetary exchanges are converted at the exchange rate in effect on the current year's closing date.

To use the historical rate method for balance sheets, monetary entries must be differentiated from non-monetary elements.

- Non-monetary elements include tangible and intangible assets, and inventory. These are elements without rights to receive or deliver a set amount of monetary units. They are converted at the historical exchange rate, meaning the rate in effect on the item's entry date in the company. To be consistent, the depreciation is calculated on the basis of this value as well.
- Monetary elements, such as accounts receivable, cash and debt are either rights to receive or obligations to deliver a set amount of monetary units. They are translated at the exchange rate in effect as of the year's closing date.

For the income statement, income and expenses are translated at the exchange rate in effect at the date of the transaction, or an average rate for a period of time can be used instead. To be consistent with the balance sheet, depreciation expenses are translated at the historical exchange rate at the acquisition date of the corresponding assets. Equity is converted at the exchange rate in effect on the date of recognition of the change in equity. The respective historical exchange rate is used for each increase or decrease of subscribed capital, and for each transfer to or withdrawal from reserves.

Using different exchange rates within the same balance sheet and the same income statement creates discrepancies referred to as **translation adjustments**. These differences come from applying the historical rate method and are recognized through profit and loss. They measure the effect on the local company's financial situation of translating the local currency into the functional currency. The example of Vodafone in Figure 8.11 illustrates the treatment of translation adjustments between the local and functional currencies.

APPLICATION 8.6

Translation to Functional Currency

Breyton is a subsidiary of Mounier's group. Its local accounting system is run in the local currency, "DE". After having analyzed the business of the subsidiary, it can be concluded that its functional currency is the one of Mounier, i.e. the euro. This involves translation from local currency to euros according to the historical rate method.

All fixed assets have been acquired at the creation of the subsidiary at 01/02/2005.

Inventories on 12/31/2008 have been bought at an average rate of 1 DE = €0.85.

Reserves are from the net income:

- of year 2005 for €180,000
- of year 2006 for €220,000
- of year 2007 for €200,000

DE rates have been the following:

- 01/02/2005: 1 DE = €0.75
- 12/31/2005: 1 DE = €1.30
- 12/31/2006: 1 DE = €1.10
- 12/31/2007: 1 DE = €0.95
- 12/31/2008: 1 DE = €0.80

DE average rates have been the following:

- 2005: 1 DE = €0.95
- 2006: 1 DE = €1.20
- 2007: 1 DE = €1.00
- 2008: 1 DE = €0.90

Please find below the balance sheet and the P&L of Breyton in thousands of DE:

Balance sheet on 12/31/2008

Assets	
Fixed assets	2,700
Inventories	180
Trades receivable	1,500
Cash	400
Total assets	**4,780**
Shareholders' equity and liabilities	
Subscribed capital	2,000
Reserves	600
Net income	200
Debts	1,980
Total SE & Liabilities	4,780
P&L	
Sales	2,100
Cost of materials	(1,050)
Other expenses	(900)
Depreciation expenses	(200)
Financial revenues	250
Net income	200

What are the exchange rate to pick out for the different lines of the balance sheet and the P&L?

Assets

Fixed assets	Non-monetary : acquisition historical rate: 0.75
Inventories	Non-monetary : acquisition historical rate: 0.85
Trades receivable	Monetary : closing rate: 0.80
Cash	Monetary : closing rate: 0.80

Shareholders' equity and liabilities

Subscribed capital	Non-monetary : acquisition historical rate: 0.75
Reserves	Non-monetary : weighted average of historical rate : 0.95 for 2005, 1.20 for 2006, 1.00 for 2007
Net income	Difference between Liabilities and Assets
Debts	Monetary : closing rate: 0.80

P&L

Sales	Average rate of the year: 0.90
Cost of materials	Average rate of the year: 0.90 (even if a part of the inventories has been bought at 0.85)
Other expenses	Average rate of the year: 0.90
Depreciation expenses	Acquisition historical rate: 0.75
Financial revenues	Average rate of the year: 0.90

Financial statements of Breyton in thousands of euros:

Balance sheet on 12/31/2008

Assets

Fixed assets	$2,700 \times 0.75 = 2,025$
Inventories	$180 \times 0.85 = 153$
Trades receivable	$1,500 \times 0.80 = 1,200$
Cash	$400 \times 0.80 = 320$
Total assets	**3,698**

Shareholders' equity and liabilities

Subscribed capital	$2,000 \times 0.75 = 1,500$
Reserves	$(180 \times 0.95 = 171 + 220 \times 1.20 = 264 + 200 \times 1.00 = 200) = 635$
Net income	-21
Debts	$1,980 \times 0.80 = 1,584$
Total SE and liabilities	**3,698**

P&L

Sales	$2,100 \times 0.90 = 1,890$
Cost of materials	$-1,050 \times 0.90 = -945$
Other expenses	$-900 \times 0.90 = -810$
Depreciation expenses	$-200 \times 0.75 = -150$
Financial revenues	$250 \times 0.90 = 225$
Translation adjustment	-231
Net income	**-21**

The functional currency involves a new assessment of the performance of the firm. A DE 200,000 profit becomes a €21,000 loss.

Translation into the Reporting Currency: The Closing Rate Method

---

Closing rate method: The financial statements denominated in the functional currency are translated into the group's reporting currency using the exchange rate in effect on the year's closing date.

Closing rate: The exchange rate at the financial statements' closing date.

The **closing rate method** is used to translate financial statements denominated in the functional currency into the group's reporting currency. The goal is to maintain the initial equilibrium within the financial statements to allow the entity's performance to be assessed. The financial risk associated with exchange rate variations appears under the heading *Equity translation adjustment* in Other comprehensive income, without altering profit or loss.

For example: the functional currency for an American subsidiary is the dollar (USD), while for its French parent company, it is the euro, and the group's financial statements are presented in euros. The subsidiaries' accounts are translated using the closing rate method according to the following rules:

- Assets (assets, inventory, accounts receivable, cash) and debts are translated at the exchange rate in effect at the balance sheet **closing date**.
- Income and expenses are translated at the exchange rate in effect at the time of the transactions. However, to make things easier, an average rate for the period can be used instead.
- The resulting translation adjustment is recognized as a special item within Other comprehensive income.

For PSA Peugeot Citroën the fact that the local currency is the functional currency of the subsidiary is the common case. Financial statements of these subsidiaries are translated to euro according to the closing rate method, as mentioned under "A. Standard method" in Figure 8.12. Nevertheless, there are some subsidiaries for which the local currency is not the functional currency but the euro. Their financial statements are translated into euro according to the historical rate method, as indicated under "B. Specific method".

As is the case in Application 8.6, Application 8.7 is also based on the example of Breyton, but this time the functional currency is the same as the local currency.

APPLICATION 8.7

Reporting Currency Translation

We supposed that Breyton's local currency is its functional currency (DE). Its annual accounts perfectly represent the economic performances of the firm in the group. The closing rate method does not change the balance sheet's or the income statement's structure.

The financial statements of Breyton converted according to the closing rate method are presented below (all in thousands of euro).

Balance sheet on 12/31/2008

Assets

Fixed assets	$2,700 \times 0.80 = 2,160$
Inventories	$180 \times 0.80 = 144$
Trade receivable	$1,500 \times 0.80 = 1,200$
Cash	$400 \times 0.80 = 320$
Total assets	**3,824**

Shareholders' equity and liabilities

Subscribed capital	$2,000 \times 0.75 = 1,500$
Reserves	$(180 \times 0.95 = 171 + 220 \times 1.20 = 264 + 200 \times 1.00 = 200) = 635$
Net income	$200 \times 0.90 = 180$
Translation adjustment	-75
Debts	$1,980 \times 0.80 = 1,584$
Total SE and liabilities	**3,824**

Income statement

Sales	$2,100 \times 0.90 = 1,890$
Cost of materials	$-1,050 \times 0.90 = -945$
Other expenses	$-900 \times 0.90 = -810$
Depreciation expense	$-200 \times 0.90 = -180$
Financial revenues	$250 \times 0.90 = 225$
Net income	$\mathbf{200 \times 0.9 = 180}$

The variations of the currency rate are listed in the currency gap line Other comprehensive income and do not impact the net profit or loss. That gap measures the difference between the capital invested by the shareholders (valuated at their historical rate) and assets/liabilities converted at the closing rate.

A. Standard Method

The Group's functional currency is the euro (€), which is also the presentation currency in the consolidated financial statements. The functional currency of most foreign subsidiaries is their local currency, corresponding to the currency in which the majority of their transactions are denominated. The balance sheets of these subsidiaries are translated at the year-end exchange rate and their income statements are translated on a monthly basis at the average exchange rate for each month. Gains and losses resulting from the translation of financial statements of foreign subsidiaries are recorded in equity under "Translation reserve". Goodwill arising on the acquisition of these subsidiaries is measured in their functional currency.

B. Specific Method

The functional currency of some subsidiaries outside the euro zone is considered to be the euro because the majority of their transactions are denominated in this currency. Non-monetary items in these subsidiaries' accounts are translated at the historical exchange rate and monetary items at the year-end rate. The resulting translation gains and losses are recognised directly in profit or loss.

Figure 8.12 PSA Peugeot Citroën, Annual report 2008.

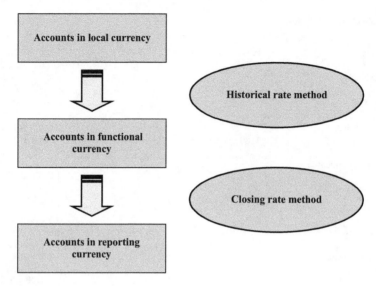

Figure 8.13   Steps to translate subsidiaries' accounts denominated in a foreign currency.

Figure 8.13 summarizes the translation procedure for subsidiary accounts denominated in foreign currency according to the closing rate method.

Special Treatment for Companies in Countries with Hyperinflationary Economies   IAS 21 specifies procedures for subsidiaries based in countries where inflation is especially high, termed hyperinflationary economies. Such an economic situation complicates the comparision of financial statements. The IAS provisions involve translating financial statements into the functional currency, regardless of the currency denomination initially used to prepare the financial statements of the local entity. Adjustments are then made for the inflationary effects since the functional currency is a melting local currency. Finally, the closing date method is applied.

8.5   CONSOLIDATING INTERCOMPANY TRANSACTIONS

Intercompany transactions: Intercompany transactions between subsidiaries within the same business group, which are removed from financial statements during the consolidation process.

A business group is an economic entity in its own right, and the consolidated financial statements must exclusively represent its transactions with third parties. **Intercompany transactions** (internal purchase, sales, and financing transactions) entered in the separate financial statements for the member companies of the group in question are therefore excluded. These accounts are simply canceled out by each other so that only the incoming and outgoing cash flows to/from outside the group appear. The treatment to consolidate these reciprocal transactions becomes overly complicated if earnings are generated internally. At the group-level, it is considered to be 'false' profits or losses since they were not gained via transactions with an external partner. Therefore, the effects on net income related to these operations must be removed from the consolidated financial statements. Insofar as such re-statements concern net income for previous periods, the effects will impact previous years' net income, i.e. the reserves. This mechanism and the reason behind it will be illustrated below for the cases of income on inventory, the disposals of non-current assets, as well as for the dividends paid to companies within the group.

- **Dividends paid to parties within the group.** Dividends paid by a subsidiary to its parent company will increase the parent company's profits and cash. The dividends received are recognized as financial income in the parent company's income statement. As part of the consolidation procedure, they must be removed from the current year's income since they come from revenues generated and recognized during the previous year in the subsidiary's income statement. As a compensation, the amount removed from the current year's net income will be added to the group reserves, since it represents previous year's income that is still within the group.
- **Income from inventory.** If goods exchanged within a group have not been resold to external customers, they appear under the purchasing company's inventory. It is necessary therefore to eliminate the profits, or losses included in the inventory acquisition cost. These earnings are cleared by crediting the inventory and in exchange debiting the appropriate item in the income statement (cost of goods, etc.). The final inventory will become the initial inventory level of the following year and will be cleared by the reserves that include, by definition, the profits and losses recorded for the previous years. The income for the seller will be eliminated even if the inventory is physically located at the purchasing company. This adjustment is important for correctly distributing earnings between the group and non-controlling interests.
- **Gains and losses on disposals of non-current assets.** Effects on net profit of the disposal of an asset within a group are eliminated so that the asset appears on the consolidated balance sheet at its 'historical' amortized cost with the following consequences:
  - The disposal gain or loss is eliminated in the seller's income statement. In subsequent years, this amount will be allocated to reserves.
  - In the acquiring company's accounts, the disposal income is deducted from the cost of the asset. Depreciation will therefore be calculated based on the "historical" cost when the asset entered the group rather than on the cost for the acquiring company.

Consequently, the depreciation expense recorded for in the separate financial statements of the company are adjusted in order to be consistent with the cost from the group perspective. However, disposals within the group can occur due to circumstances that justify changing the depreciation plan (useful life, depreciation method...)

If the transaction generates an internal loss, it must in theory be cleared. However, such a loss may be an indicator for an impairment of that asset and therefore may lead to an impairment test according to IAS 36.

Application 8.8 graphically illustrates accounting procedures for transactions within the group.

APPLICATION 8.8

Intercompany Operations Consolidation

Firma is a subsidiary of Martin. The following operations occurred during 2008 (thousands of euros):

- Martin bought products from an external supplier for 1,400.
- Martin sold these products to Firma for 1,640 and so realized a margin of 240.
- Firma sold a part of these products to external customers for 1,500.
- At the end of the year, Firma's inventory is valued at 410, it corresponds to the remaining 25% of the products bought from Martin.
- The tax rate is 33.33%.

These operations are realized in accrual accounting and are listed as follows in the accounts of Martin and Firma.

P&L of Martin

Sales	1,640
Purchases	(1,400)
Operating result	240
Income tax	(80)
Net Income	160

P&L of Firma

Sales	1,500
Purchases	(1,640)
Inventory variation	410
Operating result	270
Income Tax	(90)
Net Income	180

Extract of Martin and Firma accounts: consolidation elimination process

- Elimination of reciprocal revenues and expenses

Sales		1,640	
	Purchases		1,640

- Elimination of reciprocal receivables and payables

Suppliers		1,640	
	Receivables		1,640

- Elimination of internal gain on inventory

75% of the goods bought from Martin for 75% of 1,640 = 1,230 have been sold again to external customers for 1.500. The margin of 75% × 240 = 180 realized on the sale from Martin to Firma has been accounted for and has even been increased by 1,500 − 1,230 = 270 thanks to the sale to external customers.

However, 25% of the goods have not been sold again. The margin realized by Martin when it sold these goods to Firma (25% of 24,060) has not yet been "validated" by the sale to an external customer and has to be eliminated from the group operating result. Thus, inventory in the balance sheet will be reduced, while inventory variation in the P&L will be increased.

Cost of goods		60	
	Inventory		60

- Adjustment of the tax expense – deferred tax

The profit eliminated in the operation above had increased Martin's net income and had also been subject to corporate tax. Therefore, the group tax expenses have to be adjusted as well. According to the available information, we can consider that this is just a time difference between the consolidated net income and the entity's net income as the related goods are supposed to be sold to a third party in a near future.

The adjustment will reduce the tax expense in the consolidated P&L, and as compensation, an asset "Deferred tax" will be recorded in the balance sheet. This asset will disappear when the goods will be sold to a third party. The tax expense on the final margin on this sale (one third) will then be recognized in the consolidated accounts.

Deferred tax – Asset		20	
	Deferred tax		20

The addition of expenses and revenues of Martin and Firma allow the preparation of an extract of the consolidated P&L after the eliminations mentioned above. That allows a better understanding of the impact of intercompany transactions.

Consolidated P&L	
Sales	1,500
Purchases	(1,400)
Inventory valuation	350
Operating result	450
Income tax	(170)
Deferred tax	20
Net income	300

The income before tax amounts to 450 and is composed of the margin of 180 realized by Martin on the sale to Firma and the margin of 270 realized by Firma on the sale to external customers.

It is important to be aware that consolidated income tax expense amounts to $170 - 20 = 150$ and corresponds to:

Martin tax	80
Firma tax	90
Deferred tax	(20)
Total	150

In practice, the reciprocal accounts don't always cancel one another out for two reasons. The flow of information between companies within the group can sometimes be faulty. The resulting differences can be limited through thorough and regular reconciliation of the reciprocal accounts. Differences can also be due to transactions that straddle the closing date. This would be the case, for example, for a funds transfer that a lending company recognizes when it is credited from the bank account and recognizes a corresponding receivable at the same date, but for which the borrowing company does not receive the amount before the closing date and therefore does not book for anything. An adjustment has then to be made to the accounts to clear the transaction.

8.6   ACQUISITION OF A SUBSIDIARY

A parent–subsidiary relationship between companies can arise when the parent company creates a new company, or when it acquires a pre-existing company. The latter case is referred to as a business combination. IFRS 3 describes the accounting procedures for business combinations.

The acquirer is the company that assumes control of the other company (the acquiree). The acquisition date is when the control over the acquiree's activities is officially transferred to the acquirer. The acquisition cost is valued as of the date on which the acquirer legally transfers the consideration. In the case of successive buy outs, the acquisition cost is assessed at the date when the acquirer obtains the control of the acquiree.

The cost of the business combination is equivalent to the fair value of the contributions made by the acquirer in exchange for the control of the acquired company. Since the most recent revision of IFRS 3, the costs directly associated with the transaction (external costs such as consulting fees, auditors, evaluators, and lawyers) previously included in the cost of acquisition are now entered as expenses.

The payment of an acquisition can be realized through cash payments, or an exchange of securities (shares, obligations, etc.). Application 8.9 illustrates these forms of acquisition payment for the combination of Approl and Respla.

APPLICATION 8.9

Exchange Process for Acquisitions

Approl wants to take control of Respla. Respla currently has floating shares and convertible bonds. Approl suggests the following exchange modes:

- For the shares: 1 share of Approl in exchange for 5 shares of Respla
- For the convertible bonds: 1 bond convertible into 5 shares of Respla in exchange for 3 shares of Approl plus €3 cash.

When a company is acquired, the challenge in terms of accounting consists in reconciling the acquisition cost recognized in the parent company's balance sheet with the assets and liabilities on the subsidiary's balance sheet.

Usually, the acquisition cost of the subsidiary's securities significantly exceeds the company's net accounting value or the acquired share of it for three main reasons:

- The carrying amount of certain assets and liabilities does not represent their fair value. For assets, the balance sheets often include accounting values below the fair value. Thus, property acquired years ago and valuated at the historical acquisition cost is often undervalued compared to its current market value. The difference is taken into account in determining the acquisition cost.
- Some assets, especially intangible assets, do not appear on the acquiree's balance sheet even though the post-reconciliation statement must include all identifiable assets and liabilities. For example, the value of a brand created by the target company itself is not recognized on its balance sheet since self-created brands are not recognized. The brand's value is, nonetheless, estimated at the time of acquisition and is included in the price paid by the acquirer.
- For most acquisitions, one final part of the acquisition cost cannot be allocated to either the assets or liabilities. This difference reflects the present value of the expected financial benefits from unidentifiable assets and can include the value of expected synergies generated by the acquisition. Some existing departments in both companies will be redundant and can be combined, and some neighbouring sales outlets in the distribution network and even production sites can be closed to avoid limiting the new business combination's capacity to generate future economic benefits. This is usually termed **goodwill**.

The following sections in this chapter explain in detail the three steps involved in acquisition cost allocation. The acquirer has a limit of 12 months from the initial transaction date to complete the allocation.

Goodwill: The accounting purchase discrepancy between the acquisition cost for a new subsidiary purchase and its recognized value on the parent company's books.

8.6.1 Revaluation of a Subsidiary's Assets and Liabilities

On the acquirer's balance sheet, the subsidiary's assets and liabilities must be valuated at their fair value after reconciliation. This corresponds to the price that an asset or liability would have been worth under normal conditions between unrelated, consenting well-informed parties. There are several methods that can be used to determine fair value, including the following (in order of preference):

- Reference to an observable transaction for identical items recently exchanged in an active market.
- Market price adjustment observed on the acquisition date for a similar asset or liability.
- Application of several valuation methods and estimation techniques based on hypothetical situations determined by the entity itself.

This initial value is the basis for subsequent measurement taking into account depreciation, amortization or impairment. It also has repercussions on gains or losses if the group proceeds to a disposal at a later date.

APPLICATION 8.10

Post Acquisition Value

Santepharma takes the control of 80% of Clinica on December 31, 2008. At this time, the shareholders' equity of Clinica was up to £500,000. Its fixed assets are composed of a building measured at its depreciated (historical) cost of £100,000. An independent expert estimates the fair value of this building up to £200,000.

The building is measured at £200,000 in the consolidated balance sheet.

8.6.2 Identifying New Assets and Liabilities

The post-acquisition balance sheet should feature all of the acquiree's identifiable assets and liabilities, including any contingent liabilities. Thus any items that appear only under certain conditions and therefore are not disclosed on the target company's balance statement are recognized as a liability after the combination, as long as their fair value can be reliably measured.

Experience proves that mainly two new categories of items beyond those already disclosed on the target company's balance sheet appear on the consolidated balance sheet after reconciliation:

- Intangible assets that did not meet the criteria for recognition in the separate financial statements of the acquired entity,
- Provisions for corporate restructuring planned as part of the business combination process in the interest of increasing synergy between the two entities and improve overall profitability.

Intangible Assets

Intangible assets are non-monetary assets without physical substance.

By definition, intangible assets are more difficult to identify than tangible assets. Tangible assets are resources with a physical substance together with a right to property, or at least a right of use, and with a known market value. In contrast, **intangible assets** are non-monetary assets that cannot be seen, touched or physically measured. In addition, some of them are generated internally and are therefore not recognized on the balance sheet (brands, patents, etc.).

As part of the acquisition process, the acquirer must recognize each tangible asset belonging to the acquiree separately at the date of acquisition. Each item must qualify as an asset, which means that it must:

- Be identifiable:
  - meaning that it can be separated or detached from the entity and sold, transferred, licensed, rented or exchanged as an asset or liability, either separately or as part of a contract;

- or result from contractual or legal rights, regardless of whether the rights are transferable or separable from other rights and obligations.

- Grant the entity control over a resource. Control is defined as the entity's capacity to obtain future economic benefits associated with the asset and to restrict access to these benefits to a third party.
- Generate future economic benefits such as sales revenue from products or services, cost reduction, or other benefits associated with its use.
- Have a fair value that can be measured reliably.

All items that meet these conditions must be recognized separately without being combined with other elements. The IFRS provide a list of identifiable intangible assets, some examples are:

- Brands.
- Magazines.
- Registered internet domain names.
- Commercial agreements (contracts).
- Customer lists (separable).
- Licenses, franchises, broadcasting rights.
- Concession agreements (toll roads, water distribution, etc.).
- Research and development projects (separable).

Market share and human capital are not on this list because they are neither separable from the company nor legally recognized. However, they are indirectly recognized and measured when identifying goodwill.

The table in Figure 8.14 shows the breakdown of purchase cost allocation in the case of Vodafone Essar acquisition by Vodafone. Fair value adjustments are particularly important for intangible assets whose value rises from £121m to £3,189m.

APPLICATION 8.11

Brand Valuation

The Ski-Rossignol Group discloses in its 2004 annual report the brands Look, Lange and Never Compromise for a total value of approximately €12m. The Rossignol brand is not recognized because the group had created it internally. It therefore does not match the criteria for an asset, in particular the fair value measurement.

In 2005, the American group Quicksilver acquired Ski-Rossignol. That transaction between Quicksilver and the Rossignol's former shareholders could give a reliable value to the Rossignol brand and so assign a part of the acquisition cost to the value of the brand. Thus, in the 2005 Quicksilver balance sheet, the Rossignol brand is valued approximately $95m.

Since then, the situation changed a lot and the Rossignol brand lost a big part of its value. Quicksilver sold the whole Ski-Rossignol Group in November 2008 for $50m to an investment fund run by Rossignol's former CEO.

Vodafone Essar Limited (formerly Hutchison Essar Limited)

On 8 May 2007, the Group completed the acquisition of 100% of CGP Investments (Holdings) Limited ("CGP"), a company with indirect interests in Vodafone Essar Limited ("Vodafone Essar"), from Hutchison Telecommunications International Limited for cash consideration of US$10.9 billion (£5.5 billion). Following this transaction, the Group has a controlling financial interest in Vodafone Essar.

	Book value £m	Fair value adjustments £m	Fair value £m
Net assets acquired:			
Identifiable intangible assets	121	3,068	3,189[1]
Property, plant and equipment	1,215	(155)	1,060
Other investments	199	–	199
Inventory	5	(2)	3
Taxation recoverable	5	–	5
Trade and other receivables	277	13	290
Cash and cash equivalents	51	–	51
Deferred tax asset/(liability)	36	(512)	(476)
Short and long term borrowings[2]	(1,467)	(16)	(1,483)
Provisions	(11)	–	(11)
Trade and other payables	(534)	(35)	(569)
	(103)	2,361	2,258
Minority interests			(936)
Written put options over minority interests[2]			217
Goodwill			3,950
Total consideration (including £34 million of directly attributable costs)[3]			5,489

Notes:
(1) Identifiable intangible assets of £3,189 million consist of licences and spectrum fees of £3,045 million and other intangible assets of £144 million. The weighted average lives of licences and spectrum fees, other intangible assets and total intangibles assets are 11 years, two years and 11 years, respectively.
(2) Included within short term and long term borrowings are liabilities of £217 million related to written put options over minority interests.
(3) After deducting cash and cash equivalents acquired of £51 million, the net cash outflow related to the acquisition was £5,438 million, of which £5,429 million was paid during the 2008 financial year.

Figure 8.14 Vodafone, annual report 2008.

Restructuring Provisions Acquiring companies are often tempted to set aside provisions for corporate restructuring to anticipate costs that come with integrating a new subsidiary into the group. These expenses can be related to everything associated with economies of scale (reducing the number of employees, concentrating the capacities of production or the structure of distribution, etc.). Such restructuring costs can only be recorded as identifiable liabilities if they represent liabilities for the target company no later than at the date the acquirer takes control. In other words, restructuring plans must be detailed and announced as soon as the acquisition takes place.

Anticipated operating losses are not grounds for provisions. Assets are measured at their market value which, by definition, does not include the acquirer's intentions (transfer, reorganization, etc.). The impact of the new operating conditions will be represented in the income statements over subsequent years as changes in depreciation expenses etc. An impairment loss is recognized if the recoverable amount is less than the value recorded for at the date of acquisition.

8.6.3 Goodwill

Goodwill refers to the residual value from the acquisition cost of an entity after its allocation to the fair values of all of the subsidiary's identifiable assets and liabilities. It is an excess cost assumed by the acquirer. However, IFRS 3 as revised in 2007 grants companies a "full goodwill" option. The purpose is to recognize a goodwill that also includes an amount attributable to non-controlling interests. This method is based on the concept of the group as an "economic entity" belonging to two types of owners.

The true goodwill value is difficult to assess because it is mainly based on the subsidiary's growth potential after the combination. Goodwill includes, for example:

- Valuation of expected economic benefits from unidentifiable assets (research, human capital, a sales network, market share, synergies, etc.).
- Anticipated losses on the part of the acquirer or contingent liabilities on the part of the subsidiary entered in the balance sheet after the business combination.
- The consequences from overbidding, or from a well-negotiated bargain deal.

Goodwill can therefore be positive or negative. If it is positive, it is recognized as an asset that may represent a relatively significant part of the non-current assets on the consolidated financial statements.

APPLICATION 8.12

Goodwill Calculation

Santepharma took control of 100% of Innovpharma on 12/31/*N* for £10,000. Innovpharma's shareholders' equity is up to £8,000. Its assets and liabilities are reliably valued. According to IFRS 3, a goodwill for £2,000 has to be disclosed in the consolidated balance sheet of the group.

Positive Goodwill   Goodwill is recognized as an intangible non-current asset. An acquisition is usually strategically motivated by the anticipated long-term effects, future economic benefits (economy of scale, synergy, expertise, etc.) over a long period of time that is difficult to estimate and depends on a variety of factors. It is therefore not possible to estimate the useful life of goodwill; its useful life is indefinite. As a consequence, goodwill is not amortized, but subject to a yearly impairment test.

The impairment test can be carried out at any time between two closing dates and attempts to assess goodwill based on the current cash flow.

Goodwill cannot be dissociated from other assets since it does not generate cash flow in and of itself. It is therefore included in a cash-generating unit,[3] which is the smallest group of assets and liabilities to which cash flows can be attributed.

If the recoverable value of the cash-generating unit is less than its net book value, the loss is first allocated to goodwill. If the goodwill cannot absorb all of the loss, the balance is allocated to the other identifiable assets of the cash-generating unit, proportionally to their carrying amount or another appropriate method.

Figure 8.15 shows the methodology used by British Petroleum and disclosed in its 2008 annual report. One of the assumptions to set concerns the interest rate used for discounting cash flows. These kinds of assessment must be updated yearly.

Other assumptions concern evolutions of future prices. Especially in a highly volatile market like the oil and gas market, these assumptions are very difficult to assess, and may be subject to important changes from one year to another, with potential significant consequences for the

---

[3] *See Chapter 5.*

The group calculates the recoverable amount as the value in use using a discounted cash flow model. The future cash flows are adjusted for risks specific to the cash-generating unit and are discounted using a pre-tax discount rate. The discount rate is derived from the group's post-tax weighted average cost of capital and is adjusted where applicable to take into account any specific risks relating to the country where the cash-generating unit is located. Typically rates of 11% or 13% are used (2007 11% or 13%). The rate to be applied to each country is reassessed each year. A discount rate of 11% has been used for all goodwill impairment calculations performed in 2008 (2007 11%).

Figure 8.15 British Petroleum, annual report 2008.

result of the impairment test, as the excerpt from the British Petroleum report shows (Figure 8.16).

Given these risks of important changes in key assumptions, some groups disclose a sensitivity analysis for some of these key data and/or for selected data. The British group Vodafone (Figure 8.17) uses four key assumptions, and it indicates for two countries, Germany and Italy, the isolated changes of each of these assumptions which would be necessary to equal carrying amount and value in use of the related cash generating units.

For the purposes of impairment testing, the group's Brent oil price assumption is an average $49 per barrel in 2009, $59 per barrel in 2010, $65 per barrel in 2011, $68 per barrel in 2012, $70 per barrel in 2013 and $75 per barrel in 2014 and beyond (2007 average $90 per barrel in 2008, $86 per barrel in 2009, $84 per barrel in 2010, $84 per barrel in 2011, $84 per barrel in 2012 and $60 per barrel in 2013 and beyond). Similarly, the

group's assumption for Henry Hub natural gas prices is an average of $6.16/mmBtu in 2009, $7.15/mmBtu in 2010, $7.34/mmBtu in 2011, $7.62/mmBtu in 2012, $7.60/mmBtu in 2013 and $7.50/mmBtu in 2014 and beyond (2007 average of $7.87/mmBtu in 2008, $8.33/mmBtu in 2009, $8.26/mmBtu in 2010, $8.12/mmBtu in 2011, $8.00/mmBtu in 2012 and $7.50/mmBtu in 2013 and beyond). The prices for the first five years are derived from forward price curves at the year-end. Prices in 2014 and beyond are determined using long-term views of global supply and demand, building upon past experience of the industry and consistent with a number of external economic forecasts. These prices are adjusted to arrive at appropriate consistent price assumptions for different qualities of oil and gas.

Figure 8.16 British Petroleum, annual report 2008.

31 March 2008

As of 31 January 2008, the date of the Group's annual impairment test, the estimated recoverable amount of the Group's operations in Germany and Italy exceeded their carrying value by £2,700 million and £3,400 million respectively. The table below shows the key assumptions used in the value in use calculation and the amount by which each key assumption must change in isolation in order for the estimated recoverable amount to be equal to its carrying value in both cases.

	Assumptions used in value in use calculation		Change required for carrying value to equal the recoverable amount	
	Germany	Italy	Germany	Italy
	%	%	Percentage points	Percentage points
Pre-tax adjusted discount rate	10.2	11.5	1.6	2.7
Long term growth rate	1.2	0.1	(1.7)	(3.0)
Budgeted EBITDA[1]	(2.2)	1.4	(2.0)	(4.2)
Budgeted capital expenditure[2]	7.5 to 8.7	5.8 to 9.5	4.2	6.6

Notes:
(1) Budgeted EBITDA is expressed as the compound annual growth rates in the initial five years of the Group's approved management plans.
(2) Budgeted capital expenditure is expressed as the range of capital expenditure as a percentage of revenue in the initial five years of the Group's approved management plans.

Figure 8.17 Sensitivity analysis for key assumptions – Vodafone, annual report 2008.

An impairment loss on goodwill cannot be recovered, even if the recoverable amount of the cash-generating unit increases in the future. Therefore, the impairment test may have major consequences for the group since it represents a permanent decline in the group's earnings and consequently in its equity, and therefore has an immediate impact on the group's financial structure and profitability.

Negative Goodwill

> **Negative goodwill** is a gain occurring when the acquisition cost is less than the fair value of its net assets.

Negative goodwill is generated when the acquisition cost is less than the fair value of its net assets. If such a value appears, the accounting methods used to assess the fair value of the identifiable assets and liabilities should be checked in order to make sure that no error has been made.

If, after this verification, negative goodwill persists, it is added to the earnings for the period. At first glance, it seems like a good deal for the acquirer. However, this seemingly advantageous difference for the acquirer actually may represent anticipated losses and is not proof of a profit.

APPLICATION 8.13

Map Group Acquisition Process and Valuation

The most relevant fact of the Map group last year has been the completion of the acquisition of Geo on 07/01/2007 (all values in this application are in millions of pounds). The acquisition contract forecasts that Map takes the control of 75% of Geo for a total amount of £3,000.

On 06/30/2007, the summarized balance sheet of Geo has been disclosed as follows:

Assets		*SE & Liabilities*	
Intangible fixed assets	760	Shareholders' equity	2,900
Tangible fixed assets	370	Provisions	50
Other fixed assets	200	Deferred tax	30
Inventories	1,650	Liabilities	2,000
Trade receivable	1,500		
Cash and cash equivalent	500		
Total	**4,980**	**Total**	**4,980**

Here are a few pieces of information about the restatement of the balance sheet:

- Measurement at fair value noticeably has significant impact on net carrying amounts in the balance sheet.
- A brand has been identified and its value can be reliably measured.
- A "deferred tax – liability" no longer exists but the audit of the accounts points out a "deferred tax – asset".

The following table summarizes the fair values of Geo's assets and liabilities as identified by Map during the consolidation process:

Asset	Fair value
Intangible fixed assets	350
Tangible fixed assets	760
Brand created by Geo	700
Other fixed assets	190
Inventories	1,390
Trade receivable	1,500
Cash and cash equivalent	500
Deferred tax – assets	140
Liabilities	
Provisions	330
Debts	2000

At the acquisition date (07/01/2007) net assets are evaluated at £3,200 (total assets – provisions – debts).

Map pays £3,000 to take the control of 75% of the net assets of Geo: 75% × 3200 = 2400. The difference between cost and Geo's share in net fair value of assets and liabilities is goodwill (600). This value will be disclosed in the consolidated balance sheet as goodwill if Map applies the partial goodwill method.

However, Map can adopt the full goodwill method. In that case, the fair value of the non-controlling interests has to be measured. If the shares of the acquired company are listed on a stock market, the market price of the shares will be the basis for the measurement. If there is no active market, the buyer uses techniques of measurement appropriate to that category of shareholders. Indeed, the fair value of the share of the controlling shareholders can be different from the one of non-controlling interest shareholders. This can be explained, for example, by a prime due to the control of the firm. It would be theoretical to determine the fair value of the non-controlling interest by a simple calculation proportional to the acquirer's cash outflows.

In the case of Map and Geo, the fair value of the non-controlling interest (25% of the shares) may be evaluated to 900.

The complete goodwill is the excess between on the one hand, the difference between the sum of the fair value of the shares that give control of the firm and the fair value of the non-controlling interest and, on the other hand, the net fair value of the acquired assets and identifiable liabilities.

Complete goodwill is calculated as follows:

Map cost to get 75% of Geo (I):	3,000
Fair value of the non-controlling interest (25% of the Geo shareholders' equity) (II):	900
Total (I) + (II) (a):	3,900
Fair value of identifiable net assets (b):	3,200
Full goodwill [(a) – (b)]:	700

The full goodwill method allows the company to avoid impacts on the assets and the net income when the percentage of control is modified.

The acquisition of Geo is recorded for in the consolidated balance sheet of Map as follows:

	Balance sheet MAP before acquisition	Balance sheet GEO at fair value	Consolidated balance sheet MAP + GEO with partial goodwill	Consolidated balance sheet with full goodwill
Assets				
Goodwill			600	700
Tangible fixed assets	1,000	350	1,350	1,350
Intangible fixed assets	540	1,460	2,000	2,000
Other fixed assets	5,000*	190	2,190**	2,190**
Inventories	0	1,390	1,390	1,390
Trade receivables	500	1,500	2,000	2,000
Cash	900	500	1,400	1,400
Deferred tax		140	140	140
Total assets	**7,940**	**5,230**	**11,070**	**11,170**
SE & Liabilities				
Shareholders' equity	4,000	2,900	4,000	4,000
Non-controlling interests			800	900
Provisions	940	330	1,270	1,270
Debts	3,000	2,000	5,000	5,000
Total liabilities	**7,940**	**5,230**	**11,070**	**11,170**

*included Geo's equity investment for 3,000

** In the consolidated balance sheet, Map's equity investment in Geo is eliminated because its value is replaced by the fair values of Map's assets and liabilities.

Figure 8.18 summarizes the allocation of the acquisition cost of Geo's shares (partial goodwill method).

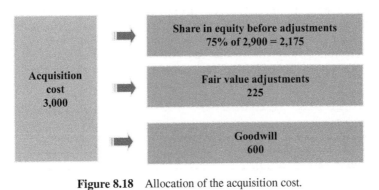

Figure 8.18 Allocation of the acquisition cost.

8.7 ACCOUNTING TREATMENT OF EQUITY INVESTMENTS

Full consolidation is a consolidation method that conveys the parent company's control by integrating the subsidiaries' assets and liabilities to clear the subsidiaries' equity investment and capital.

Full consolidation is a consolidation method that conveys the parent company's control by integrating the subsidiaries' assets and liabilities to clear the subsidiaries' equity investment. Because of the consolidation, the subsidiaries no longer exist in economic and financial terms. The procedure for clearing investments also applies for the proportionate consolidation method.

8.7.1   Shareholding in a Subsidiary: Full Consolidation

In this section, we first discuss the underlying rationale of restating investments for a parent–subsidiary relationship. We then explain the technical details involved in restatement in the case of indirect holding.

Rationale   Eliminating stock ownership and equity shared between the group and non-controlling interests establishes the consolidated equity and is the final step in the consolidation process. Since the transaction is complex, the group issues a statement of changes in shareholders' equity that explains the changes from one year to the next. This helps to avoid any mistakes or confusion.

The full consolidation method involves combining the accounts for just the controlled companies. Reciprocal transactions are then eliminated. The parent company thus incorporates all of the assets and liabilities, as well as the subsidiaries' revenues and expenses. The parent company's investment recorded as an asset is a legal construct for intermediary control over the subsidiary's assets, inventories, accounts receivable, debts, etc. According to the principle of economic substance, the investment can no longer be justified as an asset for the group and is replaced by the subsidiary's assets and liabilities now controlled by the parent company.

In contrast, any non-controlling interests in the subsidiary are maintained and restated as a **non-controlling interest**, which is included in the group's equity, though the parent company's shareholders do not provide this capital. Non-controlling interest represents a claim on capital, reserves and net profit corresponding to the share owned by the non-controlling interest in the subsidiary. Consequently, also on the group's income statement, profits and losses are split into two shares: the non-controlling interest share, and the parent company's share.

Non-controlling interest: Ownership shares in a subsidiary's net assets and net profit of an entity not held by the parent company, nor directly or indirectly by other subsidiaries.

APPLICATION 8.14

Equity Investment Elimination

In 2003, Berbis bought 60% of Picot for £7,500,000. At the acquisition date, the fair value of Picot shareholders' equity, after revaluation of its identifiable assets and liabilities, was up to £10,000,000.

What is the goodwill value (partial goodwill method)?

Answer   The share of Berbis in Picot's shareholders' equity is £6,000,000 (60% of £10,000,000). A part of the £7,500,000 paid by Berbis cannot be allocated to identifiable assets or liabilities: £1,500,000 (=7,500,000 − 6,000,000). The goodwill is positive.

At the end of 2007, after having reinvested regularly a part of its net profits, Picot's shareholders' equity amounts to £14,000,000.

What are the book entries to do in order to correctly retreat Picot's equity investment and shareholders' equity in the consolidated accounts of Berbis on 12/31/2007?

Answer

- Elimination of equity investment and the share in the historical shareholders' equity as at acquisition date, and allocation of the goodwill;

Goodwill	1,500,000
Shareholders' equity – group part	6,000,000
Equity investments	7,500,000

- Non-controlling interests (40% of the total shareholders' equity: 40% × 14,000,000 = 5,600,000)

Shareholders' equity – group part	5,600,000
Shareholders' equity – non-controlling interests	5,600,000

6,000,000 + 5,600,000 = 11,600,000 out of 14,000,000 Picot's shareholders' equity has been retreated. The difference (i.e. 2,400,000) are maintained in shareholders' equity of the group; they correspond to reserves of Berbis accumulated since the date of acquisition.

Indirect Investment   This section presents two methods for consolidating subsidiaries in indirect holding situations. In the simplest scenario, a parent company controls one single subsidiary that in turn controls a sub-subsidiary. Both methods are based on a technique that consolidates the sub-subsidiary into the parent company's consolidated statements, and both yield the same results.

According to the *consolidation by level* method, an initial consolidation procedure is carried out for the subsidiary with controlling interest in the sub-subsidiary. Then, these consolidated statements are incorporated into the parent company's consolidated financial statements.

According to the *direct consolidation method*, the sub-subsidiary's statements are incorporated directly into the parent company's consolidated financial statements, proportionally to parent company's shares in the sub-subsidiary. These shares measure the group's equity holdings for the company in question.

Application 8.15 illustrates the procedures for these two methods.

APPLICATION 8.15

Indirect Equity Investment Elimination

Zeus owns 80% of company Olymp, the shares had been acquired for £12,000,000 at the beginning of 2007. At the same date, Olymp acquired 60% of company ATN for £6,000,000.

On 12/31/2007, the balance sheets of these firms disclose these pieces of information:

- Zeus: Capital & Reserves = 20,000,000; 2007 net profit = 2,400,000
- Olymp: Capital & Reserves = 15,000,000; 2007 net profit = 2,000,000
- ATN: Capital & Reserves = 10,000,000; 2007 net profit = 1,000,000

For both subsidiaries, the fair values of assets and liabilities are the same as the values disclosed in their respective balance sheet (amortized cost at the acquisition of the investments). There is no goodwill.

How can Zeus proceed to consolidate the ATN subsidiary, using the "by level" method?

First Step: Full Consolidation of ATN in the Consolidated Financial Statements of Olymp   £6,000,000 exactly corresponds to 60% of ATN shareholders' equity (net assets value at the acquisition date).

1. Elimination of equity investment and the part in the shareholders' equity:

Capital and reserves	6,000,000	
Equity investment		6,000,000

2. Non-controlling interests:

The Non-controlling interest part is composed of 40% of shareholders' equity and reserves and 40% of the net income of ATN.

Shareholders' equity – group part	4,000,000	
Net profit	4,000,00	
Shareholders' equity – Non-controlling interests		4,400

ATN's capital and reserves have been fully eliminated. Only Olymp's capital and reserves are in the sub-group consolidated balance sheet.

Olymp's capital and reserves are disclosed as follow on 12/31/2007:

- Capital and reserves: 15,000,000
- Net profit: 2,600,000
- Non-controlling interests: 4,400,000

Second Step: Full Consolidation of the Sub-group Accounts Including ATN in Zeus' Consolidated Accounts

3. Elimination of equity investments and the quote-part in the shareholders' equity:

Capital and reserves	12,000,000	
Equity investment		12,000,000

4.   Non-controlling interests:

The non-controlling interest part is composed of 20% of shareholders' equity and reserves and 20% of the net income of Olymp sub-group: $20\% \times 15,000,000 = 3,000,000$ and $20\% \times 2,600,000 = 520$. The sum (3,520) is added to the sub-group's non-controlling interests.

Shareholders' equity – group part	3,000,000
Net profit	520,000
Shareholders' equity – Non-controlling interests	3,520,000

Olymp sub-group's capital and reserves have been fully eliminated. Only Olymp capital and reserves are in the sub-group consolidated balance sheet.

Non-controlling interests are composed of Olymp's non-controlling shareholders (3,520,000) and ATN's non-controlling shareholders (4,400,000).

Zeus group's shareholders' equity is disclosed at 12/31/2007 as follows:

- Capital and reserves: 20,000,000
- Net profit: 4,480,000
- Non-controlling interests: 7,920,000

How can Zeus proceed to consolidate the ATN subsidiary, using the direct method?

The percentage of interests of Zeus is up to:

- 80% in Olymp (non-controlling interests are up to 20%)
- 80% of 60% = 48% in ATN (non-controlling interests are up to 56%)

The consolidated net income is composed of Zeus' net income (2,400,000), 80% of Olymp's net income (1,600,000) and 48% of ATN's net income (4,800,000). The total is up to 4,480,000.

Non-controlling interests are composed of 20% of Olymp's shareholders' equity, reserves and net income (3,400,000) and 52% of ATN's shareholders' equity, reserves and net income (5,720,000). That latter amount has to be adjusted by 20% of Olymp's equity investment in ATN, which corresponds to Olymp's Non-controlling interests in ATN: $20\% \times 6,000,000 = 1,200,000$. The total amount of non-controlling interests is up to: $3,400,000 + 5,720,000 - 1,200,000 = 7,920,000$.

Zeus group shareholders' equity on 12/31/2007 is disclosed as follow:

- Capital and reserves: 20,000,000
- Net income: 4,480,000
- Non-controlling interests: 7,920,000.

8.7.2   Holdings in an Associate Company: The Equity Method

Equity method: a procedure for the revaluation of a particular category of equity investments.

The equity method is not a consolidation method per se, but a way to revaluate a particular category of an investor's investments. IAS 28 specifies that interest in an entity providing significant influence over this entity to the investor should be treated according to the equity method.

This method is used in two situations:

- Its use is required for the treatment of associate companies, meaning those in which an investor holds a significant interest.
- It is optional for treating jointly controlled companies. IAS 31 leaves investors a choice between the equity method and proportionate consolidation.

The equity method involves replacing in the holding company's balance sheet the book value of the shares by the share in the target company's equity at the closing date. The target company's equity should be determined according to group accounting principles of the holding company. The difference between this share in the target company's equity at the balance sheet date, and the corresponding value at the previous year's closing date should appear clearly as such on the holding company's income statement. As there is no control relationship, this method does not provide for the recovery of assets and liabilities, nor of revenues and expenses on the holding company's financial statements.

The value of the equity and that of the associate company's net profit must be calculated according to methods that comply with those used by the holding company so that the accounting methods remain consistent. For transactions between the two companies, the proportionate interest in reserves and net profit that corresponds to the holding company's investment is eliminated. For example, if the interest is 30%, then 30% of the earnings from transactions conducted between the two companies is eliminated.

Application 8.16 shows how the equity method is applied.

APPLICATION 8.16

Equity Method: Matt Company

First Part   On 01/01/2007, Algo, whose shareholders' equity is up to £60,000,000, is created and Matt acquires 25% of Algo's shares for £15,000,000 (25% of £60,000,000).

What are the effects on Matt's balance sheet related to these events considering that Matt paid the shares cash by bank transfer?

Matt owns 25% of Algo and therefore is presumed to have a significant influence on that firm. The equity method has to be applied to that case. The only book entry related to this operation is as follows:

Investments in entities accounted for by the equity method	15,000,000	
Bank		15,000,000

Second Part   Algo has begun to run well and realized a £8,000,000 net profit in 2007. Thus, its shareholders' equity on 12/31/2007 is composed of £60,000,000 (capital) and £8,000,000 (net income).

What are the consequences of that evolution on Matt's accounts on 12/31/2007?

The value of Matt's share in Algo shareholders' equity is now up to 25% of £68,000,000 = £17,000,000. That increase by £2,000,000 compared to the one at the beginning of 2007 represents for Matt a 2007 financial revenue. It has to be recorded for on a specific line in the P&L: "Share in net income of investments accounted for by equity method." The corresponding Debit booking increases the amount of the investment in the balance sheet.

Investments in entities by the equity method	2,000,000
Share in net income of investments accounted for by equity method	2,000,000

The value of the investment in the balance sheet amounts to 15,000,000 + 2,000,000 = 17,000,000 on 12/31/2007.

When shares in pre-existing companies are acquired, the acquisition cost can include goodwill similar to the goodwill generated by subsidiaries, as described above. Its accounting treatment is comparable to that for subsidiaries, except that positive goodwill is not recognized separately on the holding company's balance statement. Instead, it is integrated into the investment value. It nonetheless conforms to the same valuation rules as goodwill of subsidiaries, especially in terms of non-amortization and impairment test. As for subsidiaries, goodwill is not an asset to which cash flows can be directly attributed. An impairment test is therefore always performed for the overall investment value.

If there is negative goodwill, it is directly allocated to the company's earnings. This reduces the investment value recognized on the balance sheet.

Application 8.17 illustrates accounting treatment for goodwill using the equity method.

APPLICATION 8.17

Equity Method with Goodwill : Filo Company

First Part   On 01/01/2007, Filo bought 30% of Sofi for £5,200,000. At that time, Sofi's shareholders' equity is up to £12,000,000 and is composed of £8,000,000 (capital) and £4,000,000 (reserves).

The equity investment rate of 30% gives to Filo a significant influence on Sofi and therefore Filo will use the equity method. Filo and Sofi will use homogeneous accounting methods and Filo also has to identify Sofi's assets and liabilities' fair values at the acquisition date in order to correctly allocate the acquisition cost of the equity investment to its shareholders' equity and to a potential goodwill.

After an assessment on assets' and liabilities' fair values, several elements in the Sofi balance sheet have been revaluated for a total amount of £3,000,000. The adjusted shareholders' equity value is now up to £15,000,000. Fair value adjustments in this example only concern non-depreciable assets, and particularly land.

Which is the value of goodwill related to the Sofi equity investment that should be accounted for in Filo's balance sheet?

The part of Filo in the adjusted shareholders' equity of Sofi represents 30% of £15,000,000 = £4,500,000. The positive difference between the acquisition cost (£5,200,000) and the fair value (£4,500,000) is the goodwill (£700,000)

Second Part   At the end of 2007, Sofi's shareholders' equity is disclosed as follow:

- Capital: 8,000,000
- Reserves: 4,000,000
- Net profit: 1,200,000
- Shareholders' equity: 13,200,000

No indication for an impairment loss has been pointed out since the acquisition.

What are the consequences of Sofi's evolution for the accounts of Filo on 12/31/2008?

As there is no indication for an impairment loss, the revaluation adjustment is maintained at £3,000,000. The share of Filo in the adjusted shareholders' equity of Sofi amounts to 30% of (13,200 + 3,000) = £4,860,000.

The same method is applied to the goodwill, whose value keeps being up to £700,000.

Filo equity investment in Sofi:

- Interest in the revaluated shareholders' equity of Sofi: £4,860,000
- Goodwill: £700,000
- Total: £5,560,000

The evolution of the equity investment value during the year (£360,000) is recorded in the P&L line: "Share in net income of investments accounted for by equity method".

Investments in entities accounted for by the equity method	360,000	
Share in net income of investments accounted for by equity method		360,000

8.7.3   Eliminating-Investment with Proportionate Consolidation

Proportionate consolidation is one of the two consolidation methods used for jointly controlled companies.

Proportionate consolidation is one of the two consolidation methods that may be applied to jointly controlled companies. According to this method, the consolidating company's percentage of interest in the fair values of assets and liabilities of the jointly controlled entity replaces the book value of the equity investment. The transactions are the same as those for full consolidation. However, inventory, non-current assets, accounts receivable and debts, income and expenses are recognized only partially, i.e. proportionally to the interest of the (jointly) controlling entity in the joint venture. Eliminating intercompany transactions takes into account the relationships between the group and the other controlling entities. Only the group's share is eliminated. Thus, the consolidated financial statements represent the relationships between the group and the other jointly controlling entities via their common subsidiary.

APPLICATION 8.18

Proportionate Consolidation

If a firm shares the control of another entity up to 30%, the turnover up to 6,000,000 realized with the common subsidiary will involve an elimination of the sales and purchases for 1,800,000. The remaining 4,200,000 will be maintained in the accounts and represent the operations realized with the other controlling entities. The proportionate consolidation of that subsidiary will include 70% of its net profit in the group's net income and 70% of the change of reserves since its entry in the scope of consolidation.

8.8 SUMMARY

This chapter describes the financial statements that business groups must establish. A business group comprises two or more legally independent companies, including a parent company that controls the others, which are referred to as subsidiaries.

To take into account the close economic ties that exist between these companies, the group must also prepare financial statements with the goal of presenting a view of the group as if it was a single corporate entity.

These financial statements are called consolidated financial statements since they involve combining the annual financial statements of all of the companies that belong to the group, and then eliminate all of the transactions carried out between the companies within the group (consolidation). Once recognized and measured according to harmonized accounting methods, the elements on the balance sheet and income statement of the controlled company are entirely incorporated into the group's statements. Non-controlling interests in subsidiaries appear under a special heading in the group's statements.

Before combining the various financial statements, harmonization procedures are necessary. The reporting and valuation methods must be identical for all of the comparable elements that appear on the group's financial statements. The subsidiaries' annual financial statements denominated in foreign currency are either directly translated into the group's reporting currency, or after an initial translation into the subsidiary's functional currency.

All of the transactions carried out between the companies within the group are consolidated. In addition to non-current assets, inventory, accounts receivable, liabilities, purchases, sales, dividends and other transactions, this concerns above all the elimination of the investment of the parent company in exchange for the proportionate interest in the subsidiary's adjusted equity. If there is goodwill, it is recognized as an asset and is subject to impairment tests each year.

In addition to controlled companies, there are also jointly controlled companies and those over which the holding company exerts significant influence. Since the holding company does not directly control the latter two types of companies, their annual financial statements are not entirely integrated into the consolidated financial statements. For jointly controlled companies, proportionate consolidation is used to claim the proportionate interest that corresponds to the investment level in each accounting element. Conversely, the parent can also simply use the equity method for the investment in a given company. In the case of significant influence, only the equity method is permitted.

8.9   ACTIVITIES

1. Consolidation   Figure 8.19 discloses the Jal group structure.

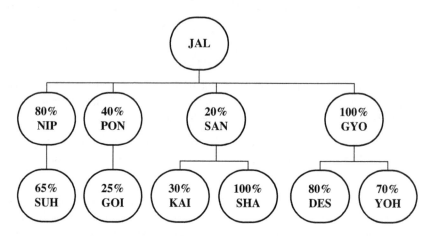

Figure 8.19   JAL group structure.

Jal contractually controls Pon even if it only has 40% of the shares. San also contractually controls Kai. In all other cases, there is not control if a firm does not hold at least 50% of the shares.

How should the firms Suh, Goi, Kai, Des and Yoh be consolidated in the group?

2. Account Retreatment   A group applying IFRS consolidates an SME that applies British standards.

List five elements that could be restated in order to be consistent with the group accounting policy.

3. Foreign Currency Adjustment   A foreign subsidiary of a European group discloses the followings accounts (in millions of dollars):

Balance sheet at 12/31/2008

Gross Fixed assets	4,000	Capital	1,500
Depreciations	3,000	Reserves	150
Net fixed assets	1,000	Net profit	150
Inventories	300	Debts	700
Trade receivables	800		
Cash	400		
Total assets	**2,500**	**Total SE &**	**2,500**
		liabilities	

P&L

Purchases	200	Sales	1,000
Inventory variation	50	Financial revenues	200
Others expenses	550		
Depreciation expenses	200		
Net income	200		
Total expenses	**1,200**	**Total revenues**	**1,200**

At the historical exchange rate, net fixed assets are up to €1,100m. Reserves had been added for $80m in 2008 and for $70m in 2007. The capital has been paid in 2005.

Relevant exchange rates are the follows:

- 12/31/2008: €0.80   2008 average: €0.85
- 12/31/2007: €0.90   2007 average: €0.95
- 12/31/2006: €0.85   2006 average: €0.90
- 12/31/2005: €0.75   2005 average: €0.70

1. *Using the historical rate method set up the subsidiaries' accounts in millions of euros. Which is the amount of the translation adjustment?*
2. *Using the closing rate method set up the subsidiaries' accounts in millions of euros. Which is the amount of the translation adjustment?*

4. Intercompany Eliminations   In 2008, Seki bought goods for €120m. It sold them to its parent company Kaa for €150m. Kaa sold 90% of those goods to a third party for €180m.

1. *Considering a 33% tax rate and disregarding other costs, how much will the income tax paid by Seki and Kaa at the end of 2008 in respect of these operations?*
2. *Considering that these sale and purchase operations are accrual operations and have not generated any cash flow, which are the adjustments to operate in order to prepare the group accounts?*
3. *Which will be the amount of the deferred tax related to these operations?*

5. Goodwill Calculation   Locaplus acquired 100% of Transcar for €10m. The fair values of assets and liabilities of Transcar are estimated at €7m.

1. *Determine the goodwill to be disclosed in the Locaplus group accounts.*
2. *Will that goodwill be different if Locaplus only purchases 80% of Transcar? If yes, why, and which will be the amount of the goodwill? Explain.*

Tangible assets	700	Capital	1,500
Intangible assets	300	Reserves	150
Inventories	300	Net income	150
Trade receivables	800	Debts	700
Cash	400		
Total assets	**2,500**	**Total SE & liabilities**	**2,500**

6. Goodwill   On 12/31/2008, Keio balance sheet is disclosed as follows (in thousands):

During the consolidation process, the fair values of Keio's identifiable assets and liabilities have been estimated as follows (thousands):

Tangible assets	400	Debts	700
Intangible assets	600	Provisions	200
Inventories	350		
Trade receivables	800		
Cash	400		
Deferred tax asset	120		

1.   *At the acquisition date, which is the amount of Keio's net assets at fair value?*
2.   *Which is the amount of goodwill for Keio if an investor paid 2,000,000 to get 100% of Keio?*

7. Consolidation Process   In 2007, at the creation of Basteau, Astra has acquired 90% of the shares of this company. Neither firm pays dividends during year 2007, and on 12/31/2007, the balance sheets of both firms are as follows (thousands):

Astra

Tangible assets	700	Capital	1,500
Intangible assets	300	Net income	500
Equity investments	2,700	Debts	2,100
Trade receivables	100		
Cash	300		
Total assets	**4,100**	**Total SE & liabilities**	**4,100**

Basteau

Tangible assets	500	Capital	400
Intangible assets	200	Net income	200
Trade receivables	100	Debts	400
Cash	200		
Total assets	**1,000**	**Total SE & liabilities**	**1,000**

1.   *Calculate the net profit of the group.*
2.   *Prepare a consolidated balance sheet of the Astra group.*

9 FINANCIAL ANALYSIS AND COMMUNICATION

Financial statements reveal a company's performance and financial situation. For listed companies subject to pressure from financial markets, it is especially important to be able to provide information to contributors, shareholders, and creditors. However, not all stakeholders need the same information. Creditors aim to determine the company's risk of default by analyzing its current situation and fundamental **financial equilibrium** as represented on its financial statements (section 9.1). The shareholders are also interested in the profitability of their investment and look for a certain number of indicators to assess the company's economic performance (section 9.2). Regardless of whether the stakeholder is a shareholder or creditor, the need for detailed information to assess risk or profitability necessitates access to a financial analysis of the company. The goal is to be able to interpret the financial statements including the balance sheet, income statement and notes, and cash flow statement to be able ultimately to form an opinion on the company's performance. This process relies on financial ratios, uses accounting information and other types of financial data, and is based on comparisons over time (looking at a company over several years) and space (competitors, sector, industry, etc.). Several financial indicators are inseparable from financial communication (section 9.3).

> **Financial equilibrium:** When a company's long-term financial resources equal its long-term assets.

9.1 ANALYZING THE FUNDAMENTAL FINANCIAL EQUILIBRIUM

A creditor conducts a financial analysis by closely examining the company's fundamental financial equilibrium to form an initial idea of the level of financial risk it presents. Creditors are primarily interested in estimating the risk of default or bankruptcy. Even if it still reports profits, a company can be forced to go out of business if it has a cash flow deficit. A financial equilibrium study based on the working capital requirements and working capital can allow creditors to assess the company's cash flow and financial strategy and, consequently, the factors that determine the risk of default.

9.1.1 Working Capital Requirement

> **Working capital requirement:** The fraction of cyclical capital need or requirements not financed by cycles (as opposed to long-term resources).

The **working capital requirements** determine a business's short-term cash flow needs for financing its operations. It is important to differentiate long-term financial resources, such as equity and financial debt, from short-term payables. In parallel, long-term capital employed

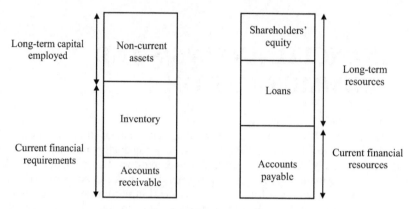

Figure 9.1   Financial requirements and resources.

(non-current assets) should be distinguished from current financial requirements (inventory and short-term claims). See Figure 9.1.

Current financial requirements are usually greater than the short-term financial resources, hence the existence of working capital requirements. For example, this is the case for a company that gives its customers a 60-day payment limit, while the company itself has a deadline of only 30 days to pay its supplier for the merchandise.

Therefore, the company's net financing requirements are not covered by the same types of financial resources. This net current financing requirement results from the delay between the time the company pays its current expenses and when it records incoming cash flow from its ordinary activities (see Figures 9.2 and 9.3).

In some industries, this is not always the case. In particular, in the hypermarket and mass distribution sector, the opposite situation can occur: merchandise inventory turnover can be very rapid, and while customer accounts may be paid in cash immediately, the corresponding suppliers are sometimes paid in 60, or even 90 days. This generates additional working capital as opposed to working capital requirements (see Figure 9.4).

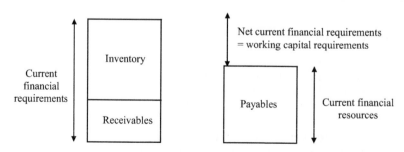

Figure 9.2   Working capital requirements.

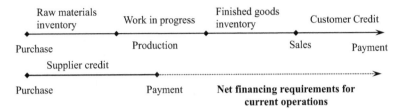

Figure 9.3   Financing requirements.

APPLICATION 9.1

Working Capital Requirement

Ardeco Corp. buys and sells furniture. On January 1, it buys four tables purchased for £2,000 each to its supplier. The invoice has to be paid within 30 days. Two weeks after the deal, the firm sells the four tables for £4,000 each. One table has been paid cash. The other three are to be paid within 2 months at the latest.

On January 15, Ardeco gets only £4,000 cash. At the end of January, it will have to pay an invoice of £8,000 although it has only £4,000 on its bank account. Its working capital requirement will be up to £4,000, which is the difference between its only one current asset of £12,000 (3 × 4,000) and a current liability up to £8,000. On January 31, Ardeco will have to pay its supplier. Therefore, the company needs to finance its operating activities.

9.1.2   Working Capital

Working capital: The resources available to meet the working capital requirements. If the working capital amount is the same as the working capital requirements, the cash position is zero. In all other cases, there is either a cash position surplus or deficit.

Analyzing a company's **working capital** helps to determine the extent to which a company's long-term financial requirements are covered by financial resources of the same nature (long term). When long-term financial resources match the long-term assets, the situation is considered one of "financial equilibrium". The company can then finance its long-term investments with its long-term financial resources, but it does not have a safety net in the case of a shortfall in cash assets from its sales. However, a company that has a surplus in its long-term financial resources (greater than its long-term requirements) can cover a portion of its working

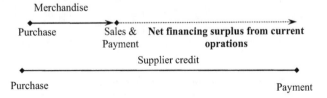

Figure 9.4   Net financing surplus.

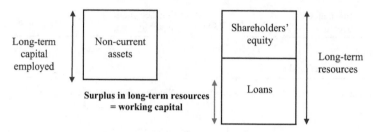

Figure 9.5   Surplus in long-term financial resources.

capital (its financial requirements for current operations). The surplus in long-term financial resources is referred to as the working capital (Figures 9.4 and 9.5).

Working capital is rarely equal to the working capital requirements.

When the working capital equals the working capital requirements, the net cash flow balance, meaning that the difference between the cash assets and cash credit (or bank overdraft) is zero. In all other cases, there is either a cash position surplus or deficit (see Figure 9.7).

Cash position is the difference between the working capital and the working capital requirements.

The cash position is defined as the difference between the working capital and the working capital requirements:

Cash position = Working capital − Working capital requirements = Cash − Overdraft

This formula illustrates the concept of the **operating cycle**. In order to produce and sell its products, a company has to be able to acquire its merchandise inventory, raw materials, etc. This inventory is transformed into sales, which are in turn transformed into cash and cash equivalents when customers pay their invoices (see Figures 9.6 and 9.7). Practically speaking,

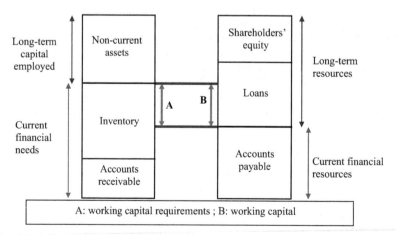

Figure 9.6   Equilibrium between working capital requirements and working capital.

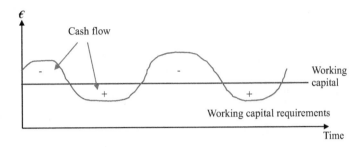

Figure 9.7 The relationship between working capital, working capital requirements, and cash flow.

the length of this cycle varies depending on the company and industry. The company relies on its short-term financial resources to finance its operating cycle, which are mostly accounts payable coming from credit obtained by suppliers. The transformation of sales into cash makes it possible to settle short-term liabilities, especially amounts owed to suppliers. If the operating cycle experiences a slowdown, the company can no longer cover its short-term liabilities, which can lead to a risk of default or bankruptcy. Businesses therefore need the security offered by a surplus in working capital. Application 9.2 illustrates the concept of financial equilibrium and the issues it raises.

APPLICATION 9.2

Financial Equilibrium Study

Val group is doing business in the transportation sector. At year end, its balance sheet (*in thousands*) is as follows:

Tangible and intangible assets	5,500	Shareholders' equity	4,800
Financial assets	1,700	Provisions	1,000
Stock, trade receivable and other assets	4,600	Loans	4,200
Cash and cash equivalent	600	Trade payables and other debts	2,400
Total asset	**12,400**	**Total liability**	**12,400**

This simplified balance sheet shows that Val group's long-term resources are the addition of three elements: shareholders' equity, provisions and loans. Non-current assets are the addition of tangible and intangible assets and financial assets. The working capital requirement can be split as below:

Long-term capital employed	7,200	Long-term financial resources	10,000

As we can see, the firm has a long-term financial resources exceeding its long-term needs of an amount of 10,000 − 7,200 = 2,800. This working capital only has sense in relation to the working capital requirement. The latter is the difference between current assets and liabilities.

Current assets	4,600	Current liabilities	2,400

Val group has a current total asset of 4,600 while its current liabilities are up to 2,400. Its working capital requirement is up to $4,600 - 2,400 = 2,200$.

The working capital amounts to 2,800 and the working capital requirement amounts to 2,200. We then have a surplus of $2,800 - 2,200 = 600$. It corresponds to Val's cash.

A fundamental element of the financial balance appears: Every firm whose working capital requirement is higher than its working capital has negative treasury. On the contrary, if the working capital is higher than the working capital requirement, the entity's treasury is positive. Therefore, Val's financial structure seems to be wealthy.

The factors that improve or worsen financial equilibrium need to be explained in detail. A closer look at the changes that can occur in the elements that constitute the working capital requirements and working capital provides some clues. Thus, for example, for an analysis of the working capital requirements, it is important to look at changes in inventory and the sales strategy through the amount of trade accounts receivable. As for any financial investigation, the most important task is to identify the reasons behind the changes. A competition study can help to determine whether the company's balance sheet is consistent with other businesses in the same industry.

9.1.3 The Cash Flow Statement

The **cash flow statement** provides additional information to the balance sheet and income statement indicating the origins of the year's cash and cash equivalents and how they are used.

The **cash flow statement** provides additional information to the balance sheet and income statement indicating the origins of the year's cash and cash equivalents and how they are used. This statement divides the company's activities into three basic categories:

- **Operating activities.** Cash flow that comes from operating activities should explain the difference between the cash on the company's balance sheet at the beginning of the year with those at the closing date. Cash includes available funds (and demand deposits), as well as cash equivalents such as liquid investments easily convertible into a known amount with no risk of significant variation. These investments are usually short term so that the company can meet its short-term cash flow commitments.

  Cash flow associated with operating activities can be determined indirectly from profit or loss (see Chapter 1). However, profit includes expenses and revenues that do not affect the cash flow. Therefore, profit or loss can be restated by eliminating the impact of revenues and expenses with no effect on cash. For expenses, this concerns depreciation, amortization and impairment of assets as well as expenses for provisions. Adjustments of revenues are operated for reversals of provisions or impairments. Finally, gains and losses from disposal of assets are also eliminated since they do not concern the company's operating activities. At this stage, the cash flow obtained is the one generated by the company's operating activities independently from its customer (and supplier) credit policies. It is therefore necessary to subsequently adjust the cash provided by operations amount according to other income and expenses that do not affect the year's cash flow. This is especially the case for sales and purchases made on credit (see Chapter 1). Once all these elements taken into account, the amount obtained is the **cash flow from operations**.

Cash flow from operations indicates the cash flow generated by the company's operating activities.

APPLICATION 9.3

Operating Activities Cash Flow

Please find below information about the balance sheet of Extra Corp (*thousands*).

Balance sheet	*12/31/08*	*01/01/08*
Cash	32,000	1,000
Trade receivables	16,000	9,000
Inventory	6,000	3,000
Trade payables	11,000	20,000
P&L		
Turnover	48,000	
Raw materials	(27,000)	
Wages	(17,000)	
Depreciation/Amortization	(5,000)	
Loss on disposal	(1,000)	
Loss	(2,000)	

According to these figures, the accountant of the firm can prepare the first part of the cash flow statement (*thousands*).

Loss	(2,000)
+ depreciation/amortization	5,000
+ loss on disposal	1,000
Increase in trade receivable	(7,000)
Increase in inventory	(3,000)
Decrease in trade payables	(9,000)
Cash flow from operations	**(16,000)**

- **Investing activities.** Cash flows linked to acquisitions of non-current assets indicate how much the entity spent for evolution of its business and/or for the assets renewal. Cash flow from operating activities is a consequence of:
  - the cash flows related the acquisition of tangible, intangible and financial assets (without the debt on these non-current assets), including assets created by the company, and
  - the cash flows from disposals of tangible, intangible and financial capital assets (possibly net of capital gains tax).

- **Financing activities.** Cash flow from financing that helps to identify financing sources (for example, capital increases, or loan issue) and related cash outflows (dividends paid, share buybacks, and loan repayments).

APPLICATION 9.4

Cash Flows from Financing and Investing Activities

During the year 2008, Extra Corp. sold a land for £50,000 and bought a vehicle for £20,000. The firm also paid a dividend of £2,000 to its shareholders and borrowed £10,000 from its bank. According to these pieces of information, the accountant completed the two final parts of the cash flow statement.

Purchase of a vehicle	(20,000)
Proceed from land's sale	50,000
Investing activities	**30,000**
Financial debt	10,000
Dividends paid	(2,000)
Financing activities	**8,000**
Change in cash	22,000

The final amount indicates the change in cash of the accounting year and equals the cash increase. The cash earned by operating activities is negative (see application 9.3) and is therefore insufficient to cover the company's investments (without the land's sale) and the payment of the dividends.

9.1.4   Analyzing Fundamental Equilibrium

Demonstrating a company's fundamental equilibrium is one of the first steps in analyzing its financial situation. In particular, it identifies how urgent its cash asset requirements are, and its capacity to meet these requirements in the long term. Once proven, analyzing this equilibrium is the next step in the process.

- Analyzing the components of the working capital is a way to evaluate the company's solvency, meaning its debt capacity and the level of risk taken by contributors. Close examination of the balance sheet is one important source of information that shows the relative proportions of various financing sources that make up the total amount of resources. This information can indicate whether the company has had to use debt in order to finance its development and its acquisitions. A few different ratios are used to measure the proportion of assets in relation to indebtedness:

$$\frac{\text{Net financial debt}}{\text{Liabilities} + \text{Equity}} \quad \text{or} \quad \frac{\text{Net financial debt}}{\text{Equity}}$$

- This measure of indebtedness is commonly referred to as the **gearing ratio** (see Figure 9.8). The importance of this ratio is demonstrated in the reference documents from Club Med (see Figure 9.8) below. The group has a line of credit of €120m. One of the conditions for using this credit is the maintenance of a gearing ratio of less than 1.00, or 100%, which means that the net debt level must remain below that of the net assets. The group recorded a gearing ratio of 60% on October 31, 2008, well within the limits of this contract clause.

Rating: The estimated level of debt default risk for a listed company.

19.5.2. LIQUIDITY RISK OF FINANCIAL LIABILITIES AND DEBT COVENANTS

Liquidity risk is managed by using diversified sources of financing. Some of the Group's debt facilities include early redemption clauses that are triggered if debt covenants are breached or assets are sold. Disposals made during the fiscal year did not trigger early redemptions or changes in the limit of the syndicated line of credit. This line of credit could be repaid in its entirety if the amount of divested assets outside of the Group's ordinary course of business exceeded €252 million.

The most restrictive debt covenants relate to the €120 million syndicated line of credit.

- Off-balance sheet commitments: less than €200 million

- Gearing (net debt/equity): less than 1

- Leverage (net debt/EBITDA Leisure[1]): less than the following:

	31 October
2008	3.5
2009 and beyond	3.0

- Fixed charge cover (EBITDAR Leisure / (rents + net interest)): greater than the following:

	31 October
2008	1.35
2009 and beyond	1.45

At 31 October 2008, the covenants had been met:
- Off-balance sheet commitments: less than €200 million €121 million
- Gearing: less than 1 0.60
- Leverage (net debt/EBITDA as defined above)): less than 3.5 2.72
- Fixed charge cover: greater than 1.35 1.51

CLUB MÉDITERRANÉE Ψ

Figure 9.8 Excerpt from the Club Med annual report, 2008.

• Investors are particularly sensitive to changes in debt levels and its relation to the company's net assets. Financial markets are very attentive to what is referred to as the company's credit **rating**. Ratings are set by independent, specialized agencies (Moody's and Standard & Poor's, for example) and impact lending terms, and also its cost. The greater the indebtedness ratios, the higher is the company's default risk. In the case of a high indebtness, the company is not certain to be able to pay the interest on its loans, or to be able to pay back its creditors if it goes bankrupt. The following ratios measure a company's reimbursement capacity:

$$\frac{\text{Net financial debt}}{\text{Cash flow from operations}} \qquad \frac{\text{Total indebtedness}}{\text{CF from operations}}$$

$$\frac{\text{Operating profit before depreciation and amortization}}{\text{Cash earnings}}$$

These ratios emphasize the consequences of indebtedness in relation to the company's capacity to generate cash through its operating activities independently from its credit policies.

APPLICATION 9.5

Shareholders' Equity and Indebtedness

Dubois group operates in the industrial equipment field. The study of its balance sheet on the three last weeks enabled us to extract the data below:

(thousands of euros)	2006	2007	2008
Shareholders' equity	8,200	9,000	10,500
Long-term financial debts	7,500	7,000	5,000

This table shows the evolution of shareholders' equity and the long-term indebtedness of the Dubois group. During all the three years, the firm was increasing its equity whereas it managed to reduce its amount of debt. In 2006, the amount of financial debts almost equalled the total shareholders' equity. The gearing ratio was 7,500/8,200, that is to say 91%. In 2007, the ratio was approximately 78% whereas it represents 47% at the end of 2008. The financial situation has been steadily improving over the past three years.

The analysis of the reasons of this improvement shows that shareholders' equity has strongly increased during the past three years (28%) whereas the level of debt has remarkably decreased (33%). Without knowing the reasons of the increase in capital, it can be stated that the firm had a successful policy of debt-reducing. This improvement in the financial structure has a positive impact on the opinion about Dubois on financial markets.

Credit rating agencies (such as Standard & Poor's) run analysis about listed companies' financial situation and they give their opinion about the credit risk. The grade that is attributed to the company has an impact on new loan conditions that a firm can get on the financial markets. The better financial structure displayed by the Dubois group in 2008 may contribute to get lower interest rates on future loans.

- The analysis of the working capital requirements is focused on issues concerning the company's liquidity. Examining current assets and liabilities enables the company to analyze its liquidity with the aim of determining if it can, in the short term, meet all its payment obligations. This can help to assess the company's credit default risk.

The assets that can quickly be converted into cash have to be identified in order to anticipate the working capital requirements. Several ratios can be used to do so, in particular those that measure the turnover for the elements that constitute the working capital requirements.

$$\text{Inventory turnover} = \frac{\text{Material inventory} \times 360}{\text{Purchases}} \text{ or } \frac{\text{Finished goods' inventory} \times 360}{\text{Sales}}$$

$$\text{Debt turnover} = \frac{\text{Operating debt} \times 360}{\text{Purchases (VAT included)}}$$

$$\text{Receivables turnover} = \frac{\text{Accounts receivable} \times 360}{\text{Turnover (VAT included)}}$$

A ratio like the receivables turnover, for example, expresses the average length of customer credit as a number of days. They help to quickly interpret a company's financial situation and are useful analysis indicators. Thus, a company with substantial current working capital requirements has an interest in reducing the amount and length of credit it extends to its customers and/or extend the length of credit with its suppliers.

- Analyzing the financial situation also requires looking at cash flow changes over a given period to complement the information provided in the balance sheet.

APPLICATION 9.6

Cash Flow Statement and Investing Cycle

Verbois group produces and sells farm tools. The summarized cash flow statements of the past 3 last years are as follows:

(*thousands of euros*)	2006	2007	2008
Cash flow from operating activities	3,980	4,500	5,200
Cash flow from investing activities	(4,300)	(3,000)	500
Cash flow from financing activities	2,000	1,200	(1,000)

This chart displays relevant information about investing and financing: the first 2 years, the firm invested a lot. Cash flows from operating activities could not finance all the acquisitions of the first year; hence additional cash inflows came from financial activities. These acquisitions seem to have been relevant because of the great increase in operating cash inflows between the first and third years. The 2008 figures show that the firm sold non-current assets which enabled it to start reimbursing some of its debts.

The above application illustrates the logic of the investing and financing cycle. At first, an investing company usually has to seek financial resources to cover the acquisitions considered for its development. Once these acquisitions generate the desired operating cash flow, the resulting cash flow surplus will make it subsequently possible to reduce the company's level of indebtedness. This can create a so-called "virtuous circle". Close examination of the cash flow statement is essential for understanding how investing and financing cash flows are generated. However, another financial statement provides more detailed information for the analysis: the statement of changes in shareholders' equity (see Chapter 6). This statement helps us to understand the relationship between the company and its shareholders and the extent to which it relies on them to finance its growth.

9.2   ANALYSIS OF PROFITABILITY

Shareholders' equity contributors need to be able to assess the profitability of their investment, or, in other words, the resources available to the company that ensure its continued operation given the level of risk involved. Indicators that help to assess the company's economic performance are primarily based on the analysis of the income statement and balance sheet.

9.2.1   Preparing Financial Statements

To conduct a break-even analysis that gives an overall financial perspective on the company, the financial statements need to be restated. The information needed for the analysis, namely the available resources classified by their origin, needs to be identified and extracted. Elements associated with operational activities need to be distinguished from those associated with financing.

Balance sheet

Non-current assets	Shareholders' equity
Inventory	Financial debt
Accounts receivable	
Cash assets	Non-financial debt
Total assets	**Total liabilities & equity**

> **Financial balance sheet** (restated) represents the net worth of the company's assets and liabilities and its relation to the total equity.

Establishing a **financial balance sheet** involves differentiating purely financial entries from other accounting entries. Non-financial entries can then be considered by default as operational elements necessary to maintain the company's ordinary activities. This is the case for most of the entries on the accounting balance sheet. The financial balance sheet is prepared by offsetting assets and liabilities of the same nature. For example, non-financial debt reduces the total amount of operational assets. Similarly, financial assets including short-term and other types of financial investments reduce the amount of financial debt, thus revealing the net indebtedness. Short-term investments can be liquidated quickly and used to reimburse loans, thus reducing the company's "real" indebtedness.

A financial balance sheet is usually presented as follows:

Financial balance sheet

Non-current assets	Shareholders' equity
	Net financial debt
Working capital requirements	
Financial net worth	**Financial liability**

The income statement also needs to be restated. Even though the earnings from ordinary activities already appear on the financial statements (as well as in the operating income), the respective amount after tax needs to be determined. If the company finances all of its operations with its shareholders' equity, it would not have any interest expense, and the income from its ordinary activities would then be higher. Therefore, the amount of tax that the company must pay needs to be calculated to determine the theoretical net income (without taking the financing elements into account). Similarly, the operating income must be calculated after tax to determine the real cost of financing activities. Since interest expenses are tax-deductible, the tax savings reduces the cost of a loan and the real cost of the loans or other financing activities is lower than the interest expenses as disclosed in the financial section of the income statement.

The operating income is determined after taking into account depreciation, impairment and provision expenses. In order to ensure that a company's investing strategy does not affect the analysis, the operating income can be calculated without taking these elements into account; this is commonly known as EBITDA (Earnings Before Interest, Taxes, Depreciation and Amortization). This amount is less subject to creative accounting practices than other data issued by the company, which helps to explain why it is so widely used.

9.2.2 The Relationship Between Return on Assets and Return on Equity

> **Return on assets or rate of return:** The ratio between the wealth produced by the company's ordinary activities (operating income after tax) and the financial resources used to generate it.
>
> **Return on equity:** the ratio of net income to shareholders' equity.

Two types of profitability can be identified: **return on assets (ROA),** also referred to as the **rate of return,** and **financial profitability**. The ROA is the ratio between the wealth produced by the company's ordinary activities (operating income after tax) and the resources used to generate it. These resources are the **net assets**. The ratio between the wealth created by the net assets with the financial resources used is the ROA:

$$\text{ROA rate} = \text{ROA} = \frac{\text{Operating income}}{\text{Net assets}}$$

Shareholders assess the performance of the only equity contributions (shareholders' equity). The relevant ratio is the **Return on Equity** and it is measured as follows:

$$\text{ROE} = \text{Return on equity} = \frac{\text{Operating income}}{\text{Shareholders' equity}}$$

If the shareholders are the only financial contributors, meaning that there is no financial debt (loans, etc.), then the ROA is equal to the ROE.

Thus the financial balance sheet is as follows:

Financial balance sheet

Non-current assets	Shareholders' equity
Working capital requirements	
Net assets	**Financial liabilities**

In consequence, the shareholders are the sole beneficiaries of the economic benefits generated by the net assets. The operating income is equal to the net income since there are no interest expenses. However, if ever the shareholders decide to finance new projects by relying on loans, the operating income will, at least in part, be used to reimburse creditors through interest payments. This situation is acceptable for shareholders as long as the interest expenses (the cost of the loan) are less than the benefit surplus generated by the new project (creating an operating income surplus). This relationship is referred to as financial leverage:

$$\text{ROE} = \text{ROA} + \frac{\text{Financial debt}}{\text{Shareholders' equity}} \times (\text{ROA} - k)$$

$$\text{ROE} = \text{ROA} + \text{LEV} \times (\text{ROA} - k)$$

where

        ROE = return on equity
        ROA = return on assets (after taxes)
        LEV = financial debt
         k = debt cost (after taxes)

Application 9.7 illustrates the concept of financial leverage.

APPLICATION 9.7

Leverage Effect

UBC discloses its balance sheet and its P&L. A quick analysis based on the gearing ratio can explain how the profitability is made (*in thousands of euros*).

Balance sheet

Fixed assets	1,000	Shareholders' equity	12,000
Working capital requirement	5,000	Net financial debt	3,000
Net economic assets	15,000	Financial liabilities & SE	15,000

P&L

Operating income	2,600
Interests on debts	(200)
Tax	(720)
Net income	1,680

The average tax rate in this case is 30%. The economic profitability rate and the cost of indebtedness (after tax) is as follows:

Return on assets:

$$\frac{1,680}{12,000} = 14\%$$

Economic profitability rate:

$$2,600 \times \frac{1 - 0.30}{15,000} = 12.13\%$$

Cost of indebtedness :

$$k = 200 \times \frac{1 - 0.30}{3,000} = 4.67\%$$

The link with the gearing ratio can be confirmed like this:

Return on assets:

$$12.13\% + \frac{3,000}{12,000}(12.13\% - 4.67\%) = 12.13\% + 0.25\% \times 7.46\% = 14\%$$

Wealth created by operating activities generates a lower profitability than that one of shareholder's equity. If the firm was only financed by equity, the equity profitability would be only 12.13%. However a part of the economic assets of the firm is financed by debt. This way of financing only costs 4.67% after tax to the shareholders. The extra profitability (7.46% = 12.13% − 4.6%) is given to shareholders, proportionately to the gearing ratio (debt/equity).

In these conditions, if nothing changes, the shareholders should keep on financing their projects with debt, in order to increase the equity profitability. They would still make 7.46% profitability on all the projects they do not finance themselves.

There are limits to the debt strategy. The company's default risk increases at the same rate as its level of indebtedness. Creditors therefore adjust the interest rate to reflect the level of risk so that the cost of the existing debt is equivalent to the company's ROA. Consequently, shareholders will no longer have an interest in loan financing. The resulting financial leverage in this case is negative (ROA rate $< k$).

The ROE is a positive function of the ROA. It is interesting to examine the origins of the ROE, especially through a detailed analysis of the income statement. The income statement should indicate whether the company has, for example, managed its costs and maintained its gross margin (the gross margin is the difference between net sales and cost of sales). The various economic indicators that take into account the operating activities should be studied as part of an overall review of all relevant indicators. However, certain operating ratios can be determined in the perspective of more accurately assessing the effectiveness of the management strategies in place. For example, the **gross margin rate** can only be revealing, as is the case for any ratio, if the values are compared over time or with those of competitors or the sector.

The **gross margin rate** is the difference between net sales and cost of sales expressed as a percentage of net sales.

APPLICATION 9.8

Calculation and Interpretation of Gross Margin

A firm has a turnover of £800,000 with a gross margin of £500,000 (difference between the turnover and the cost of sales). The gross margin rate is 62.5%. This ratio does not have any special meaning in itself but it is making more sense if one relates it to the events of the previous years. Does this rate mean better management efficiency or not? In this case, it is a matter of time comparison. The meaning of this ratio also becomes very interesting when several firms of the same sector and same size are compared with each other. Comparisons about management efficiency are then allowed.

This example clearly shows the ambiguity of financial analysis. Each data has to be compared with others while being sure that operating conditions can be compared from one year to another.

9.2.3   Financial Analysis Integrated into Financial Statements

The IFRS do not require financial analysis components to be added to financial statements. However, many experts believe that the publication of one or several financial ratios lead to a better understanding of the company's financial situation. For this reason, groups often include additional statements in their financial statements. This section deals with just two types of indicators:

- Indicators based exclusively on the income statement that help to assess economic performance.
- Indicators that express a form of profitability by comparing income indicators (economic performance) with invested capital indicators (identified using data found on the balance sheet).

It is important to be aware that these indicators are not officially defined by the IFRS, or anywhere else. Their definitions and components can therefore vary from one company to another depending on specific corporate management and operational needs or interests. This diversity of definitions can make comparisons between companies more difficult, or even impossible.

Economic Performance Indicators   One of the most commonly used indicators for multinationals is the *Operating Result*. Its publication was even mandatory according to IAS 1 up until the end of 2003. But the standard did not provide a precise enough definition of this indicator, and it is not even really possible to give one. The consequence was that *Operating Result* was removed from the list of elements to publish in the income statement. As of 2004, this requirement was made optional and companies can now publish the intermediary results of their choice as long as they provide the accompanying definitions.

The main purpose of the *Operating Income* indicator is to provide information on the company's overall operational performance, in a way that is not impacted by the financing structure (reflected by certain financial elements, interest expenses in particular) or income tax. This very general definition nevertheless creates allocation problems, especially for non-recurring elements where consolidation into the operating income can distort estimations of the company's future economic performance. Suez Environnement has found a transparent way to resolve this problem. In its 2008 annual report, along with the Operating Result, called *Income from Operating Activities*, the company publishes another indicator called *Current Operating Income*. The difference between the two is detailed in the notes (Figure 9.9).

With the same goal in mind, other multinationals differentiate an *Operating Margin* from the *Operating Income* by specifying the difference between these two indicators also in the notes. This is the case for Capgemini in its 2008 annual report (see Figure 9.10).

9.2.2 **COMPARISON BETWEEN THE FISCAL YEARS ENDED DECEMBER 31, 2008 AND 2007**

(in millions of euros)	2008	2007
Revenues	12,363.7	12,034.1
Purchases	(2,677.2)	(2,210.1)
Personnel costs	(3,062.2)	(3,140.1)
Depreciation, amortization and provisions	(776.0)	(754.9)
Other operating income and expenses	(4,789.2)	(4,867.6)
Current operating income	**1,059.1**	**1,061.4**
Mark-to-market on operating financial instruments	3.2	(5.7)
Impairment	(1.7)	(35.4)
Restructuring costs	(20.9)	(12.3)
Expenses linked to the initial public offering and change of logo	(50.8)	
Disposals of assets	46.9	181.4
Income from operating activities	**1,035.8**	**1,189.4**
Financial expenses	(420.8)	(365.7)
Financial income	91.0	103.0
Net financial loss	**(329.8)**	**(262.7)**
Income tax expense	(92.7)	(273.5)
Share in net income of associates	34.0	22.6
Net income	**647.3**	**675.8**
Minority interests	114.1	184.1
Net income Group share	**533.2**	**491.7**

Other income statement items:

(in millions of euros)	2008	2007
EBITDA	**2,101.9**	**2,061.4**

Figure 9.9   From Suez Environnement 2008 annual report, p. 160.

Schneider Electric uses another term for its intermediary results on its income statement. While disclosing the *Operating Results*, as is done on the statements of other companies, Schneider Electric also specifies that it measures its performance according to the EBITA indicator, which corresponds to an adjusted *Operating Result*, but does not take into account part of the amortization expenses.

In contrast to the Schneider Electric example, Accor shows that it's also possible that a particular term can be used, but can refer to calculations that are entirely different from what might be expected. Accor applies a much wider definition to the term *Operating Profit before tax* to include all items on the income statement except for the amount of income tax, and therefore includes the total financial income (see Figure 9.12). In addition to the *Operating Income* indicator, Accor includes four other intermediary results that reflect the company's

CONSOLIDATED FINANCIAL STATEMENTS					
in millions of euros	2004 (1)	2005	2006	2007	2008
REVENUES	**6,235**	**6,954**	**7,700**	**8,703**	**8,710**
OPERATING EXPENSES	6,259	6,729	7,253	8,063	7,966
OPERATING MARGIN	**(24)**	**225**	**447**	**640**	**744**
% of revenues	(0.4%)	3.2%	5.8%	7.4%	8.5%
OPERATING PROFIT/(LOSS)	**(281)**	**214**	**334**	**493**	**586**
% of revenues	(4.5%)	3.1%	4.3%	5.7%	6.7%
PROFIT/(LOSS) FOR THE YEAR	**(534)**	**141**	**293**	**440**	**451**
% of revenues	(8.6%)	2.0%	3.8%	5.1%	5.2%
EARNINGS/(LOSS) PER SHARE					
Number of shares at December 31	131,383,178	131,581,978	144,081,808	145,425,510	145,844,938
Earnings/(loss) per share at December 31 (in euro)	(4.07)	1.07	2.03	3.03	3.09
Dividend per share for the year (in euros)	-	0.50	0.70	1.00	1.00*
NET CASH AND CASH EQUIVALENTS AT DECEMBER 31	**285**	**904**	**1,632**	**889**	**774**
AVERAGE NUMBER OF EMPLOYEES	**57,387**	**59,734**	**64,013**	**79,213**	**86,495**
NUMBER OF EMPLOYEES AT DECEMBER 31	**59,324**	**61,036**	**67,889**	**83,508**	**91,621**

(1) Restated in accordance with IFRS.
* Subject to approval by the Extraordinary Shareholders' Meeting of April 30, 2009.

Figure 9.10   From Capgemini's 2008 annual report, p. 69.

internal management: EBITDAR, EBITDA, EBIT and operating profit before tax and non-recurring items. Each of these indicators is detailed in the notes.

An Example of a Profitability Indicator: ROCE   Return on Capital Employed (ROCE) is an indicator that combines the concept of economic performance (operating income, or intermediary results) with the value of the resources employed to obtain it, in particular the current and non-current operating assets minus operating liabilities. Since neither the indicator itself nor its components is defined by the IFRS, the definitions that companies use can vary greatly, sometimes even within the same business group, depending on the industry and other factors.

PSA Peugeot Citroën uses two different definitions for "capital employed": one for its industrial and sales activities and another for its financing activities. The components included in capital employed are listed in an explanatory note included with the consolidated financial statements (see Figure 9.13).

The capital employed determined this way is compared with the "Economic profit after tax" which is in essence the net income after tax, but without the "Financial results after tax" (see

(in millions of euros except for earnings per share)		2008	2007
Revenue	*(note 21)*	18,311	**17,309**
Cost of sales		(10,896)	(10,210)
Gross profit		7,415	**7,099**
Research and development expenses	*(note 22)*	(402)	(417)
Selling, general and administrative expenses		(4,120)	(3,978)
Other operating income and expenses	*(note 24)*	(139)	(142)
EBITA (*)		2,754	**2,562**
Amortization and impairment of purchase accounting intangibles	*(note 25)*	(174)	(79)
Operating profit		2,580	**2,483**
Finance costs, net		(246)	(247)
Other financial income and expenses		(68)	(19)
Finance costs and other financial income and expense, net	*(note 26)*	(314)	**(266)**
Share of profit /(losses) of associates	*(note 6)*	12	4
Profit before tax		2,278	**2,221**
Income tax expense	*(note 11)*	(555)	(600)
Profit for the period		1,723	**1,621**
- Attributable to equity holders of the parent		1,682	1,583
- Attributable to minority interests		41	38
Basic earnings per share (in euros)	*(note 13.3)*	7.02	6.78
Diluted earnings per share (in euros)	*(note 13.3)*	7.00	6.70

* EBITA (Earnings Before Interest Taxes and Amortization of purchase accounting intangibles).
The accompanying notes are an integral part of the consolidated financial statements.

Figure 9.11   From Schneider Electric's 2008 annual report.

Figure 9.14). The way it is calculated is also specified in the notes, and it is indeed possible to re-establish the relationship between this concept and the various items on the income statement:

The ROCE is thus presented as follows (see Figure 9.15).

The ROCE value of −2.5% in 2008 is not comparable with Accor's value of 14.1% for the same period because the two companies use significantly different definitions of the term ROCE.

For Accor, the ROCE is based on the capital that was initially invested. Thus it maintains the gross (historical) values for assets as components of the capital employed. The working capital

(in million of euros)	Notes	2006 (*)	2007	2008
Revenue		7,533	8,025	7,610
Other operating revenue		74	96	129
CONSOLIDATED REVENUE	3	**7,607**	**8,121**	**7,739**
Operating expense	4	(5,523)	(5,800)	(5,449)
EBITDAR	5	**2,084**	**2,321**	**2,290**
Rental expense	6	(836)	(931)	(903)
EBITDA	7	**1,248**	**1,390**	**1,387**
Depreciation, amortization and provision expense	8	(436)	(419)	(446)
EBIT	9	**812**	**971**	**941**
Net financial expense	10	(96)	(92)	(86)
Share of profit of associates after tax	11	11	28	20
OPERATING PROFIT BEFORE TAX AND NON RECURRING ITEMS		**727**	**907**	**875**
Restructuring costs	12	(69)	(58)	(56)
Impairment losses	13	(94)	(99)	(57)
Gains and losses on management of hotel properties	14	109	208	111
Gains and losses on management of other assets	15	15	188	12
OPERATING PROFIT BEFORE TAX		**688**	**1,146**	**885**
Income tax expense	16	(258)	(234)	(272)
Profit or loss from discontinued operations	17	104	-	-
NET PROFIT	43	**534**	**912**	**613**
NET PROFIT, GROUP SHARE		**501**	**883**	**575**
Net Profit, Minority interests	27	33	29	38
Weighted average number of shares outstanding (in thousands)	25	224,738	225,013	221,237
EARNINGS PER SHARE (in euros)		**2.23**	**3.92**	**2.60**
Diluted earnings per share (in euros)	26	2.17	3.78	2.59
DIVIDEND PER SHARE (in euros)		1.45	1.65	1.65 (**)
EXCEPTIONAL DIVIDEND PER SHARE (in euros)		1.50	1.50	-
Earnings per share from continuing operations (in euros)		1.77	3.92	2.60
Diluted earnings per share from continuing operations (in euros)		1.74	3.78	2.59
Earnings per share from discontinued operations (in euros)		0.46	N/A	N/A
Diluted earnings per share from discontinued operations (in euros)		0.43	N/A	N/A

(*) In accordance with IFRS 5, Carlson Wagonlit Travel (CWT) profits or losses have been recognised in Profit or loss from discontinued operations (see Note 17).
(**) Proposed to the Combined Ordinary and Extraordinary Shareholders' Meeting.

Figure 9.12　From Accor's 2008 annual report.

requirements are then added to this amount. In addition, the income indicator does not include the year's depreciation expenses and does not take into account other "calculated" expenses, such as impairment losses or provision expenses.

This calculation is explained in a note accompanying the company's 2008 financial statements (see Figure 9.16).

The examples above prove that the analysis of financial ratios is a delicate task, even in an economic context where most multinationals apply the same financial standards (IFRS).

39.1. Capital Employed

Capital employed corresponds to the operating assets or liabilities employed by the Group. The definition of capital employed depends on whether it relates to manufacturing and sales companies or finance companies.

Capital employed is defined as representing:

- all non-financial assets, net of non-financial liabilities, of the manufacturing and sales companies, as reported in the consolidated balance sheet;
- the net assets of the finance companies.

Based on the above definition, capital employed breaks down as follows:

(in million euros)	Dec. 31, 2008	Dec. 31, 2007	Dec. 31, 2006
Goodwill	1,237	1,488	1,488
Intangible assets	4,061	3,885	3,947
Property, plant and equipment	14,064	14,652	15,221
Investments in companies at equity	732	725	687
Investments in non-consolidated companies	48	47	53
Other non-current assets	152	126	96
Deferred tax assets	468	428	499
Inventories	7,757	6,913	6,826
Trade receivables - manufacturing and sales companies	2,001	2,857	3,043
Current tax assets	189	169	210
Other receivables	1,897	1,782	1,719
Other non-current liabilities	(2,793)	(2,886)	(2,759)
Non-current provisions	(876)	(1,109)	(1,383)
Deferred tax liabilities	(1,321)	(1,689)	(1,854)
Current provisions	(2,053)	(2,132)	(1,747)
Trade payables	(8,428)	(10,600)	(10,481)
Current taxes payable	(76)	(158)	(152)
Other payables	(3,795)	(4,241)	(4,075)
Net assets of the finance companies	2,919	2,894	2,652
Accounts between the manufacturing and sales companies and the finance companies	(10)	8	141
TOTAL	16,173	13,159	14,131

PSA PEUGEOT CITROËN

Figure 9.13 From PSA Peugeot Citroën's 2008 annual report, p. 278.

Based on this definition, economic profit is as follows:

(in million euros)	2008	2007	2006
Consolidated profit for the year	(500)	826	70
Interest income	(247)	(283)	(178)
Finance costs	343	306	234
Net gains on disposals of short-term investments	-	-	(26)
Tax on financial income and finance expenses	6	28	9
ECONOMIC PROFIT AFTER TAX	(398)	877	109

PSA PEUGEOT CITROËN

Figure 9.14 From PSA Peugeot Citroën's 2008 annual report.

39.3. Return on Capital Employed

Return on capital employed, corresponding to economic profit expressed as a percentage of total capital employed at December 31, is as follows:

	Dec. 31, 2008	Dec. 31, 2007	Dec. 31, 2006
	(2.5%)	6.7%	0.8%

PSA PEUGEOT CITROËN

Figure 9.15   From PSA Peugeot Citroën's 2008 annual report.

This is due to the fact that the IFRS do not deal with financial analysis, and the choice of how to define financial ratios remains at the discretion of those who prepare the financial statements (or those who will analyze them), even if these ratios are included within statements established according to the IFRS. The only reliable comparisons that can be made between these IFRS-compliant ratios are therefore those made over time within the same company.

Return On Capital Employed (ROCE) is a key management indicator used internally to measure the performance of the Group's various businesses.

It is also an indicator of the profitability of assets that are either not consolidated or accounted for by the equity method.

It is calculated on the basis of the following aggregates derived from the consolidated financial statements:

▶ Adjusted EBITDA: for each business, EBITDA plus revenue from financial assets and investments in associates (dividends and interest);

▶ Capital Employed: for each business, the average cost of non-current assets, before depreciation, amortization and provisions, plus working capital.

ROCE corresponds to the ratio between EBITDA and average capital employed for the period. In December 2008, ROCE stood at 14.1% versus 13.6% in fiscal 2007 and 11.9% in fiscal 2006.

(in million of euros)	Dec. 2006 (*)	Dec. 2007	Dec. 2008
Capital employed	10,779	10,519	10,308
Adjustments on capital employed [1]	78	44	(316)
Effect of exchange rate on capital employed [2]	(50)	43	97
RESTATED AVERAGE CAPITAL EMPLOYED	**10,807**	**10,606**	**10,089**
EBITDA	1,248	1,390	1,387
Interest income on external loans and dividends	17	9	8
Share of profit of associates before tax (see Note 11)	18	38	28
RESTATED ADJUSTED EBITDA	**1,283**	**1,437**	**1,423**
RESTATED ROCE (ADJUSTED EBITDA/CAPITAL EMPLOYED)	**11.9%**	**13.6%**	**14.1%**

(*) ROCE presented above have been adjusted to exclude Carlson Wagonlit Travel (CWT), in accordance with IFRS 5.

(1) For the purpose of calculating ROCE, capital employed is prorated over the period of EBITDA recognition in the income statement. For example, the capital employed of a business acquired on December 31 that did not generate any EBITDA during the period would not be included in the calculation.

(2) Capital employed is translated at the average exchange rate for the year, corresponding to the rate used to translate EBITDA.

Figure 9.16   From Accor's 2008 annual report.

9.3 ANALYZING FINANCIAL STATEMENTS AND PROFITABILITY

Examining a company's financial statement is generally accompanied by an analysis of its profitability, in particular for the shareholders. Financial statements provide a great deal of information that allows shareholders to conduct a detailed analysis: the annual comprehensive income statement (section 9.3.1), the statement of changes in shareholders' equity (section 9.3.2), the notes (section 9.3.3), information by business segment (section 9.3.4), earnings per share (section 9.3.5), and information provided on discontinued operations (section 9.3.6).

9.3.1 The Statement of Comprehensive Income

The comprehensive income refers to all changes in equity during a period, except for those resulting from transactions with owners in their capacity as owners (for example, as part of a share capital increase or a reduction of capital).

IFRS identify two definitions of income that should not be confused with one another:

- *Profit or loss*: Income less expenses, excluding the components of other comprehensive income,
- *Total comprehensive income*: Profit or loss, plus the other components of comprehensive income.

Other components of comprehensive income include income and expenses that the IFRS either permit or require to be excluded from the *Profit or Loss*. They represent increases and reductions in wealth for equity owners, even if they do not appear in the income statement, and it is due to their impact on the owners' earnings that they are taken into account in the *Total comprehensive income*.

The revised version of IAS 1, applicable for fiscal years beginning January 1, 2009, lists five components of other comprehensive income:

(a) Changes in the *revaluation surplus* from revaluations of non-current tangible and intangible assets according to IAS 16 and IAS 38 (see Chapter 5).
(b) Actuarial gains and losses recorded as part of benefit and retirement plans in accordance with IAS 19 (see Chapter 4).
(c) Gains and losses arising from translating the financial statements of a foreign subsidiary denominated in a foreign currency according to IAS 21 (see Chapter 8).
(d) Gains and losses associated with the revaluation of available-for-sale financial assets in accordance with IAS 39 (see Chapter 5).
(e) The effective portion of gains and losses on hedging instruments in a cash flow hedge according to IAS 39 (see Chapter 5).

Thus the total comprehensive income has six components in all: the *Profit or Loss*, plus the five other components listed above.

The excerpt below, from Lafarge's 3rd quarter 2009 interim report (see Figure 9.17), is already established according to the revised version of IAS 1. Its content is a good illustration of the difference that can exist between the recorded *Profit or Loss* of €1,029m (called here "Net income") and the *Total comprehensive income* of €548m.

Consolidated statement of comprehensive income

(million euros)	9 months		3rd quarter		December 31,
	2009	2008	2009	2008	2008
Net income	1,029	1,824	496	741	1,939
Available for sale investments	265	(204)	50	13	(338)
Cash-flow hedge instruments	21	(9)	6	(63)	(53)
Actuarial gains / (losses)	(414)	(88)	(45)	-	(384)
Currency translation adjustments	(460)	234	(266)	1,249	(836)
Income tax on other comprehensive income	107	13	12	16	126
Other comprehensive income for the period, net of income tax	(481)	(54)	(243)	1,215	(1,485)
Total comprehensive income for the period	548	1,770	253	1,956	454
Out of which part attributable to:					
- Owners of the parent of the Group	*358*	*1,507*	*181*	*1,780*	*148*
- Non-controlling interests	*190*	*263*	*72*	*176*	*306*

The accompanying notes are an integral part of these consolidated financial statements.

Figure 9.17   Lafarge, 2009 3rd quarter interim report.

9.3.2   Statement of Changes in Shareholders' Equity

While the comprehensive income for the period just measures the impact of transactions with non-shareholders on the shareholders' equity, the statement of changes in shareholders' equity analyzes the changes in all of the various equity components. Beyond the effects from the total comprehensive income, these changes can come from increase or reductions of subscribed capital, distribution of dividends, or transactions with treasury shares. The effect of each of these changes is presented for each equity component including:

- Subscribed capital.
- Share premiums.
- Reserves.
- Each of the five other components of the comprehensive income (see above, section 9.3.1).
- Non-controlling interests.

Thus, the statement of variations in shareholders' equity provides information on the factors that influence the amount of wealth ultimately available to the shareholders over the course of the year. It gives a perspective on capital transactions and cash flows that have impacted the shareholders' equity, and hence the transfers of funds between the company and its shareholders.

The excerpt in Figure 9.18 from the statement of changes in shareholders' equity in Accor's 2008 annual report illustrates the level of detail required. The columns represent the different

In € millions	Number of shares outstanding	Share capital	Additional paid-in capital	Currency translation reserve (1)	Fair value adjustments on Financial Instruments reserve (2)	Reserve related to employee benefits	Reserve for actuarial gains/losses	Retained earnings and profit for the period	Share-holders' equity	Minority interests	Conso-lidated share-holders' equity
AT DECEMBER 31, 2007	**221,527,644**	**665**	**2,276**	**(145)**	**66**	**59**	**(19)**	**789**	**3,691**	**61**	**3,752**
Fair value adjustments on financial instruments	-	-	-	-	(72)	-	-	67	(5)	-	(5)
Currency translation adjustment	-	-	-	(222)	-	-	-	-	(222)	(45)	(267)
Change in reserve for actuarial Gains/losses	-	-	-	-	-	-	(4)	-	(4)	-	(4)
Profit for the period	-	-	-	-	-	-	-	575	575	38	613
Recognised income and expense	-	-	-	*(222)*	*(72)*	-	*(4)*	*642*	*344*	*(7)*	*337*
Issues of share capital											
On exercise of stock options	204,578	1	7	-	-	-	-	-	8	-	8
Capital reduction (4)	(1,837,699)	(6)	(57)	-	-	-	-	-	(63)	-	(63)
Dividends paid	-	-	-	-	-	-	-	(698)	(698)	(22)	(720)
Change in reserve for employee benefits	-	-	-	-	-	23	-	-	23	-	23
Effect of scope changes	-	-	-	-	-	-	-	-	-	226	226
AT DECEMBER 31, 2008	**219,894,523**	**660**	**2,226**	**(367)**	**(6)**	**82**	**(23)**	**733**	**3,305**	**258**	**3,563**

Figure 9.18   From Accor 2008 annual report.

components of the shareholders' equity, and each line indicates the impact of each source of change on the respective components. Thus, the change in the fair value of the financial instruments over the year (−€72m) did more than exhaust the reserves generated over previous years and set aside for this purpose, bringing them from €66m to −€6m. Changes in foreign currency exchange rates also contributed to a reduction in shareholders' equity by decreasing the balance sheet *Translation difference* by €222m from −€145m to −€367m. The most significant changes for the year were due to 2008's net income of €575m allocated to the *Retained earnings and profit for the year* column, as well as the distribution of dividends totaling €698m in 2008 for 2007 also allocated to *Retained earnings and profit for the year* column.

APPLICATION 9.9

Statement of Changes in Equity

A metal firm discloses its statement of changes in equity:

(in thousands of euros)	Capital	Share premium	Reserve	Accumulated incomes	Total
At January 1, 2008	10,700	49,600	163,000	23,400	246,700
Increase in capital	180	1,200			1,380
Net income of the year				29,200	29,200
Allocation to reserves			8,120	(8,120)	
Dividends				(4,500)	(4,500)
At December 31, 2008	10,880	50,800	171,120	39,980	272,780
Increase in capital					
Net income of the year				22,500	22,500
Allocation to reserves			8,500	(8,500)	
Dividends				(6,000)	(6,000)
At December 31, 2009	10,880	50,800	179,620	47,980	289,280

The first year, the firm increased capital by 1,380 whereas it paid 10,500 dividends during both years. A financial analyst could wonder about the relevance of making an increase of capital; it would have been sufficient not to pay any dividend to the shareholders.

This example underlines financial and investing issues on two points:

- The impact of the investing policy, that is to say the efficiency of the investments made that is visible through the net income of the year and the evolution of retained earnings (reserves).
- Did the company rely on the shareholders to finance its investments? This can be analyzed through the increase in capital. The increase in capital from the former shareholders (inflows) does not prevent the payment of dividends (outflows) during the next two years.

9.3.3   Accounting Methods and Other Explanations: Notes

The Notes are a required component of financial statements and must include three types of information:

1. Information on the standards used to establish the financial statements (for example, a declaration of compliance with the IFRS) and the specific accounting methods used.
2. Information required by the IFRS that is not provided elsewhere in the financial statements.
3. Information that does not appear elsewhere in the financial statements, but is important for their interpretation.

In addition, the four financial statements (the statement of financial position, the statement of comprehensive income, the statement of changes in shareholders' equity, and the statement of cash flows) must include cross-references to information in the notes whenever possible.

Danone (Figure 9.19) provides a good example of a table of contents of the notes in its annual report 2008.

The first note is relatively long (about 5 pages). In addition to the declaration of compliance with the IFRS, it outlines the accounting standards in effect, especially the accounting and consolidation methods that the company has chosen to use. Note also that paragraph 25 insists on the importance of the assumptions, estimations and assessments made as part of the preparation of the financial statements. They convey the corporate management's perception of the economic situation and introduce an element of subjectivity in the accounts that users should be aware of, especially for accounts established according to the IFRS. Danone's declaration of compliance with the IFRS and the note regarding estimations appear in Figure 9.20. This is just an example; IFRS do not require any particular wording. For comparative purposes, the right-hand column features the corresponding notes in PSA Peugeot Citroën's annual report. Peugeot's notes are a bit more explicit in terms of the risks associated with uncertainties and specify the balance sheet items that are more affected.

Notes 2 and 3 deal with changes in the group's composition (changes in the scope of consolidation and discontinued operations). Notes 4 to 24 provide in-depth details on information presented in the balance sheet and the income statement, while note 26 gives additional information on the cash flow statement.

● ● ● TABLE OF THE NOTES

DANONE

Figure 9.19   From Danone 2008 annual report.

Note 25 covers transactions with related parties detailed in a particular IFRS standard (IAS 24). The purpose is to inform users of the quantity and terms of transactions between the company and individuals and corporate entities associated with it, in particular:

- Companies included in full consolidation, proportionate consolidation, or by the equity method.
- Members of administrative bodies such as the Executive Committee and Board of Directors.
- Companies subject to significant influence on the part of a member of one of these administrative bodies (or a close family member).

The information that must be provided according to this standard deals with compensation for members of administrative bodies (salaries, subsequent employment advantages, contract termination compensation, payment in shares, etc.), and also regarding any other agreement between the company and its related parties.

The consolidated financial statements of Groupe Danone have been prepared in compliance with IFRS *(International Financial Reporting Standards)* as adopted by the European Union, available on the web site of the European Commission (http://ec.europa.eu/internal_market/accounting/ias_fr.htm).

The accounting principles applied by the Group comply with the IFRS recommendations of the IASB *(International Accounting Standards Board)* not adopted at European level.

The Group's consolidated financial statements for 2008 have been prepared in accordance with International Financial Reporting Standards (IFRS) adopted for use in the European Union[1].

International Financial Reporting Standards include IFRSs and IASs (International Accounting Standards) and the related interpretations as prepared by the Standing Interpretations Committee (SIC) and the International Financial Reporting Interpretations Committee (IFRIC).

1.4. Uses of Estimates and Assumptions

The preparation of financial statements in accordance with IFRS requires management to make estimates and assumptions in order to determine the reported amounts of certain assets, liabilities, income and expense items, as well as certain amounts disclosed in the Notes to the financial statements relating to contingent assets and liabilities.

25. USE OF ESTIMATES

The preparation of consolidated financial statements requires management to make estimates and assumptions that affect the reported amounts of assets and liabilities and disclosures at the date of the consolidated financial statements, especially regarding the valuation of intangible assets, investments accounted for under the equity method, deferred tax assets, financial liabilities relating to put options granted to minority shareholders, provisions for risks and liabilities, provisions for commercial agreements and pension liabilities. Those estimates and assumptions, assessed based on current situation as of the end of the financial period presented, are detailed in the corresponding notes. Actual amounts could differ from those estimates, including in a context of economic and financial crisis.

The estimates and assumptions used are those deemed by management to be the most pertinent and accurate in view of the Group's circumstances and past experience.

Nevertheless, given the uncertainty inherent in any projections, actual results may differ from initial estimates.

To reduce uncertainty, estimates and assumptions are reviewed periodically, and the effects of any changes are recognised immediately.

The main items determined on the basis of estimates and assumptions are as follows:

- pension obligations;
- provisions (particularly vehicle warranty provisions, restructuring provisions and provisions for claims and litigation);
- the recoverable amount and useful life of property, plant and equipment and intangible assets;
- the recoverable amount of finance receivables, inventories and other receivables;
- the fair value of derivative financial instruments;
- deferred tax assets;
- sales incentives.

Figure 9.20   From Danone and PSA Peugeot Citroën annual reports 2008.

NOTE 25 - Related Party Transactions

The main related parties are the affiliated companies, the members of the Executive Committee and the members of the Board of Directors.

Affiliated companies are those companies in which the Group exercises a significant influence and that are accounted for under the equity method.

Transactions with affiliated companies are usually performed at arm's length.

The table below gives the breakdown of the amount of the transactions conducted with affiliated companies in 2007 and 2008:

(In € millions)	2007	2008
Operating income	137	165
Operating expense	(1)	-

The table below gives the breakdown of the amount of receivables and payables with affiliated companies as of December 31, 2007 and 2008:

(In € millions)	2007	2008
Long and short-term loans	2	1
Operating receivables	28	20
Operating payables	1	-

MEMBERS OF THE EXECUTIVE COMMITTEE AND OF THE BOARD OF DIRECTORS

Total compensation paid to the members of the Executive Committee amounted to € 17.5 million in 2008 (€ 12 million in 2007). In addition, as of December 31, 2008, the number of stock options granted to members of the Executive Committee amounted to 3,602,966.

As of December 31, 2008, the amount of pension provisions relating to the members of the Executive Committee amounted to € 41.6 million (€ 46 million as of December 31, 2007).

In addition, on July 21, 2004, the Board of Directors set the indemnification conditions of the members of the Executive Committee in certain cases where they cease their mandates or functions. The indemnity would correspond to twice the annual gross compensation (fixed, variable and in-kind) they received over the last 12 months before they cease their functions. On February 13, 2008, the Board of Directors decided to terminate those for the indemnities that were due to the Company's four corporate officers. The General Meeting of April 29, 2008 authorized the granting to these four corporate officers of new terms of indemnification, leaving the amounts and cases of payability unchanged, but subordinating the payment of these indemnities to conditions of performance.

The Board of Directors also decided to grant new terms of indemnification for these four corporate officers, leaving the amounts and cases of payability unchanged, but subordinating the payment of these indemnities to conditions of performance. In accordance with the provisions of the French Commercial Code (*Code de commerce*), the terms of indemnification of the four corporate officers will be subject to the approval of the next General Meeting. Finally, the directors' fees paid to the members of the Board of Directors amounted to 388,000 euros in 2008 (382,000 euros in 2007).

DANONE

Figure 9.21   From Danone annual report 2008.

In the case of Danone (Figure 9.21), the related parties are essentially associate companies, and members of the Executive Committee and the Board of Directors.

Note 27 outlines the contractual obligations and commitments not included in the balance sheet, such as future financial commitments associated with purchasing or leasing agreements in effect.

Finally, notes 28 and 29 contain information broken down by industry and geographic area (see section 9.3.4 below). Note 30 gives information about subsequent events as well, while note 32 deals with more Danone-specific topics, which are legal and arbitration proceedings. The last note, 32, features a list of companies included in the group's consolidated financial statements.

The number of notes can vary from one company to another. For example, Accor's 2008 annual report includes 49 notes, while Vodafone 2008 annual report featured 37, and Air France's, 41 notes.

Some multinationals include other types of information that they consider relevant for understanding the financial statements. For example, they may feature information on the financial ratios used internally to track the company's transactions. An example is note 39 in PSA Peugeot Citroën's annual information form, which details the composition of the ROCE, an especially important financial indicator for the group.

9.3.4   Segment Reporting

> **Segment reporting:** information that a company must provide on its business segments.

Analyzing a company's financial profitability and return on investment is not enough when the company's activities involve various activities in several geographical areas, all of them being subject to various risks. This is why users of financial information must be provided with information to evaluate the nature and financial effects of the company's activities, and the economic environments in which they operate. To do that, first, by looking at the group's internal structure, its main operating segments need to be identified (section 9.3.4(a)). If necessary, these segments are then combined in reportable segments (section 9.3.4(b)). The company then provides specific information on each reportable segment (section 9.3.4(c)). Finally, taking into account the fact that segmentation criteria can vary greatly from one company to another, and in the interest of ensuring that a minimum of comparable information should be provided for all companies, IFRS 8 requires disclosure of segment-specific information on each industry, geographic area, and the company's major customers (section 9.3.4(c)).

(a) Identifying Operating Segments   Companies are required to break their operations down into different segments. An operating segment is defined as a specific area of activity that:

- generates income and expense,
- yields operating profits that are regularly reviewed by operational decision-makers as part of their managerial capacities, and for which
- specific financial data is available.

Segmentation can be applied to industries and geographic areas, or a combination of the two. For example, activities can be segmented by industry within a particular area (Europe, for example), but grouped together for all the other geographic areas if the business volume there is less significant, but nonetheless diversified outside of Europe. It is also possible to identify one or several sectors for certain customers if the customers in question are significant enough to be tracked internally by the company and they meet the criteria listed above.

It is also possible to identify an activity that does not yet generate any sales revenue as an operating segment in and of itself. This may arise in the case of a new activity launch. This would be the case, for example, for an agri-food multinational, which launches a new activity of pharmaceutical products, or if a company decides to launch business operations in a new geographic area.

It should also be noted that it is not necessary to allocate all assets and liabilities to specific operating segments. For example, administration of the company's headquarters and certain other managerial functions are often not attributed to particular operating segments because they serve many, or even all of the company's business segments.

Thus, the nature and scope of operating segments can vary immensely (by industry, geographic area, customers, etc.) within the same business activity. This is allowed by the IFRS since what prevails in this context is how the company itself manages its transactions internally. Industry-specific information that is consistent with the internal management structure is what is most relevant for users of the financial information in question.

The German company, Deutsche Telekom, identifies three main business activities: mobile phone communications, broadband and fixed network telecommunications, and business customers. Its other activities are combined in a segment it calls "group headquarters and shared services". However, the industry-specific information for the "mobile communications" activities is split into two reporting segments according to a geographic criterion: Europe and USA, which reflects the company's internal organization. Therefore, the segmentation is based on a combination of criteria, i.e. on business activity and geographic area (Figure 9.22).

(b) Reporting Operating Segments   Not all of a company's operating segments are presented in its financial statements, only those that exceed a certain size. This is determined according to:

- the relative volume of its reported revenue: the segment represents at least 10% of the company's total internal and external reported revenues for all operating segments;

In contrast to the former reporting structure, Deutsche Telekom reports on five operating segments, which are independently managed by bodies responsible for the respective segments depending on the nature of products and services offered, brands, sales channels, and customer profiles. The identification of Company components as business segments is based in particular on the existence of segment managers who report directly to the Board of Management of Deutsche Telekom AG and who are responsible for the performance of the segment under their charge. In accordance with IFRS 8, Mobile Communications Europe and Mobile Communications USA are reported separately as operating segments, since internal reporting and management channels in the Mobile Communications operating segment have been changed. Prior-year figures have been adjusted accordingly.

Figure 9.22   From Deutsche Telekom's 2007 annual report.

- the relative amount of its profit or loss: the segment represents at least 10% of the absolute value of the whichever of the following is greater:
  - the cumulative profit for profit-making operating segments, or
  - the cumulative loss for operating segments with shortfall, or
- the value of its assets: the segment represents at least 10% of the cumulative value of the assets for all operating segments.

If an operating segment exceeds at least one of these three criteria, it is considered a segment to be presented separately as part of segment-specific information reporting procedures.

If the total reported revenue determined according to these criteria for the reportable segments reaches at least 75% of the entity's reported revenue, all other operating segments can be combined under the category "Other segments". If, however, the threshold of 75% is not met, some segments will need to be reassigned to create additional reportable segments. This recombination of segments should meet a certain number of criteria so that the operating segments that the company combines together meet all of the following conditions:

- They have similar economic characteristics.
- They are similar in terms of:
  - the type of products and services they deal with
  - their manufacturing process
  - the type or category of customers that their products and services target
  - the methods used to distribute products and provide services, and
  - if relevant, the regulatory context (for example, for a bank, insurance company, or public services).

Operating segments must be recombined as long as the 75% reported revenue threshold is not met, even when the segments to report fall below the 10% limits mentioned above.

In addition, in the interest of guaranteeing the quality of segment information, the company should avoid reporting separate information for too many different segments. In general, there should not be more than a total of 10 segments.

As is illustrated in Figure 9.23, the 75% criteria are easily met by four of Deutsche Telekom's operating segments. The "Other" category, called here "Group Headquarters & Shared Services", represents not even 1% of the group's net revenue.

(c) Information to Disclose for Reportable Segments The segment information provided should reflect the way the company manages its operations. This is also true for the information given for each business segment, as well as for the assessment procedures used to obtain data. This is important for two reasons:

- The information that must be provided, with few exceptions, is the same information that is regularly presented to the primary operational decision-makers.
- The assessment procedures are the same as those used internally to calculate indicators prepared for the primary operational decision-makers. Thus they do not necessarily comply with the IFRS.

millions of €   Net revenue

Mobile Communications Europe	2008	19,978
	2007	20,000
	2006	17,700
Mobile Communications USA	2008	14,942
	2007	14,050
	2006	13,608
Broadband/ Fixed Network	2008	17,691
	2007	19,072
	2006	20,366
Business Customers	2008	8,456
	2007	8,971
	2006	9,301
Group Headquarters & Shared Services	2008	599
	2007	423
	2006	372
Total	**2008**	**61,666**
	2007	**62,516**
	2006	**61,347**
Reconciliation	2008	–
	2007	–
	2006	–
Group	2008	61,666
	2007	62,516
	2006	61,347

Figure 9.23   From Deutsche Telekom's 2008 annual report.

Only two indicators must be provided in all cases for each reportable segment:

1. An income indicator.
2. A total assets indicator.

However, the following 12 indicators must be provided only if they are regularly reviewed by the primary operational decision-makers, regardless of whether they are included in the two indicators mentioned above, or provided separately:

- For income:

   3. Ordinary revenue generated by external customers (external sales).
   4. Ordinary revenue from other divisions within the company (internal sales).
   5. Interest income.
   6. Interest expense.
   7. Depreciation of tangible and non-tangible assets.

8. Significant revenue and expenses reported in accordance with IAS 1.97.
9. The entity's proportionate interest in earnings of affiliated companies and joint-venturers recorded for according to equity method.
10. Income tax expenses or earnings.
11. Major elements without cash consideration other than depreciation of tangible and intangible assets (for example, write-downs, estimated expenses, etc.).

- For the balance sheet:

12. A liability indicator.
13. The amounts of cost to acquire non-current assets (other than financial instruments, assets for retirement plan coverage, income tax assets, and benefits related to insurance policies).
14. The carrying amount of participation in affiliated companies and joint-ventures accounted for according to the equity method.

Companies must indicate the composition of the indicators used, especially for income and asset indicators, but also for liabilities and acquisitions, and all other reported items.

The obligation to present segment information has certain consequences for the company's organizational structure. It necessitates efforts to gather and present data, which sometimes lead to information systems modifications. For example, to determine a company's income for a particular segment, it may be necessary to identify the transactions carried out internally. Practically speaking, the company's transfer prices are used. For accountability purposes, the financial information published by the company must indicate how these transfer prices are set, and to what extent they have changed from year to year.

Another issue stems from allocating assets to the various segments, since assets are often used by several segments. In this case, rules set down as part of the company's internal management practices apply to the reported segment information in a way that is consistent with the general approach of the IFRS.

Deutsche Telekom's annual report gives a good example of a description of measurement principles and definitions regarding business segments in the financial statement notes (Figure 9.24).

The example of Deutsche Telekom in Figure 9.25 shows that this group meets these requirements. The group has even added additional information on a voluntary basis, such as the number of employees per segment, as well as the cash flow from operating activities, investments and financing for each segment. All of the segment information restated for an additional year, 2006, is also provided. Given how high some of the amounts are, the column showing the impairment losses should not be considered voluntary information, but rather as information to be disclosed in keeping with point number 11 described above.

It should be noted that the level of detail required for the income indicators is very close to the requirements in IAS 1 for the company's entire income statement. Those who analyze the statements therefore can get a fairly accurate idea of the economic performance of each of the company's operating segments. This information can then be compared with figures on the invested assets and liabilities associated with each segment, which makes profitability analysis such as calculating the ROCE possible.

The measurement principles for Deutsche Telekom's segment reporting structure are based on the IFRSs adopted in the consolidated financial statements. Deutsche Telekom evaluates the segments' performance based on their profit/loss from operations (EBIT), among other factors. Revenue generated and goods and services exchanged between segments are calculated on the basis of market prices.

Segment assets and liabilities include all assets and liabilities that are attributable to operations and whose positive or negative results determine profit/loss from operations (EBIT). Segment assets include in particular intangible assets; property, plant and equipment; trade and other receivables; and inventories. Segment liabilities include in particular trade and other payables, and significant provisions. Segment investments include additions to intangible assets and property, plant and equipment.

Figure 9.24   From Deutsche Telekom's 2008 annual report.

Finally, the information on acquisitions by segment allows for an estimation of future evolutions and the direction that the company hopes to take for its activities.

This information is not necessarily presented according to the accounting procedures used for the company's balance sheet or income statement, and the scope of the items included is usually different as well. To establish a relationship between the company's financial statements and the segment information provided, IFRS 8 requires reconciliation to be presented for at least the total ordinary revenue, the indicators for income by segment, the assets and liabilities by segment, and any other significant element reported for each segment:

- The ordinary revenue of reportable segments are to be reconciled with the company's income from its ordinary activities.
- All segment income indicators are to be reconciled with the company's income before tax and discontinued operations.
- The total assets of reportable segments are to be reconciled with the company's total assets.
- The total liabilities of reportable segments (if there are any) are to be reconciled with the company's total liabilities.
- The same goes for other significant elements reported for each segment.

Deutsche Telecom provides segment information in compliance with the IFRS (Figure 9.26). Therefore, restatement to comply with accounting procedures is not necessary. However, reconciliations due to differences in the scope of items included in the indicators allow us to compare the segment information with the company's financial statements for net income, asset and liability indicators (Figure 9.27).

(d) Information to Provide on the Scope of a Company's Activities   The required segment information described in the previous section is directly based on the company's internal organizational structure and accounting methods. Differing evaluation methods and presentation guidelines can make comparisons difficult. This can run contrary to the main argument

millions of €		Net cash from (used in) operating activities	Net cash (used in) from investing activities	Of which: cash capex*	Net cash (used in) from financing activities
Mobile Communications Europe	2008	6,711	(2,313)	(1,807)	(6,192)
	2007	6,494	(3,537)	(1,938)	447
	2006	4,882	(3,168)	(1,950)	(3,049)
Mobile Communications USA	2008	3,740	(2,880)	(2,540)	(852)
	2007	3,622	(2,714)	(1,958)	(831)
	2006	3,388	(5,291)	(5,297)	1,904
Broadband/Fixed Network	2008	7,847	(2,405)	(3,134)	(2,350)
	2007	6,673	909	(2,805)	(2,895)
	2006	8,812	(2,575)	(3,250)	(4,802)
Business Customers	2008	782	(10)	(929)	(955)
	2007	553	(654)	(921)	1,191
	2006	816	(1,523)	(795)	475
Group Headquarters & Shared Services	2008	6,096	(3,337)	(435)	(1,397)
	2007	854	(3,766)	(471)	(6,933)
	2006	3,208	(3,952)	(500)	(1,866)
Total	2008	25,176	(10,957)	(8,845)	(12,747)
	2007	18,196	(9,962)	(8,093)	(9,021)
	2006	21,106	(16,507)	(11,800)	(7,338)
Reconciliation	2008	(9,808)	(421)	138	9,650
	2007	(4,482)	1,908	78	2,896
	2006	(6,884)	2,202	(6)	5,277
Group	2008	15,368	(11,384)	(8,707)	(3,097)
	2007	13,714	(8,054)	(8,015)	(6,125)
	2006	14,222	(14,305)	(11,806)	(2,061)

* Cash outflows for investments in intangible assets (excluding goodwill) and property, plant and equipment, as shown in the cash flow statement.

		Segment assets	Segment liabilities	Segment investments	Investments accounted for using the equity method*	Depreciation and amortization	Impairment losses	Employees (average)
		millions of €	millions of €	millions of €	millions of €	millions of €	millions of €	
Mobile Communications Europe	2008	30,441	4,879	1,882	3	(3,626)	(249)	29,237
	2007	35,151	5,263	2,249	0	(3,903)	(338)	30,802
	2006	36,950	5,187	3,231	0	(3,342)	(25)	25,345
Mobile Communications USA	2008	34,362	4,001	3,615	14	(1,863)	(21)	26,076
	2007	30,146	3,441	2,203	10	(1,883)	(9)	31,855
	2006	33,162	3,070	5,200	6	(1,958)	(33)	28,779
Broadband/Fixed Network	2008	25,939	7,943	3,390	83	(3,545)	(67)	94,287
	2007	25,668	7,235	3,176	86	(3,605)	(70)	97,690
	2006	26,913	6,106	3,251	157	(3,744)	(96)	107,006
Business Customers	2008	7,860	4,799	866	46	(789)	(16)	52,479
	2007	9,352	4,699	987	18	(882)	(25)	56,566
	2006	9,333	4,869	1,223	31	(939)	(7)	56,595
Group Headquarters & Shared Services	2008	11,675	7,994	603	3,411	(704)	(127)	72,808
	2007	11,946	8,536	565	4	(708)	(259)	27,023
	2006	11,882	7,808	594	2	(710)	(237)	30,755
Total	2008	110,218	29,616	10,356	3,557	(10,527)	(480)	234,887
	2007	112,263	29,174	9,180	118	(10,981)	(701)	243,736
	2006	118,240	28,840	13,499	196	(10,693)	(397)	248,480
Reconciliation	2008	(3,551)	(3,719)	(239)	0	32	0	–
	2007	(3,201)	(3,619)	(103)	0	48	23	–
	2006	(2,963)	(3,142)	(84)	1	69	(13)	–
Group	2008	106,667	25,897	10,117	3,557	(10,495)	(480)	234,887
	2007	109,062	25,555	9,077	118	(10,933)	(678)	243,736
	2006	115,277	25,698	13,415	197	(10,624)	(410)	248,480

* Prior-year figures adjusted. Accounting change in accordance with IFRIC 12. For explanations, please refer to "Summary of accounting policies/Change in accounting policies."

millions of €		Net revenue	Intersegment revenue	Total revenue	Profit (loss) from operations (EBIT)	Interest income	Interest expense	Share of profit (loss) of associates and joint ventures accounted for using the equity method*	Income taxes*
Mobile Communications Europe	2008	19,978	685	20,663	3,188	435	(500)	0	(146)
	2007	20,000	713	20,713	2,436	208	(495)	0	635
	2006	17,700	755	18,455	2,746	168	(514)	77	13
Mobile Communications USA	2008	14,942	15	14,957	2,299	61	(577)	6	(694)
	2007	14,050	25	14,075	2,017	99	(457)	6	(519)
	2006	13,608	20	13,628	1,756	68	(408)	3	651
Broadband/Fixed Network	2008	17,691	3,640	21,331	2,914	643	(62)	6	(48)
	2007	19,072	3,618	22,690	3,260	522	(62)	46	(84)
	2006	20,366	4,149	24,515	3,356	256	(41)	31	(241)
Business Customers	2008	8,456	2,554	11,010	(6)	112	(60)	41	(10)
	2007	8,971	3,016	11,987	(323)	91	(99)	1	(47)
	2006	9,301	3,568	12,869	(935)	61	(99)	(78)	(50)
Group Headquarters & Shared Services	2008	599	2,974	3,573	(1,198)	1,341	(3,833)	(441)	(574)
	2007	423	3,445	3,868	(1,973)	1,015	(3,309)	2	(1,361)
	2006	372	3,386	3,758	(2,138)	1,055	(3,043)	(2)	342
Total	2008	61,666	9,868	71,534	7,197	2,617	(5,027)	(388)	(1,472)
	2007	62,516	10,817	73,333	5,407	1,935	(4,422)	55	(1,375)
	2006	61,347	11,878	73,225	4,885	1,608	(4,105)	31	715
Reconciliation	2008	–	(9,868)	(9,868)	(157)	(2,200)	2,132	0	44
	2007	–	(10,817)	(10,817)	(121)	(1,674)	1,647	0	2
	2006	–	(11,878)	(11,878)	402	(1,311)	1,268	1	255
Group	2008	61,666	–	61,666	7,040	408	(2,895)	(388)	(1,428)
	2007	62,516	–	62,516	5,286	261	(2,775)	55	(1,373)
	2006	61,347	–	61,347	5,287	297	(2,837)	32	970

* Prior-year figures adjusted. Accounting change in accordance with IFRIC 12. For explanations, please refer to "Summary of accounting policies/Change in accounting policies."

· · · · · **T** · · ·

Figure 9.25   From Deutsche Telekom's 2008 annual report.

Reconciliation of the total of the segments' profit or loss to profit after income taxes.

millions of €	2008	2007*	2006*
Total profit (loss) of reportable segments	7,197	5,407	4,885
Reconciliation to the Group	(157)	(121)	402
Profit from operations (EBIT) of the Group	7,040	5,286	5,287
Profit (loss) from financial activities	(3,588)	(2,833)	(2,675)
Income taxes	(1,428)	(1,373)	970
Profit after income taxes	2,024	1,080	3,582

* Prior-year figures adjusted. Accounting change in accordance with IFRIC 12. For explanations, please refer to "Summary of accounting policies/Change in accounting policies."

Figure 9.26   From Deutsche Telekom's 2008 annual report.

Reconciliation of segment assets and segment liabilities.

millions of €	Dec. 31, 2008	Dec. 31, 2007*	Dec. 31, 2006*
Total assets of reportable segments	110,218	112,263	118,240
Reconciliation to the Group	(3,551)	(3,201)	(2,963)
Segment assets of the Group	106,667	109,062	115,277
Cash and cash equivalents	3,026	2,200	2,765
Current recoverable income taxes	273	222	643
Other current financial assets (excluding receivables from suppliers)	1,997	1,862	1,677
Investments accounted for using the equity method	3,557	118	197
Other non-current financial assets (excluding receivables from suppliers)	1,386	599	657
Deferred tax assets	6,234	6,610	8,952
Assets in accordance with the consolidated balance sheet	123,140	120,673	130,168
Total liabilities of reportable segments	29,616	29,174	28,840
Reconciliation to the Group	(3,719)	(3,619)	(3,142)
Segment liabilities of the Group	25,897	25,555	25,698
Current financial liabilities (excluding liabilities to customers)	10,052	8,930	7,374
Income tax liabilities	585	437	536
Non-current financial liabilities	36,386	33,831	38,799
Deferred tax liabilities	7,108	6,675	8,083
Other liabilities	–	–	–
Liabilities in accordance with the consolidated balance sheet	80,028	75,428	80,490

* Prior-year figures adjusted. Accounting change in accordance with IFRIC 12. For explanations, please refer to "Summary of accounting policies/Change in accounting policies."

Figure 9.27   From Deutsche Telekom's 2008 annual report.

for adopting the IFRS in the first place, which is to facilitate comparative analysis. For segment information, it is hard to find many groups that have completely comparable operating segments. Major multinationals are often so different from one another that an attempt to standardize all of the details of their segment information is not realistic and would not even provide information that is useful or more comparable between groups.

To ensure a minimum of comparability between companies, IFRS 8 requires the disclosure of specific information that does not necessarily follow the same logic as the segment information detailed above. The required information:

- must be presented in all cases, regardless of whether it is regularly analyzed by the main operational decision-makers or not,
- must be documented according to the procedures used to establish the financial statements, rather than the methods used internally within the company to prepare segment information.

There are three types of information to provide for this purpose:

- Information concerning the nature of products and services

  - Income from ordinary activities generated by transactions with external customers for each product and/or service.

- Information on geographic areas:

  - Revenues from ordinary activities generated by transactions with external customers with distinctions between those:

    o allocated to the country where the company's headquarters is located (the parent company for a business group),
    o allocated to all other countries,
    o allocated to one particular country if its revenue is substantial.

  - Non-current assets with the same scope as for the assets for the reportable operating segments with distinctions between assets located:

    o in the country where the company's headquarters is located (the parent company for a business group),
    o in all other countries,
    o in one particular country if the value of the assets located there is substantial.

- Information on major customers, specifically those from whom the company generates at least 10% of its income from ordinary activities:

  - Indication of existence of one (or several) existing customers in this case (no requirement to specify their names).
  - Indication of the total amount of sales recorded from transactions with all major customers, or individually for each customer in question if there are several.
  - Indication of the reported operating segments that these sales concern without specifying sales by segment.

The required information described here does not need to be reported separately, but should be included with the reported segment information. For this reason, and because it does not list any "major customers" in its financial statements, Deutsche Telekom limits itself to information

Information by geographic area.

millions of €	Non-current assets			Net revenue		
	Dec. 31, 2008	Dec. 31, 2007*	Dec. 31, 2006*	2008	2007	2006
Germany	44,385	44,817	47,457	28,885	30,694	32,460
International	55,227	52,702	57,151	32,781	31,822	28,887
Of which:						
Europe (excluding Germany)	23,854	25,238	26,786	17,324	17,264	14,823
North America	31,298	27,407	30,344	14,931	14,159	13,700
Other countries	75	57	21	526	399	364
Group	99,612	97,519	104,608	61,666	62,516	61,347

* Prior-year figures adjusted. Accounting change in accordance with IFRIC 12. For explanations, please refer to "Summary of accounting policies/Change in accounting policies."

Figure 9.28   From Deutsche Telekom's 2008 annual report.

listed by geographic area (for revenues from ordinary activities and non-current assets). It's apparent that about half of the group's net revenue is generated from sales in Germany (€29 billion), with the remaining half distributed nearly equally between other European countries (€17 billion) and North America (€15 billion). The percentage of sales in Germany sharply declined from 2006 to 2008 (−11%), while international sales increased by over 13% for the same period (Figure 9.28).

APPLICATION 9.10

Segment Information

Men & Pets Corp. has to disclose segment information according to IFRS 8. Its business is split in three different activities (DIY, gardening, pet shop). The company operates in three different geographic areas (UK, EU without UK, Eastern Europe). Each of the nine segments Business/Geographic area is regularly reviewed by the COO. The IT department is able to disclose separate financial information (in thousands of euros) for each segment.

	Total turnover by segment	*Net income by segment*	*Assets by segment*
DIY	4,000	150	4,200
Gardening	3,600	400	3,000
Pet shop	2,400	360	1,500
UK	**10,000**	**910**	**8,700**
DIY	2,500	100	2,500
Gardening	3,000	350	2,500
Pet shop	2,020	300	1,000
EU without UK	**7,500**	**750**	**6,000**
DIY	1,500	60	1,400
Gardening	1,400	150	1,300
Pet shop	900	150	700
Eastern Europe	**3,800**	**360**	**3,400**
Total	**21,300**	**2,020**	**18,100**

According to this table and on the basis on the information given above, what are the different segments to be disclosed (reportable segments)?

One of the main rules concerns the 10% threshold, be it in total turnover, total net income, or total assets. As soon as one of these three criteria is reached, the segment has to be disclosed.

(thousands of euros)	Total Turnover : 21,300	Total Net income : 2,020	Total Assets : 18,100	Segment disclosure
Disclosure point	2,130	202	1,810	
DIY UK	4,000	150	4,200	Yes
Gardening UK	3,600	400	3,000	Yes
Pet shop UK	2,400	360	1,500	Yes
DIY EU without UK	2,500	100	2,500	Yes
Gardening EU without UK	3,000	350	2,500	Yes
Pet shop EU without UK	2,020	300	1,000	Yes
DIY Eastern Europe	1,500	60	1,400	No
Gardening Eastern Europe	1,400	150	1,300	No
Pet shop Eastern Europe	900	150	700	No

Six segments have been identified. Their accumulated turnover reaches 82% of total turnover. The 75% threshold is exceeded so there is no reason to add other segments.

The segment information should be split in seven different segments with the six identified segments and a segment labelled as 'Other' that would aggregate Eastern Europe activities. Depending on the information reviewed by the COO, 2 to 14 elements of information should be disclosed for each segment.

Which elements of information are to be disclosed at the entity level?

IFRS 8 requires disclosing turnover by activity if this information is not already disclosed by segment. In this case the revenues can only be partly disclosed because the Eastern Europe data for all activities are gathered in only one segment. Additional information should be disclosed, specifying the total revenues for each activity in Eastern Europe.

Men & Pets Corp. has to disclose information by geographic area separating at least the main country (UK) and all the other countries. The data to be disclosed should be the 10,000 sales and 8,700 assets for the British segment, as well as the 11,300 turnover and the 9,400 assets for the other countries.

Financial analysis should shed light on a group's corporate strategy. Reliable segment information is one of the keys to this process: it makes it possible to move beyond a general, company-wide financial analysis to get a closer look at each operating activity. The company's development strategy will then be apparent and its future opportunities can be more easily estimated. Segment-specific analysis lends a perspective on the company's operating segments that resembles the company's own vision. Analyzing the evolution of the various segments helps identify the company's strengths and weaknesses, and therefore its chances for successfully meeting its strategic objectives.

At this stage, financial analysts can compare portfolios for different activities and determine the company's competitive advantages, which can vary greatly from one company to another. A competitive advantage can be technological, due to high-performing distribution networks, or a leadership position in a particular market. The income statement can be studied segment by segment to provide answers to questions raised by analysts. Of course, analyzing corporate strategy and the different operating segments does not need to end with a diagnostic report of the present situation. The most important task lies in determining and anticipating future developments.

9.3.5 Earnings per Share

> **Earnings per share:** A company's net revenue divided by the number its shares in circulation.

The amount of a company's **earnings per share** allows shareholders to identify how much wealth has been generated and can potentially be distributed in relation to the number of shares owned. It is a ratio where the numerator is the net revenue for the period, and the denominator is the weighted average of the number of common shares in circulation during the period in question, as detailed in IAS 33. This standard also requires the publication of the **diluted earnings per share**, which takes into account accretive and dilutive instruments (stock option grants and convertible bonds) that would impact the earnings per share if exercised. This definition seems simple, but the earnings-per-share calculation procedure is actually quite complex.

Earnings per Share: Determining Net Income

The income used to calculate the earnings per share is the net income generated by common shares. It must be adjusted to best reflect the potential wealth that can be distributed to common shareholders.

- Usually companies issue preferred shares, rather than common shares. Preferred shares are paid out before common shares. This is the case for priority dividend shares, for example. It is therefore necessary to adjust the net revenue by the value of dividends associated with preferred shares.
- In the case of **discontinued operations**, two income amounts are disclosed: net revenue that reflects the income indicated on the income statement for the company's ongoing operations, and net revenue that takes into account the entire year's total net revenues. This dual-presentation is particularly interesting from a financial analysis perspective. The scale of the impact of discontinued operations on the company's revenues is an important factor for investors to be aware of since it can radically change the outlook for future revenue.
- Non-controlling interests must also be taken into account. Parent companies and subsidiaries do not always hold 100% ownership. Hence, the net revenue used as the numerator in the earnings per share equation corresponds only to the group's ownership share.

Earnings per Share: Determining the Common Share Value The denominator to use when calculating the earnings per share also requires some adjustment. The share value used is the weighted average of the number of common shares in circulation during the period. Three steps are necessary to arrive at this amount:

- When shares are issued, they must be recorded proportionally according to their date of issuing during the year. An example: the company Dubois has 5,500 common shares as of January 1, 2008. On July 1, a cash financing operation creates 3,000 additional common shares. The number of shares to take into account for 2008 is the weighted average of the number of shares: $(5,500 \times 12/12) + (3,000 \times 6/12) = 7,000$.
- Issued instruments with a required conversion feature on or before a contractual date. This concerns instruments such as mandatory convertible bonds. These bonds are required to be converted into the underlying common stock. Calculating the earnings per share must include these securities in the weighted average of common shares from their issue date, not from when they are converted.
- Finally, for income analysis for groups, it is important to point out that the number of common shares to use for calculations corresponds to the common stock held by the parent company's shareholders.

APPLICATION 9.11

EPS Calculation

On January 1, 2008, Duval's equity is composed of 200,000 shares, 40,000 of them with preferred dividends without voting rights. These 40,000 shares are preferred shares which procure to their holder an additional dividend of £3 each, as a compensation for the lack of voting right. On January 9, 2008, Dubois proceeds to an increase of capital through transformation of reserves into new shares. 100,000 new shares are issued. During July, Duval's pays a £4 dividend by each ordinary share and £3 additional dividend for preferred shares, that is to say a total amount of £920,000. The net income of the year is £1,200,000.

What is the EPS (Earning per Share)?

The increase in capital has been done through reserve incorporation. In this case, the former shareholders (since January 1 of the year) will benefit from that increase. This particularity must be considered to calculate the number of floating shares because the increase of capital is supposed to have been realized on January 1.

Number of floating common shares in 2008: $(200,000 - 40,000) + 100,000 = 260,000$

The amount of additional dividend must be subtracted from the net income to calculate the EPS: $1,200,000 - 120,000$ (£3 × 40,000 shares) $= £1,080,000$

Therefore, the EPS is: $1,080,000/260,000 = £4.15$

The net income calculated that way is called the "adjusted net income".

Earnings per Share: Determining the Diluted Earnings per Share   Companies often take advantage of so-called "hybrid" securities for their financing operations. Typical examples of this type of product include mandatory convertibles and bond warrants. These are loans with a conversion option (the possibility to transform bonds into shareholders' equity). Exercising this conversion option leads to a dilution of profits due to the increase in the number of shares issued. This potential dilution (if the bondholder exercises the option) must be taken into account in the diluted earnings per share. The numerator in the equation that represents the

Profit/(loss) for the financial year (millions of €)		**6,756**	(5,297)	(21,821)
Attributable to:				
– Equity shareholders	23	6,660	(5,426)	(21,916)
– Minority interests		96	129	95
		6,756	(5,297)	(21,821)
Basic earnings/(loss) per share (pence)				
Profit/(loss) from continuing operations	8	12.56p	(8.94)p	(27.66)p
Loss from discontinued operations	8, 29	–	(0.90)p	(7.35)p
Profit/(loss) for the financial year	8	**12.56p**	(9.84)p	(35.01)p
Diluted earnings/(loss) per share (pence)				
Profit/(loss) from continuing operations	8	12.50p	(8.94)p	(27.66)p
Loss from discontinued operations	8, 29	–	(0.90)p	(7.35)p
Profit/(loss) for the financial year	8	**12.50p**	(9.84)p	(35.01)p

Figure 9.29   Excerpt from Vodafone 2008 annual report.

net revenue must be increased by the amount of dividends and interest after taxes entered in the accounts for the year the potential common stock would be issued. The denominator also needs to be adjusted to take into account the potential common stock that would be created if conversion took place (see Application 9.12).

The excerpt from Vodafone 2008 annual report (Figure 9.29) illustrates how the earnings per share information is presented in the income statement. In addition to the distinction between basic earnings per share vs. diluted earnings per share, both indicators have to be presented on both a current basis and on the basis of continuing operations (see section 9.3.6 below). This latter distinction is an additional tool to highlight the risk of "loss" per share for actual shareholders due to the abandonment of activities or the disposal of significant assets.

APPLICATION 9.12

Diluted EPS Calculation

The net income of Durand at the end of 2008 (after tax) is £1,200,000. The tax rate is 33.33%. The number of common shares is 700,000. In order to finance its growth, Durand issued convertible bonds. It is specified that the annual interest is 4%. 1,600 bonds can be converted in exchange for 400 common shares.

If the conversion is realized, Durand will save financial expenses up to $4\% \times 1,600 \times £1,000 = £64,000$. The tax saving must be taken into consideration (financial fees are deductible) : $64,000 \times (1 - 0.333) = £42,688$.

The diluted EPS can be calculated: Net income + Financial expenses (after tax) = $1,200,000 + 42,688 = 1,242,688$.

Average number of floating shares risen by the new shares in case of conversion: 700,000 + 640,000 = 1,340,000.

The diluted EPS is: 1,242,688/1,340,000 = £0.92.

The (basic) EPS is: 1,200,000/700,000 = £1.71.

Investors can understand the potential consequences of the conversion of bonds on the net income per share. The conversion may have a significant dilution effect on the EPS, which would decline from £1.71 to £0.92.

9.3.6 Discontinued Operations and Financial Analysis

Discontinued operations: When a company either sells one of its components or ends its operations. The component in question must represent a major and distinct business activity or geographic region identified in operational terms and in the company's financial communications.

Companies must provide a clear presentation and specific information on operations they intend to discontinue. This independent presentation of discontinued operations is a financial reporting innovation (IFRS 5). The reporting standard for this type of transaction is not a measurement standard since the values to report can be those established according to standards other than the IFRS. The goal is clearly to isolate the items in the financial statements and to isolate all information that concern assets, liabilities, income, expenses, and cash flow that the company will no longer control within a short period of time, usually less than 12 months.

The disclosure of assets or activities to be held for disposal stops the depreciation of these assets; they will be measured in the financial statements of their transfer value less the cost of sales, etc. Such a reclassification of assets or activities therefore sends a strong signal to the third parties. When discontinuation occurs during the reference period, isolating the accounting items associated with it also isolates the profits or losses recorded at the time of discontinuation, which also will be non-recurring. This information helps to provide a more accurate perspective on the current and future financial situation of the company in question.

In practice, the information to present for operations that have been or will be discontinued includes the following:

- Balance sheet items:
  - Grouping of all assets and liabilities affected by the disposal or abandon as current (including items previously considered non-current).
- Income statement items:
  - The profits and losses generated by the discontinued operations grouped together in a single amount.
  - In the notes or in the statement itself, details on the expenses, revenues and income taxes associated with the discontinued operations.

- The cash flow attributable to the operating, investing and financing activities related to these operations.

The following example, from Danone's 2008 annual report (see Figures 9.30 and 9.31), illustrates the application of these procedures very clearly. The impact of the revenue associated with the discontinuation of "Biscuits and Cereal Products" (a total of €3.292 billion) is clearly apparent on the 2007 income statement. Details on its composition are provided in the notes. The report shows, for example, that operations that have already been or that will be discontinued in 2007 represent net revenues of €1.929 billion.

APPLICATION 9.13

Discontinued Operations and Financial Analysis

The Morin group is one of the leaders on the European mass retail distribution market. In 2006, the group acquired one of its competitors, which was by then operating in Hungary and in Romania. However, since the acquisition date, these supermarkets are losing money and they are more of a financial burden for the Morin group. The board of directors approved an abandonment plan and announced it in November, 2008. In compliance with the IFRS, the financial statements for the years 2007 and 2008 must disclose specifically the discontinued operations in Hungary and in Romania. In the 2007 financial statements, the ordinary result amounted to 6,000, while the supermarkets located in Hungary and in Romania were losing 200.

The 2008 financial statements disclose expenses linked to these dicontinued operations. The abandonment plan mentions dedicated expenses linked to the lay-off of employees working in these supermarkets for 150. Moreover, it is very likely that a loss is going to be made on the sale of the assets (100), since the disposable value is lower than the net book value. These pieces of information must be disclosed separately in the 2008 financial statements.

How important is this information for the financial analysis?

The information disclosed in the financial statements about the discontinued operations is interesting for investors in two ways :

First, they give a piece of evidence to understand the strategy of the company, both in terms of operational and geographical segments. It makes it possible to observe the axis of development chosen by the company on a long-term basis. The strategy of the company is therefore clearer.

Second, this information is very valuable to determine the profitability of the company. Having supermarkets in Hungary and in Romania was a source of losses. The fact that the operations in these areas are discontinued should enable the company to increase its operating income in relation to the assets used for the production (improving ROA). This is extremely important because one of the criteria to which the investors pay the most attention is the financial profitability. In a way, discontinuted operations are signals sent to the market about the company's strategy in order to improve the value creation for the shareholders.

9.4 SUMMARY

Financial analysis involves examining a company's working capital requirements and working capital. The working capital requirements determine the company's cash flow requirements

CONSOLIDATED INCOME STATEMENTS

		Year ended December 31	
(In € millions)	Notes	**2007**	**2008**
Net sales		**12,776**	**15,220**
Cost of goods sold		(6,380)	(7,172)
Selling expenses		(3,498)	(4,197)
General and administrative expenses		(943)	(1,297)
Research and development expenses		(121)	(198)
Other (expense) income	21	(138)	(86)
Trading operating income		**1,696**	**2,270**
Other operating (expense) income	22	(150)	(83)
Operating income		**1,546**	**2,187**
Interest income		*132*	*58*
Interest expense		*(307)*	*(497)*
Cost of net debt	23	(175)	(439)
Other financial (expense) income	23	(2)	(145)
Income before tax		**1,369**	**1,603**
Income tax	24	(410)	(443)
Income from consolidated companies		**959**	**1,160**
Net income of equity-accounted affiliates	7	87	62
Net income from continuing operations		**1,046**	**1,222**
Net income from discontinued operations	3	3,292	269
Net income		**4,338**	**1,491**
- Attributable to the Group		**4,180**	**1,313**
- Attributable to minority interests		**158**	**178**

The income statement for the discontinued operations, presented below, includes the "Biscuits and Cereal Products" activities over 11 months in 2007:

	Year ended December 31	
(In € millions)	**2007**	**2008**
Net sales	**1,929**	-
Cost of goods sold	(1,021)	-
Selling expenses	(416)	-
General and administrative expenses	(152)	-
Research and development expenses	(21)	-
Other (expense) income	(15)	-
Trading operating income	**304**	-
Other operating (expense) income [1]	3,249	257
Operating income	**3,553**	**257**
Interest income	3	6
Interest expense	(30)	-
Cost of net debt	(27)	-
Other financial (expense) income	(1)	-
Income before tax	**3,525**	**263**
Income tax	(224)	6
Income from consolidated companies	**3,301**	**269**
Net income (loss) of equity-accounted affiliates	(9)	-
Net income from continuing operations	**3,292**	**269**
attributable to the Group	*3,299*	*269*
attributable to minority interests	*(7)*	-

(1) Includes the capital gains or losses on disposals of activities.

DANONE

Figure 9.30   Excerpt from the 2008 Danone annual report.

CONSOLIDATED STATEMENTS OF CASH FLOWS

(In € millions)	Notes	Year ended December 31 2007	2008
Net income attributable to the Group		4,180	1,313
Net income attributable to minority interests		158	178
Net income from discontinued operations		(3,292)	(269)
Net income of equity-accounted affiliates		(67)	(62)
Depreciation and amortization		420	525
Dividends received from equity-accounted affiliates		30	29
Other flows with impact on cash	26	-	(113)
Other flows with no impact on cash	26	21	98
Cash flows provided by operating activities, excluding changes in net working capital		**1,430**	**1,699**
(Increase) decrease in inventories		(51)	3
(Increase) decrease in trade accounts receivable		(39)	(74)
Increase (decrease) in trade accounts payable		244	36
Changes in other working capital items		27	90
Net change in current working capital		181	55
Cash flows provided by (used in) operating activities		**1,611**	**1,754**
Capital expenditures		(726)	(706)
Purchase of businesses and other investments net of cash and cash equivalents acquired	26	(12,100)	(259)
Proceeds from the sale of businesses and other investments net of cash and cash equivalents disposed of	26	4,899	329
(Increase) decrease in long-term loans and other long-term assets		(142)	67
Changes in cash and cash equivalents of discontinued operations		171	-
Cash flows provided by (used in) investing activities		**(8,098)**	**(569)**
Increase in capital and additional paid-in capital		66	48
Purchases of treasury stock (net of disposals)		(439)	46
Dividends		(622)	(705)
Increase (decrease) in non-current financial liabilities		3,069	1,338
Increase (decrease) in current financial liabilities		2,614	(1,901)
(Increase) decrease in marketable securities		1,708	63
Cash flows provided by (used in) financing activities		**6,396**	**(1,111)**
Effect of exchange rate changes on cash and cash equivalents		**(16)**	**(31)**
Increase (decrease) in cash and cash equivalents		**(107)**	**43**
Cash and cash equivalents at beginning of period		**655**	**548**
Cash and cash equivalents at end of period		**548**	**591**
Supplemental disclosures			
Cash paid during the year:			
- net interests [1]		152	433
- income tax		369	221

(1) In 2007, net interests corresponded to interest expense on net debt ("interest") for € 252 million net of interest income on net debt for € 100 million.

The notes on pages 92 to 139 are an integral part of the consolidated financial statements.

DANONE

The contribution of the "Biscuits and Cereal Products" activities to changes in the Group's cash flow before financing operations is presented below:

(In € millions)	Year ended December 31 2007	2008
Net income	3,301	269
Depreciation and amortization	63	-
Other changes	(3,125)	(269)
Cash flows provided by operating activities, excluding changes in net working capital	**239**	**-**
(Increase) decrease in inventories	(25)	-
(Increase) decrease in trade accounts receivable	(75)	-
(Increase) decrease in trade accounts payable	58	-
Changes in other working capital items	34	-
Net change in current working capital	(8)	-
Cash flows provided by operating activities	**231**	**-**
Capital expenditure	(46)	-
Financial investments	(28)	-
Disposals and realization of assets (including debt of companies sold at date of disposal)	14	-
Cash flows used by investing activities	**(60)**	**-**
Exchange differences	-	-
Contribution to increase in cash and cash equivalents	**171**	**-**

DANONE

Figure 9.31 Excerpt from the 2008 Danone annual report.

to finance its current operations, while the working capital assures the long-term financial resource requirements. "Financial equilibrium" is reached when the non-current financial resources are equal to the non-current assets. Cash compensates for the difference between the working capital and working capital requirements. The cash flow statement supplements the information provided on the balance sheet and income statement by detailing the sources of cash flows over the course of the year. There are three main sources: cash flow generated by the company's operating, investing, and financing activities.

For shareholders, financial analysis is enhanced by studying their company's return on investment and financial profitability. This requires some additional data. In addition to the earnings per share, which appears on the income statement, the annual comprehensive income statement shows all of the variations in shareholders' equity for the period (except for capital financing or reductions). The "total comprehensive income" is a more wide-ranging measure than the "profit or loss" in this sense, since it takes into account other items such as revaluation reserves, actuarial gains and losses from retirement plans, etc. The final document that completes the company's financial information is the statement of changes in shareholders' equity, which focuses on capital transactions, dividends, and share buybacks.

The entire set of financial statements is accompanied by explanatory notes outlining the accounting principles on which the statements are based. The notes specify the accounting methods used and provide various kinds of essential information that does not appear on the financial statements themselves. It is in this context that companies are required to report on their business segments. They must provide at least one indicator for measuring income and total assets for each segment. Finally, operations that the company plans to discontinue must be detailed separately in the financial statements by identifying the assets and liabilities concerned and the profits or losses associated with the discontinuation.

9.5 ACTIVITIES

1. Cash flow statement During 2008, Finesse Corp. sold land for £40,000 and bought furniture for £15,000. The firm paid £3,000 dividends to its shareholders and borrowed £20,000 from its bank after having paid back a £10,000 debt.

Balance sheet	12/31/08	01/01/08
Cash	???	5,000
Trade receivables	8,000	4,000
Inventory	3,000	8,000
Trade payables	10,000	20,000
P&L		
Turnover	68,000	
Cost of sales	(25,000)	
Wages	(15,000)	
Depreciation/Amortization	(6,000)	
Gains on disposals	1,000	
Net income	23,000	

Based on these data, please prepare a cash flow statement.

2. EPS Boulay & Ken carried out a net income before tax of £2m in 2007. The number of common shares is 500,000. To finance its growth, Boulay & Ken issued 2,000 convertible bonds. It is specified that the interest is 5% per year and that 2,000 convertible bonds can be converted into 500 common shares. The tax rate is 40%.

1. *Calculate the net saving on financial expenses if the bonds are converted into shares.*
2. *Calculate the basic EPS.*
3. *Calculate the diluted EPS.*

3. Cash Flow Statement The Schneider group cash flow statement for the year 2007 is disclosed in Figure 9.32, and some additional information provided in the notes is disclosed in Figure 9.33. Using that information, please answer the following questions:

1. *What action produced the most important impact on cash of Schneider group in 2007?*
2. *What do you think about this statement: "Cash of Schneider group has been deteriorated from 2006 to 2007"?*
3. *How has the question 1 project been financed?*

2. Consolidated statement of cash flows

(in millions of euros)		2007	2006
I - Cash flows from operating activities:			
Profit attributable to equity holders of the parent		1,583.1	1,309.4
Minority interests		38.4	37.2
Share of (profit)/ losses of associates, net of dividends received		(4.3)	(1.9)
Adjustments to reconcile net profit to net cash provided by operating activities:			
Depreciation of property, plant and equipment		309.4	282.1
Amortization of intangible assets other than goodwill		184.9	110.4
Losses on non current assets		41.2	32.2
Increase/(decrease) in provisions		100.8	80.7
Change in deferred taxes		11.3	99.0
Losses/(gains) on disposals of assets		(80.7)	(38.0)
Other		26.6	10.2
Net cash provided by operating activities before changes in operating assets and liabilities		**2,210.7**	**1,921.3**
(Increase)/decrease in accounts receivable		(367.1)	(255.8)
(Increase)/decrease in inventories and work in process		(44.0)	(382.5)
Increase/(decrease) in accounts payable		150.6	225.0
Change in other current assets and liabilities		139.9	79.9
Change in working capital requirement		**(120.6)**	**(333.4)**
	Total I	2,090.1	1,587.9
II - Cash flows from investing activities:			
Purchases of property, plant and equipment		(403.0)	(330.1)
Proceeds from disposals of property, plant and equipment		78.7	76.6
Purchases of intangible assets		(232.7)	(225.4)
Proceeds from disposals of intangible assets		(3.1)	(2.0)
Net cash used by investment in operating assets		**(560.0)**	**(480.9)**
Purchases of financial investments - net	*(note 3)*	(5,291.1)	(897.8)
Purchases of other long-term investments		(0.3)	163.1
Increase in long-term pension assets		(25.1)	(19.6)
Sub-total		**(5,316.5)**	**(754.3)**
	Total II	**(5,876.5)**	**(1,235.2)**
III - Cash flows from financing activities:			
Issuance of long-term debt	*(note 17)*	707.7	996.8
Repayment of long-term debt		(5,159.8)	(148.7)
Sale/(purchase) of treasury shares		14.7	52.9
Increase/(reduction) in other financial debt		6,386.0	298.5
Issuance of shares		1,270.8	76.5
Dividends paid: Schneider Electric SA [(1)]		(670.4)	(502.6)
Minority interests		(28.8)	(14.6)
	Total III	2,520.1	758.8
IV - Net effect of exchange rate:	**Total IV**	(1.6)	11.5
Net increase/(decrease) in cash and cash equivalents: I + II + III + IV		(1,267.9)	1,123.0
Cash and cash equivalents at beginning of period		2,426.2	1,303.3
Increase/(decrease) in cash and cash equivalents		(1,267.9)	1,123.0
Cash and cash equivalents at end of period	*(note 13)*	1,158.3	2,426.2

(1) Includes a précompte withholding tax back payment in 2006.
The accompanying notes are an integral part of the consolidated financial statements.

Figure 9.32   Extract of the 2007 Schneider Electric annual report, cash flow statement.

Note 3 - Changes in the scope of consolidation

3.1 - Additions and removals

The consolidated financial statements for the year ended December 31, 2007 include the accounts of the companies listed in note 29. The scope of consolidation at December 31, 2007 is summarized as follows:

Number of companies	Dec. 31, 2007 France	Dec. 31, 2007 Abroad	Dec. 31, 2006 France	Dec. 31, 2006 Abroad
Parent company and fully consolidated subsidiaries	65	507	67	458
Proportionally consolidated companies	-	-	-	-
Companies accounted for by the equity method	1	3	1	2
Sub-total by region	66	510	68	460
Total	576		528	

The principal changes at December 31, 2007 were as follows:

Main acquisitions

On February 14, 2007, the Group finalized the full acquisition of American Power Conversion (APC) for around $6.1 billion. APC was consolidated as from February 15, 2007. The acquisition cost was allocated as follows:

	Before allocation of acquisition cost	After allocation of acquisition cost
Acquisition price		4,678.5
Transaction costs		33.1
Total acquisition cost		**4,711.6**
Non-current assets	263.1	2,259.0
Other current assets (excluding cash and cash equivalents)	778.5	784.6
Cash and cash equivalents	420.5	420.5
Total assets	**1,462.1**	**3,464.1**
Non-current liabilities	90.5	793.0
Current liabilities	365.3	365.3
Total liabilities (excluding equity)	**455.8**	**1,158.3**
Goodwill		2,405.8

On October 17, 2007, Schneider Electric finalized the acquisition of the entire capital of PELCO, a worldwide leader in the design, development and manufacture of video security systems, for around $1.5 billion. The acquisition cost was provisionally allocated as follows:

	Before allocation of acquisition cost	After allocation of acquisition cost
Acquisition price		1,096.0
Transaction costs		10.6
Total acquisition cost		**1,106.6**
Non-current assets	64.8	655.8
Other current assets	129.7	134.2
Cash and cash equivalents	5.0	5.0
Total assets	**199.5**	**795.0**
Long and short-term debt	2.3	2.3
Other non-current liabilities (excluding long-term debt)	-	6.2
Other current liabilities (excluding short-term debt)	48.1	48.1
Total liabilities (excluding equity)	**50.4**	**56.6**
Goodwill		368.2

Figure 9.33   Extract of the 2007 Schneider Electric annual report.

10 THE IASB AND DEVELOPMENT OF THE IFRS

The previous chapters in this book present the main accounting treatment practices that businesses use to report their current transactions. These practices are governed by internationally recognized standards for establishing corporate annual financial statements. However, these standards have been constantly evolving ever since their creation. To better understand this ever-changing process, it is important to review their history. Section 10.1 therefore presents the background and organizational structure of a private institution, the International Accounting Standards Board (IASB). Section 10.2 discusses the developments that have led to such wide-scale international adoption of the IASB standards that they are now used in the consolidated financial statements of virtually all listed European multinational corporations. Section 10.3 explains how the IASB's standards are drafted. Finally, section 10.4 explores the overall guiding principles behind these standards.

10.1 BACKGROUND AND CURRENT STRUCTURE OF THE IASB

Today's business world is entirely international in nature. The French yoghurt manufacturer Danone is now an agri-food market leader in the United States. Many cars sold in France are designed in Japan, and then assembled in the United Kingdom or Poland.

As for accounting standards, major changes first occurred in the early 1970s. For example, the foundations for the British Accounting Standards Committee (ASC) were first laid out in 1969, and the American organization, the Financial Accounting Standards Board, was founded in 1973. At the time, the European Community was working on its Fourth Directive on company law, and on an international level, the United Nations and the Organization for Economic Co-operation and Development (OECD) formed committees to study multinational corporate accounting practices. Clearly, even then there was a growing awareness of the need to establish more detailed accounting rules, especially for international transactions.

The IASB's predecessor, the International Accounting Standards Committee (IASC) was formed following a conversation between two British accountants, Douglas Morpeth and Sir Henry Benson at the World Congress of Accountants in Sydney, Australia, in 1972. Morpeth was President of the Institute of Chartered Accountants in England and Wales, and both he and Benson were partners of international auditing firms. Their idea was to set up an international standardization organization to establish accounting rules for international companies and encourage harmonization among national accounting procedures. Morpeth and Benson united a group of accounting professionals from other countries (the United States, Canada, France, Germany and Japan) to form the IASC, which was officially founded in 1973.

The IASC initially represented the accounting profession in nine countries, but progressively expanded to include a growing number of countries. Given the large number of participants (two representatives per country plus European Commission and UN observers), the decision-making process that followed working group meetings on various technical issues became increasingly difficult. At the same time, accounting standardization initiatives were being carried out independently of the accounting profession in several different countries. The IASC's system of bringing together representatives from professional organizations in different countries was therefore at odds with the way that the same countries were in the process of designing their own national standards.

The ensuing debate on how to change the organizational structure of the IASC mainly centred on a choice between two possibilities. It could become either "a consensus-seeking body", or "a small, independent group of experts in standardizing financial market procedures". The first option was based on the existing IASC structure and would have facilitated the adoption of standards in several countries since they had contributed to their development. However, the quantity of members (country representatives), each with their own preferences would have slowed down the decision-making process. In the interest of favouring a more efficient and coherent drafting process, the second option was chosen. One of the decisive factors was that the standardization of accounting procedures in the United States was based on the same principle, which facilitated cooperation between the two standardization entities, which was an essential ingredient in arriving at comparable standards across all financial markets.

The reforms made to the IASC led to the creation of several organizations and groups (see also Figure 10.1):

- The IASC Foundation (IASCF) is the organization's governing authority. Its designated Trustees are responsible for securing financial resources and appointing the members of the IASB, the International Financial Reporting Interpretations Committee (IFRIC), and the Standards Advisory Committee (SAC).
- The standards themselves are developed by the International Accounting Standards Board (IASB) whose members are appointed by the IASCF Trustees. The IASB currently comprises 15 members. IASB will be expanded to 16 members by 2012. IASB members serve a term of five years, renewable one time only.
- As of 2009, the IASCF has embarked on a gradual restructuring of the IASB. The number of members is going from 14 to 16, with quotas by geographic area. There are to be four members these three regions: Europe, North America, Asia/Pacific, one member representing South America, one is representing Africa, and the remaining two can be from any geographic area of the world. The Board members must now have proven experience in world financial markets.
- The IASB Interpretations Committee (IFRIC) is a non-profit volunteer-based organization responsible for interpreting standards. It is headed by a member of the IASB. Its members are technical staff from auditing firms, banking and investment executives and corporate accountants.
- Finally, the Standards Advisory Council (SAC) provides consulting services to the Board.
- The Trustees created a new entity in 2009 called the Monitoring Group. It is made up of representatives from the European Commission, stock market regulation authorities in the United States (the Securities and Exchange Commission) and Japan (the Japanese Financial Services Agency), the International Organization of Securities Commissions (IOSCO), the World Bank, and the International Monetary Fund. The objective of the

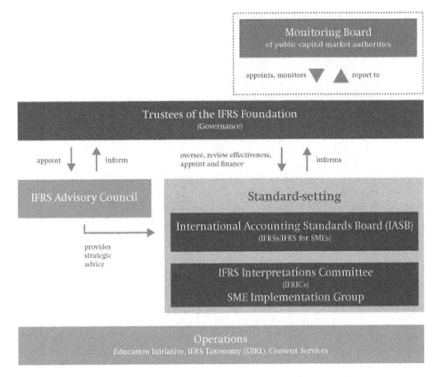

Figure 10.1   The organizational structure of the IASCF.

Monitoring Group is to provide oversight of regulatory authorities and ensure public accountability in the standard-setting process. These regulatory authorities can thus address directly to the standard setters.

The IASB meets once a month for sessions of two to four days. There are also meetings twice a year with the American standardization authority, the Financial Accounting Standards Board (FASB), three times a year with representatives from the European Financial Reporting Advisory Group (EFRAG), and an annual meeting for all standard-setting groups from member countries. IASB delegations and staff members regularly pay visits to such countries as Japan, China and Canada that hope to adopt the IFRS in the near future.

The IASC publishes the International Accounting Standards (IAS), the most recent of which was IAS 41 on agriculture issued in 2000. Since then, IASB has also published the International Financial Reporting Standards (IFRS), which are numbered from 1 onwards. Therefore, there is both an IAS 1 and an IFRS 1, each of which deal with entirely different subjects. When an IAS is revised, it is not necessarily renamed as an IFRS. Thus, the current version of the IAS was last updated after the disappearance of the IASC. For example, IAS 1 on Presentation and IAS 8 on Accounting Methods were heavily revised by the IASB, but still have their initial reference titles.

Figure 10.2   Headquarter of the IASB.

The IFRIC's mission is to answer questions raised by auditing firms, stock market regulatory authorities and other third parties on the interpretation of the existing standards. This is most often in situations that were not anticipated by the standard in question. The IFRIC's interpretations have the same degree of authority as the IFRS themselves. When the IASB revises a standard, it includes all additional interpretations in the new standard that it deems appropriate.

The acronym IFRS refers to the standards published under this name, and also more generally speaking, to the IFRS, IAS and IFRIC's interpretations.

The IASCF and IASB offices are located in London (see Figure 10.2). Meetings and events are held in English and the standards are also published in English. Official translations are issued with approval by the Trustees. In addition, European Commission publishes the standards approved for Europe in all of the official EU languages.[1]

10.2   INTERNATIONAL RECOGNITION OF THE IFRS

The IASC was entirely governed by professional organizations from different countries and published a constant stream of accounting standards. However, while these standards influenced discussions on national standards, their impact within each country remained limited. It was only in the 1990s that governments and businesses started to be convinced of the need for internationally recognized accounting standards in the interest of improving the international positioning of their own stock markets and multinationals.

---

[1]   *The European Commission Regulation No 1126/2008 of November 3, 2008 presents the most recent consolidated version of the IFRS (IAS, IFRS, SIC, IFRIC) applicable to the EU.*

The IOSCO[2] decided to facilitate listing for companies on stock exchanges outside their home countries. Each stock exchange has its own rules of operation, included for the information required of listed companies. Each listed company has a "primary" stock exchange, usually in the same country as its corporate headquarters, which makes its market monitoring easier. For this reason, many European companies are listed on more than one European stock market and also in the United States (Lafarge, for example, has its primary listing in Paris and a secondary listing on the NYSE). A company that is listed on four different exchanges must sometimes provide four different financial information reports.

The IOSCO established a single set of rules for secondary exchange listings. It looked towards the IASC as its source of inspiration for its accounting rules. Over the course of the 1990s, major improvement efforts allowed the IASC to revise the existing standards and add new standards to meet specifications established with the IOSCO. In 2000, the IASC received official approval from the IOSCO. The IAS then became the sole accounting guidelines for secondary exchange listing in the world.

Very quickly, the European Commission regarded the IAS as the required accounting rules for listed companies in Europe. Australia, New Zealand, Russia and South Africa followed the EC's example by requiring compliance with the IAS for their respective listed companies. Currently, close to 100 countries use these international standards for at least some companies. In 2007, the SEC decided to consider the IFRS as published by the IASB as equivalent to the US GAAP for foreign companies listed in the United States. Multinationals that apply the IFRS do not need to publish additional information according to the US GAAP.

Canada, Japan, India, China, Brazil and Korea will adopt the IFRS in 2011, and in the same year the United States plans to conduct forecast studies to examine possibly adopting the IFRS for its listed companies. If this measure is approved, it will be instated gradually starting in 2014. Mexico will adopt the IFRS in 2012.

The widespread adoption of the IFRS can be explained by the fact that multinationals now dominate the world's economy. For investors looking for investment opportunities in international companies, the existence of common accounting procedures (often certified by major international auditing firms) makes their investment much less risky, in particular by offering elements for economic comparison. Similarly, emerging companies based in country with a limited financial market that are willing to reach out to international investors. For example, investors might hesitate to invest in a company based in India if it only have statements presented according to Indian accounting standards. However, if this same company is listed in both London and Delhi and its financial statements are established according to the IFRS and audited by a leading auditing firm, potential investors' financial analysis will be much easier.

The European Commission's motivations were quite similar. In the 1970s, it issued its own accounting standardization initiative for annual financial statements for companies based in EC member countries, the Fourth European Directive. However, accounting directives have to be approved by each member state and numerous amendments were added. Consequently, the

---

[2] *The IOSCO represents stock exchange regulatory authorities such as the Autorité des Marchés Financiers (AMF) in France and the Securities and Exchange Commission (SEC) in the United States.*

accounting rules vary from one country to another. Using the IAS and IFRS was therefore an opportunity to have common procedures for listed companies and take a major step towards a centralized European financial market and in facilitating European companies' access to international financial markets.

So that the IFRS can be incorporated into European corporate law, the European Union had to have an IASB standard approval process, which ultimately did approve all of the standards. However, a few differences exist between the IFRS as they were first published by the IASB, and the standards that were adopted by the European Union. This is due to the fact that a few interest groups attempted to revise certain standards, which interfered with the overall convergence process.

10.3   THE STANDARD-SETTING PROCESS

The preface to the IFRS details the steps in the IASB setting process. There are 11 steps, including four required steps and seven optional ones. The required steps are shown in Figure 10.3.

---

1. Consulting the SAC about the opportunity of adding the topic to the IASB's agenda
2. Publishing for public comment an exposure draft approved by at least nine votes of the IASB
3. Consideration of all comments received within the comment period on discussion documents and exposure drafts
4. Approval of a standard by at least nine votes of the IASB and inclusion in the Published standard of any dissenting opinions

---

Figure 10.3   Required steps in the IFRS due process.

10.3.1   Adding a Topic to the Agenda (Step 1)

At first glance, how the IASB sets its agenda does not seem so important. Nonetheless, how topics are chosen and priorities set are key decisions that determine the areas of accounting that will be developed over the short term. For example, a particular group might suggest a new approach to the consideration of intangible assets since the current approach does not allow numerous such assets to be entered on the balance sheet. However, if the topic is not on the agenda, it may not be addressed for another five, or even 20 years.

How topics are added to the agenda is a subjective matter. The IASB is free to establish its agenda as it wishes. Nonetheless, it consults the Trustees and the SAC and receives suggestions from the IFRIC and the public,[3] especially from major auditing firms. The Board then decides whether or not to add the topic to the agenda "primarily according to investors' needs".

---

[3] *The term "public" refers here to all other participants in the process: accountants, auditors, financial analysts, and any one else interested in international financial information.*

Practically speaking, the agenda reflects a variety of motivations:

- Between 2001 and 2005, the top priority was to fill the gaps in the list of IAS topics to meet the needs of listed European countries that programmed to adopt the IFRS in 2005. This involved drafting a new standard for companies adopting the IFRS for the first time (IFRS 1) and interim standards for insurance policies (IFRS 4) and mineral resources industries (IFRS 6), which were not covered by any of the international accounting standards.
- In parallel, the IASB completed the "Improvements" project, which involved eliminating a certain number of anomalies and significantly revising existing standards. Substantial modifications were made to IAS 1, IAS 8 and IAS 9, and more minor changes were made to about 10 other standards. The goal was to make applying the standards easier and more logical to facilitate the work for accountants and auditors.
- In 2002, the IASB also launched a convergence program with the US GAAP. This interest in harmonization between the two systems stemmed from a desire to improve the quality of information for investors. By using a sole set of international standards, or at least comparable standards for all financial markets, making investment decisions would be easier. Many European companies were hesitant to be listed in the United States due to the high costs of preparing the US GAAP "20-F Reconciliation Form". Indeed, foreign companies listed in the United States can use their own financial statements, but they must also provide a reconciliation of their revenue and shareholders' equity with what these amounts would be according to US GAAP procedures. The European Commission estimates that this requirement costs a company between €5 and 10 million per year. In addition, the companies that agree to pay this price must publish two different revenue amounts. The convergence project effectively eliminated the need for this reconciliation. As part of this project, IFRS 5 (Non-current Assets Held for Sale and Discontinued Operations) was published to converge with its FASB equivalent. IFRS 3 (Business Combinations) was aligned with the former IAS 22 to converge with the FASB's standard 141, and an amendment to IAS 38 (Intangible Assets) made it possible to align it with the FASB's standard 142.
- IFRS 2 (Share-based Payment) was drafted with the aim of providing the most accurate information to investors. It requires companies to enter the cost of granting shares or share options to employees as expenses. The IASB deliberately made this choice to demonstrate that it is capable of taking the initiative on a global level. The United States was the only country that had a standard dealing with the cost of granting share options to employees. The standard gave companies the option to treat this cost as an expense since American companies were generally against it (in 1994, they spent at least $70 million in lobbying efforts against this proposition). The IASB was in large part inspired by the American standard in its technical approach, but its mandatory nature forced the United States to revise their own standard, making it mandatory for companies to enter these costs as expenses.

When the IASB anticipates adding a topic to its agenda, the staff drafts a technical analysis of the problem. The IASB can either directly add a topic to the agenda, or it can add it to its research plans, which functions a bit like a waiting list. The IASB can also ask national standardsetters to conduct a study on the topic before deciding whether or not to add it to its agenda. In 2005, for example, this procedure led standards organizations in Australia, Norway, Canada and South Africa to study accounting practices in their mining and mineral resources industries.

In 2008, the financial crisis created new problems for the IASB. Financial regulatory authorities realized how potentially damaging the interdependence between financial products can be. In particular, the practice of valuing financial instruments at their fair value and then using these values to define the minimum limits for the ratio to respect between shareholders' equity and financial instruments proved to be harmful. The IASB quickly responded by clarifying the application procedures for the principle of fair value when the market is no longer active and by providing more complete information on liquidity risk.

The IASB and the FASB hope to complete a series of key projects for 2011 to help new countries and users adopting their standards to avoid two successive waves of changes. The most important standards expected in 2011 deal with the presentation of financial statements, the categorization of debts, shareholders' equity, revenue recognition, lease agreements and financial instruments. The IASB also plans to revise its standard on consolidation (which also deals with elements not yet recognized on the balance sheet), as well as its standard on retirement benefit plans. The publication of a standard on insurance contracts is also on the agenda, but it is less likely to be finalized before the 2011 deadline.

10.3.2   Publishing a Discussion Document and an Exposure Draft (Step 2)

Once a topic is added to the agenda, the IASB staff (a team of specialists based in the London office) writes an initial exposure draft of the standard and a series of reports on various aspects of the topic. The staff then submits its reports to the Board for debate at a monthly public hearing.

For important topics, the Board can decide to publish a discussion document to solicit feedback from a wider audience and give the public an idea of the Board's intentions. In theory, a discussion paper can define the accounting problem and outline the various possible solutions. However, the current Board prefers to include what they call their "favourite conclusions", which reflect the preliminary analysis of what the Board would like to choose among the possible options. The public is then invited to make formal comments on the discussion document, which will be used to write the exposure draft.

Appointing a working group and drafting a discussion paper give the public the impression that they are involved in the standard setting process. These measures also protect the Board against potential criticism for being cut off from economic realities. However, these two procedures extend the standard setting process. In general, preparation, publication and analysis of comments on a discussion paper last over a year. Nonetheless, this survey process slightly reduces the time required to write the exposure draft.

Current practices have changed a great deal over recent years. The IASB now prefers to publish discussion documents on all major projects underway, which can give the impression that the Board is not willing to make any significant changes to a project as it appears in the exposure draft. In consequence, in order to be able to have any real influence on a project, all remarks, comments and suggestions now need to be made at the discussion paper stage, not later. Discussion documents usually contain preliminary points of view on a standard, though the Board may still be open to arguments showing how difficult it may be to implement and disadvantages that might ultimately result from its application. These arguments are then directly incorporated into the exposure draft. If they are mentioned during the exposure draft stage, the Board just has to respond that they have already been taken into account.

The Board can also decide to make its consultation process official by establishing "working groups" that usually include specialized accountants, auditors, users, and other stakeholders. The staff solicits the working group while they prepare the discussion document and exposure draft. Working groups have been created to focus on financial instruments, insurance policies and performance reporting.

The exposure draft is developed during a multi-step process where the staff poses important questions to the Board. Then, over the course of the decision-making process, the staff asks more detailed questions. The public can follow the process on an observer basis by reading the Board's monthly publication, *Update*, and by reading the agenda and observer notes posted on the IASB website. Articles in specialized journals also help to keep the public informed. A complete exposure draft is available only at the end of the process, and the final vote is confidential. The Board members who do not approve the draft must publish their dissenting opinions. Board decisions require approval by 9 members. Approval by 10 members will be necessary when there will be a total of 16 members.

The exposure draft is the last occasion for the public to offer comments. It details the final version of the standard, including its application guidelines and a "basis for conclusions" section that explains the reasons behind the Board's decisions. Once the final standard is approved, the official standard setting due process prohibits the Board from adding any significant elements that were not included in the exposure draft. If it wishes to add elements, it can decide to publish a new exposure draft, though the current Board avoids this practice to avoid any delay in the decision-making process. If doubts persist on a particular point, the Board usually forwards its most solid arguments in favour of the exposure draft. The exposure draft is accompanied with a series of questions to encourage comments and discussion. These questions may concern alternative suggestions, which then can be considered as having been explored.

The consultation process usually takes 90 days, but can be longer. The IASB is now committed to submitting exposure drafts to its liaison standard-setters 30 days before they are officially published so that there is time to translate them. The Board considers this a waste of time, since it believes that most of the people directly concerned by the approval and application of the standards understand the English version.

10.3.3 The Comment Period and Publication of the Final Standard (Steps 3 and 4)

The next phase of the due process involves examining the comments made on the proposed standard. This does not usually extend beyond about 100 comment letters, which are posted on the IASB website for public consultation. The staff summarizes the information received, in particular the responses to the questions that were raised in the exposure draft. This analysis groups the comments by type of author (for example, accountants, standard-setters, etc.), and by content.

The staff does not take into account comments that merely reiterate arguments that have already been made, for example, in its "basis for conclusions". Instead, it considers arguments that have not yet been studied and unanticipated conclusions. To be taken seriously, the comment letters must be clearly and logically presented and appropriate to the standard's objectives and its guiding principles (see the following section).

The Board does not hesitate to revise exposure drafts, but the vast majority of the debates occur while they are being developed. Those who want to express their opinions on the standard's contents need to participate in the project from the moment it is added to the agenda. Comments must be submitted directly to the staff, or if need be, in response to the discussion document at an earlier stage in the standard-setting process. In contrast, the exposure draft represents the final phase. At this stage, the Board only accepts comment letters that are particularly incisive and well-articulated since the main issues on the accounting topic have already been dealt with. If the Board changes a few details, it informs the public via its website so that those concerned can see the final version of the standard.

The next step is the secret ballot on the standard. Typically, the final version is sent to the members of the IFRIC and major auditing firms' IFRS offices to be proofread and checked for any mistakes. This helps to ensure that there are no potential problems that the standard could cause that have been overlooked.

Finally, the last step involves publishing the standard. Application procedures can vary greatly from one standard to the next. A standard that requires extensive changes may appear in its final version a year or longer before it is actually applied. In exceptional circumstances, a standard can be published for immediate application. Preparers must then be provided with information on the standard before it is published. During periods before a change in accounting rules, the IASB prefers to use what is called a "complete retrospective application". When a company applies the standard, it has to refer back to previous accounting periods and restate them as if the new standard had always been in effect. For example, comparative figures for 2009 published in financial statements for 2010 must comply with the version of the standards used for preparing the 2010 statements. This sometimes represents a heavy additional work load, and it implicates a restatement of shareholders' equity to absorb the effects of the changes made to previous years. However, the IASB grants exemptions if restatement is impossible when the necessary information is unavailable.

The amount of time between a topic's addition to the agenda and the publication of the final version of the standard varies greatly. It depends on how much discussion is stimulated by the questions, which can be related to the standard's degree of innovation. A major standard requires at least two years of preparation time, while a joint-project with the FASB can take anywhere from three to four years, or more (there is no upper limit). When an initial analysis has been presented for an IASB-FASB joint-project to harmonize their conceptual frameworks, the FASB staff estimates the project's duration to be 10 years, even though the FASB's conceptual framework served as the original model for drafting the equivalent IASB Framework.

10.4 CHARACTERISTICS OF THE STANDARDS

It is impossible to present an exhaustive list of all the guiding principles for the standard-setting process. The most important source is the Framework, which often serves as a basis for discussion. Those who want to contribute to the final draft of a standard have to justify their arguments with principles laid out in the IFRS Framework. Other criteria are also taken into account during the standard setting process, such as its coherence and guiding principles (see Figure 10.4).

10.4.1 Conceptual Framework

The IFRS Framework does recognize the wide variety of potential users of financial information. Nonetheless, those who have the most at stake are investors (shareholders and lenders).

Consequently, the Framework concludes that the financial information that meets investors' decision-making needs also meets the needs of other types of users (who assume fewer risks). Thus the accounting treatment for making investment decisions is the first priority in the analysis. If there is no effect, the information is not considered important and therefore does not deserve any attention. However, if the accounting treatment can potentially influence investment decisions, the Framework provides for a "cost–benefit analysis". A standard "passes" this test when the benefits associated with the information are greater than the cost incurred by obtaining it. The assessment is subjective, since the obligation of obtaining information is on the accountant, while it is the investor who reaps the benefits.

In general, the Board is sensitive to the argument that the cost of preparing information is high, and needs to be compared to the anticipated benefits that investors will gain from it. It has therefore simplified some of the information that is required in the notes to financial statements since the cost of obtaining this information is greater than the expected advantages. The same argument is also behind the request for specific rules for small and medium-sized entities (SMEs). A particular accounting treatment may have enough of an impact to influence investment decisions, but it may prove to be too costly for standard-setters to require its application.

The analysis also includes examining the effect on the company's assets and liabilities. This is the "accrual basis" approach recommended by the Framework. For example, when a retailer sells a camera from its inventory for €500 that it purchases for €300 from its supplier, there are two asset entries: cash assets increase by €500, and inventory decreases by €300. This results in an equity increase of €200. The staff has to analyze all of the transactions according to their impact on assets and liabilities, and also the net impact on shareholders' equity.

At this stage of analysis, while differing accounting treatments continue to exist, the Framework sets forth four principles with which the financial information should comply and which the standards should take into account:

- **Understandability.** The information provided in annual reports should be easily understandable for readers with a reasonable knowledge of business and economic activities.
- **Relevance.** Information is considered relevant when it influences the economic decisions of users by helping them to evaluate the company's past, present or future activities. The idea is not to provide vast quantities of information, just the most important information.
- **Reliability.** To be reliable, information must be accurate and free of any subjective bias. It should faithfully represent financial transactions and other past and future events. To this end, the information should be presented in accordance with their substance, and not merely their legal form. It must also be neutral and free of any influence or bias aimed at achieving a predetermined outcome. Finally, information must also demonstrate a certain degree of caution in the exercise of the judgements needed, and be complete, while respecting its relative importance and remaining within the bounds of cost constraints.
- **Comparability.** Users must be able to compare financial statements, both over time for the same entity, and also for the same period between different entities.

The Framework explicitly states: "The relative importance of the characteristics in different cases is a matter of professional judgment." It is therefore the Board's responsibility to weigh these criteria for alternative accounting procedures and decide which method to include in the standard.

10.4.2 Coherence

Beyond the Framework, the Board is also concerned with the overall coherence of the standards, as well as with new standards and revisions of existing standards.

- Individual standards must be consistent with the Framework.
- Standards must be consistent with the complete set of international standards of the IAS/IFRS, generally speaking.
- The text of a standard must be coherent and free of any internal contradictions.
- Finally, a standard must also be consistent with American accounting standards, in view of the convergence between the two sets of standards.

In theory, consistency between the standards of the IFRS and US GAAP should not pose any problems since the two Boards have similar conceptual frameworks, and are currently being revising them to resemble one another even more closely. Nonetheless, often this is not yet the case, especially since American standard-setters have working in a context quite different from the IASC. Conformity with the US standards was not a major concern for the previous IASC Board, whose priority was primarily to achieve consensus among its members, whereas the capacity to draft standards that are consistent with one another was one argument for the "group of experts" approach to the initial IASB reforms.

In addition, the IASB and the FASB had to make some exceptions. The standard on financial instruments (IAS 39) is a typical example. Initially, the rule was simple: all financial instruments had to be valuated at their fair value. After years of discussion, exceptions were finally granted, such as for the valuation at cost of financial instruments held to maturity. The FASB and the IASB both base their procedures on the same principle, but they grant different exceptions to it, and also have different application guidelines.

10.4.3 A Principles based Approach

The IASB's objectives, as stated in the Preface to the IFRS, are to develop high-quality, understandable and enforceable standards. This means that they should be easy to audit. Following the Enron scandal, the FASB was accused of over-simplifying life for auditors and drafting standards that were too specific for their field of application. In contrast, during its standardsetting process, the IASB tried to establish "general guiding principles" along with advice for applying its standards. Auditors have to then use their professional judgement in knowing how to best apply these principles in specific situations.

However, one aspect of the application of standards that is often raised in debates deals with the gaps that the standards leave for "creative accounting" practices and fictitious transactions. "Will it create opportunities for manipulating the balance sheet" is a recurring question raised in particular by the IASB's American members. Standard-setters assume that accountants will try to find ways around a standard and therefore test various accounting techniques to minimize the chances of encouraging fictitious transactions and take the problem into account in drafting the standards.

10.4.4 Understandable Standards

The Preface and the Framework both recommend that the IFRS be understandable, though it's not clear if the IASB actually views this criterion as a constraint! As Sir David Tweedie joked,

Characteristics of the standards
    Framework
        Usefulness for decision-making
        Cost–benefit analysis
        Impact on assets and obligations
        Understandability
        Relevance
           Relative importance
        Reliability
           Faithful representation
           Substance over form
           Neutrality
           Prudence
           Completeness
        Comparability
    Coherence
    Principled approach

Figure 10.4   Characteristics of the IFRS.

"anyone who says they understand IAS 39 hasn't actually read it". Practically speaking, the comprehensible nature of the standards is the qualitative aspect that is least respected. The above figure summarizes the main principles that the IFRS should follow.

10.5   SUMMARY

This chapter describes the context and background to the development of the IFRS. It describes how the standard-setting organizations that draft the standards – the IASC Foundation and its primary governance structure, the IASB – operate.

The standard development process involves several steps and takes place over several years. This allows all interested parties to offer their point of view. Consideration of comments from the public comes second to the standards' compliance with a series of general guiding principles.

The main principle is that the standards are drafted to help investors to make decisions, and are subject to several constraints that have an impact on their contents.

INDEX

*Index compiled by Terry
Halliday*